HOW TO DRAW ALMOST EVERYTHING VOL. 2

AN ILLUSTRATED SOURCEBOOK

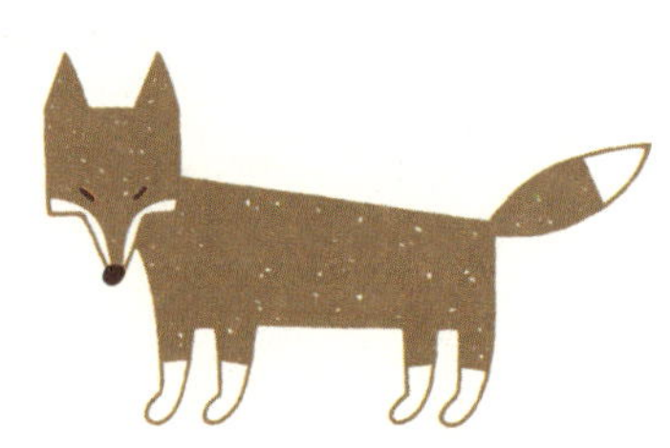

SIX POMMES

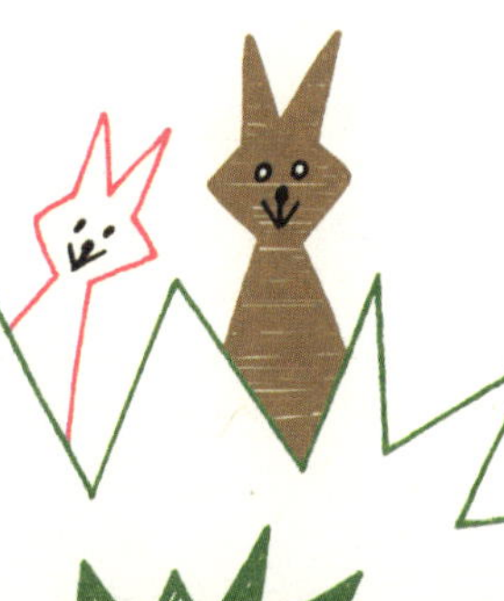

QUARRY

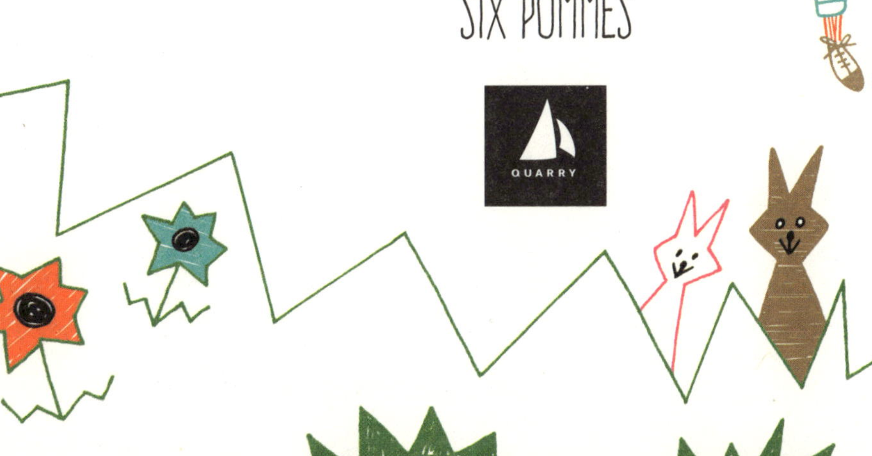

INTRODUCTION

Have you ever found yourself thinking: "I wish I could draw cute and trendy illustrations on notes, greeting cards, and calendars?"

Even if you've never considered yourself artistic, don't despair!

This book will show you just how easy it is to draw cute illustrations.

With a little practice, you'll be making adorable doodles in no time!

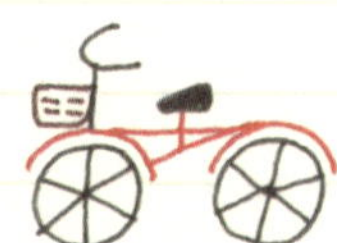

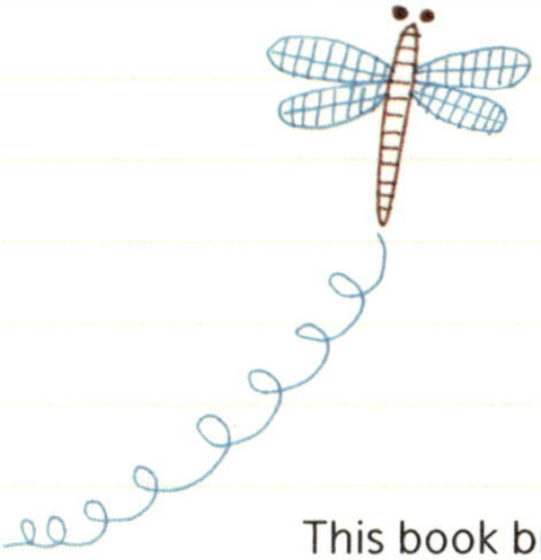

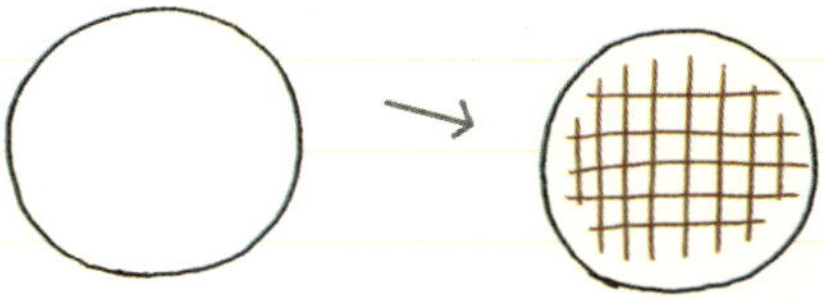

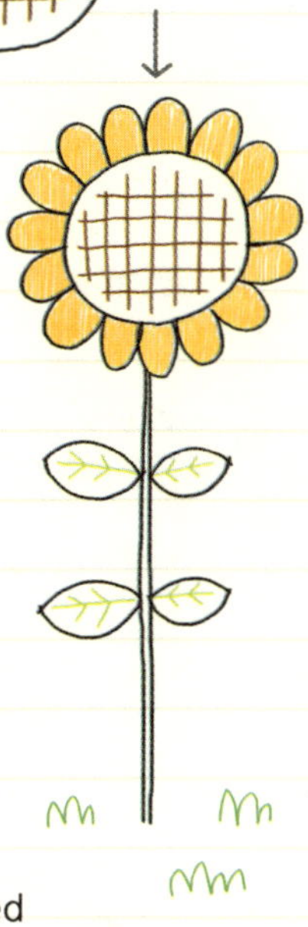

This book breaks each illustration down into easy-to-follow steps.

Plus, you'll learn how to start with basic shapes, such as circles, triangles, and squares, to create realistic illustrations.

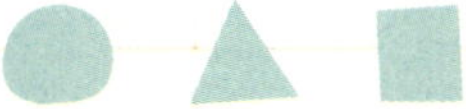

Once you learn the basic drawing methods, it's time to add special details to personalize your illustrations.

The more you practice, the more you'll be inspired to create fun and stylish one-of-a-kind illustrations!

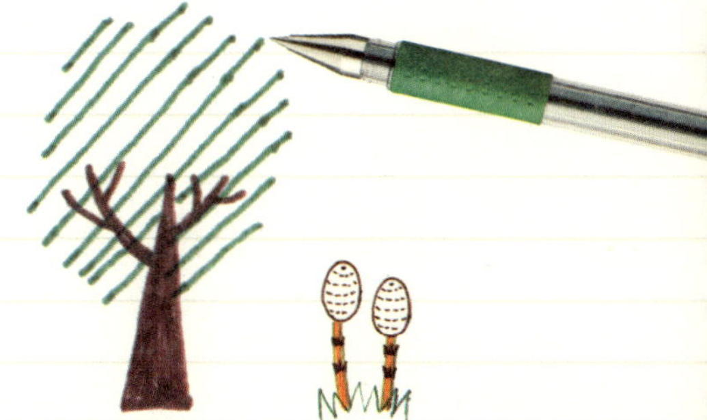

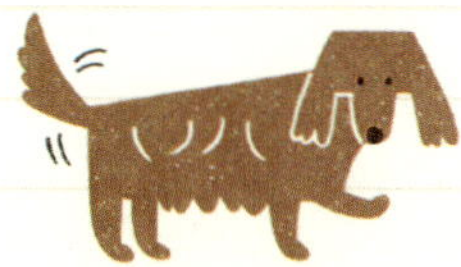

CONTENTS

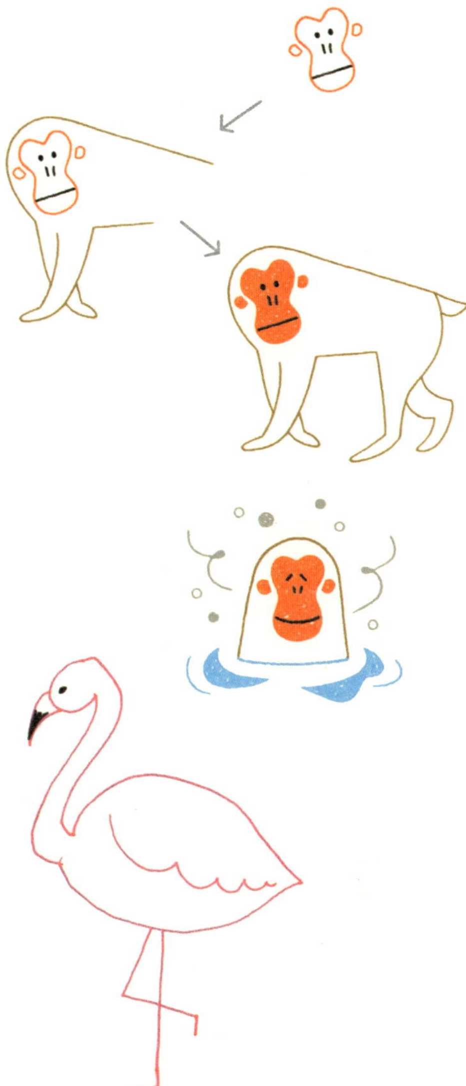

CHAPTER 2: DRAWING PEOPLE

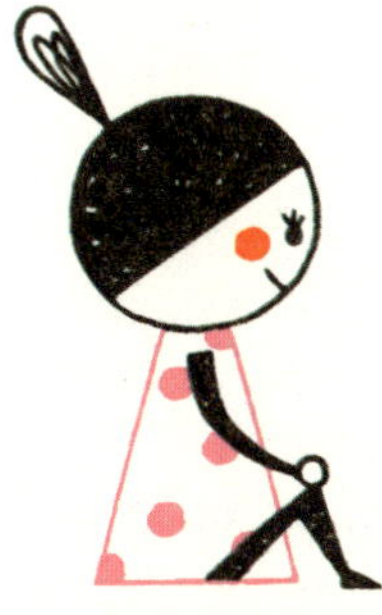

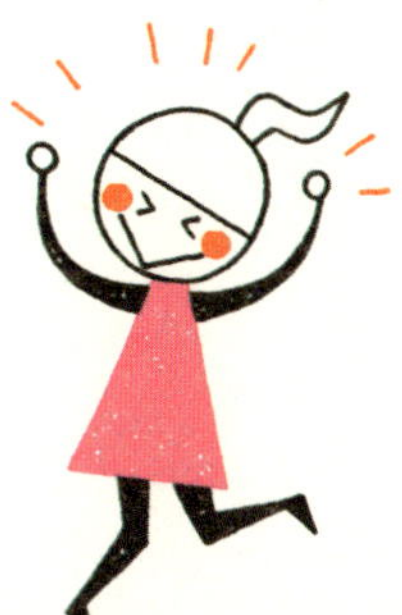

CHAPTER 3: DRAWING EVERYDAY OBJECTS

CHAPTER 4: PATTERNS & BORDERS

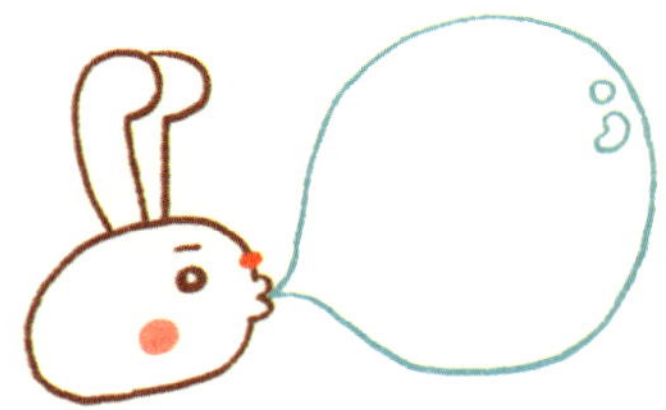

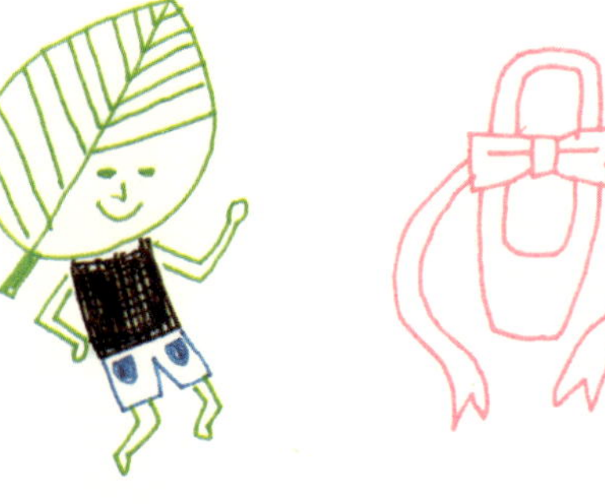

CHAPTER 5: HOLIDAYS & SEASONAL ILLUSTRATIONS

HOW TO USE THIS BOOK

Before we get started drawing, let's go over some basic information about the tools, materials, and techniques used in this book. These tips and suggestions are provided to help you create better illustrations.

About Ballpoint Pens

Most of the illustrations in this book were drawn using gel ink ballpoint pens with a size of 0.38 to 0.5 mm. Ballpoint pens are available in many different thicknesses, so choose one that is easy to draw with based on the size of the illustration.

About Paper

Most of the illustrations introduced in this book were drawn on copy paper. When you practice drawing, use paper with a somewhat smooth surface, such as copy paper or notebook paper. Papers with extremely smooth or coarse surfaces may not work well—the ink may not adhere properly or the ink may bleed. Test your paper first and select the best option based on the pens you're using and the finished use of your illustration.

The Drawing Method

In this book, each illustration is broken down into easy-to-follow steps. Follow the arrows to complete each step. You'll also find helpful tips and ideas for drawing variations included.

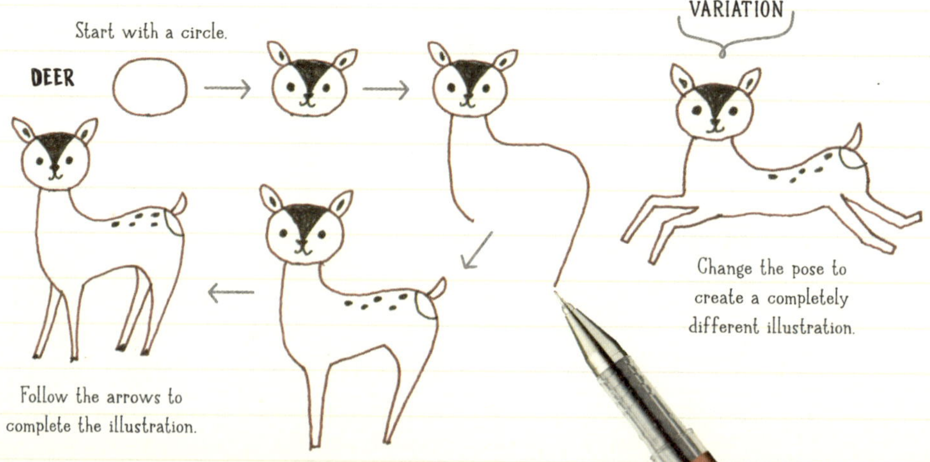

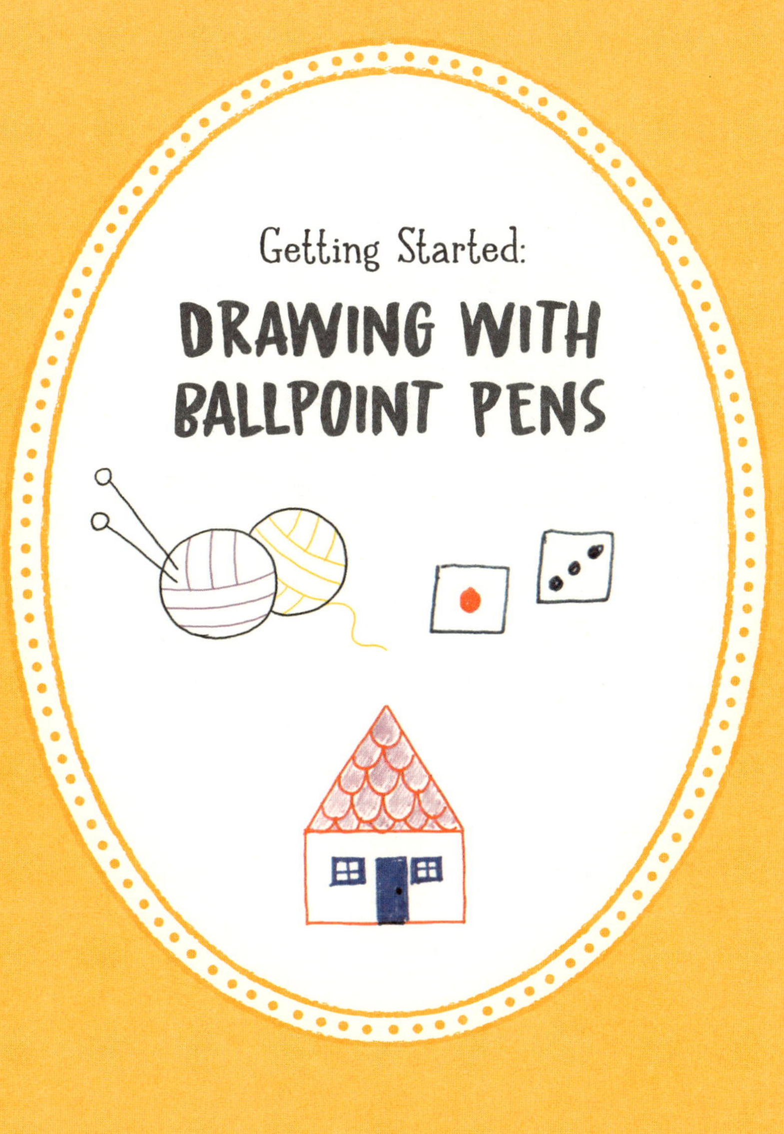

Getting Started:

DRAWING WITH BALLPOINT PENS

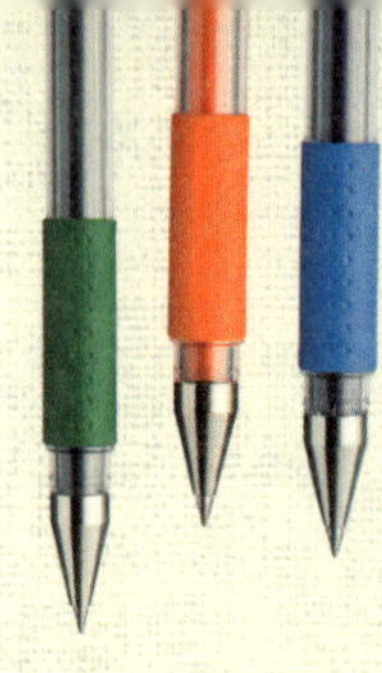

ALL ABOUT BALLPOINT PENS

Ballpoint pens are available at office supply stores, grocery stores, craft supply stores, and many other locations. When selecting a ballpoint pen for drawing, you'll want to consider both the ink type and the line thickness.

INK TYPE

Ballpoint pens are available with three different ink types: oil, water, and gel. Each type offers distinct advantages and disadvantages in regards to appearance and durability.

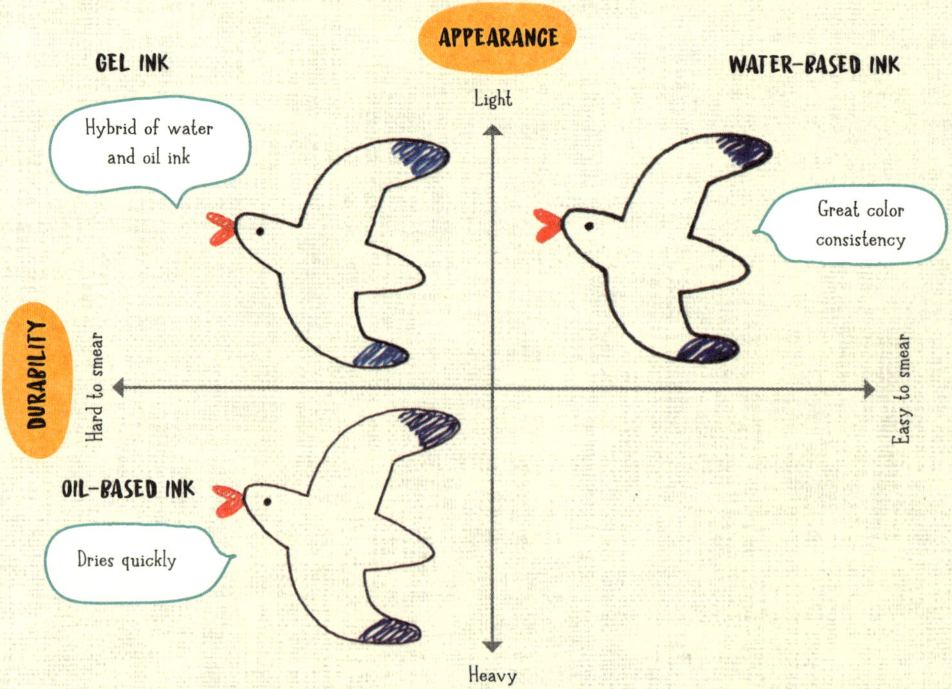

LINE THICKNESS

When shopping for ballpoint pens, you'll notice that they are available in a variety of different sizes. Keep in mind that the size numbers, such as 0.4 mm or 0.5 mm, indicate the diameter of the point, not the width of the line. Use a pen with a thickness that is suitable for your desired drawing.

0.38 mm and 0.4 mm

Suitable for drawing small illustrations.

0.5 mm

Suitable for practicing illustrations as the ink flows well. Available in a wide range of colors.

0.7 mm and 1.0 mm

Suitable for drawing large illustrations or filling large areas with color as the tips of these pens do not get caught on the paper.

BALLPOINT PEN RECOMMENDATIONS

1 For small illustrations on paper

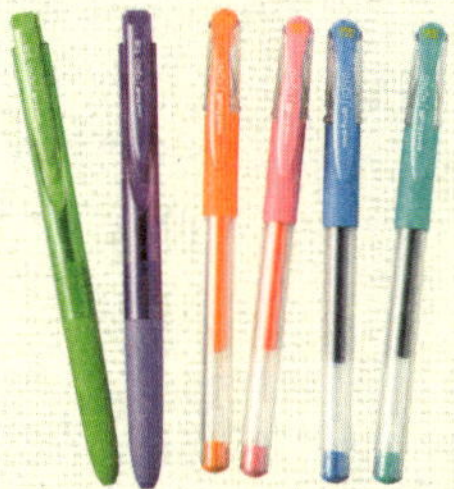

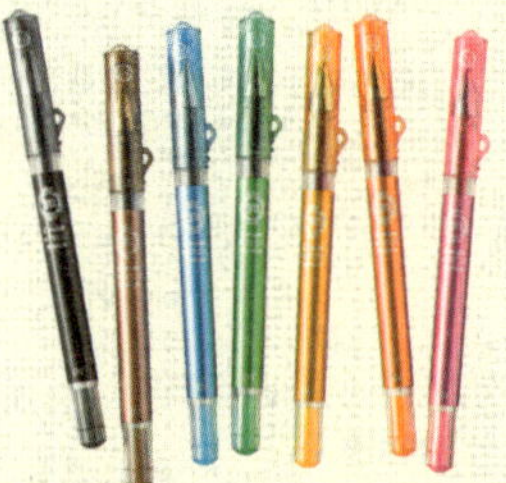

UNI-BALL SIGNO (0.38 mm) BY MITSUBISHI PENCIL

These gel ink ballpoint pens use pigment ink, which provides a very smooth appearance and vivid color. These pens are available in a wide range of colors.

HI-TEC-C MAICA (0.4 mm) BY PILOT

These pens have extremely fine tips as the width of the drawn line is 0.2 mm. These pens are ideal for small, detailed illustrations.

2 For erasable pens

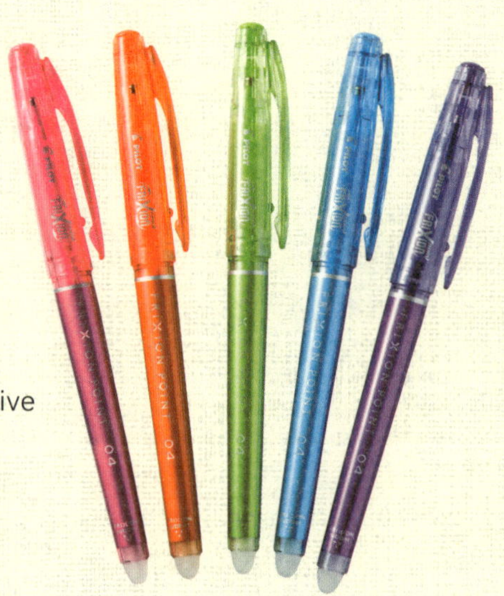

FRIXION POINT (0.4 mm) BY PILOT

These pens feature thermo-sensitive ink, allowing you to remove your mistakes with the included eraser. The heat created by the friction causes the ink to disappear!

3 For drawing on plastic, glass, and metal

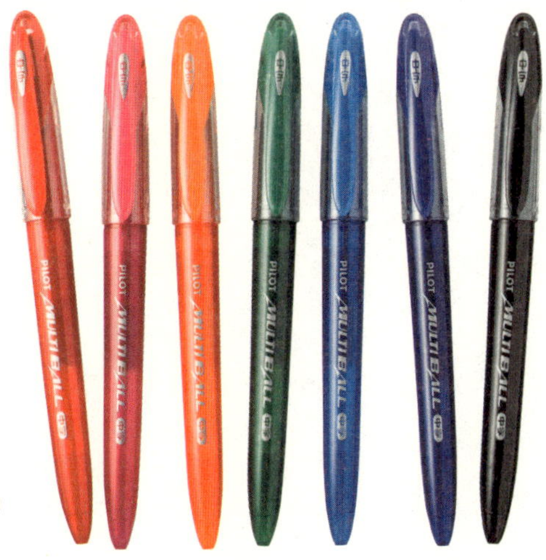

MULTI BALL (FINE AND MEDIUM) BY PILOT
These ballpoint pens with water-based pigment ink can be used to draw not only on paper, but also on surfaces that do not absorb ink, such as plastic, glass, and metal.

4 For drawing on black paper or on photos

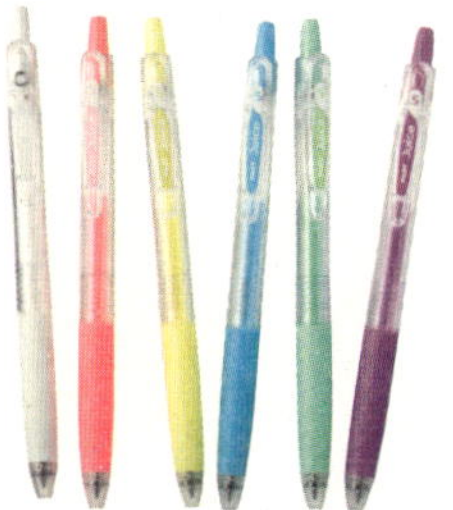

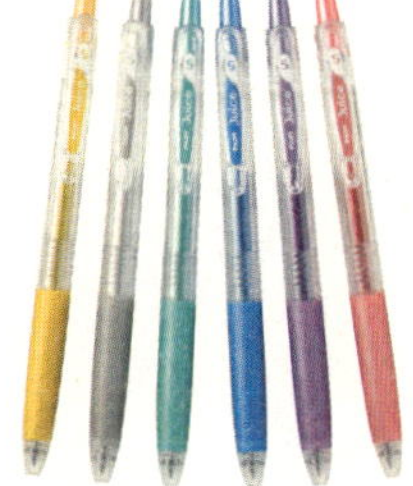

JUICE PASTEL COLORS (0.5 mm) BY PILOT
These pens can be used on black paper or photos and have a beautiful, milky color. They feature pigment gel ink, which is water-resistant.

JUICE METALLIC COLORS (0.5 mm) BY PILOT
Just like the Juice Pastel Colors, these pigment gel ink ballpoint pens can be used to draw on black paper or photos. The ink contains glitter so you can draw sparkly lines.

WARM-UP 1

DRAWING LINES

First, let's practice drawing illustrations using different types of lines such as curly, jagged, dotted, and much more.

CURLY LINES

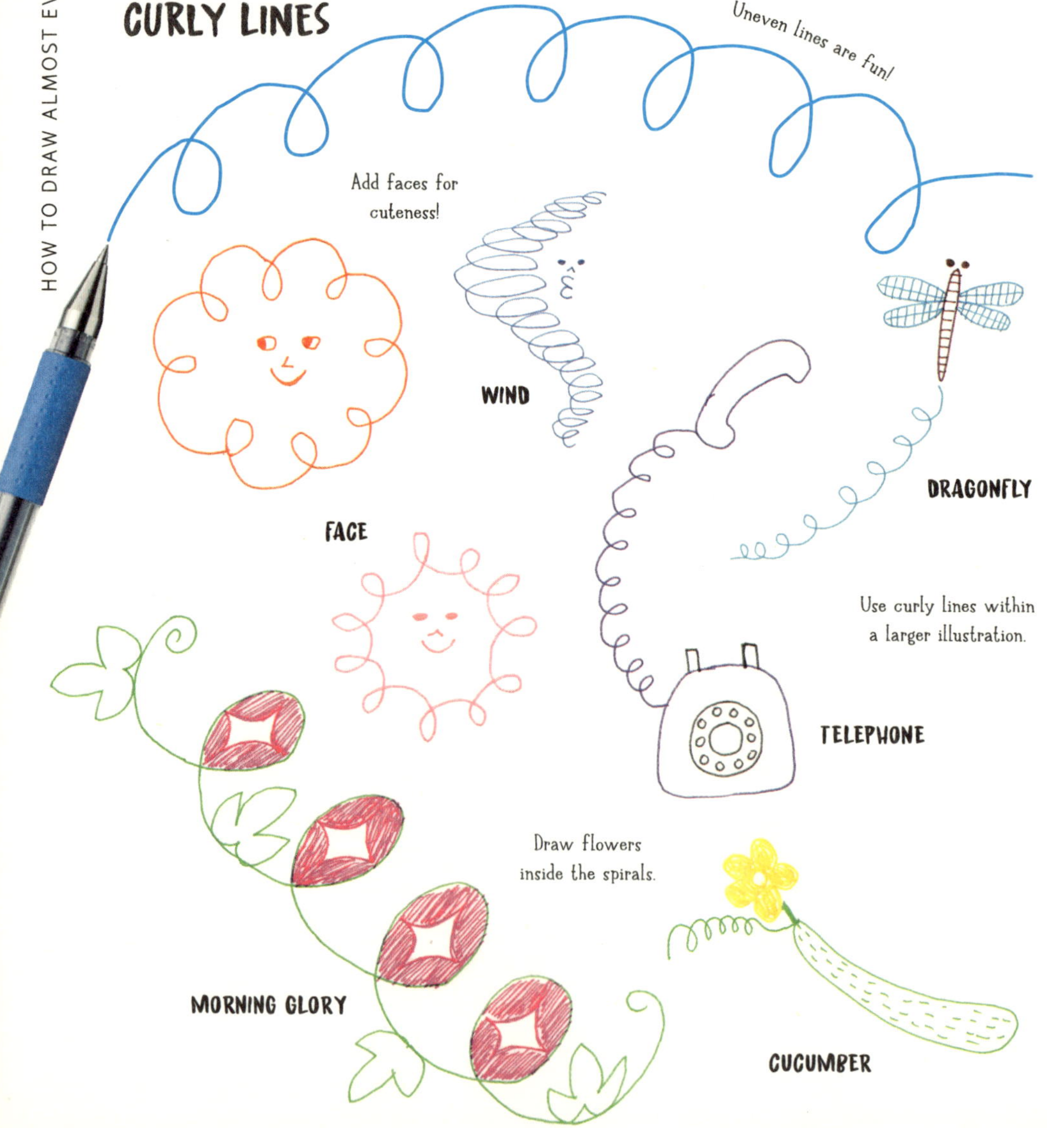

FLUFFY LINES

Vary the size for a relaxed feeling!

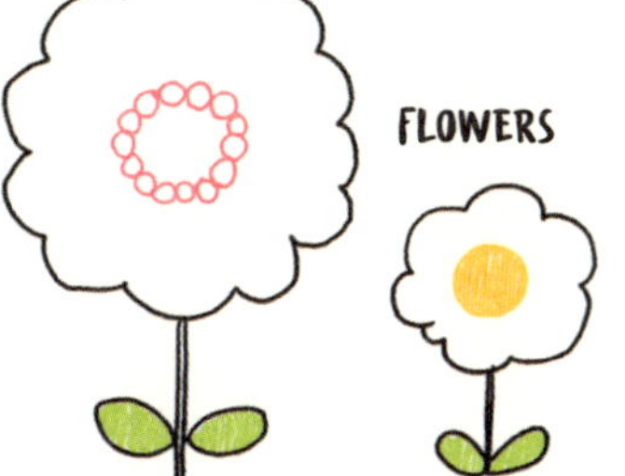

FLOWERS

Add patterns inside the fluffy lines.

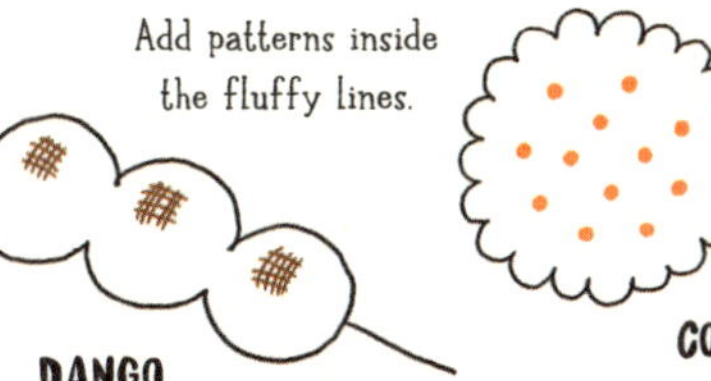

DANGO

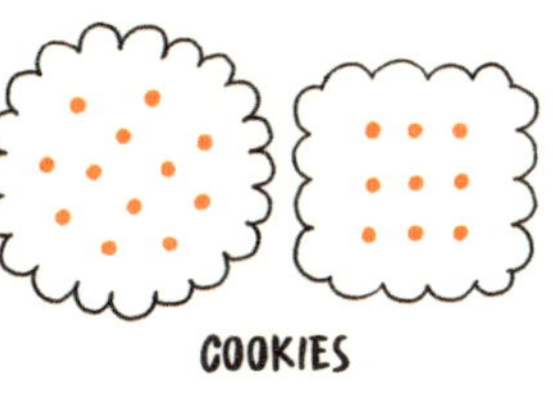

COOKIES

Use fluffy lines to draw a triangle.

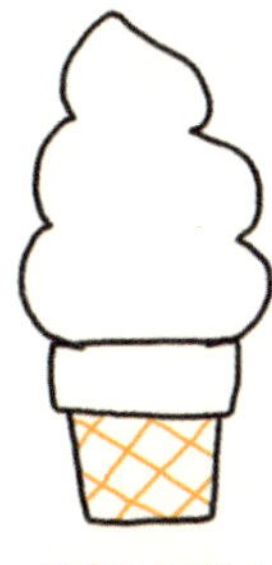

SOFT-SERVE ICE CREAM

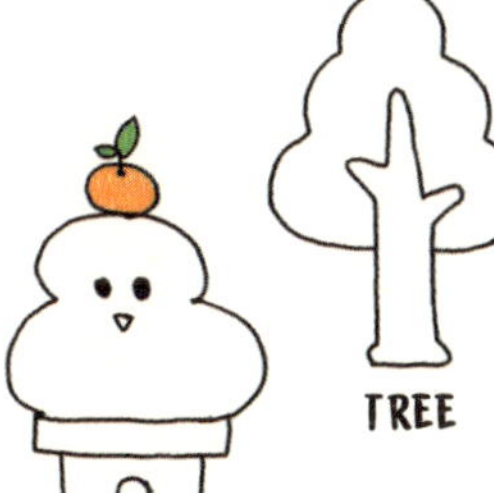

NEW YEAR'S RICE CAKE

TREE

CHOW CHOW

LION

Use fluffy lines to draw animal faces.

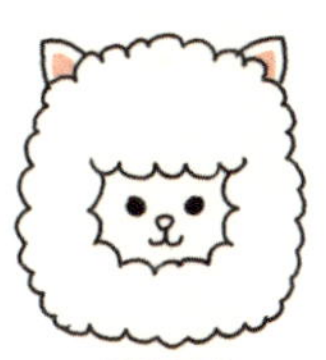

ALPACA

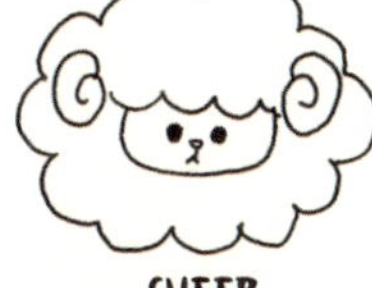

SHEEP

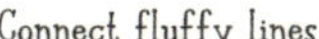

Connect fluffy lines.

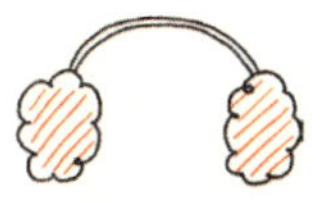

EARMUFFS

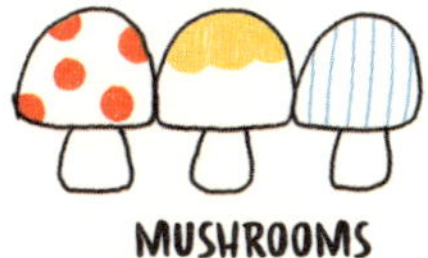

MUSHROOMS

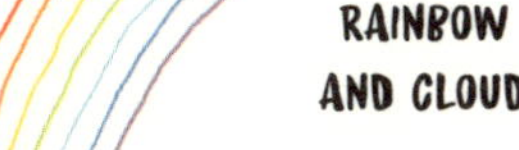

RAINBOW AND CLOUD

Draw along the edge of the paper.

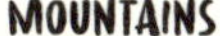

MOUNTAINS

JAGGED LINES

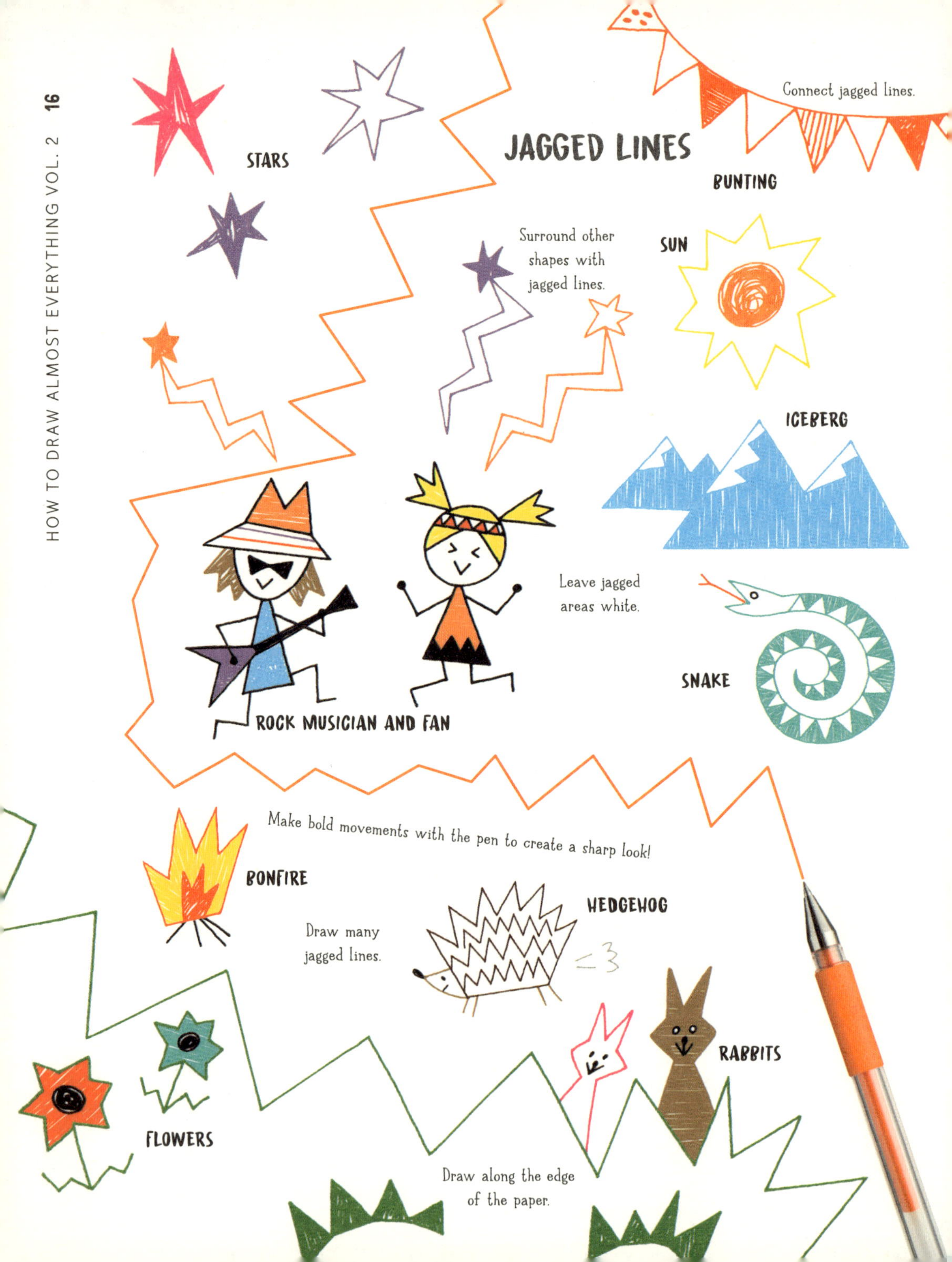

Connect jagged lines.

STARS

BUNTING

Surround other shapes with jagged lines.

SUN

ICEBERG

Leave jagged areas white.

SNAKE

ROCK MUSICIAN AND FAN

Make bold movements with the pen to create a sharp look!

BONFIRE

HEDGEHOG

Draw many jagged lines.

RABBITS

FLOWERS

Draw along the edge of the paper.

DOTTED LINES

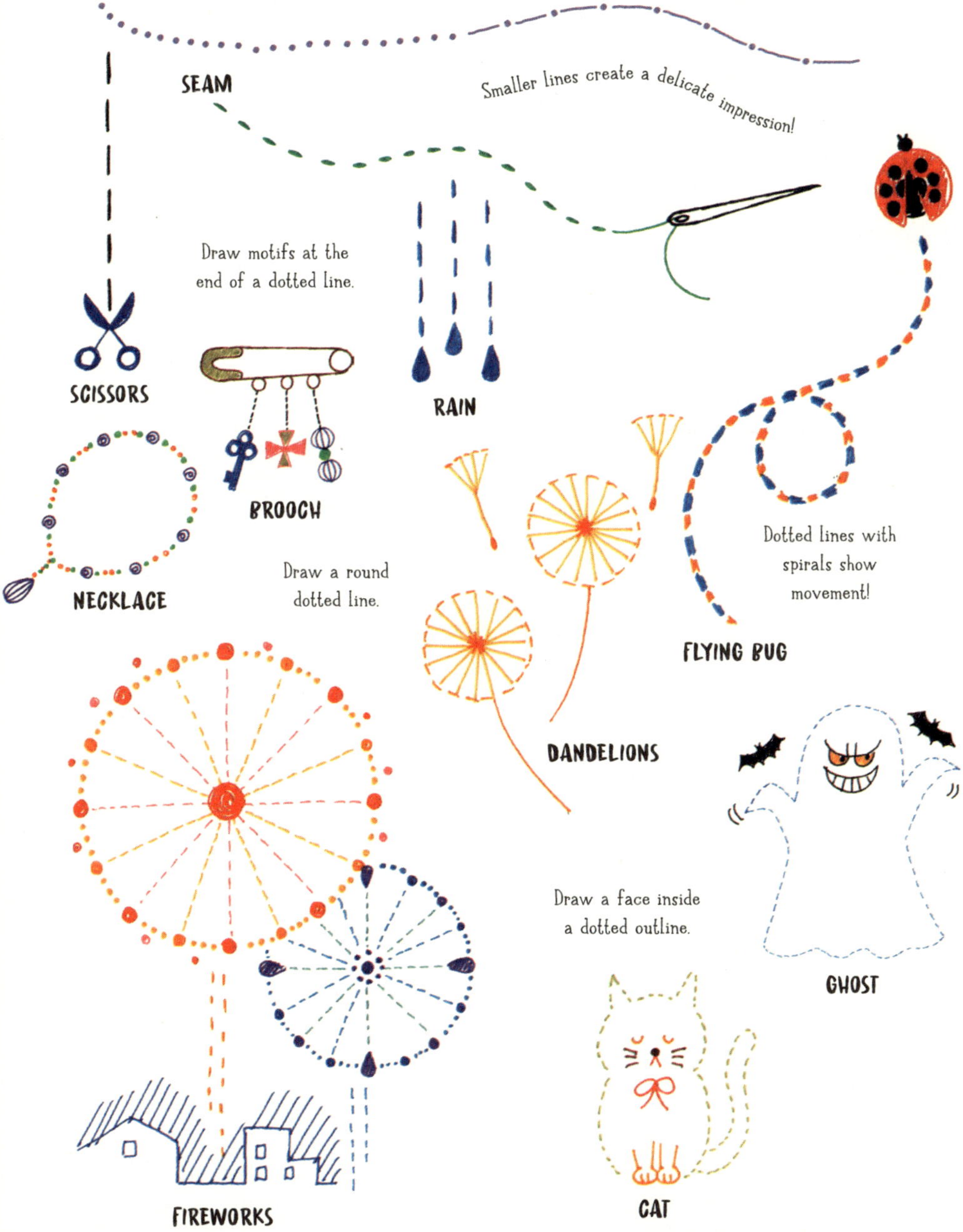

SEAM

Smaller lines create a delicate impression!

Draw motifs at the end of a dotted line.

SCISSORS

BROOCH

RAIN

NECKLACE

Draw a round dotted line.

Dotted lines with spirals show movement!

FLYING BUG

DANDELIONS

Draw a face inside a dotted outline.

GHOST

FIREWORKS

CAT

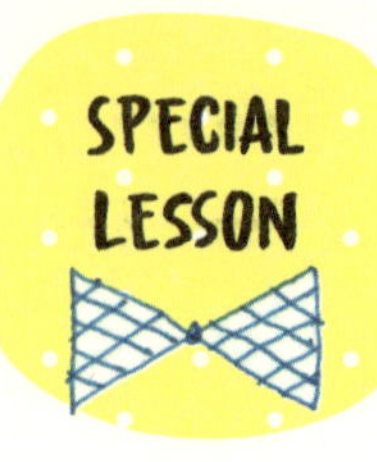

COLOR YOUR ILLUSTRATIONS USING LINES

Use the lines practiced on pages 14–17 to fill your illustrations with pattern and color. This method will create unique illustrations full of movement and texture.

TECHNIQUE 1: COLOR USING VARIOUS LINES

STRAIGHT LINES

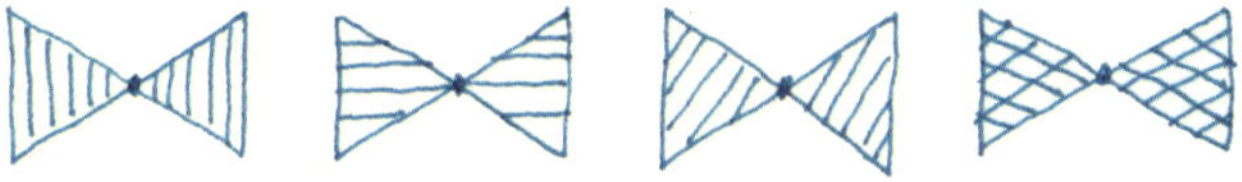

Vertical

Horizontal

Diagonal

Cross

You can change the thickness of the lines and the amount of space between lines for added interest.

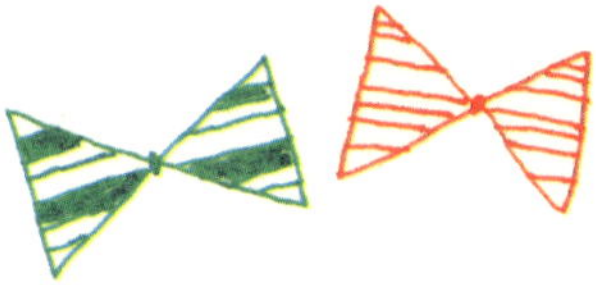

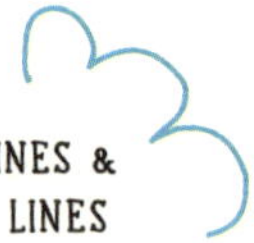

CURLY LINES & FLUFFY LINES

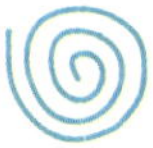

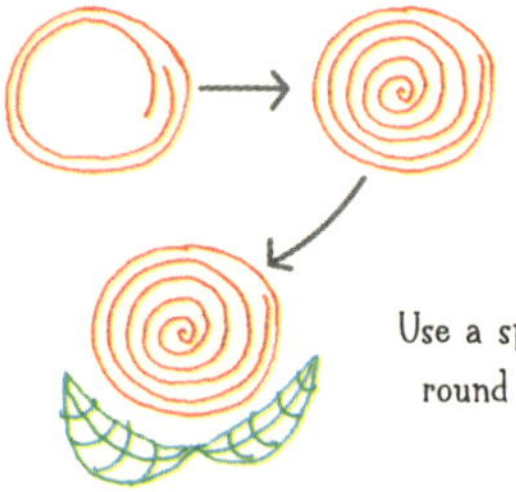

Use a spiral to fill a round illustration.

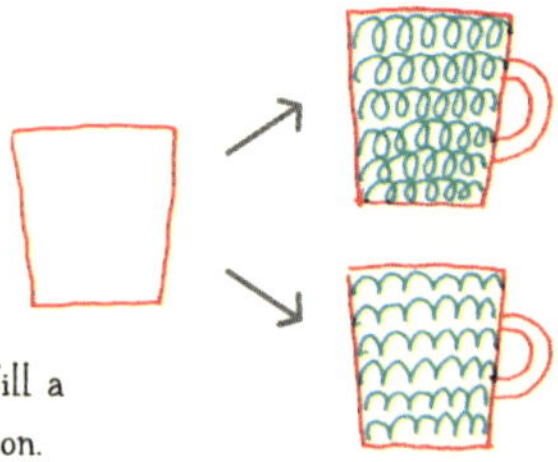

Curly lines and fluffy lines can also be used to fill in geometric shapes.

JAGGED LINES

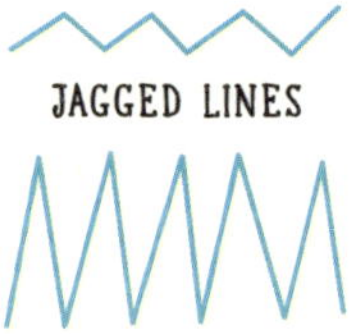

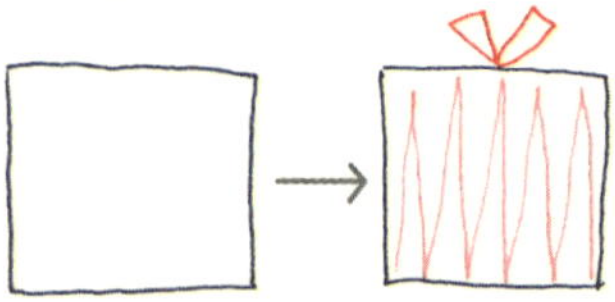

Use a single stroke for a casual look.

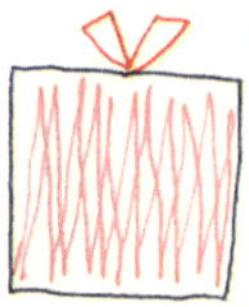

Or try layering several thin lines.

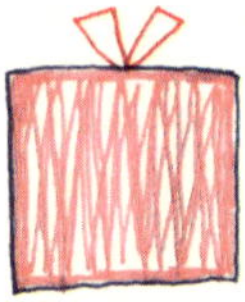

Don't forget to color along the outline of the shape.

DOTTED LINES

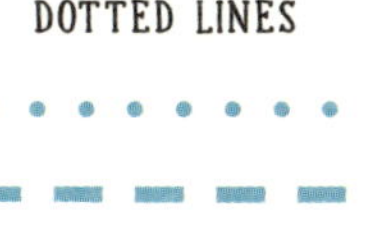

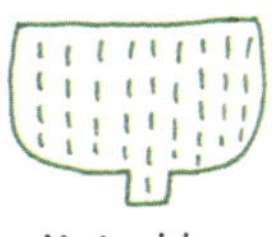

Vertical lines

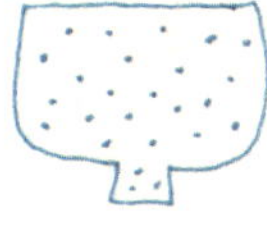

Random dots

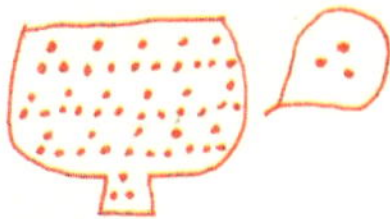

Patterned dots

Arrange the dots in a pattern as shown here.

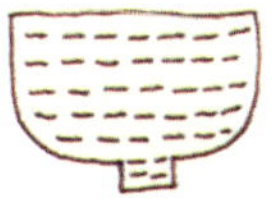

Horizontal lines

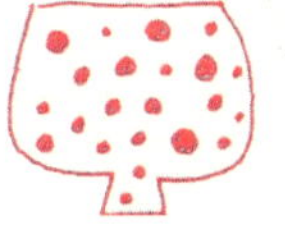

Dots of various sizes

TECHNIQUE 2: COLOR USING SPECIAL EFFECTS

COLOR FOLLOWING THE SHAPE

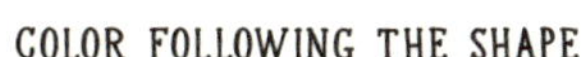

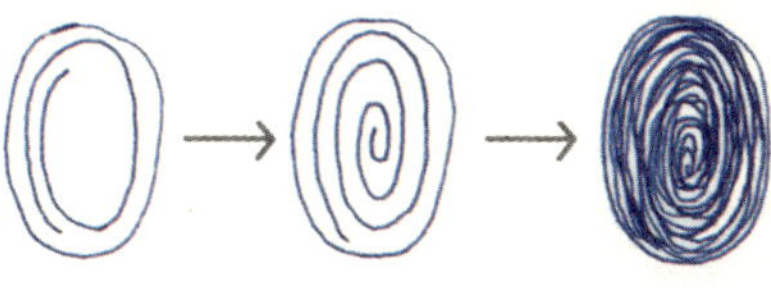

Color from the outside toward the inside of the circle.

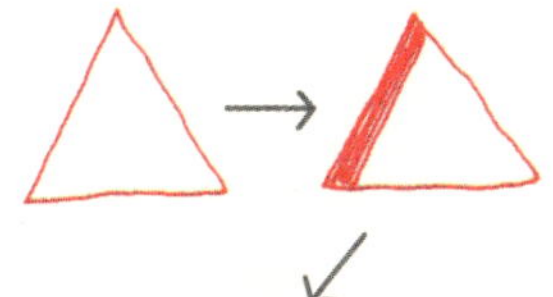

Layer straight lines along three sides of a triangle.

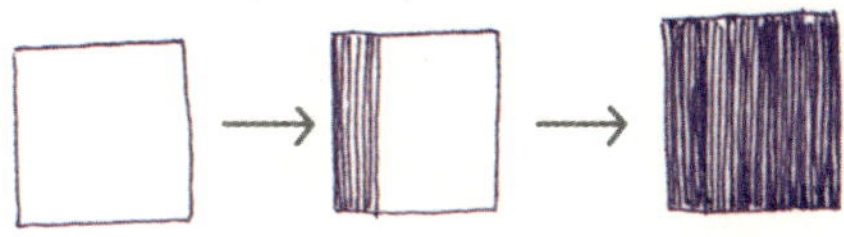

Layer straight lines along 3 sides for a square.

INTENTIONALLY SHIFT THE COLORING

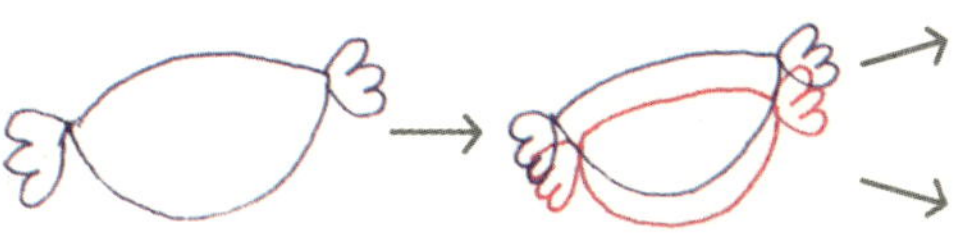

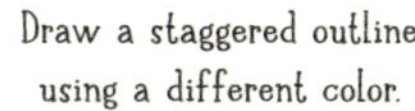

Draw a staggered outline using a different color.

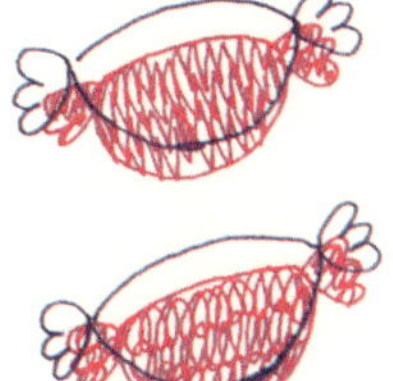

Color inside the outline with jagged or curly lines.

ADD GRADATIONS

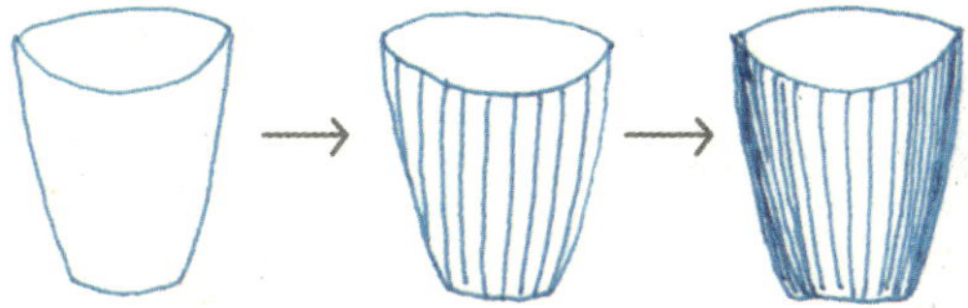

First, color with lines.

Next, layer lines where you want to show depth to create a three-dimensional finish.

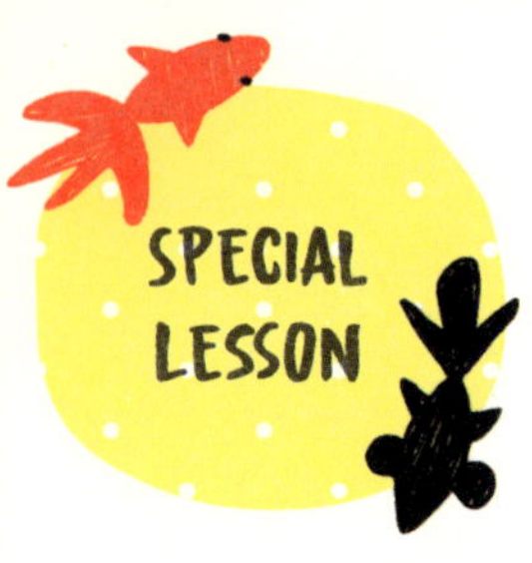

UNDERSTANDING COLOR COMBINATIONS

Color plays an important role in the overall impression of an illustration, so it's important to consider which color pens you'll use before starting your illustration. The following guide showcases some of our favorite color combinations.

TECHNIQUE 1

First, let's focus on the three most common colors of ballpoint pens: black, blue, and red.

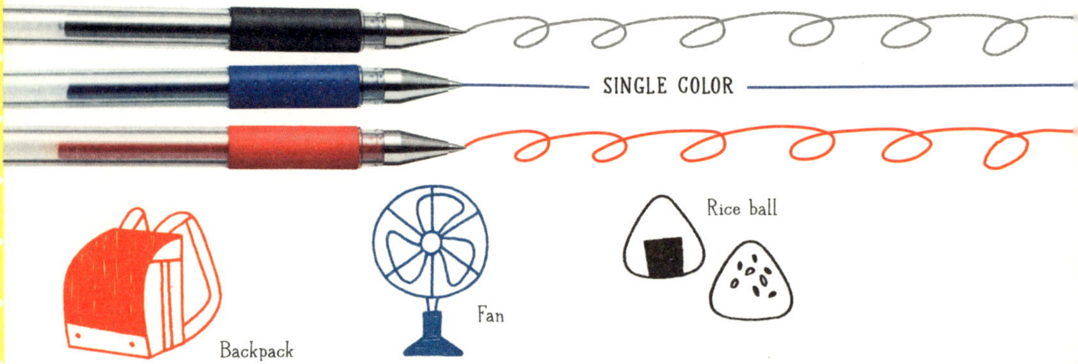

SINGLE COLOR

Backpack

Fan

Rice ball

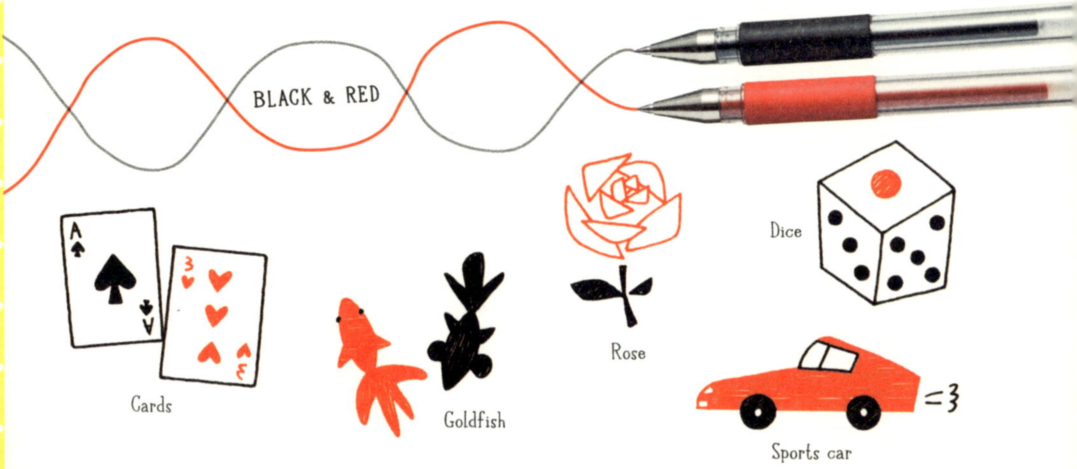

BLACK & RED

Cards

Goldfish

Rose

Dice

Sports car

BLACK & BLUE

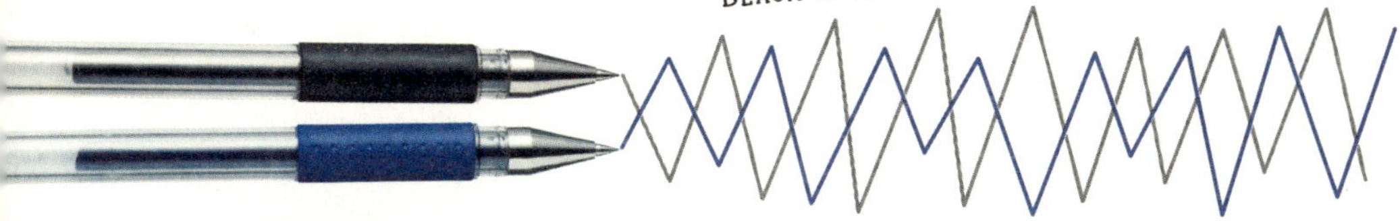

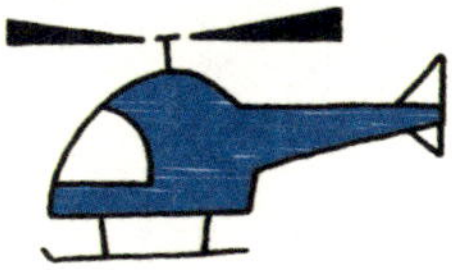

Helicopter

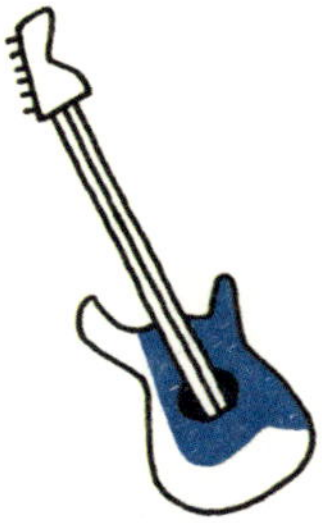

Electric guitar

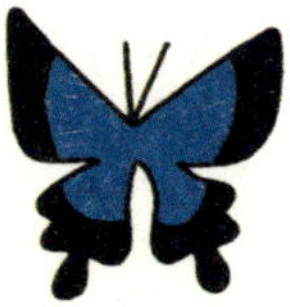

Butterfly

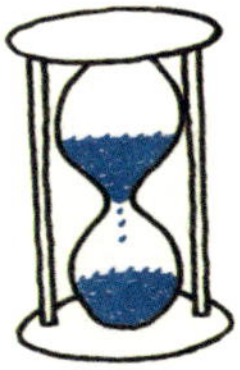

Hourglass

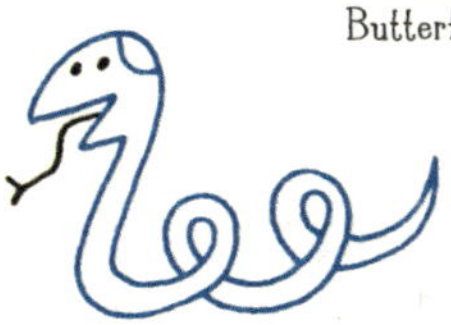

Snake

TRI-COLOR

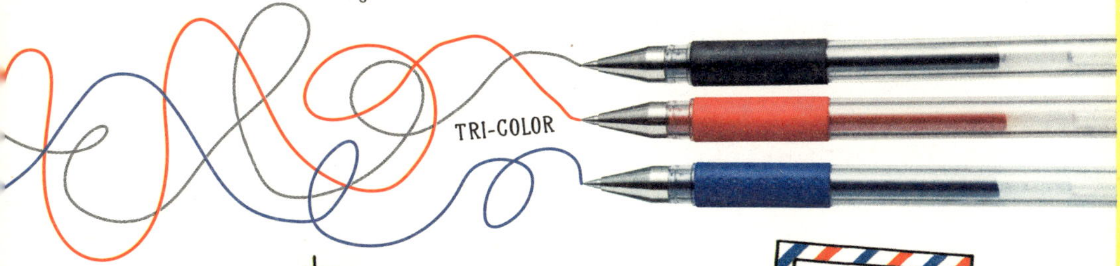

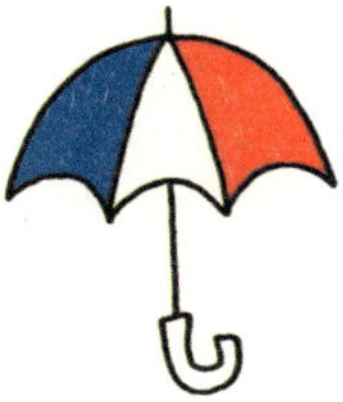

Umbrella

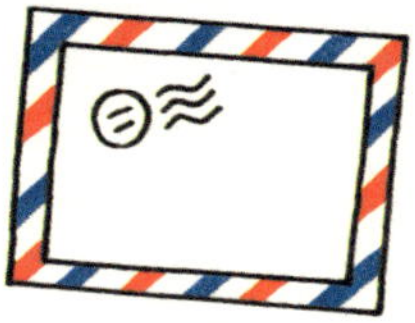

Airmail

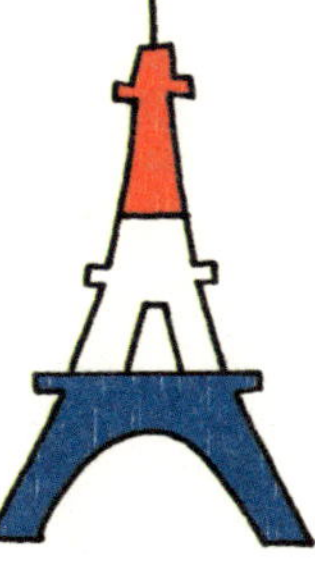

Eiffel Tower

Birthday cake

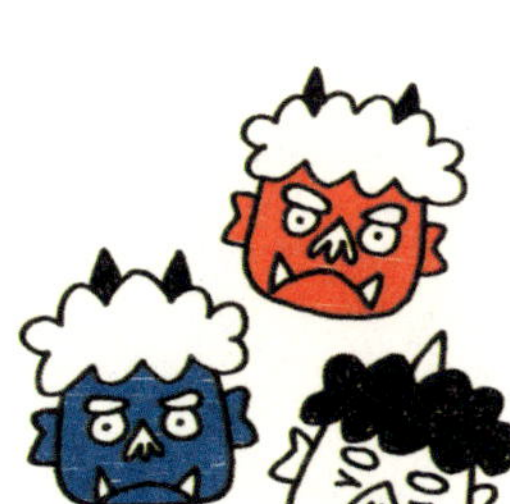

Demons

TECHNIQUE 2

It may be tempting to use a bunch of different colors when drawing with ballpoint pens, but try narrowing your palette down to just one or two shades to make a more dramatic impact.

One-Color Illustrations

Using a single color of ink can be an effective technique for creating chic, stylish illustrations. Consider the subject of your illustration when selecting your color—use brown for a steaming cup of coffee or navy for a rainy day scene.

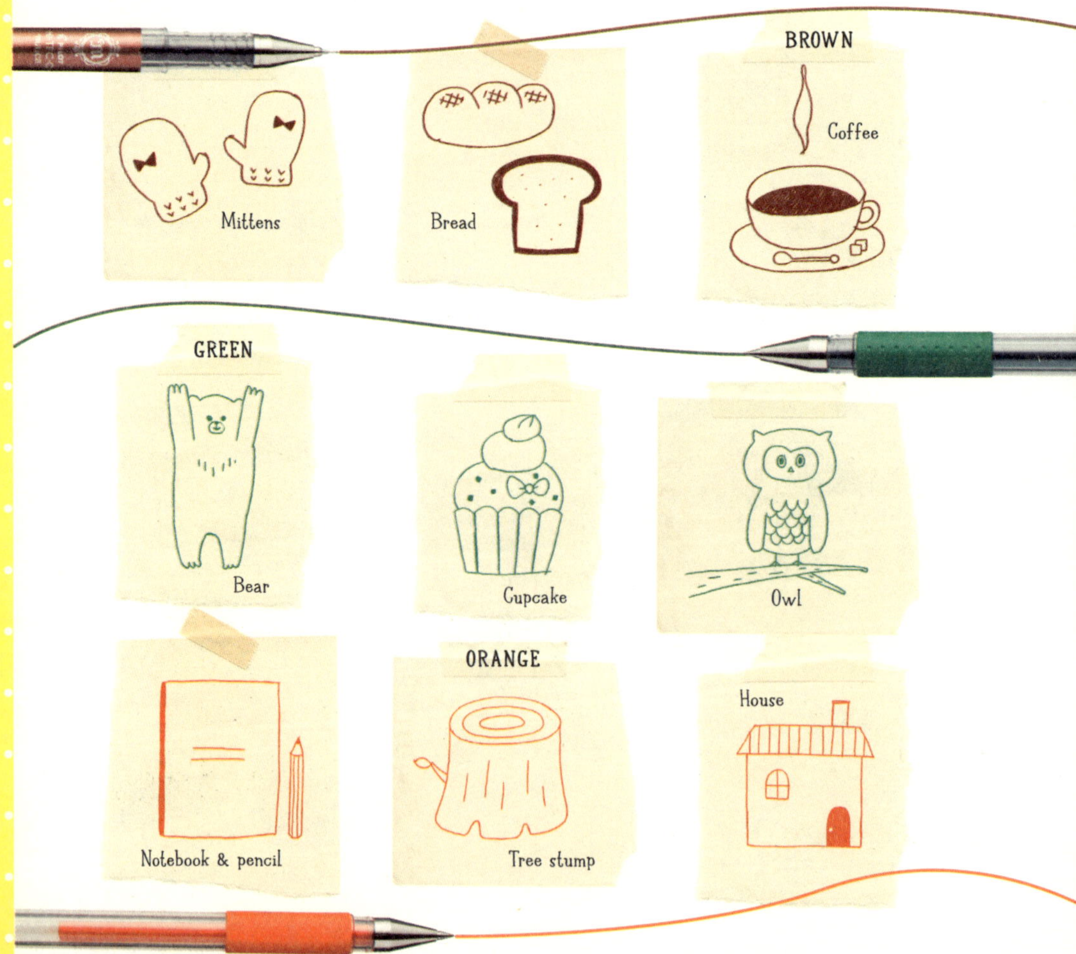

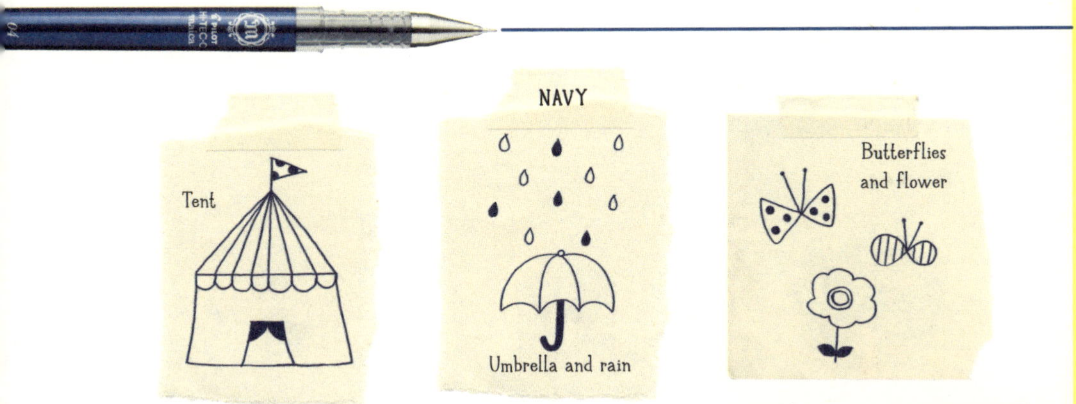

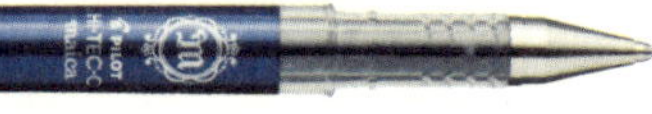

NAVY

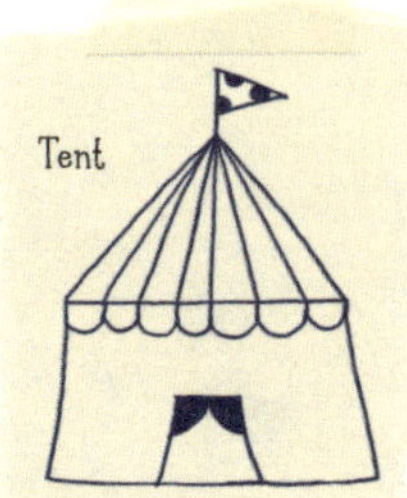

Umbrella and rain

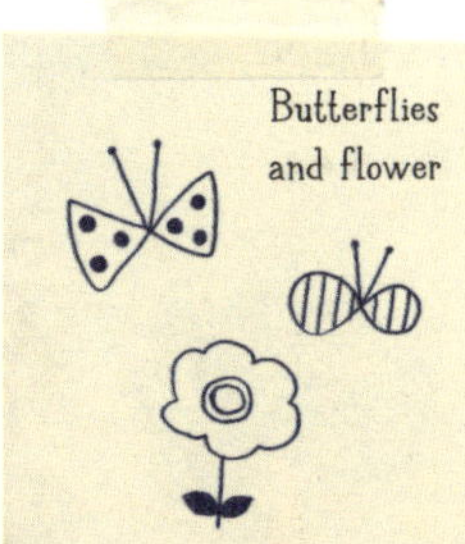

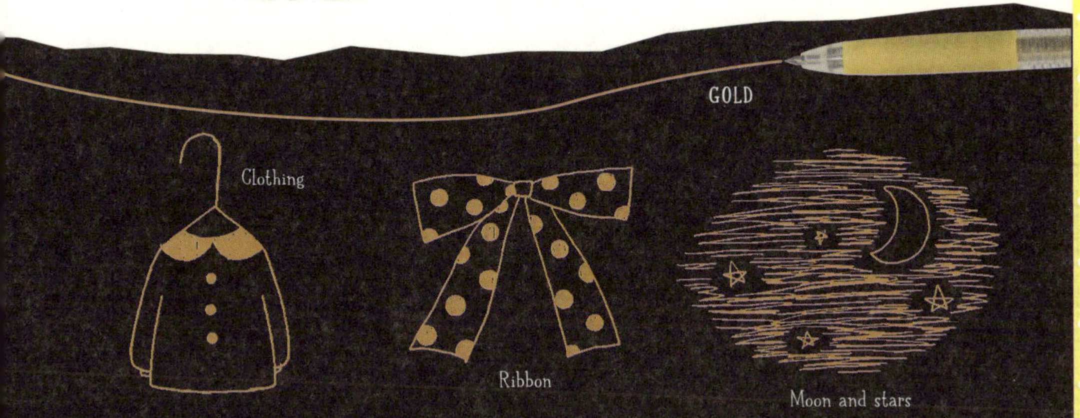

GOLD

Clothing

Ribbon

Moon and stars

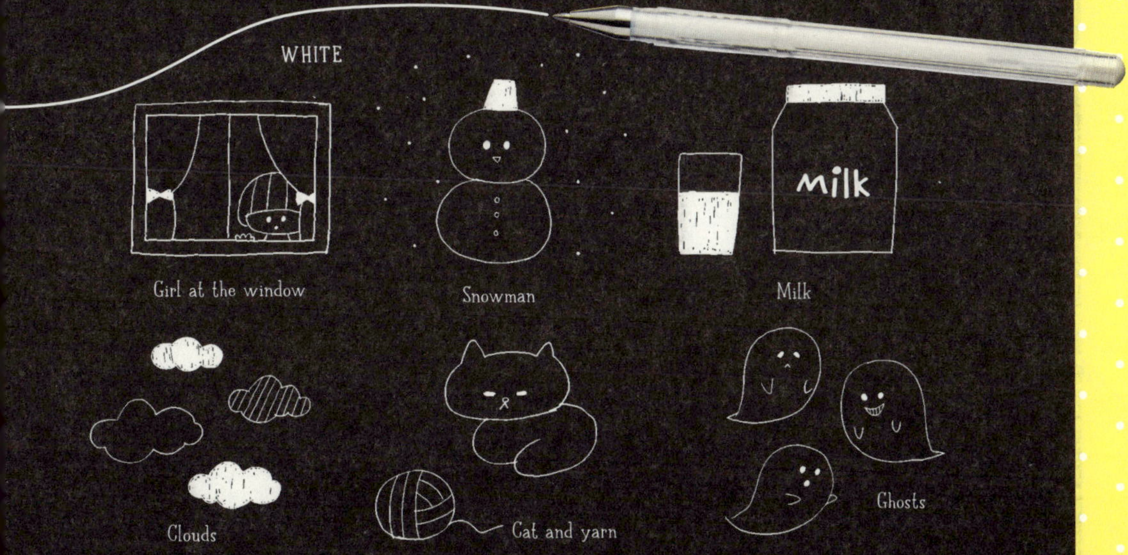

WHITE

Girl at the window

Snowman

Milk

Clouds

Cat and yarn

Ghosts

Two-Color Illustrations

Use contrasting colors to create sharp and crisp impressions or different shades of the same color to create soft impressions.

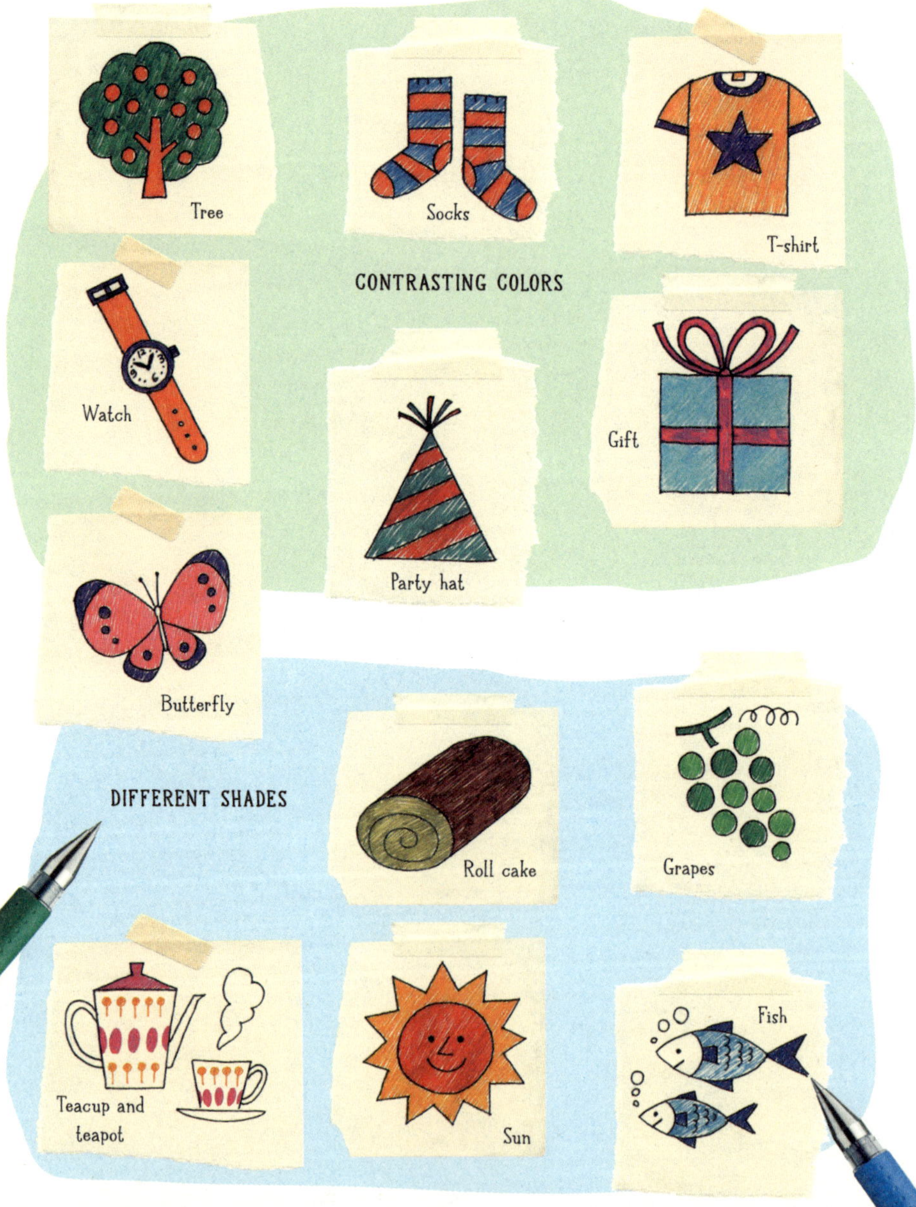

Three-Color Illustrations

When working with three colors, use the third color sparingly as an accent, or use all three colors equally to create colorful, pop-inspired images.

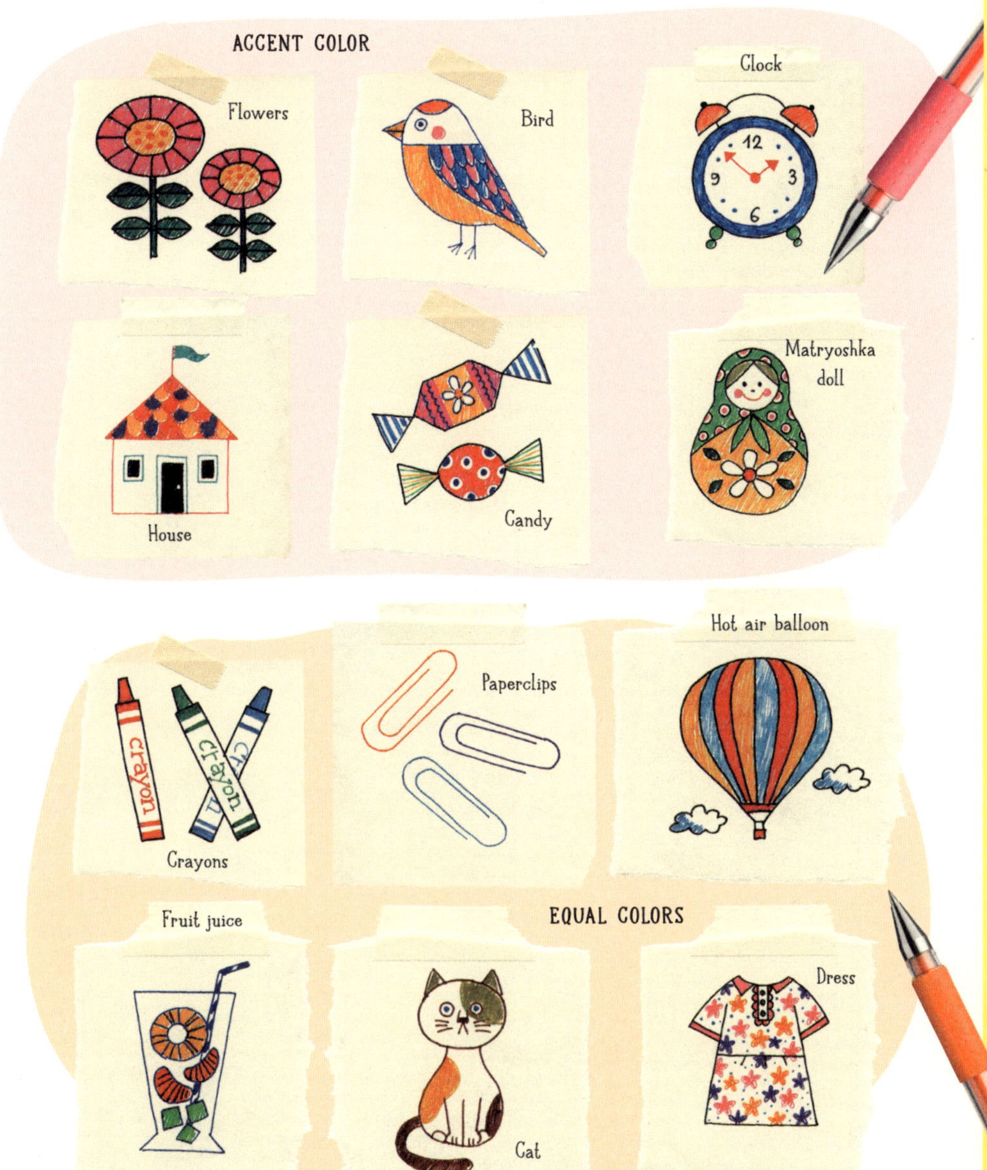

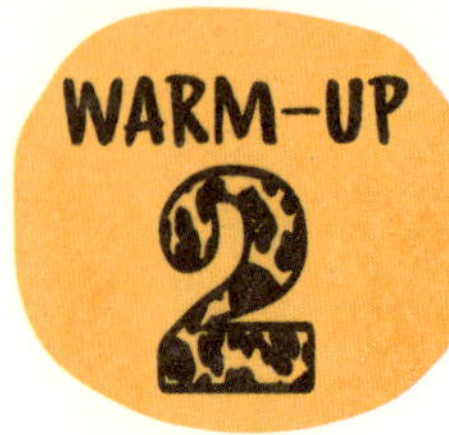

DRAWING ILLUSTRATIONS FROM BASIC SHAPES

Create cute illustrations from simple shapes, such as circles, triangles, and squares.

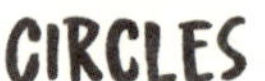

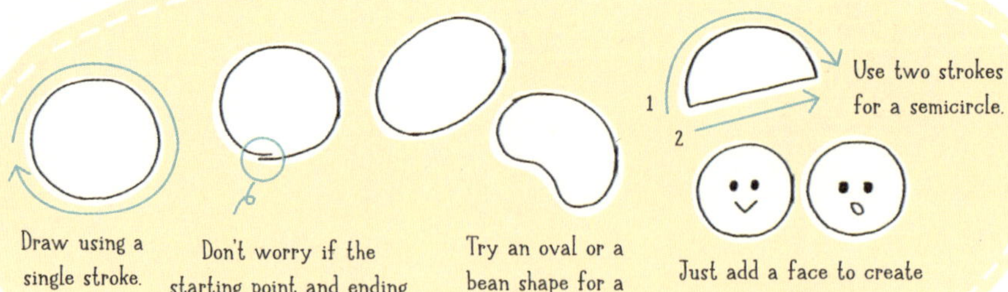

ILLUSTRATIONS BASED ON CIRCLES

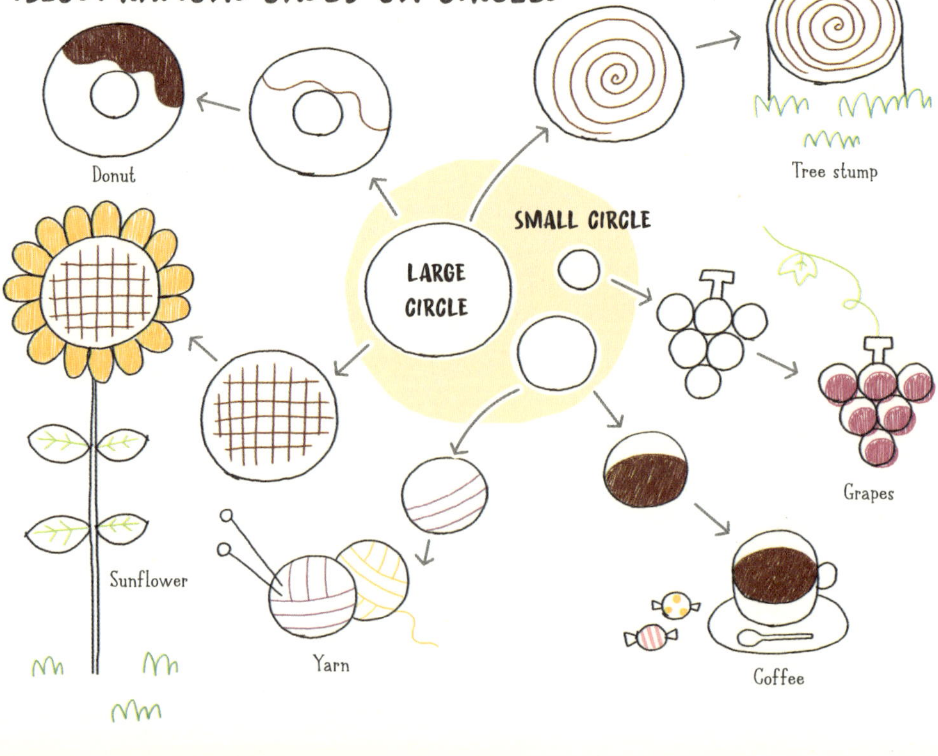

LARGE CIRCLE

SMALL CIRCLE

Donut

Tree stump

Sunflower

Yarn

Grapes

Coffee

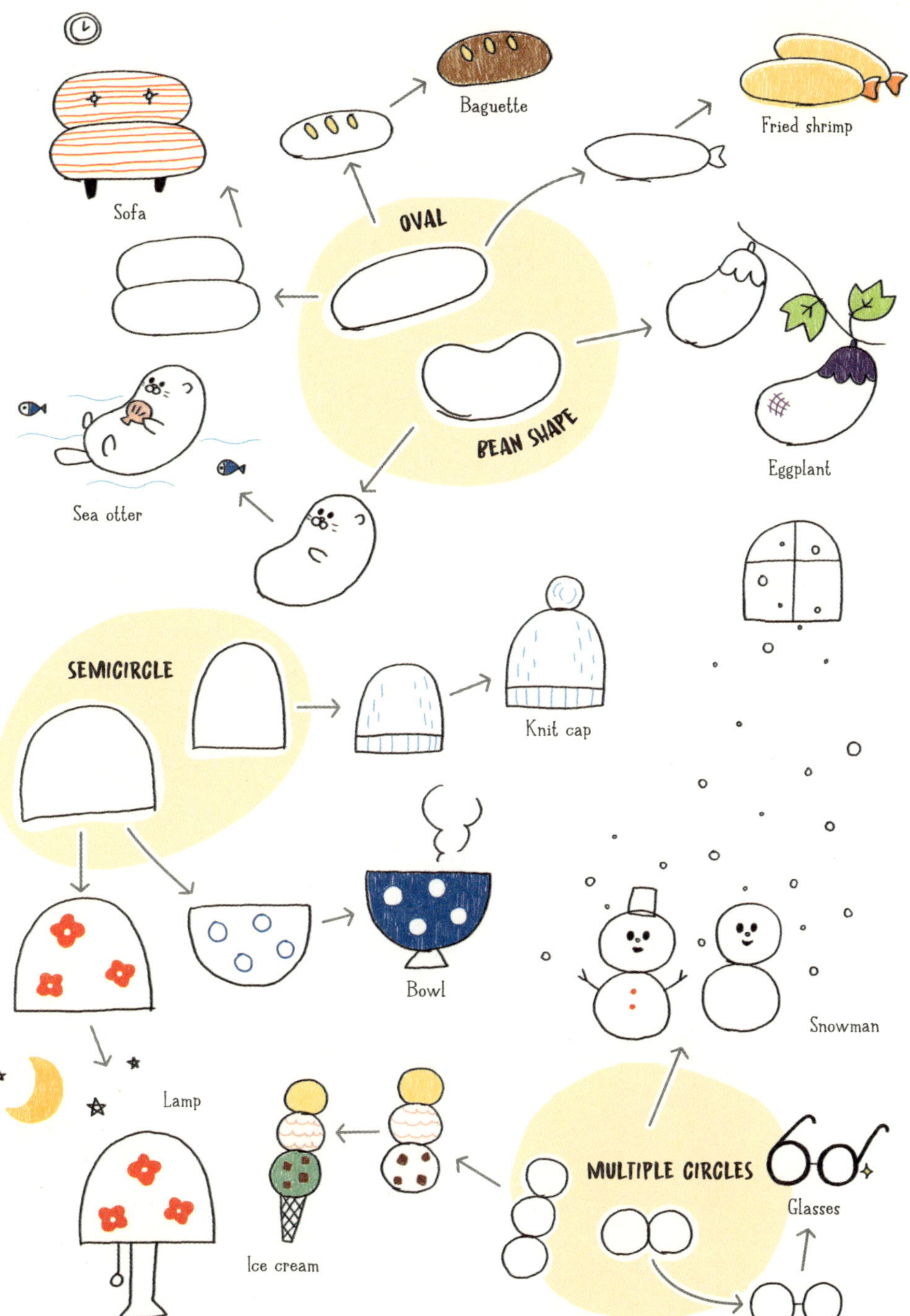
OVAL
Sofa
Baguette
Fried shrimp
BEAN SHAPE
Eggplant
Sea otter
SEMICIRCLE
Knit cap
Bowl
Lamp
Snowman
Ice cream
MULTIPLE CIRCLES
Glasses

TRIANGLES

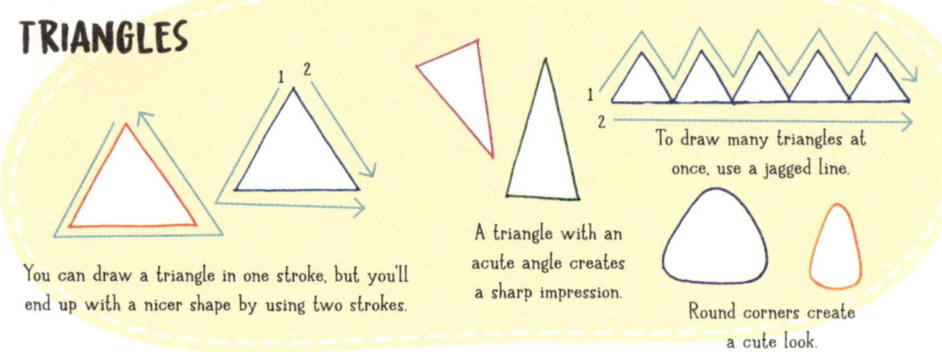

You can draw a triangle in one stroke, but you'll end up with a nicer shape by using two strokes.

A triangle with an acute angle creates a sharp impression.

To draw many triangles at once, use a jagged line.

Round corners create a cute look.

ILLUSTRATIONS BASED ON TRIANGLES

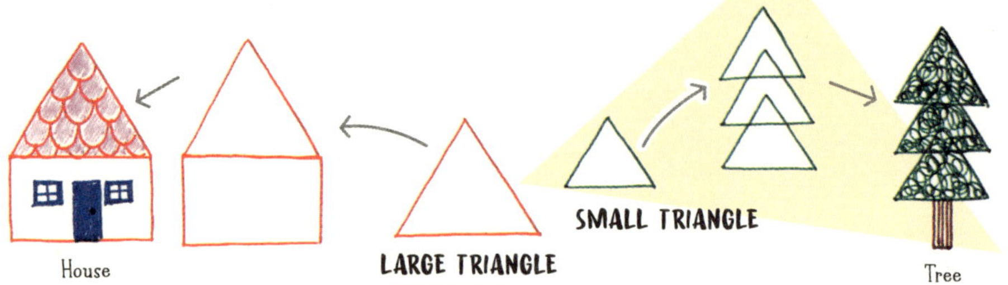

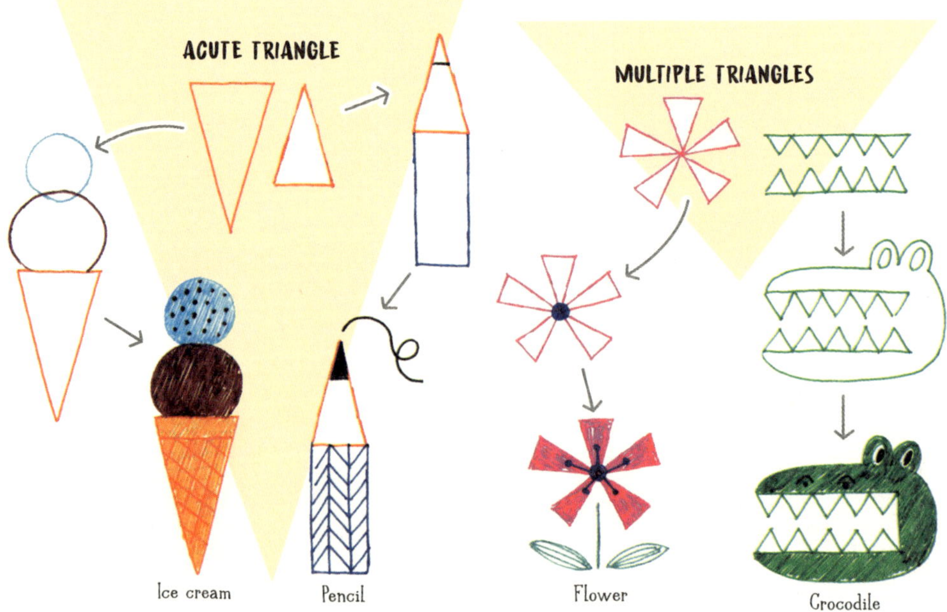

SQUARES

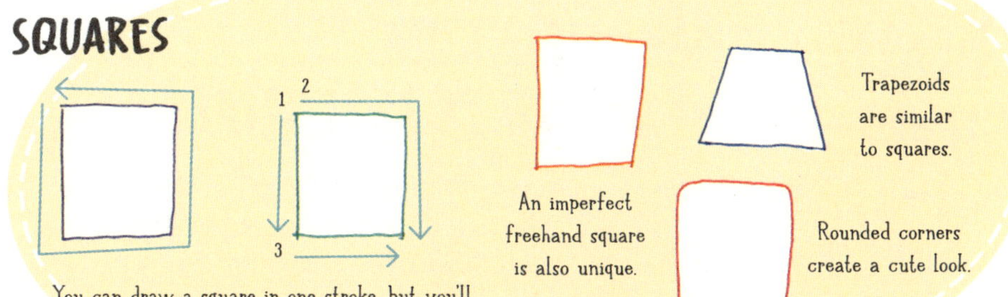

You can draw a square in one stroke, but you'll end up with a nicer shape by using three strokes.

ILLUSTRATIONS BASED ON SQUARES

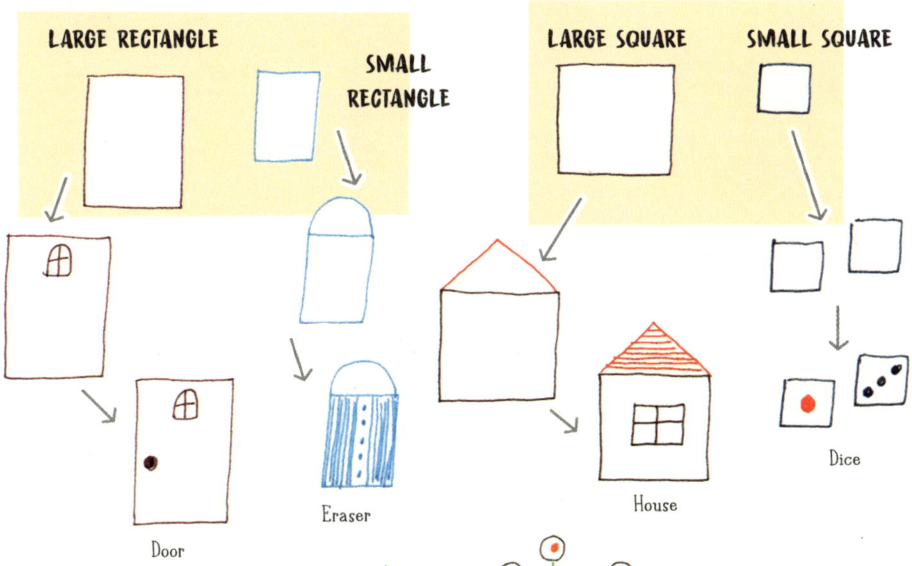

LARGE RECTANGLE

SMALL RECTANGLE

LARGE SQUARE

SMALL SQUARE

Door

Eraser

House

Dice

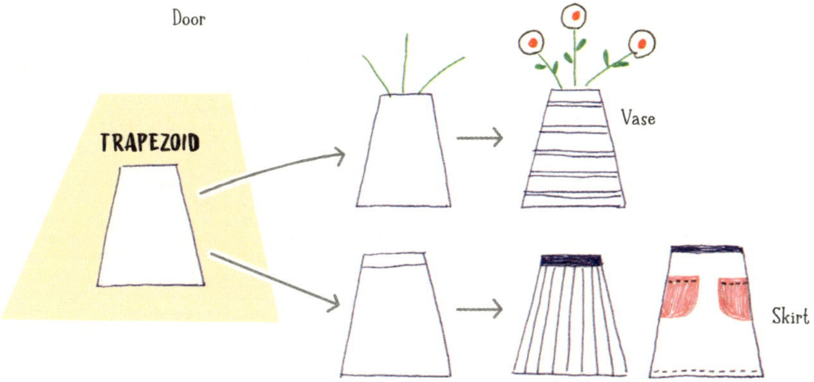

TRAPEZOID

Vase

Skirt

SPECIAL LESSON

DRAWING FROM DIFFERENT PERSPECTIVES

Changing the perspective may result in a stronger illustration. Let's learn how to draw an object from various angles, then choose the angle that best captures the characteristics of the object.

CUPCAKE

FROM ABOVE

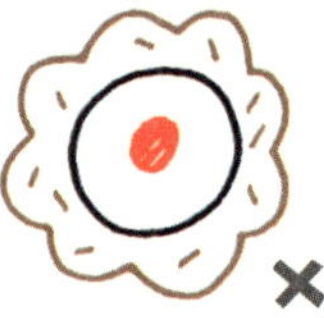

At first glance, it looks like a cookie.

FROM BELOW

You can't really tell what it is.

FROM THE SIDE

You know it is a cupcake right away when you see the shape.

FROM ABOVE AT AN ANGLE

The soft-looking cake is emphasized and looks very yummy.

BULLET TRAIN

FROM THE FRONT ✗

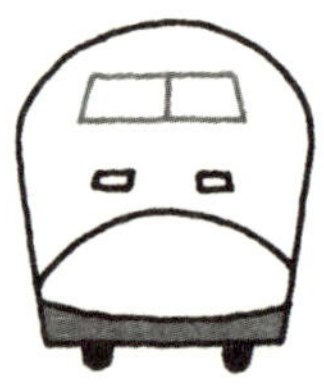

The length of the train or the speed cannot be expressed from this angle.

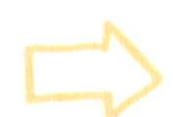

FROM THE SIDE ✓

The pattern of the car and the shape of the tip are visible, and the length of the train is obvious!

FROM ABOVE ✗

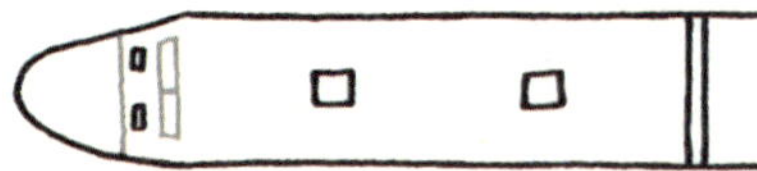

Important characteristics, such as the shape of the tip or the pattern of the car are not visible from this angle.

FROM THE SIDE AT AN ANGLE ✓

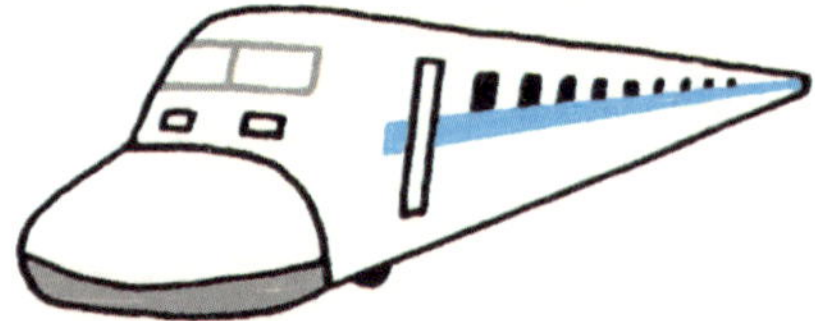

Drawing at an angle creates depth and increases the sense of speed.

Chapter 1:

DRAWING ANIMALS

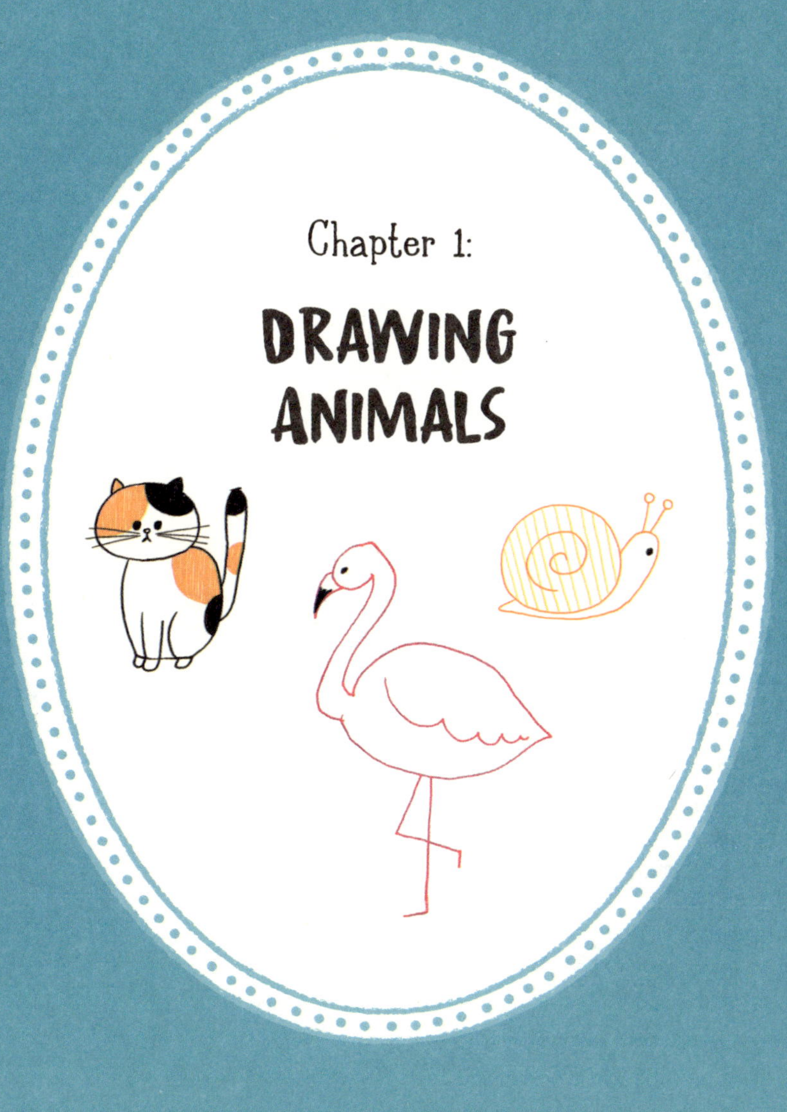

LESSON 1

DRAWING ANIMAL FACES USING BASIC SHAPES

Drawing animal faces may seem intimidating, but if you start with basic shapes, you'll see how easy it is to draw cute creatures!

CIRCLE OR OVAL

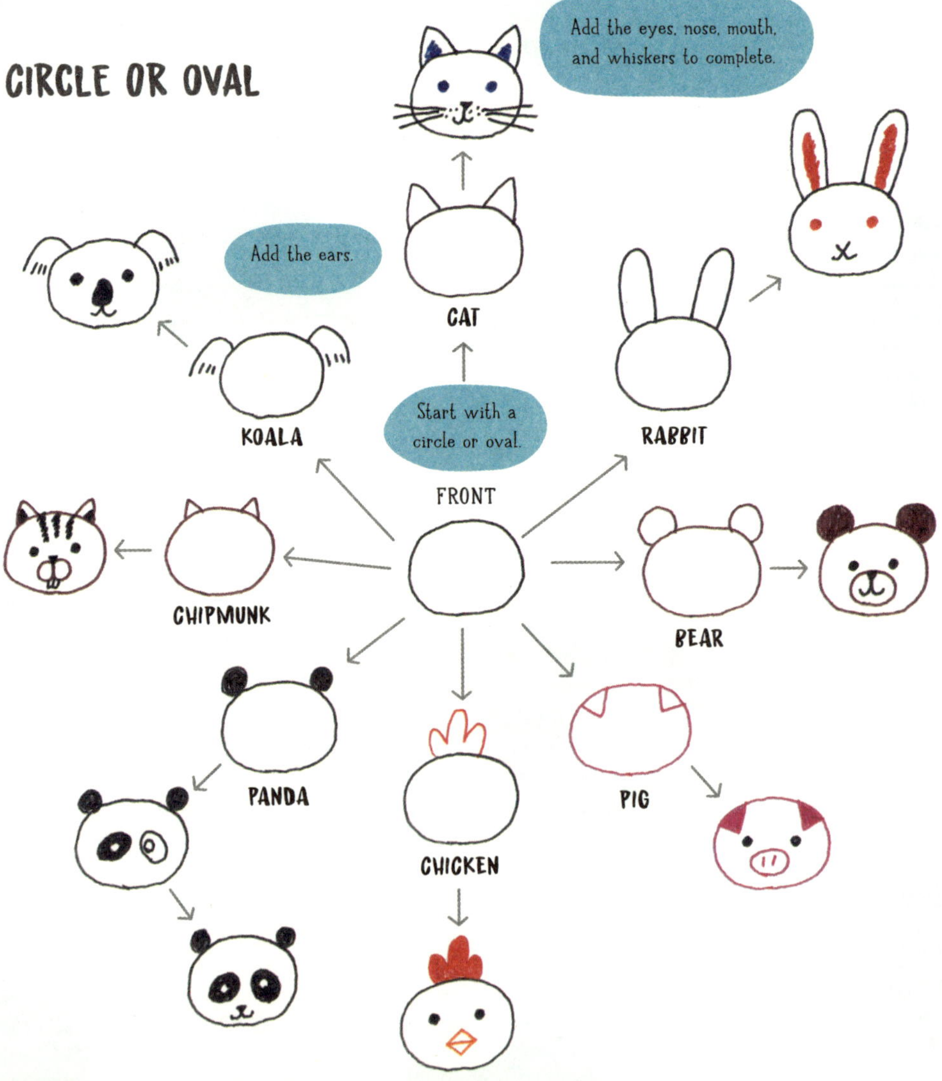

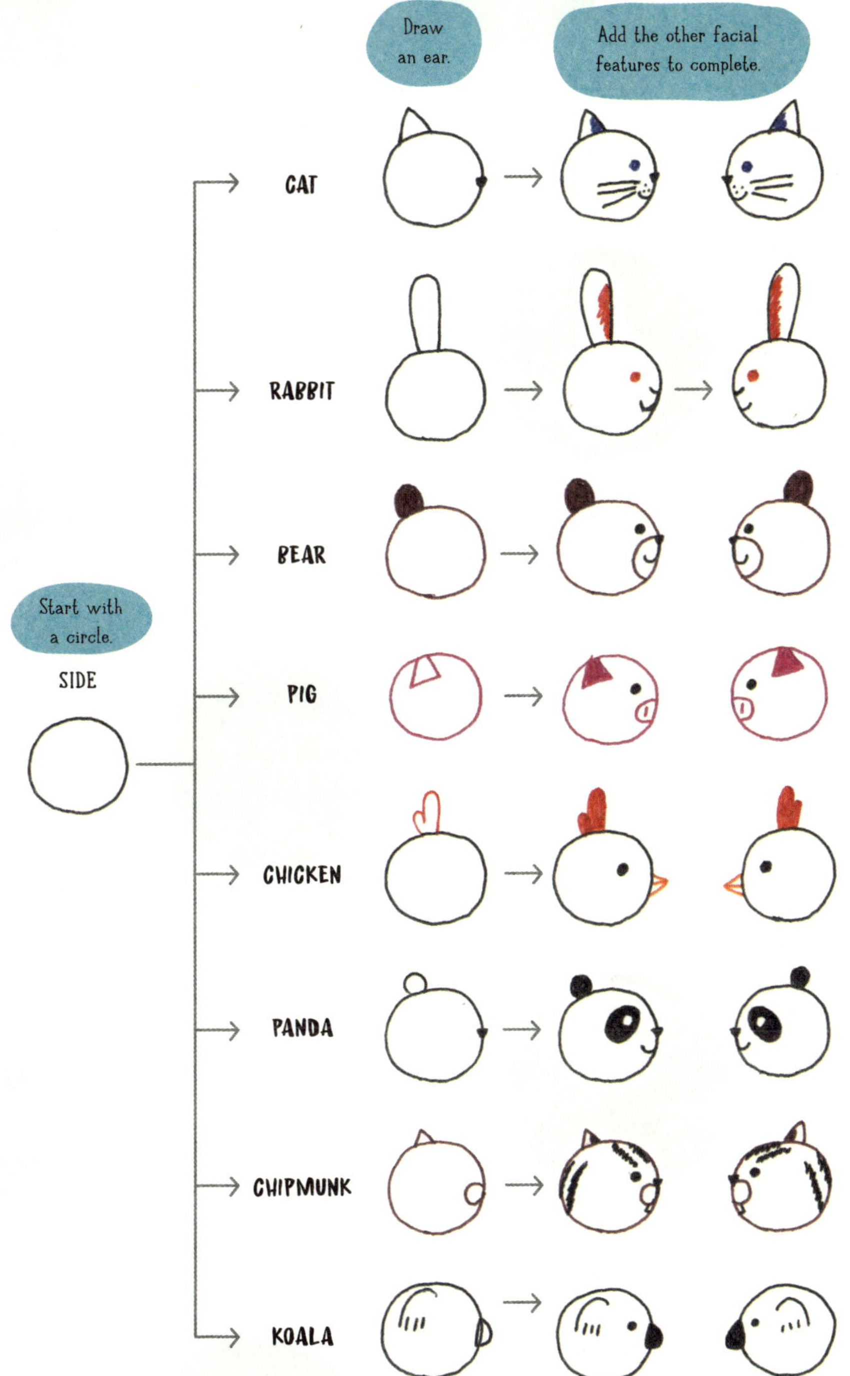
Draw an ear.
Add the other facial features to complete.
Start with a circle.
SIDE
CAT
RABBIT
BEAR
PIG
CHICKEN
PANDA
CHIPMUNK
KOALA

TRIANGLE

Start with an inverted triangle.

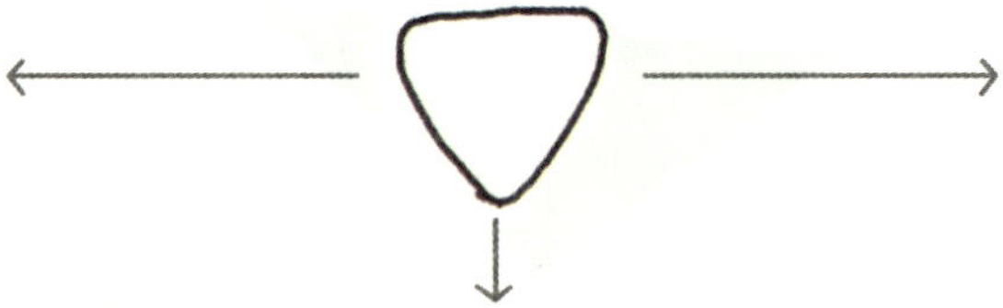

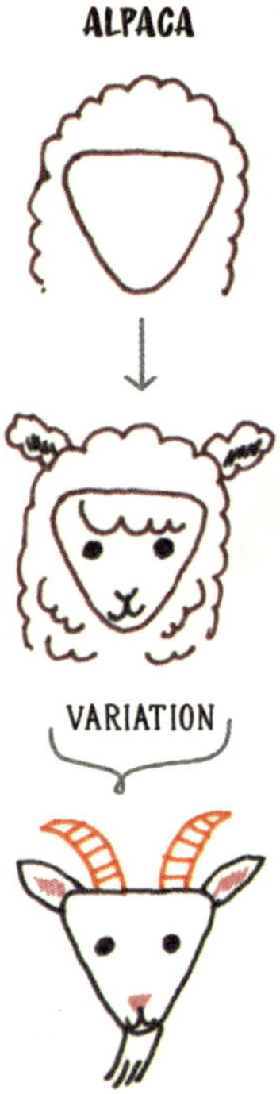

ALPACA

VARIATION

Add horns and a beard to transform into a goat.

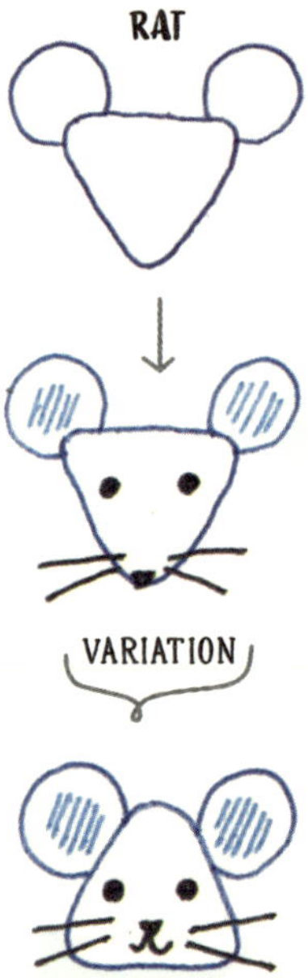

RAT

VARIATION

A rounded triangle creates a cute impression.

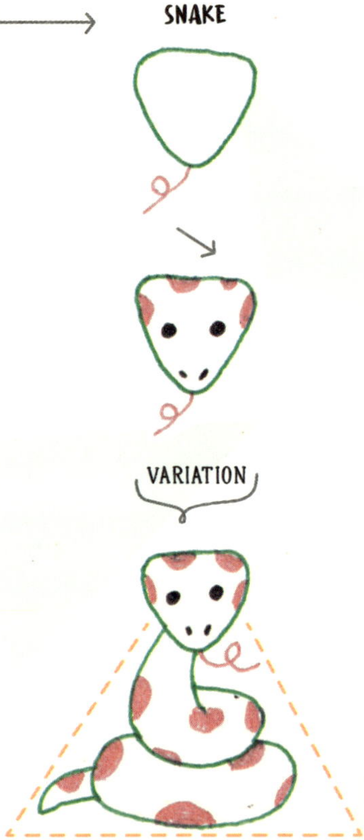

SNAKE

VARIATION

Keep a triangular shape in mind when you draw the body too.

Start with a thin triangle.

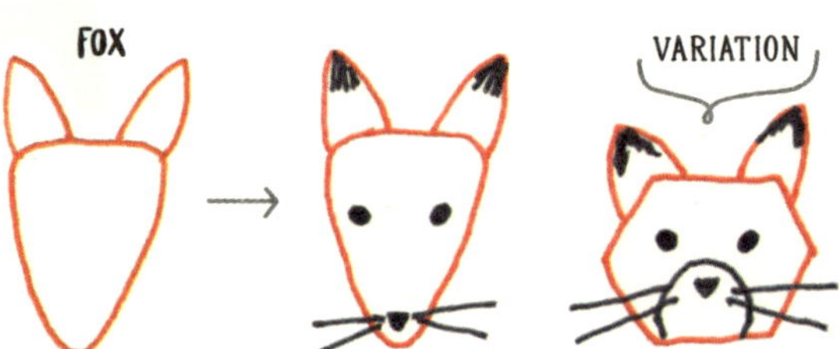

Use the same triangular ears, but change the face shape to a hexagon to draw a fox cub.

SQUARE

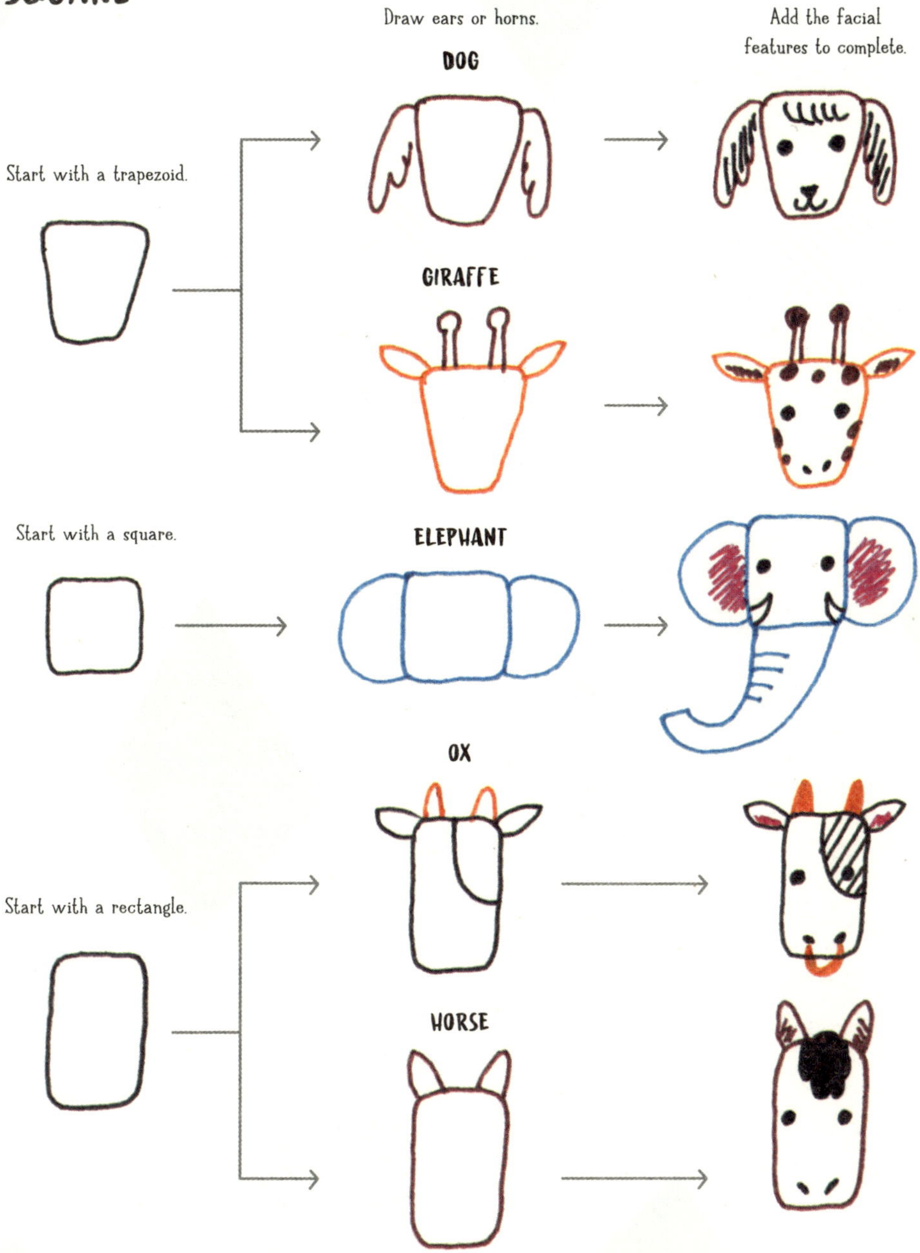

Draw ears or horns.

Add the facial features to complete.

Start with a trapezoid.

DOG

GIRAFFE

Start with a square.

ELEPHANT

Start with a rectangle.

OX

HORSE

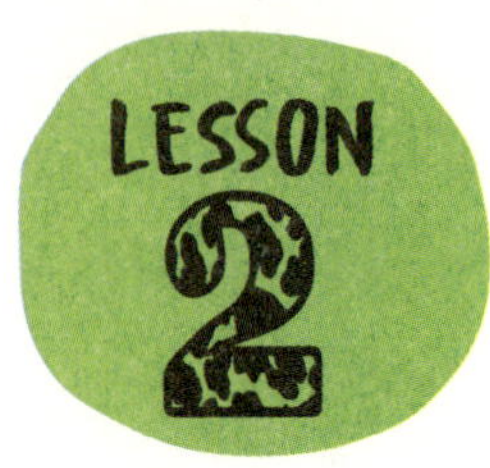

DRAWING ANIMAL BODIES

Once you master drawing animal faces, you'll be ready to tackle whole body illustrations.

1 Draw the body the same length as the face.

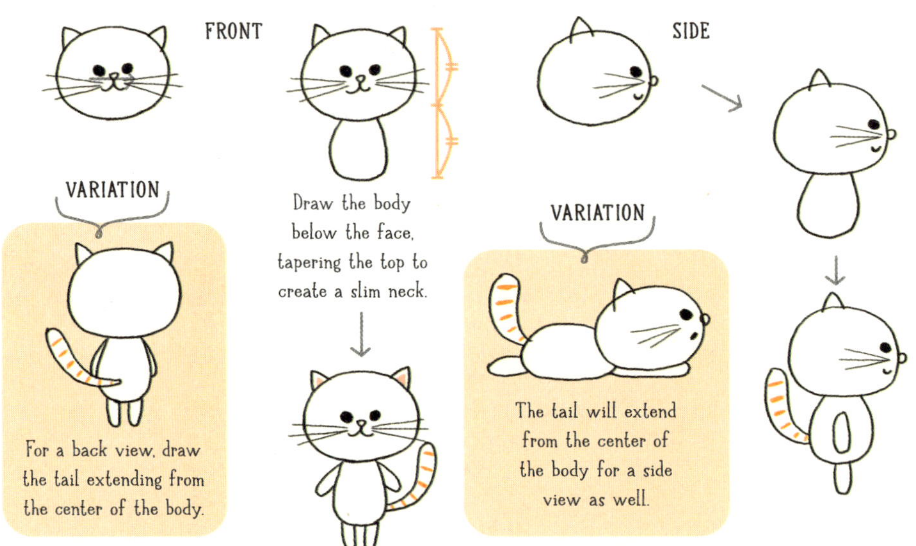

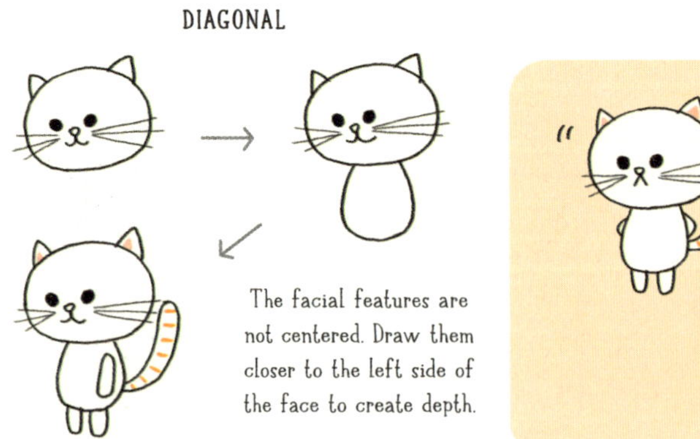

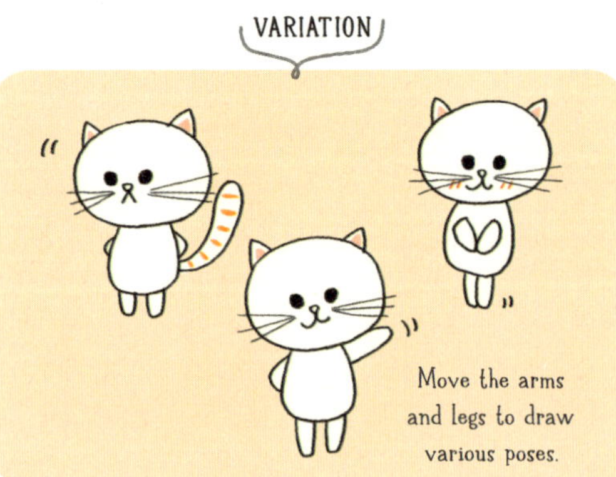

2 Add tails and special markings unique to each animal.

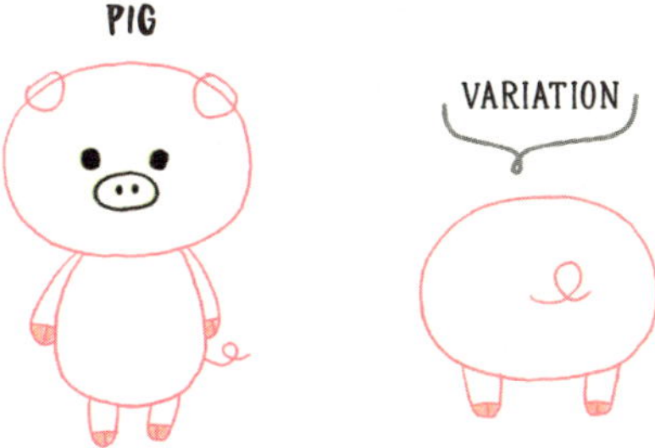

Add a "T" to create hooves at the ends of arms and legs. Don't forget a cute, curly tail.

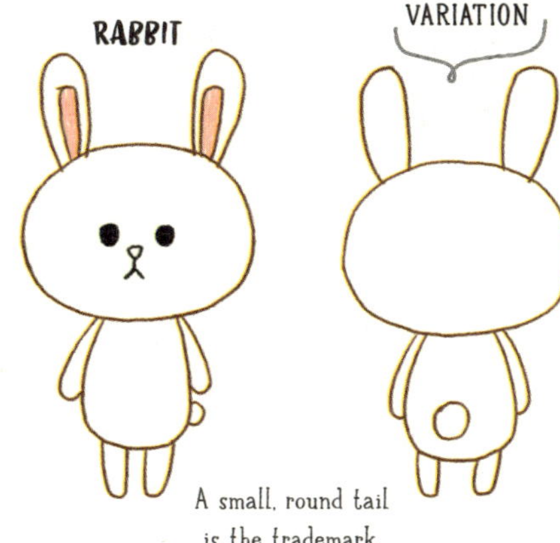

A small, round tail is the trademark.

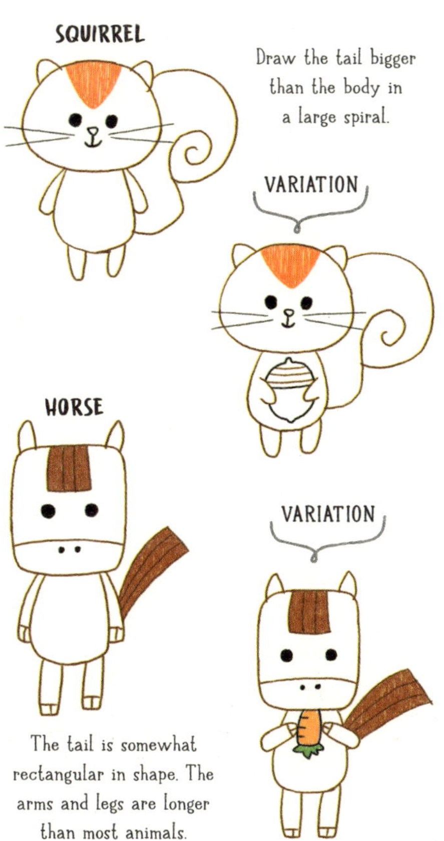

Draw the tail bigger than the body in a large spiral.

The tail is somewhat rectangular in shape. The arms and legs are longer than most animals.

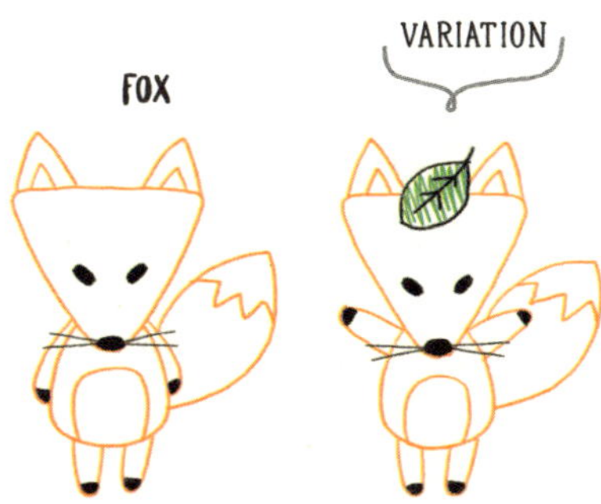

Color the ends of hands and feet black. Add a jagged line at the tip of the tail.

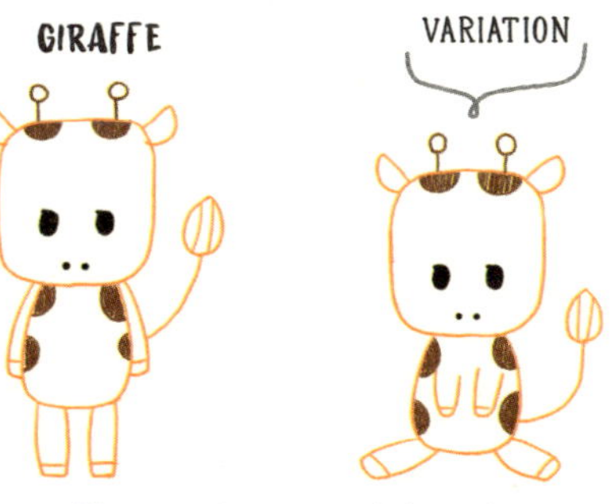

The spotted pattern and thin tail differentiate the giraffe from a horse.

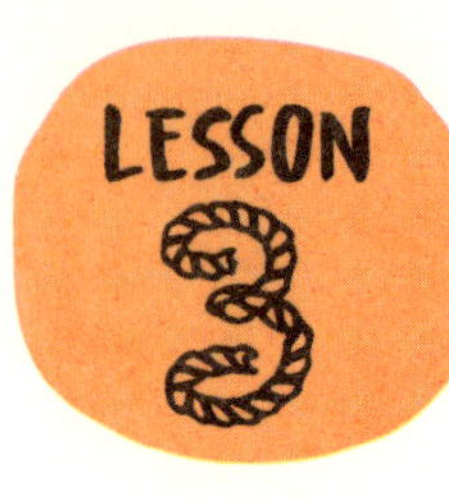

CATS

Draw cats with a rounded back for that classic feline look. Change the markings and coloring for different cat breeds.

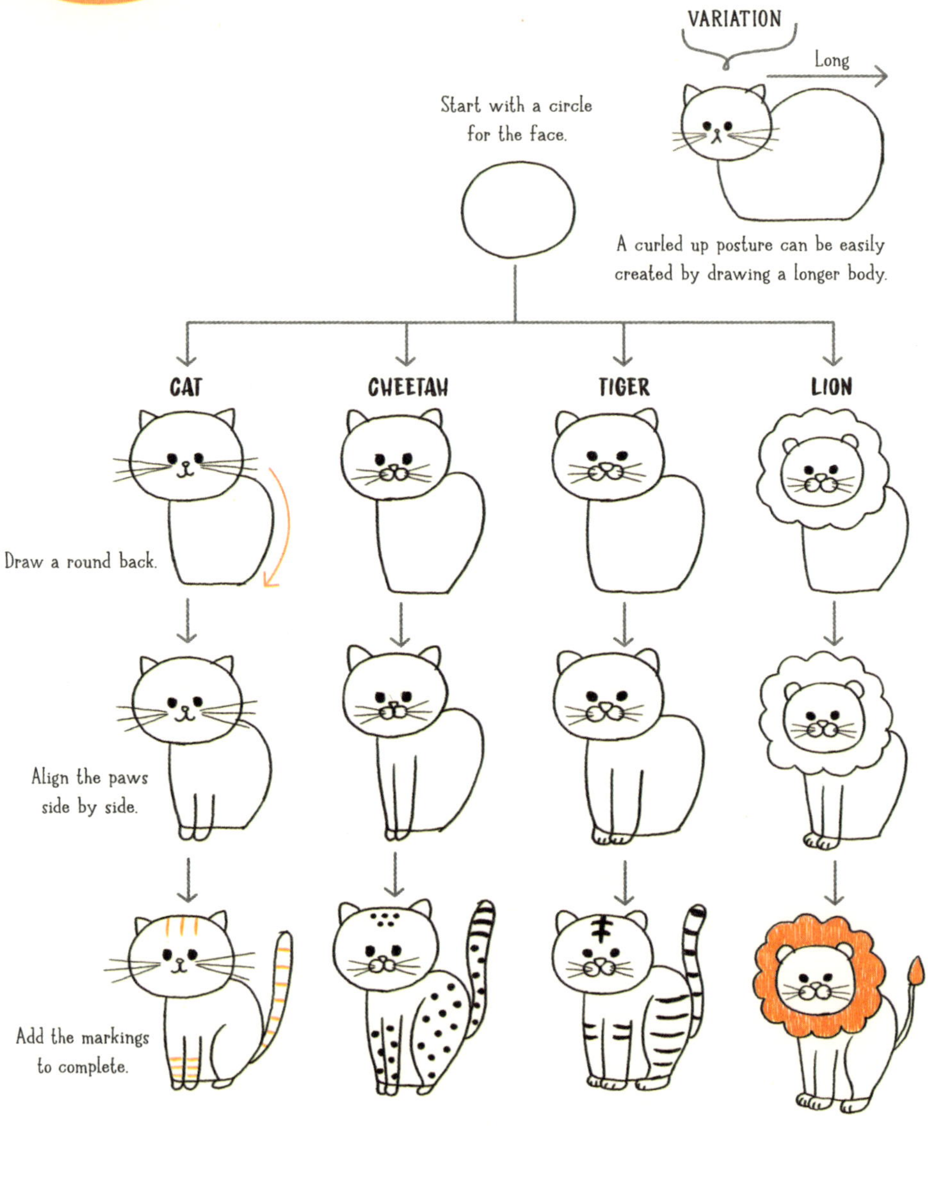

VARIATION

Long

Start with a circle for the face.

A curled up posture can be easily created by drawing a longer body.

CAT

CHEETAH

TIGER

LION

Draw a round back.

Align the paws side by side.

Add the markings to complete.

VARIATION

DRAW VARIOUS CATS BY CHANGING THE MARKINGS

The basics are the same! Change the hair color or pattern to draw various kinds of cats.

BICOLOR

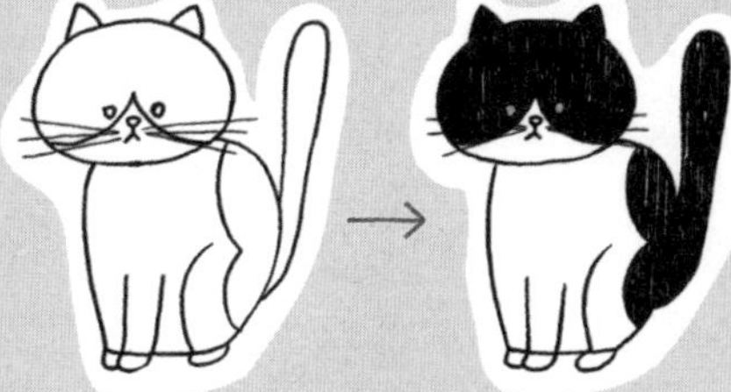

Draw an inverted V-shaped pattern on the face and body.

CALICO

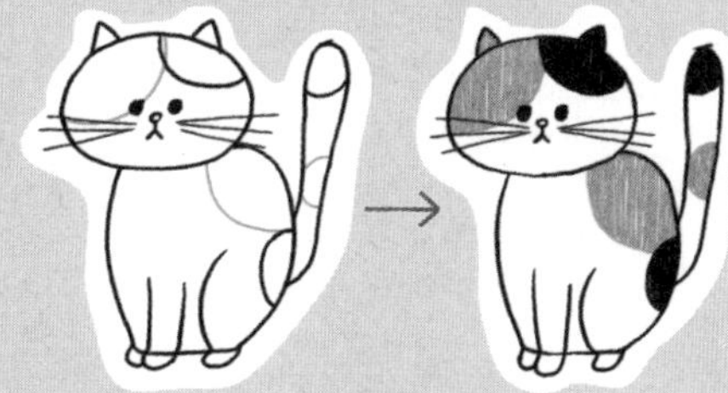

Draw patterns using white, brown, and black.

SIAMESE

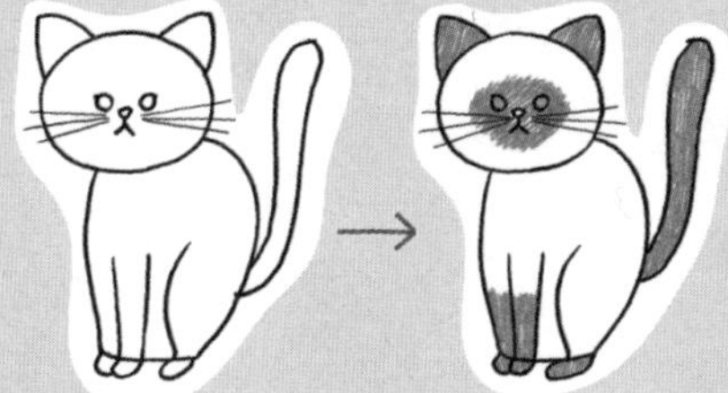

Add color at the center of the face, on the ears, tail, and ends of the legs.

RED TABBY

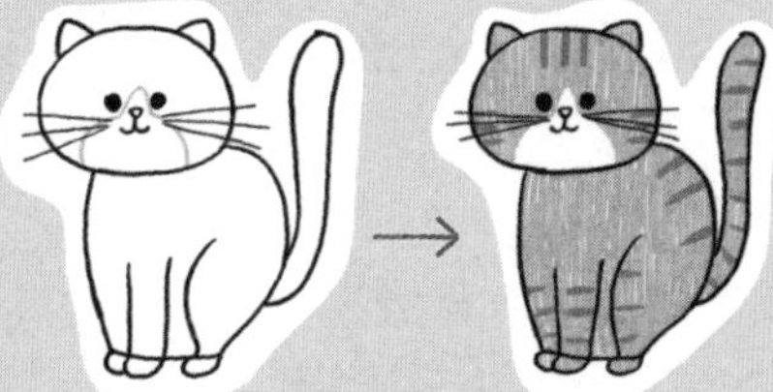

Color the whole body orange, then add stripes.

RUSSIAN BLUE

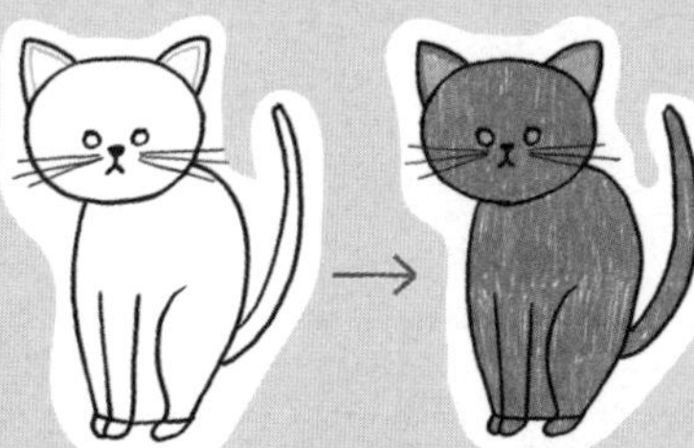

A thin body and gray hair are the main characteristics of this breed. Color the eyes green.

PERSIAN

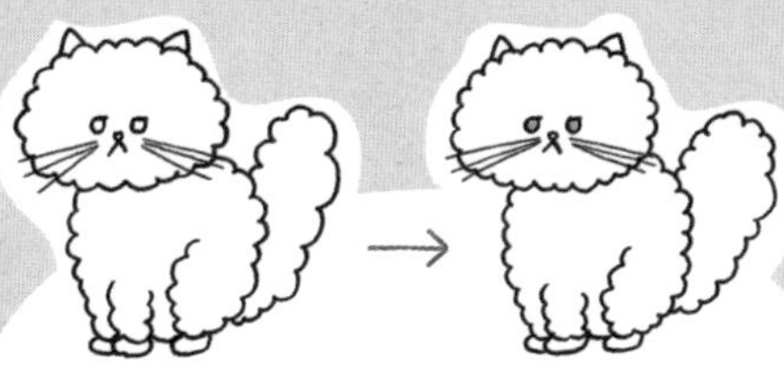

Longer hair can be expressed with fluffy lines.

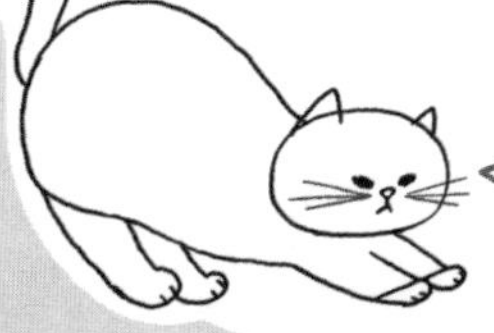

See page 43 for tips on drawing different cat postures.

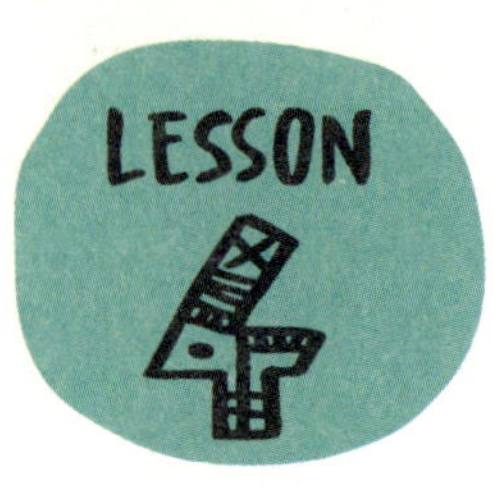

DOGS

Use a straight line to draw the flat backs of dogs and other canine creatures. Change the shape of the snout and body patterns depending upon the animal.

Start with a square for the face.

Draw a straight line for the back.

VARIATION

DOG

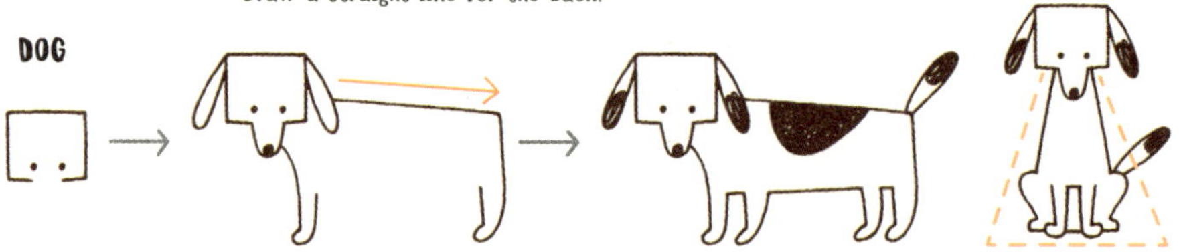

A sitting dog's body will have a triangular shape—draw the back legs on both sides of the front legs.

WOLF

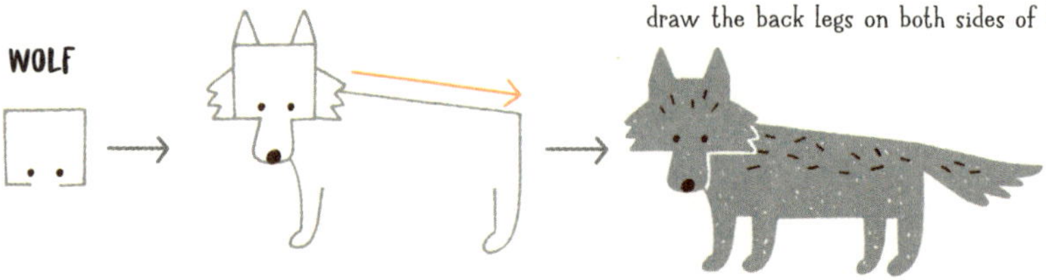

Use curly lines to color in the body, leaving a bit of white space, then add a pattern of brown lines on top.

FOX

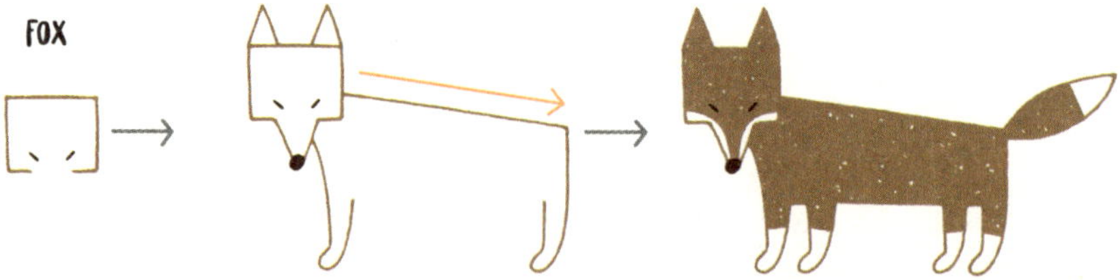

Leave the tips of the legs white, and use curly lines to fill in the body, leaving a bit of white space.

RACCOON DOG

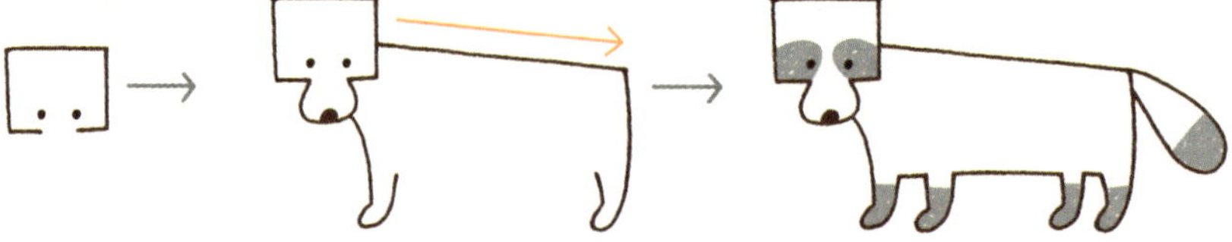

VARIATION

LET'S DRAW POPULAR DOG BREEDS

The basics are the same—just change the coloring and size of the body to draw different dog breeds.

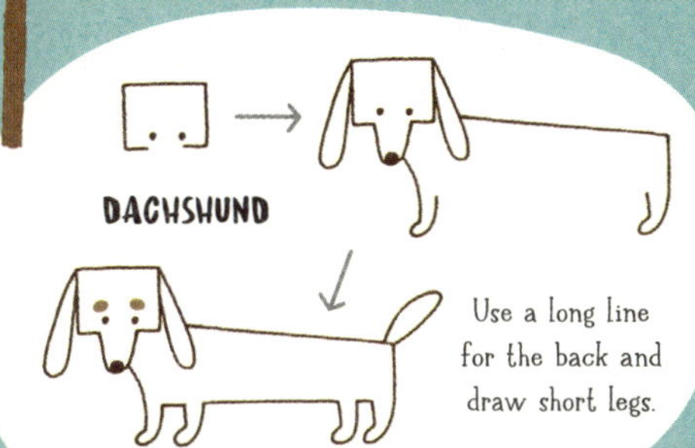

Use a long line for the back and draw short legs.

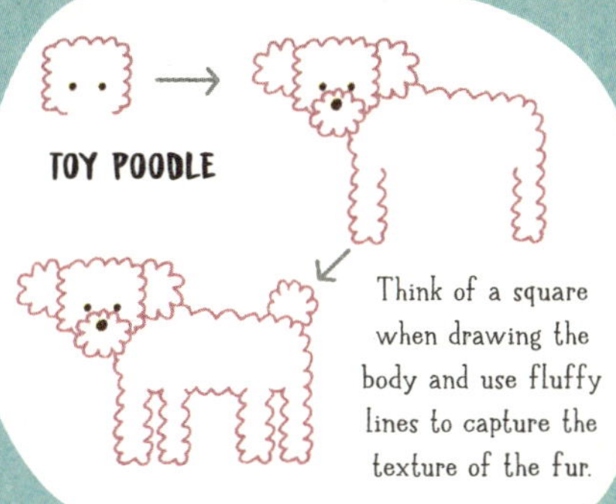

Think of a square when drawing the body and use fluffy lines to capture the texture of the fur.

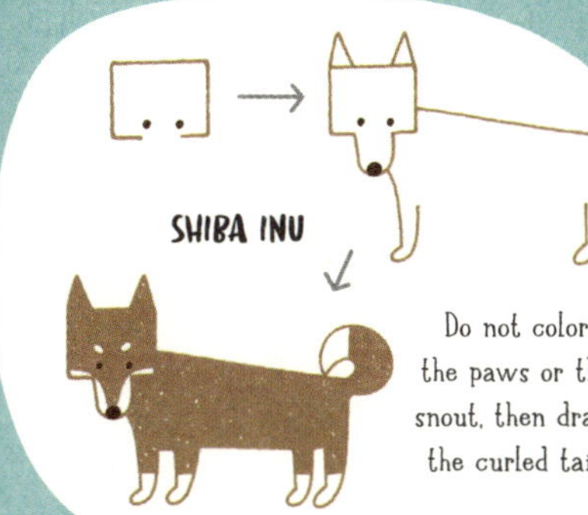

Do not color the paws or the snout, then draw the curled tail.

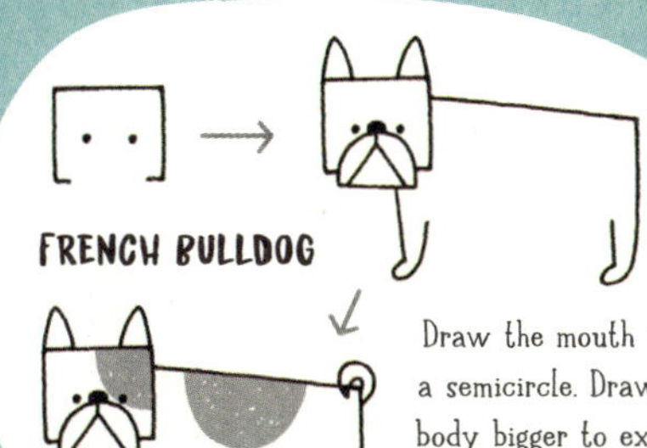

Draw the mouth with a semicircle. Draw the body bigger to express its muscular build.

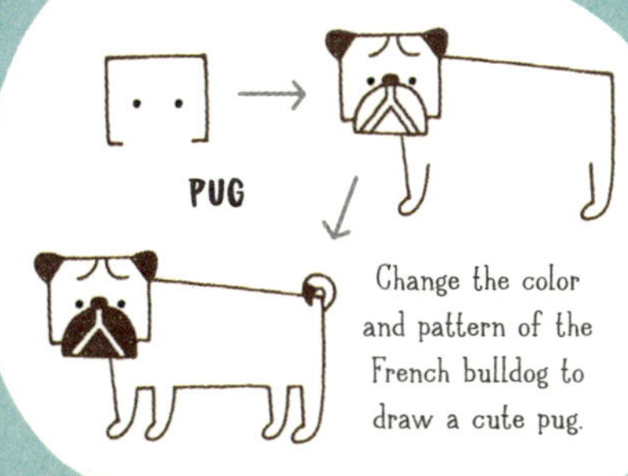

Change the color and pattern of the French bulldog to draw a cute pug.

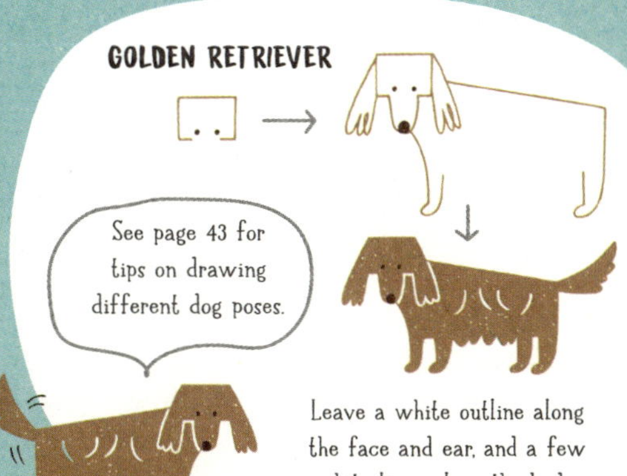

See page 43 for tips on drawing different dog poses.

Leave a white outline along the face and ear, and a few white lines along the body.

SPECIAL LESSON

TIPS FOR DRAWING CUTER CATS & DOGS

Now that you've mastered the basics of drawing cats and dogs, let's add some unique details, such as expressions and gestures, for even cuter illustrations.

TECHNIQUE 1: EXPRESSIONS

BASIC

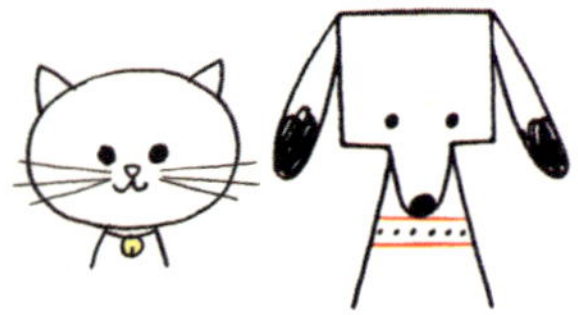

Draw the eyes with dots. The cat eyes are somewhat raised.

WHITE EYES + BLACK PUPILS

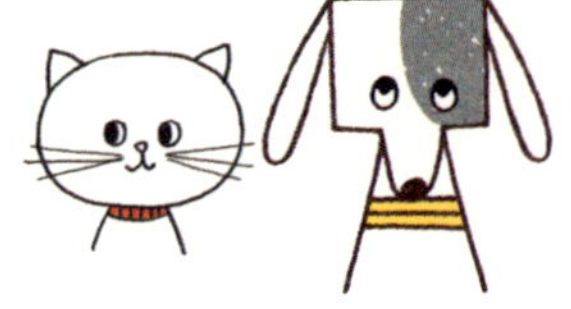

The position of the pupils indicate where the animal is looking.

EYELASHES

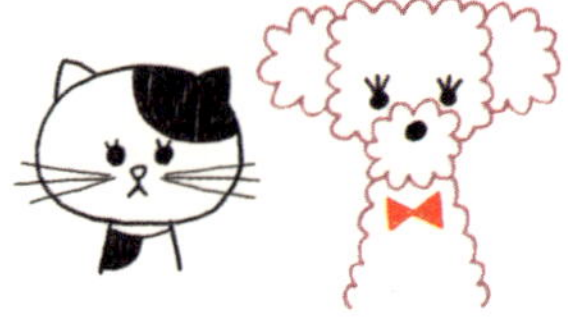

Draw three lines to add eyelashes and increase the cute factor.

EYEBROWS

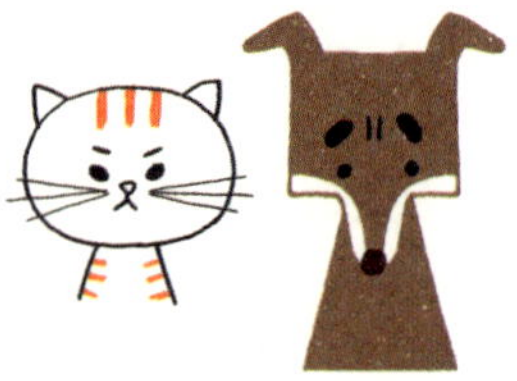

Add eyebrows for comedic effect.

SLEEPY EYES

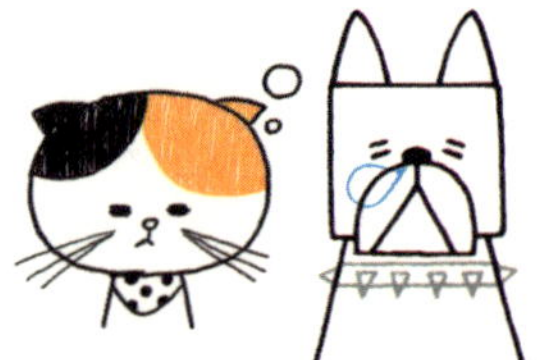

Draw the eyes with lines to create a sleepy expression.

HAPPY EYES

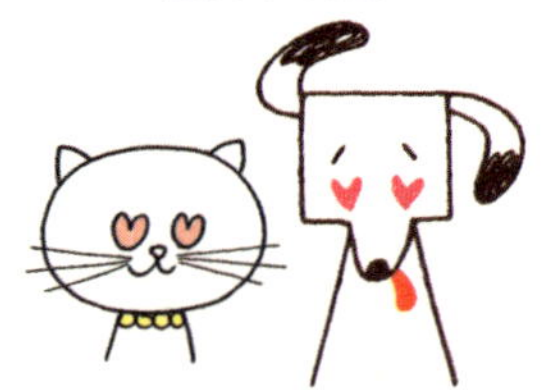

A happy expression of love can be illustrated with heart-shaped eyes.

EXCITED EYES

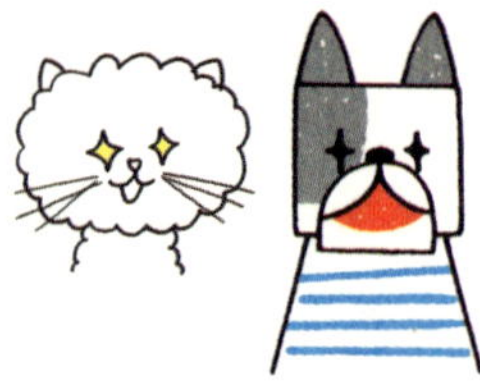

Draw diamond-shaped eyes to capture the excited expression of seeing one of your favorite things.

CRYING EYES

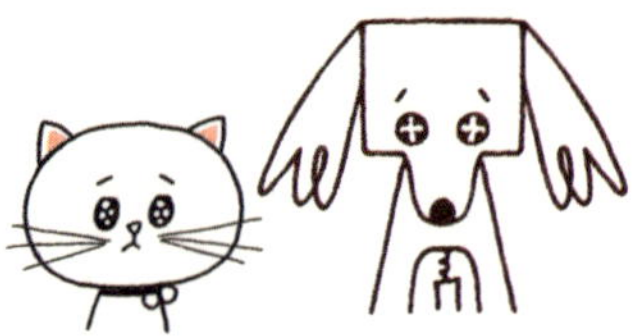

Add diamond-shaped highlights to the eyes to create the impression of tears.

SURPRISED EYES

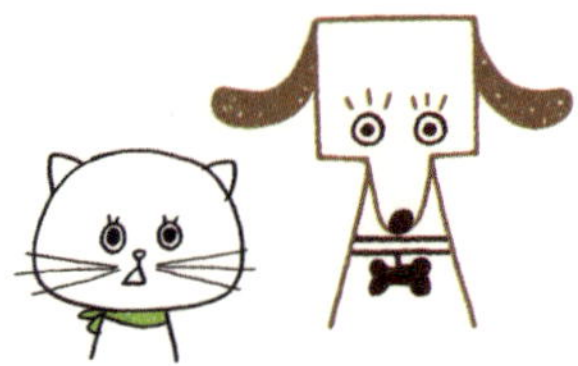

Draw large, round pupils and add long eyelashes for a wide-eyed surprised expression.

TECHNIQUE 2: GESTURES & MOVEMENTS

CAT

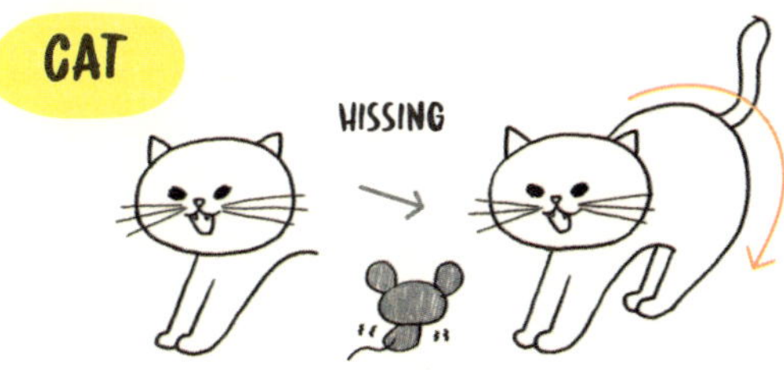

Draw an extremely rounded back. The key is to align the front and back legs.

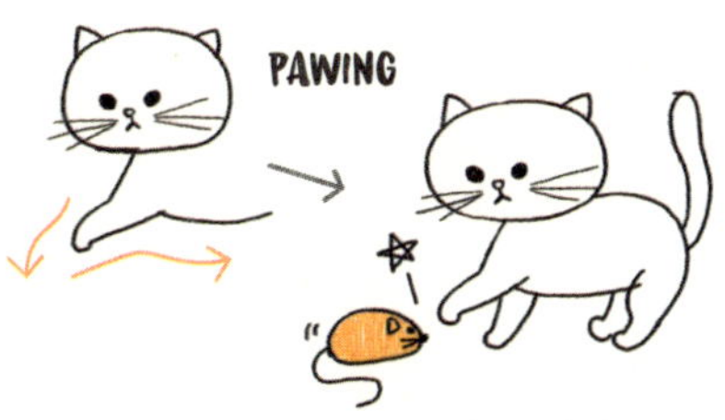

Draw the extended paw in front of the face and the tail pointing upward.

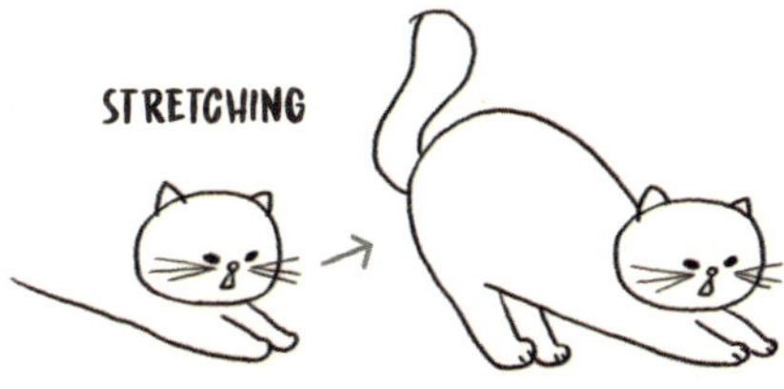

Draw the outstretched front legs extending further than with the hissing posture.

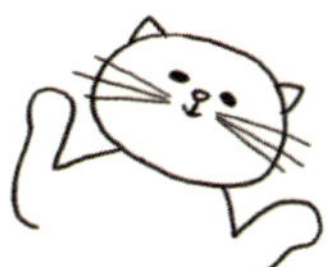

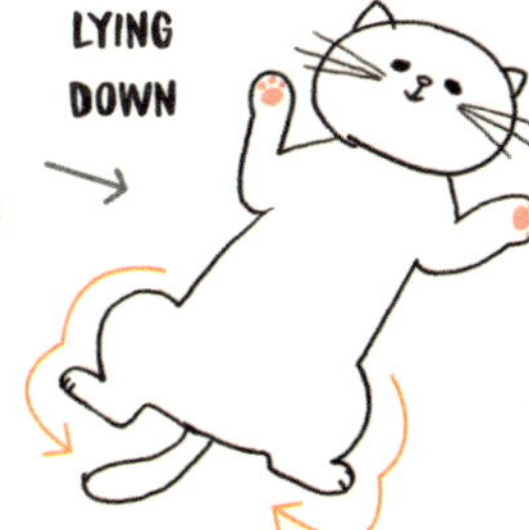

The back legs are not completely outstretched.

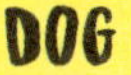

DOG

Draw two tails to express the fast movement.

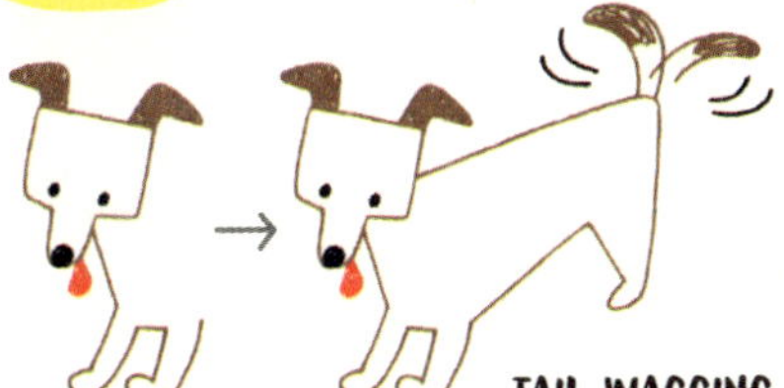

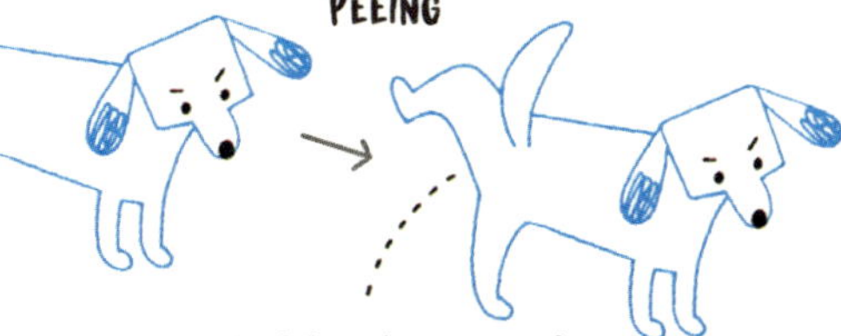

The back line slants upward due to the raised leg.

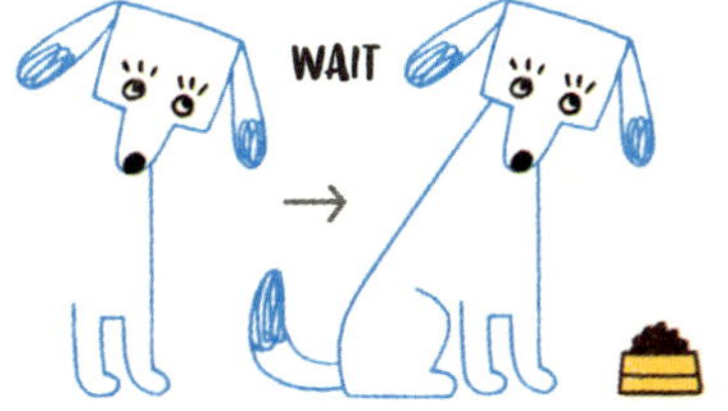

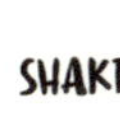

The head is slightly tilted. Draw the body with a triangle in mind.

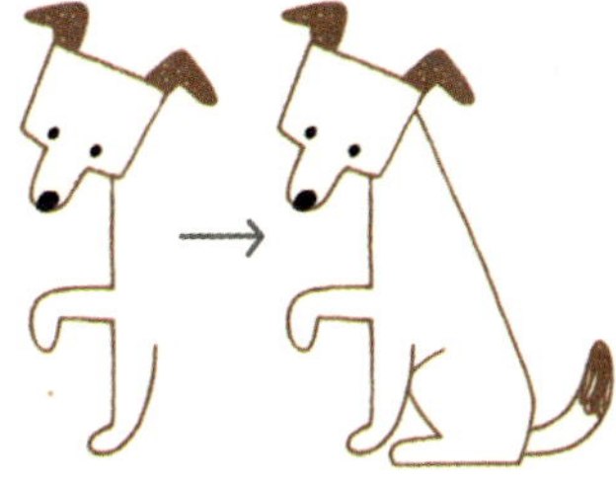

Draw the raised paw, then use a diagonal line to draw the back.

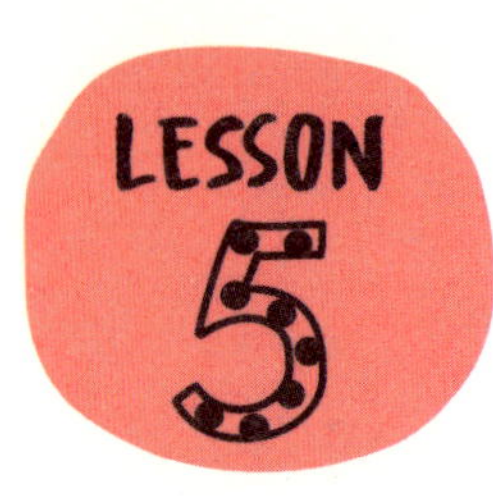

EQUINES

Horses and other relatives of this animal family are known for their long, thin legs and necks. Start by drawing the face, then add the neck and body.

THE BASICS

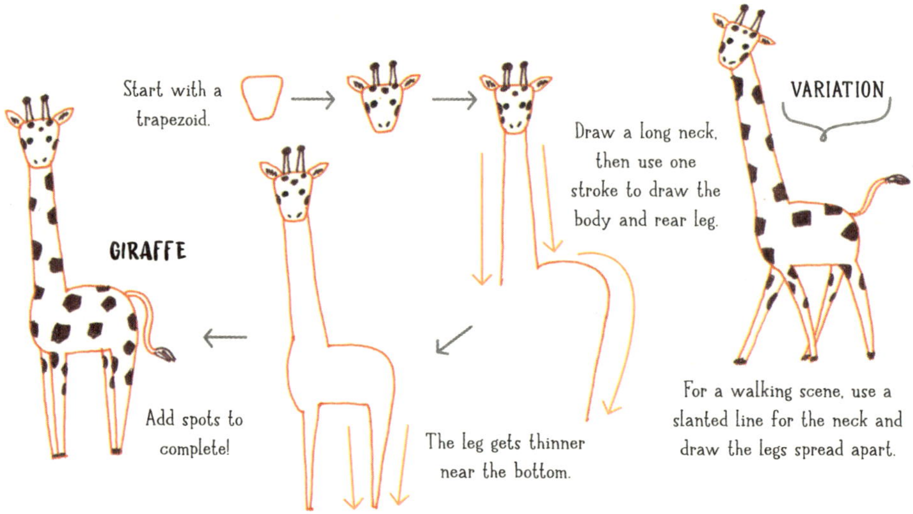

Start with a trapezoid.

Draw a long neck, then use one stroke to draw the body and rear leg.

The leg gets thinner near the bottom.

Add spots to complete!

GIRAFFE

VARIATION

For a walking scene, use a slanted line for the neck and draw the legs spread apart.

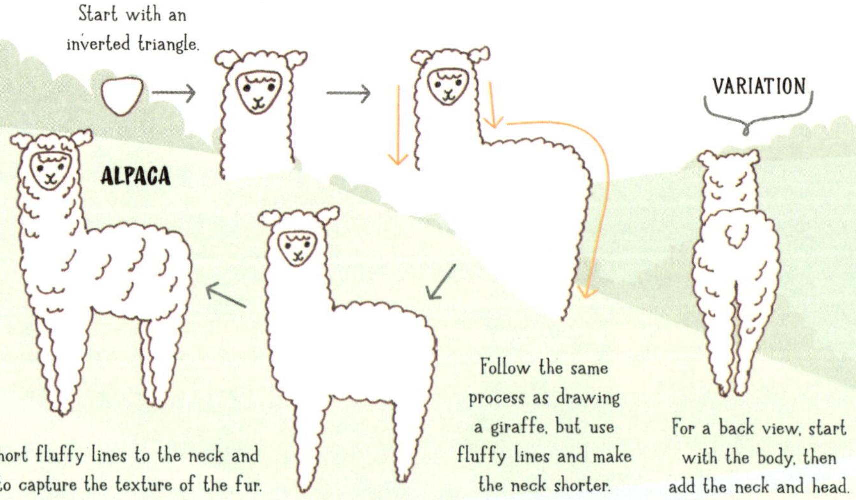

Start with an inverted triangle.

Follow the same process as drawing a giraffe, but use fluffy lines and make the neck shorter.

Add short fluffy lines to the neck and body to capture the texture of the fur.

ALPACA

VARIATION

For a back view, start with the body, then add the neck and head.

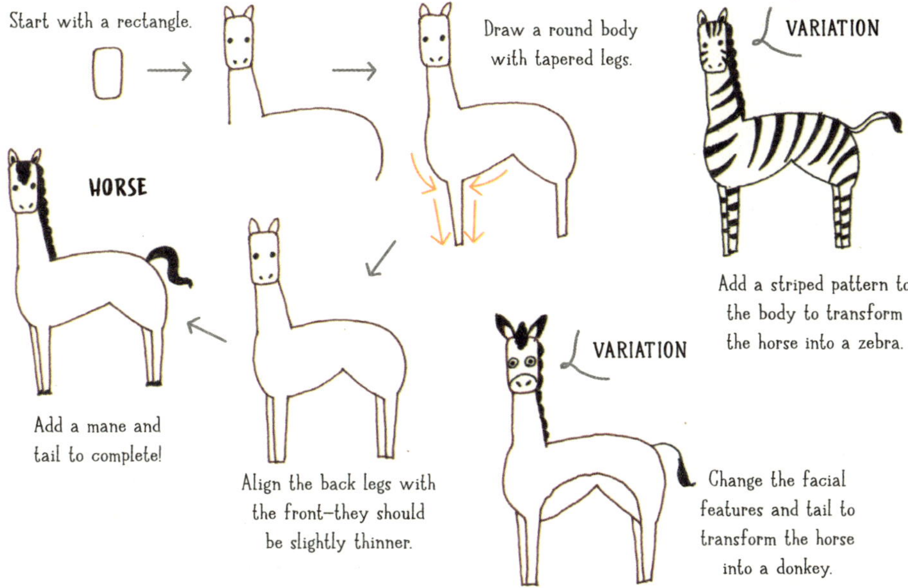
Start with a rectangle.
Draw a round body with tapered legs.
VARIATION
HORSE
Add a striped pattern to the body to transform the horse into a zebra.
VARIATION
Add a mane and tail to complete!
Align the back legs with the front—they should be slightly thinner.
Change the facial features and tail to transform the horse into a donkey.

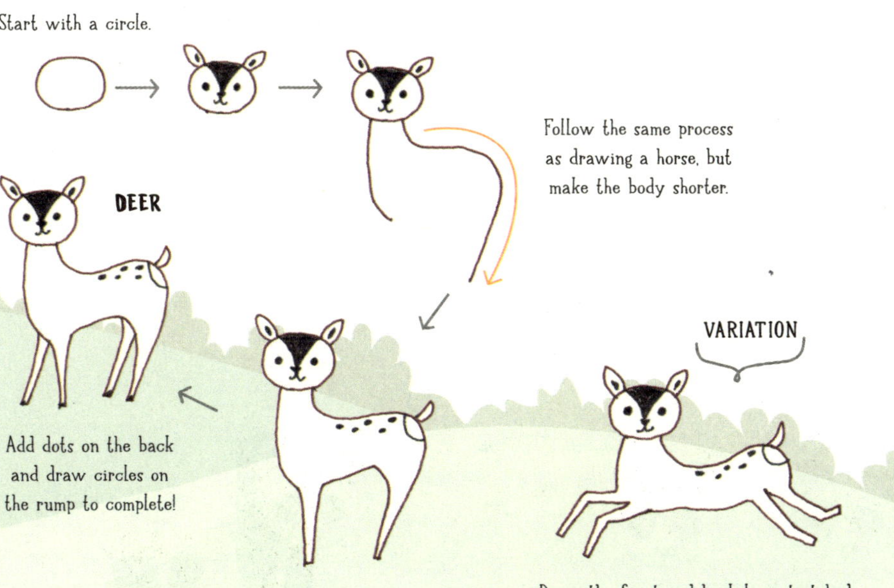
Start with a circle.
Follow the same process as drawing a horse, but make the body shorter.
DEER
VARIATION
Add dots on the back and draw circles on the rump to complete!
Draw the front and back legs stretched wide apart for a running deer.

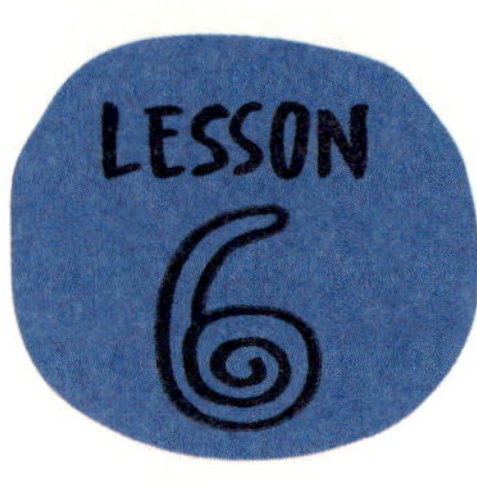

BEARS

Animals that walk on all fours, such as bears, have mountain-shaped backs that rise up higher than their heads.

BEAR

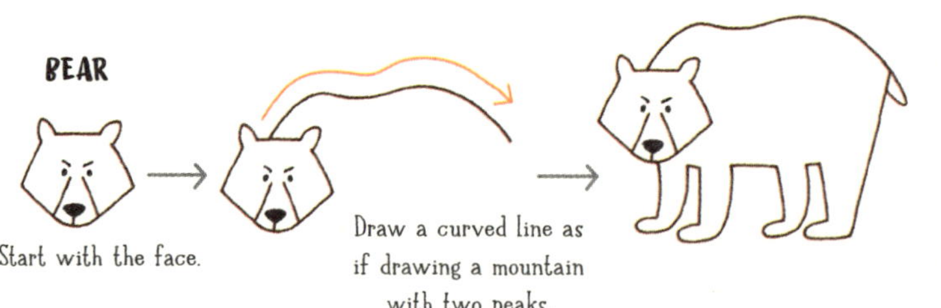

Start with the face.

Draw a curved line as if drawing a mountain with two peaks.

VARIATION

When drawing a front view, the front legs will face inward.

BLACK BEAR

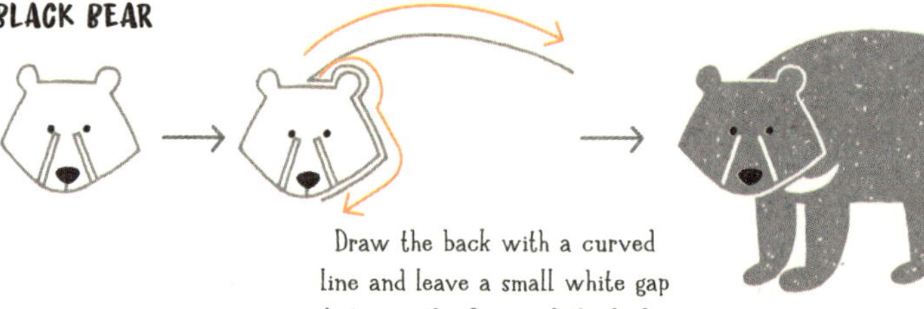

Draw the back with a curved line and leave a small white gap between the face and the body.

POLAR BEAR

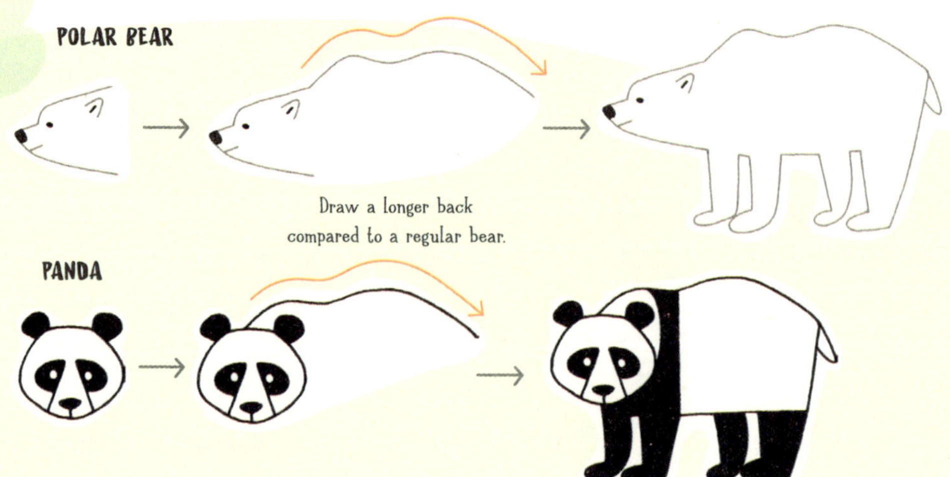

Draw a longer back compared to a regular bear.

PANDA

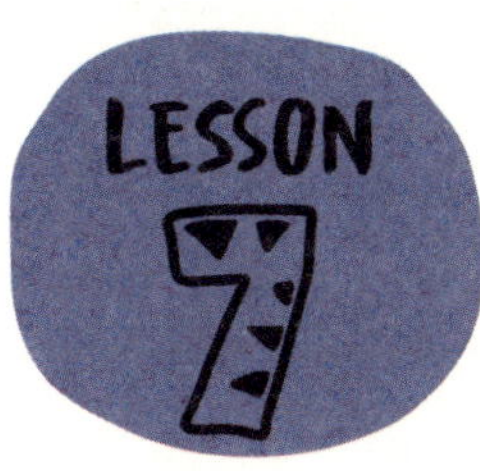

MONKEYS & GORILLAS

Monkeys are known for their long arms and legs. You can differentiate the species by adding color and changing the shape of the hands and feet.

VARIATION

MONKEY

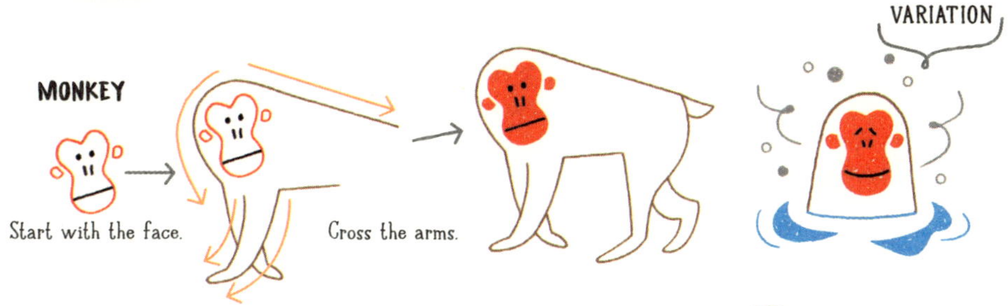

Start with the face.

Cross the arms.

CHIMPANZEE

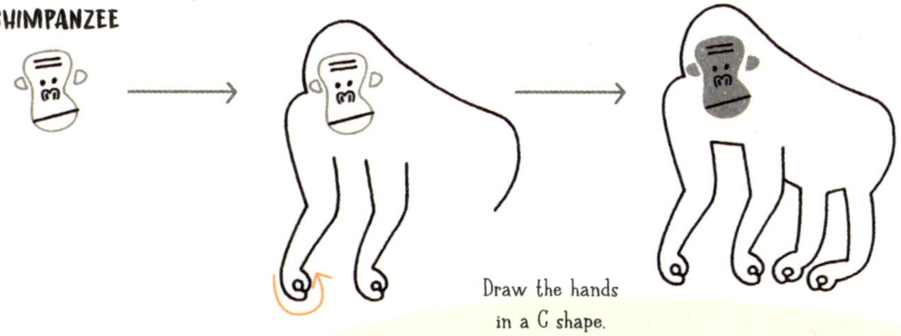

Draw the hands in a C shape.

SQUIRREL MONKEY

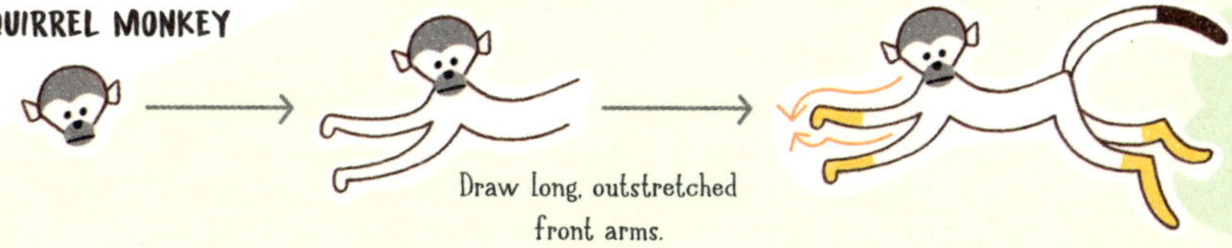

Draw long, outstretched front arms.

SLOTH

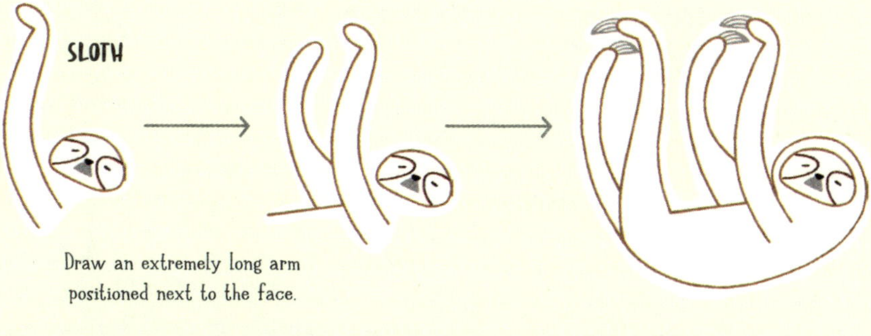

Draw an extremely long arm positioned next to the face.

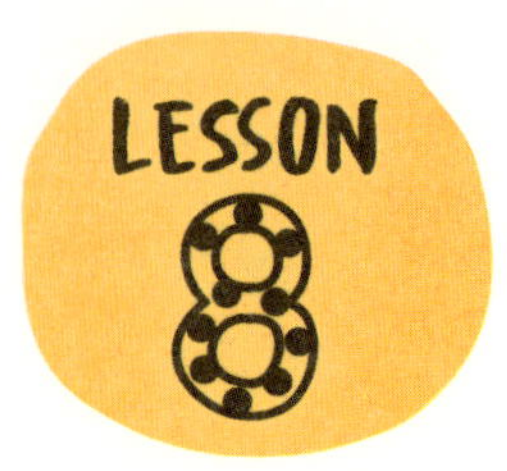

ROUND ANIMALS

Draw the face and the body as one for animals with distinctively round silhouettes. Once you understand the basics, you can draw them very easily.

1 Draw a semicircular body, then add the head and legs.

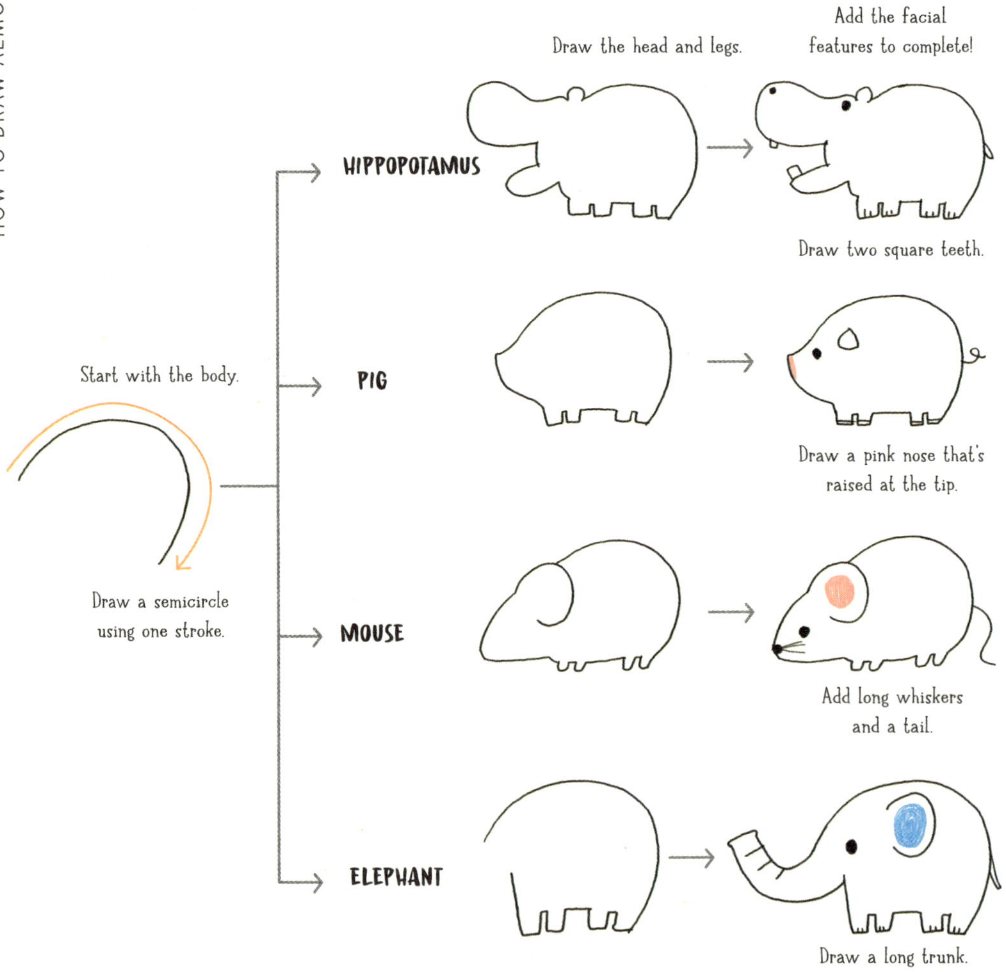

Start with the body.

Draw a semicircle using one stroke.

Draw the head and legs.

Add the facial features to complete!

HIPPOPOTAMUS

Draw two square teeth.

PIG

Draw a pink nose that's raised at the tip.

MOUSE

Add long whiskers and a tail.

ELEPHANT

Draw a long trunk.

2 Use fluffy, jagged, or dotted lines to draw a round body.

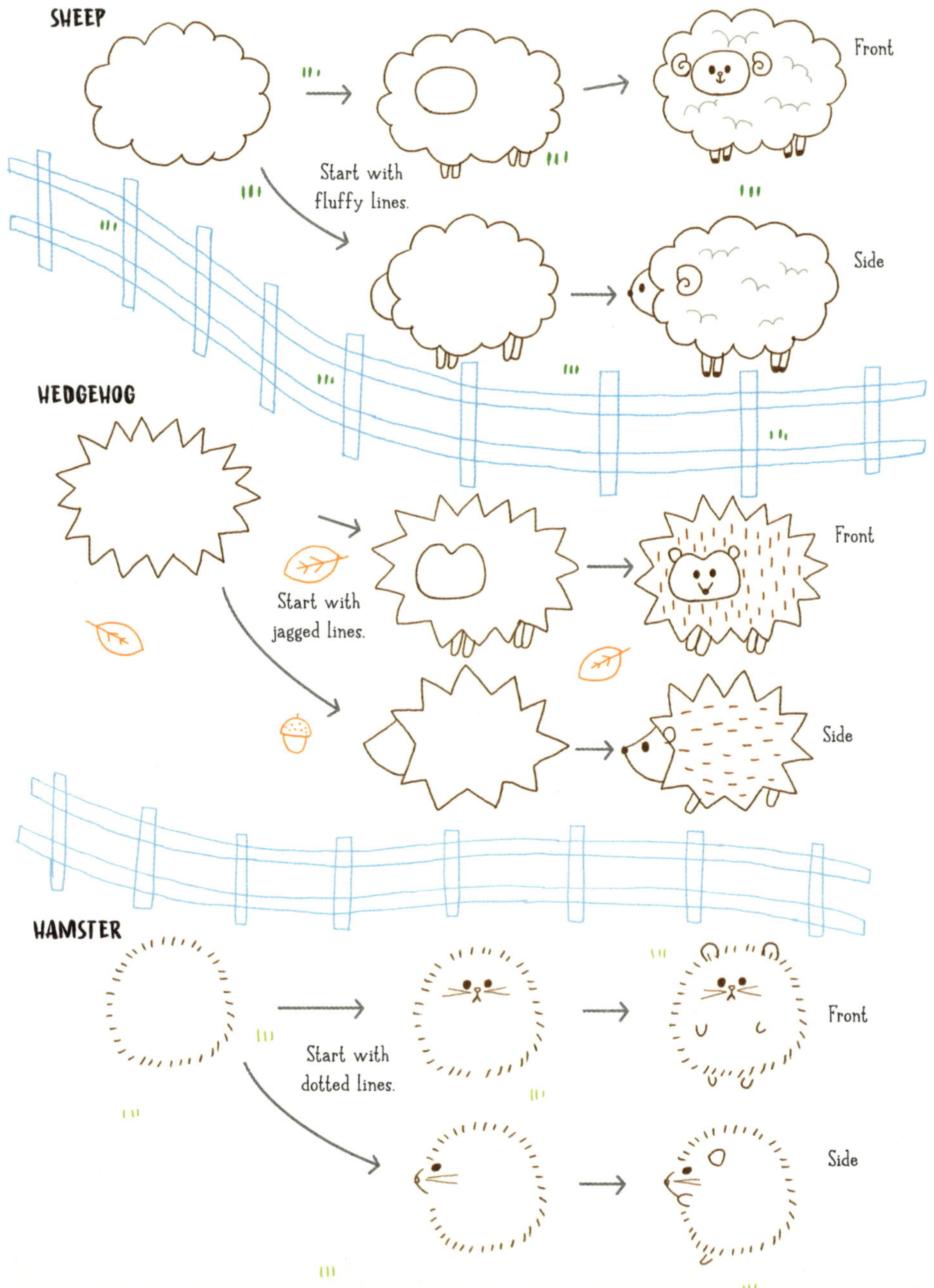

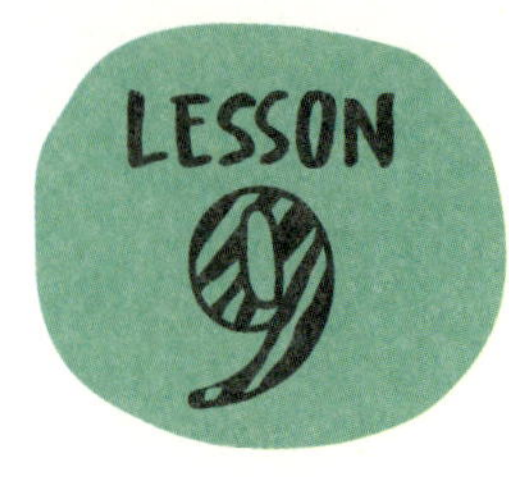

REPTILES & AMPHIBIANS

When drawing these unique creatures, consider the best angle to use in order to highlight and emphasize characteristic features, such as their shells, claws, and and tongues.

SEA TURTLE

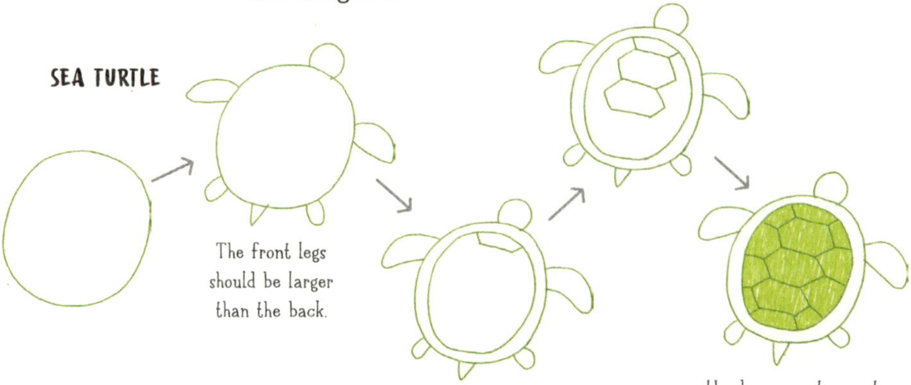

The front legs should be larger than the back.

Use hexagons to create the patterned shell.

TORTOISE

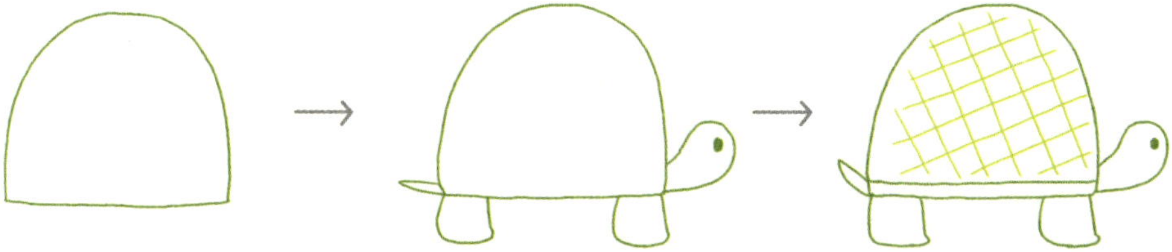

The legs should be thicker at the bottom.

Use a lattice pattern for the shell.

VARIATION

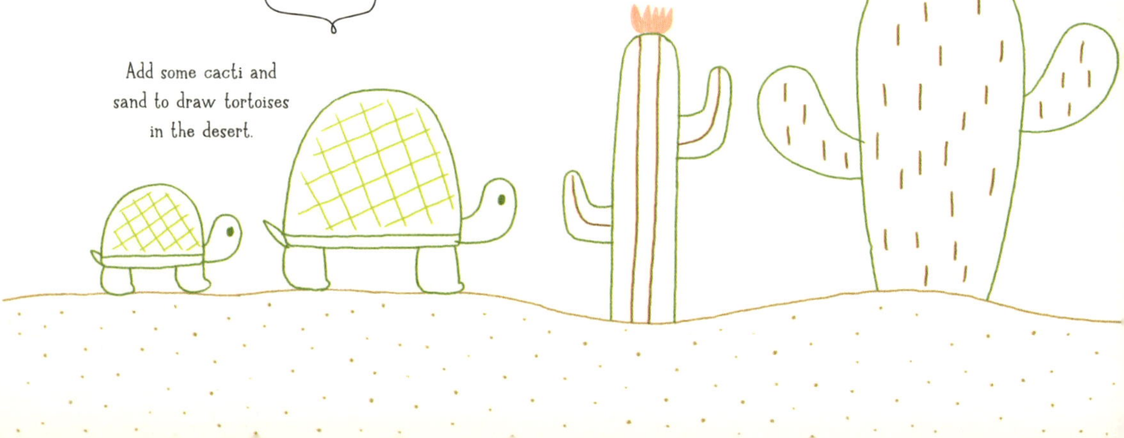

Add some cacti and sand to draw tortoises in the desert.

CHAMELEON

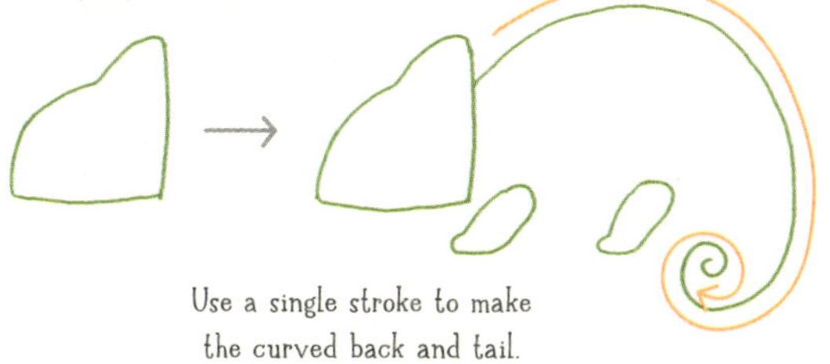

Use a single stroke to make the curved back and tail.

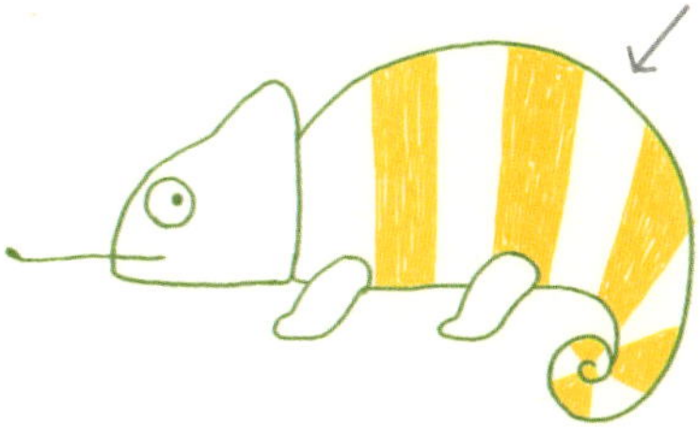

Add a long tongue and colorful stripes.

VARIATION

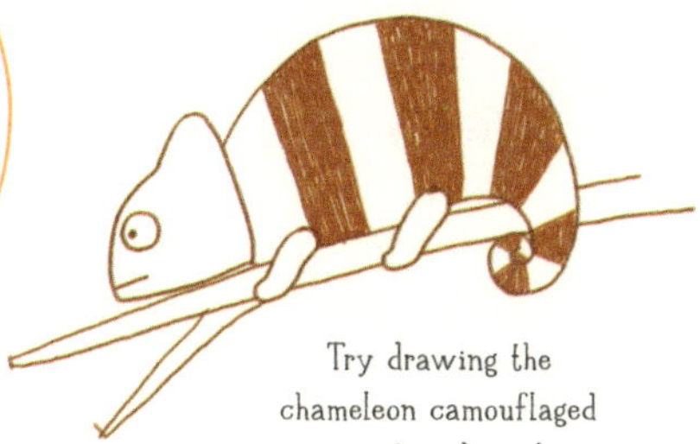

Try drawing the chameleon camouflaged on a tree branch.

FROG

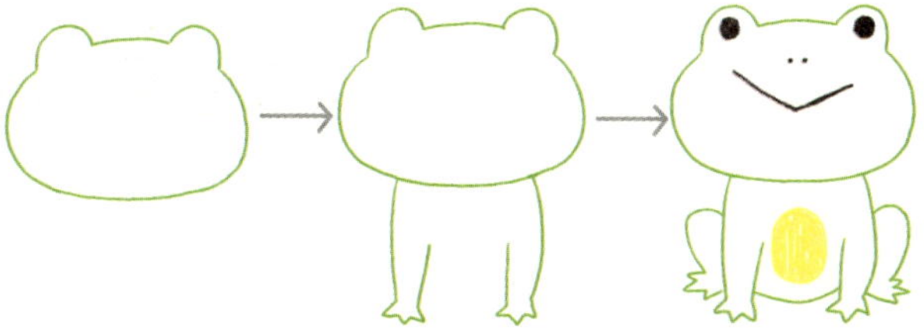

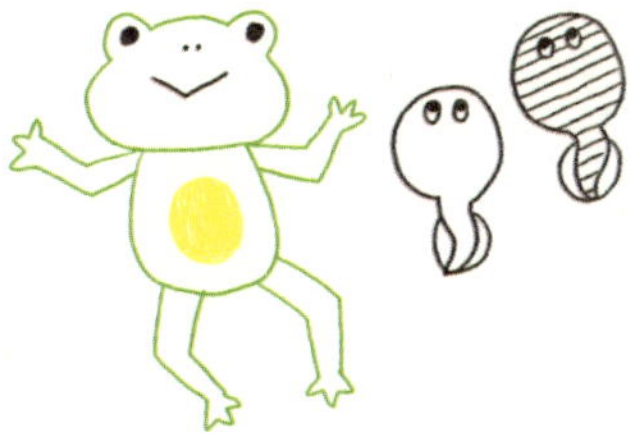

Draw the hind legs positioned on the sides of the body.

VARIATION

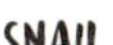

SNAIL

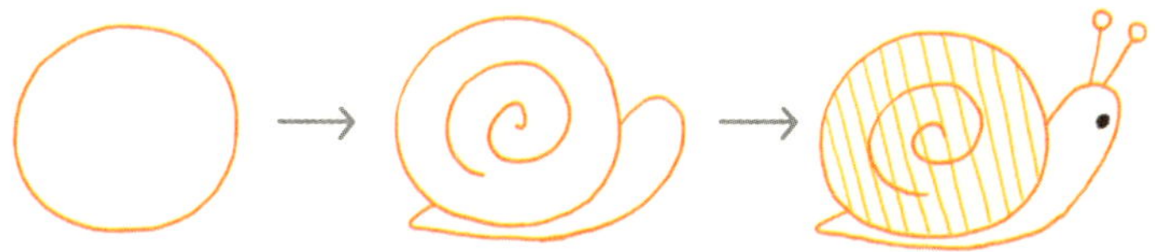

Draw a snail from a sideways angle to capture the shape of the soft body and the spiral shell.

HERMIT CRAB

For a hermit crab, draw large claws positioned in front of a fancy shell.

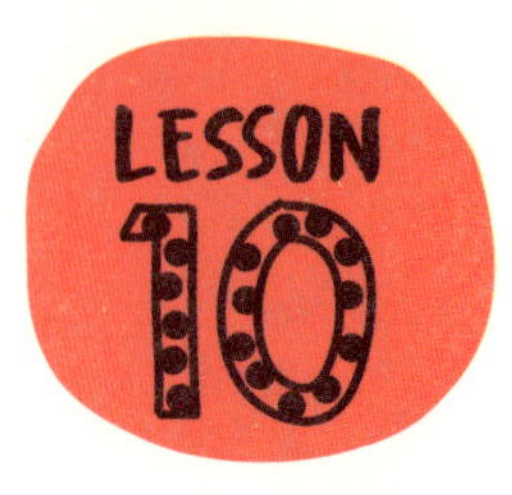

BIRDS

When learning how to draw birds, it helps to classify them into three different categories based on neck length.

1 Draw birds without necks—these birds will often have cute, gourd-shaped bodies.

CHICK

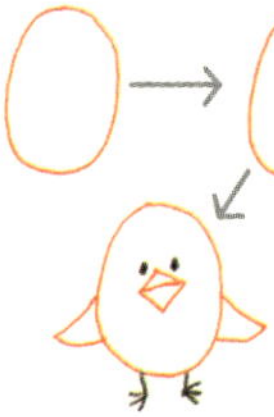

Start with an oval.

BLUEBIRD

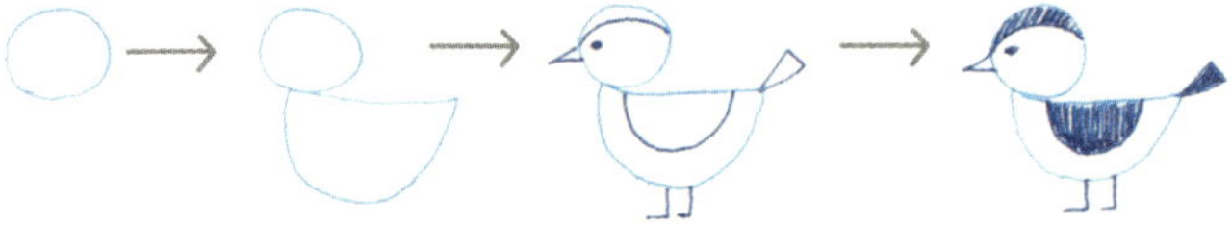

BAT

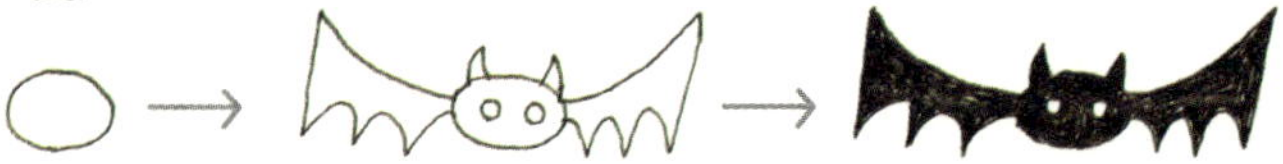

OWL

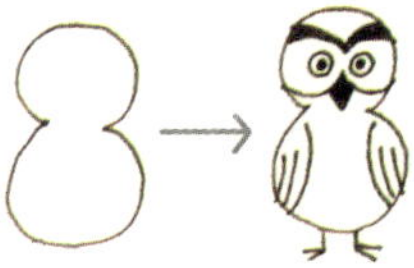

Start with a gourd shape.

PARAKEET

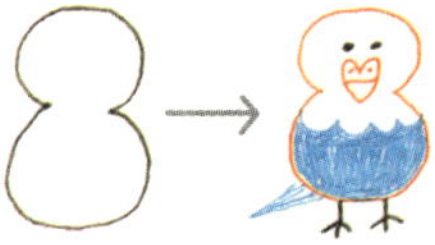

SPARROW

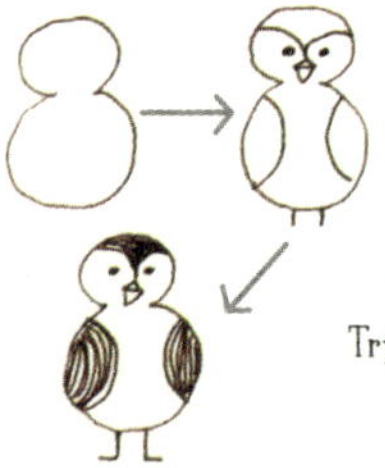

VARIATION

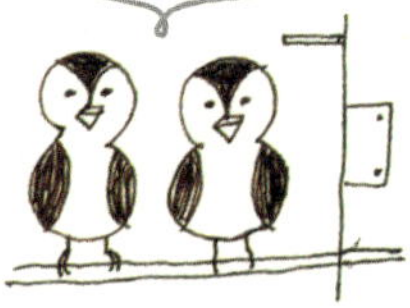

Try drawing two sparrows resting on a wire.

PARROT

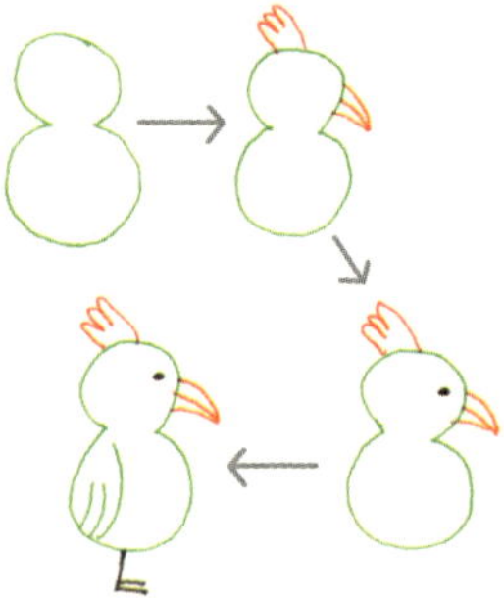

VARIATION

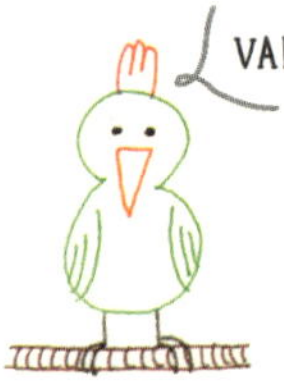

The side view and front view are very similar—just change the position of the facial features.

WOODPECKER

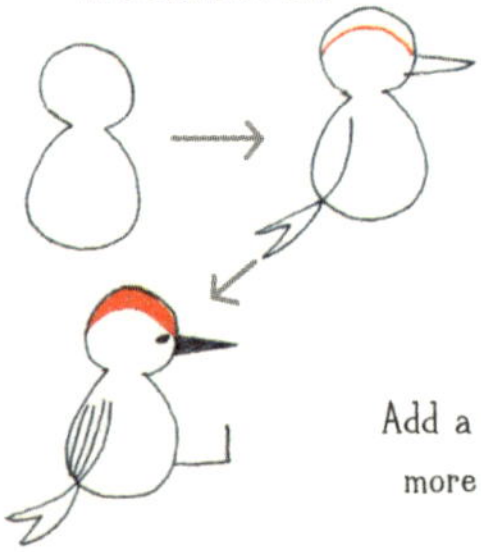

VARIATION

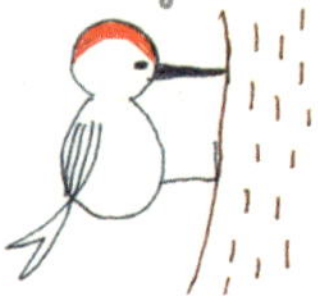

Add a tree trunk for a more realistic scene.

2 Draw birds with short necks.

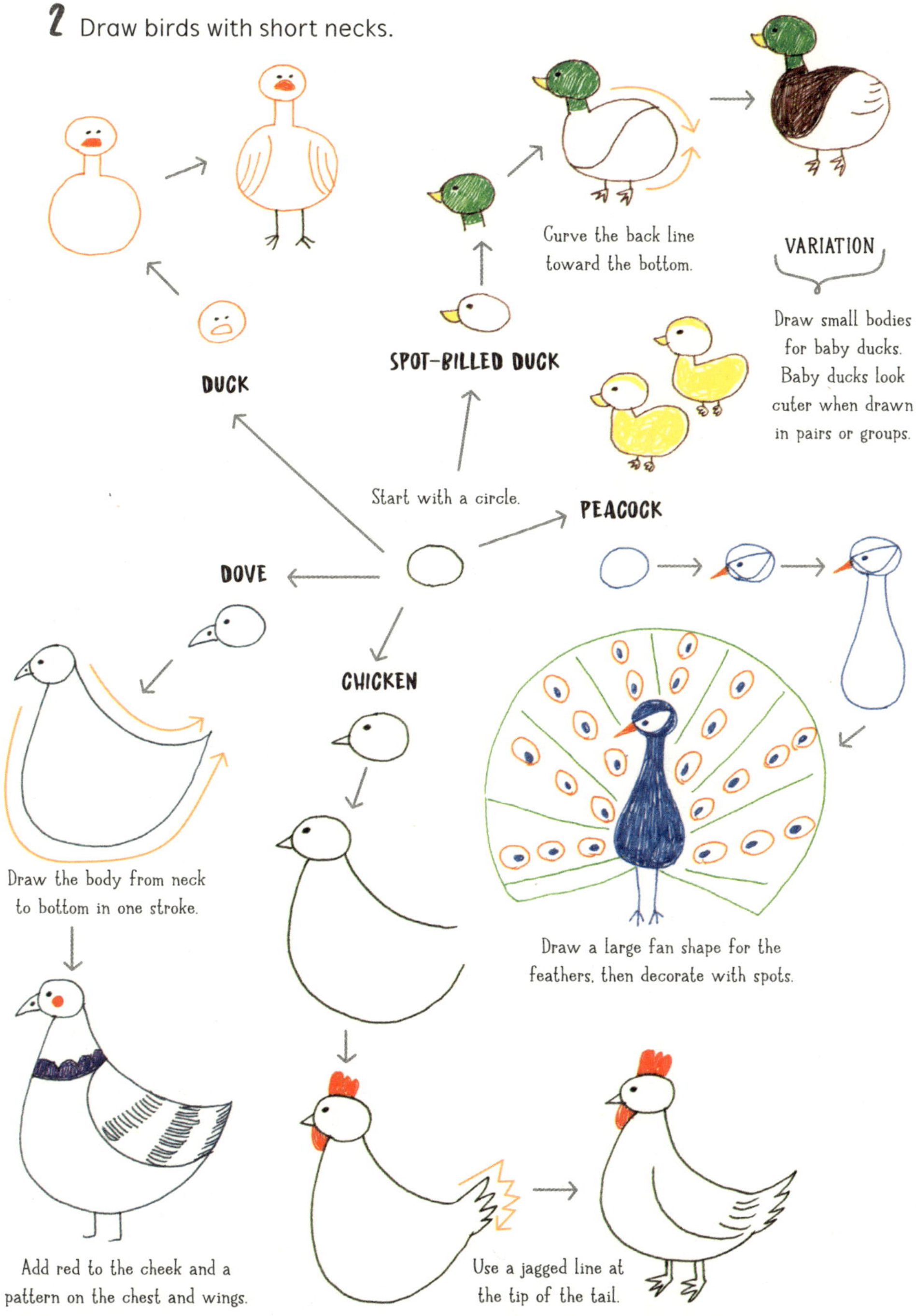

3 Draw long, flexible necks for elegant birds.

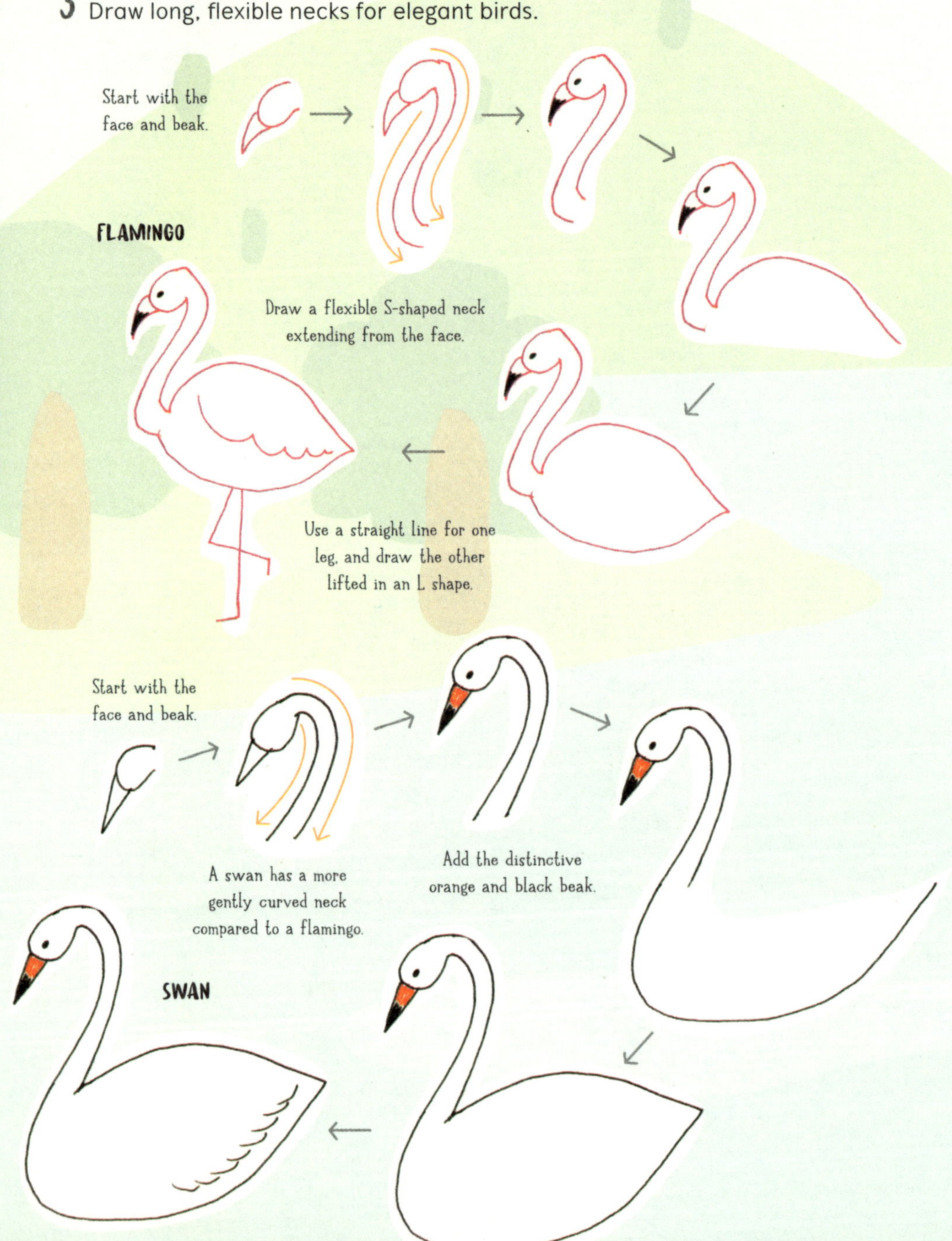

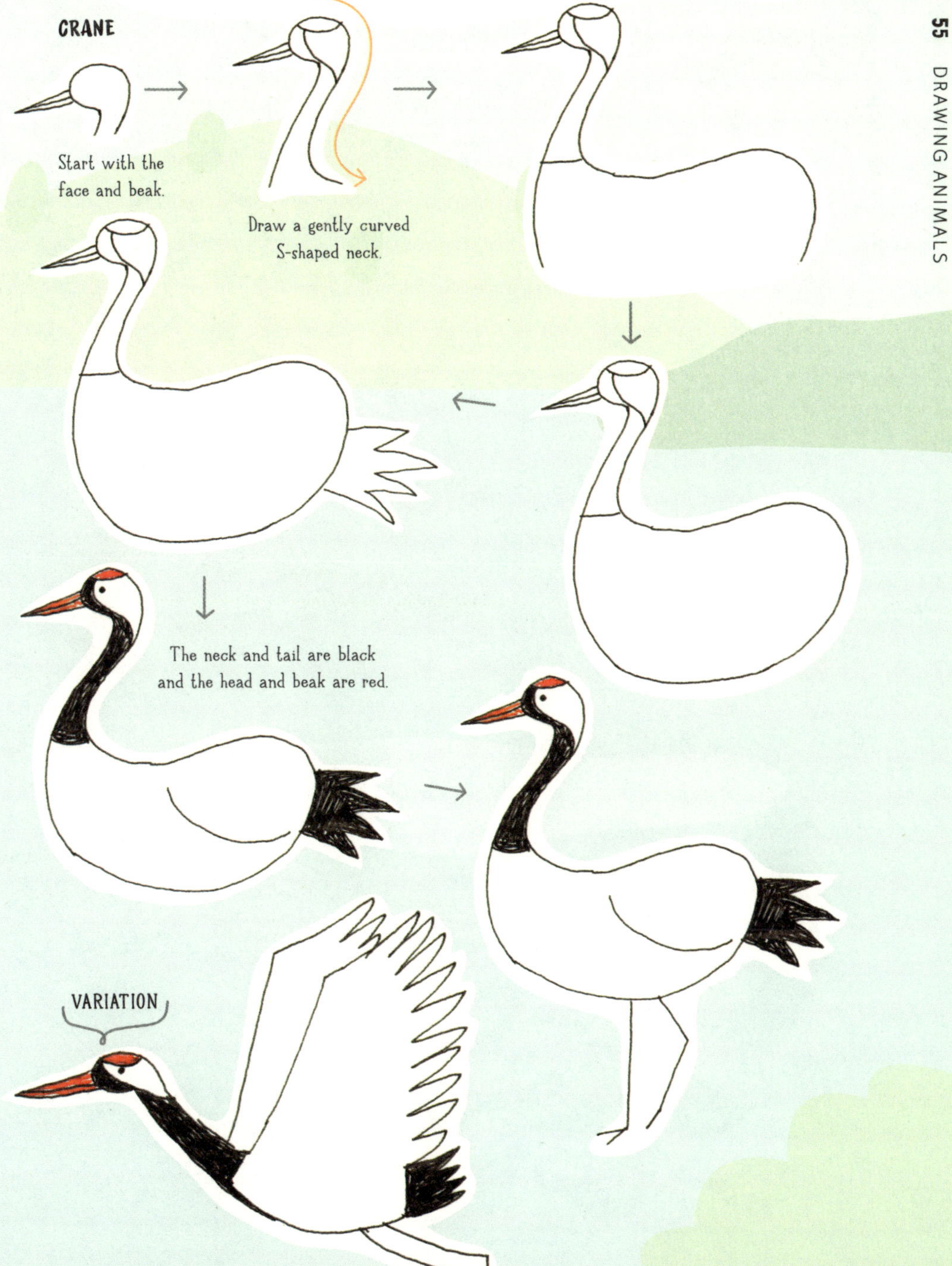
CRANE
Start with the face and beak.
Draw a gently curved S-shaped neck.
The neck and tail are black and the head and beak are red.
VARIATION

VARIATION

DRAW STYLISH PATTERNS WITH BIRDS!

Let's draw bold, modern patterns using bird motifs. Try combining flowers and birds for a fun, nature-inspired design.

FLYING BIRDS

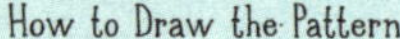

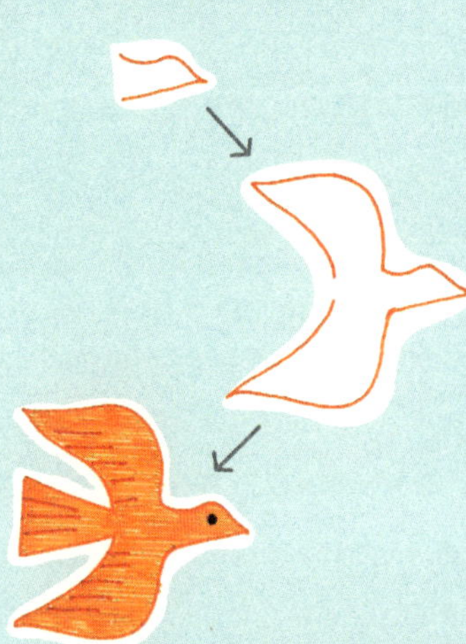

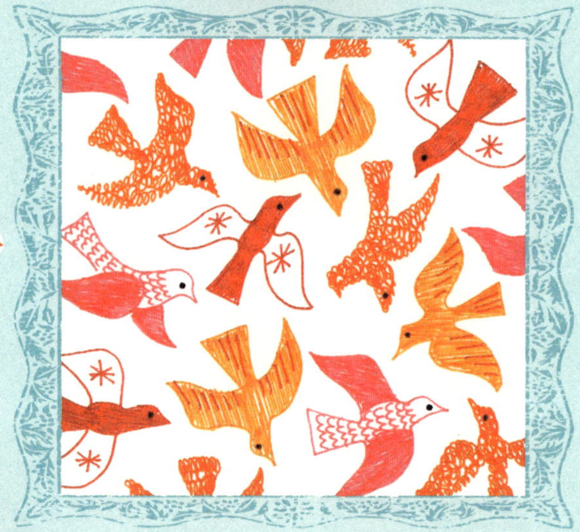

SOCIALIZING BIRDS

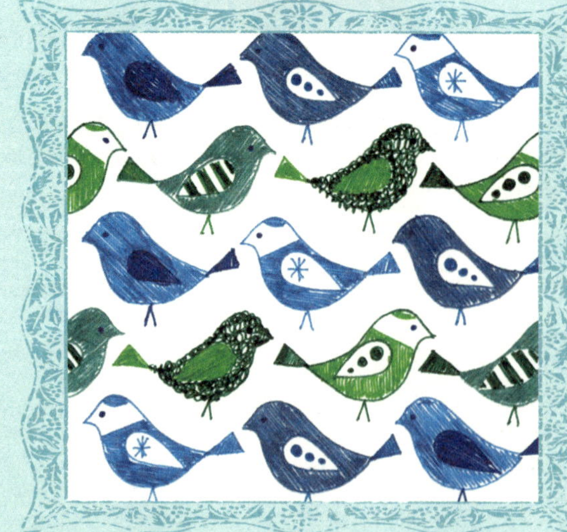

How to Draw the Pattern

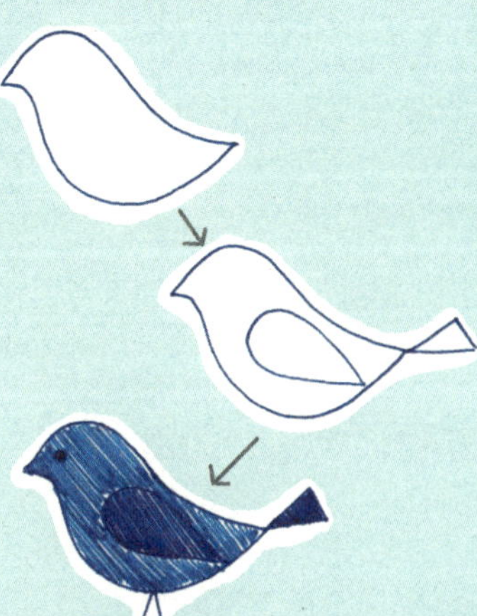

BIRDS & LEAVES

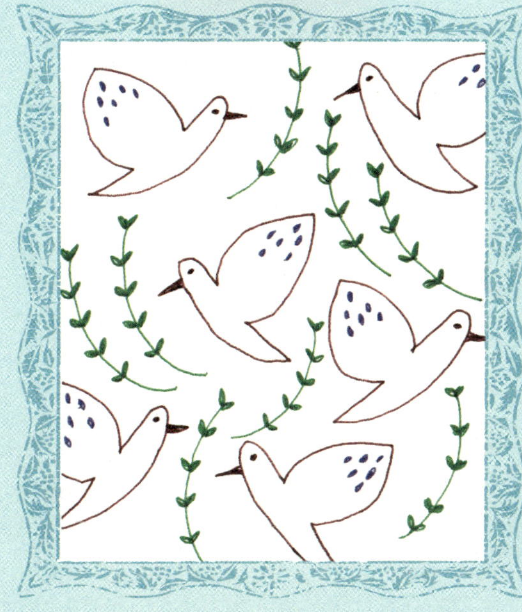

How to Draw the Pattern

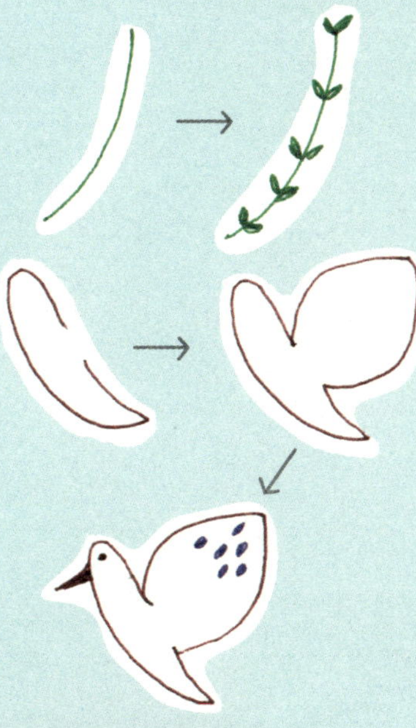

How to Draw the Pattern

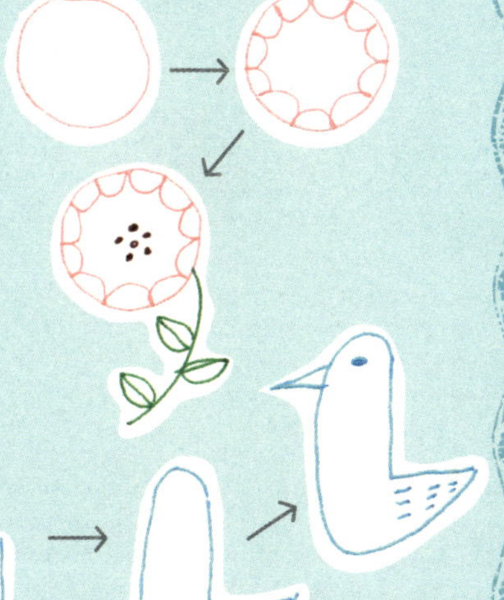

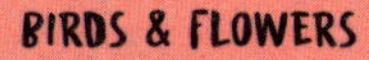

BIRDS & FLOWERS

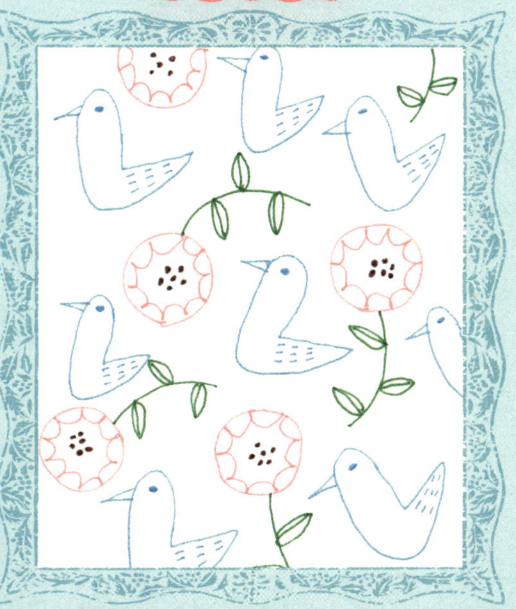

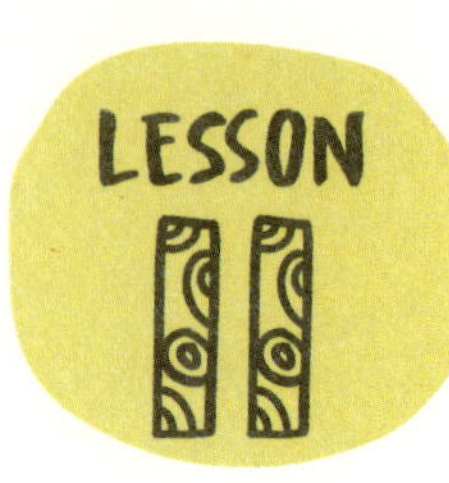

FISH & AQUATIC ANIMALS

Use simple shapes to draw water creatures such as fish. Add fins or arms and legs depending upon the animal.

1 For fish, draw the body and then add fins.

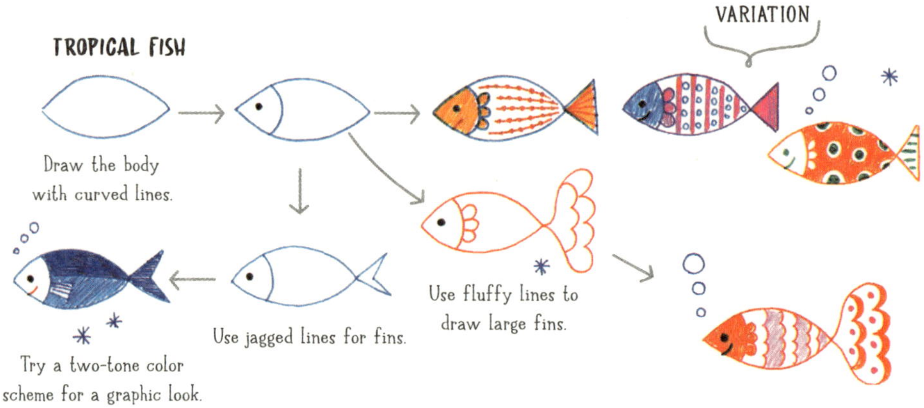

TROPICAL FISH

Draw the body with curved lines.

VARIATION

Use jagged lines for fins.

Use fluffy lines to draw large fins.

Try a two-tone color scheme for a graphic look.

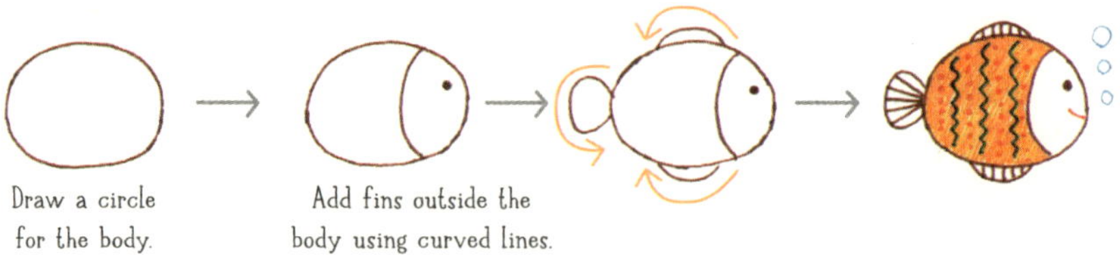

Draw a circle for the body.

Add fins outside the body using curved lines.

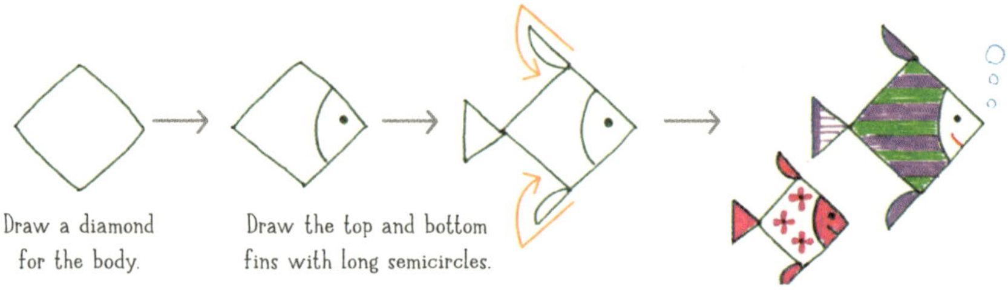

Draw a diamond for the body.

Draw the top and bottom fins with long semicircles.

2 For other aquatic animals, start with the body, then add arms, legs, and tails.

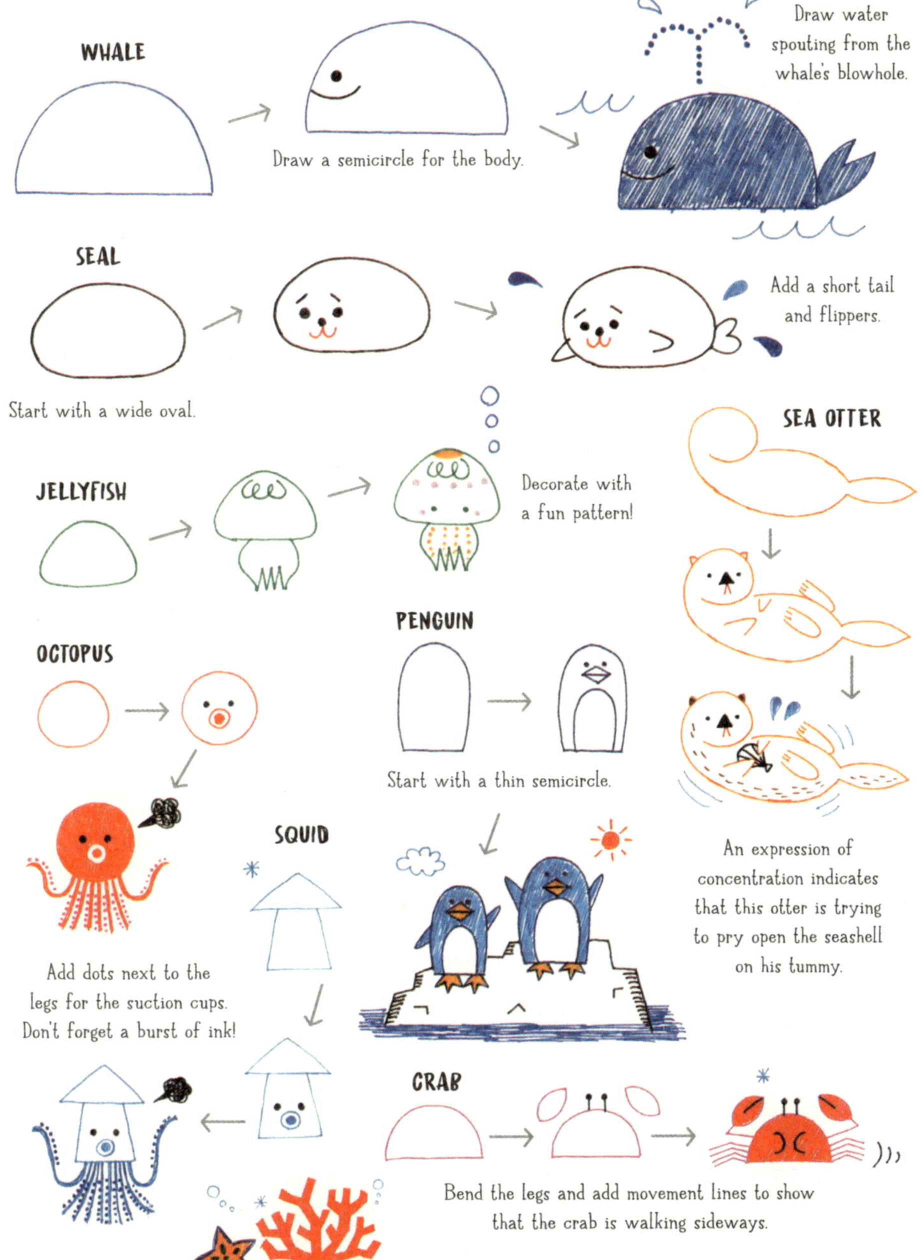

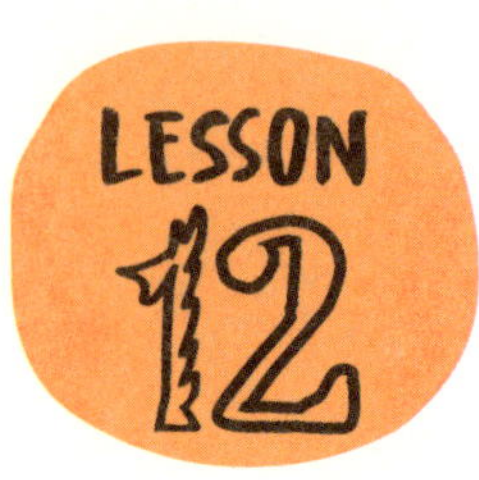

INSECTS

Insects are divided into three sections: the head, the thorax, and the abdomen. Understanding the basic structure helps create more realistic drawings.

1 Divide an oval into three sections.

Start with a thin oval.

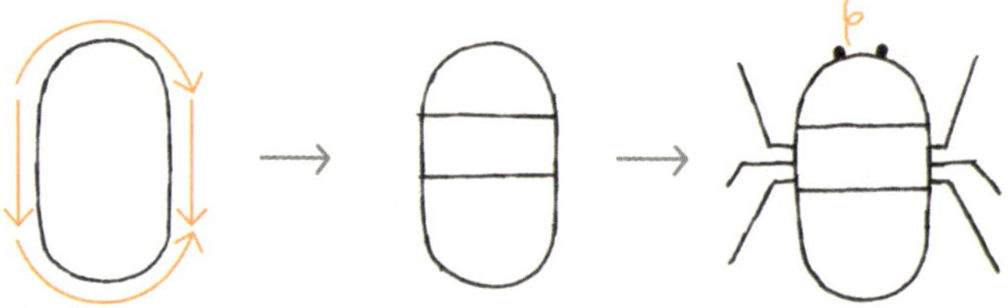

The thorax section is almost straight.

Use two lines to divide the oval into three sections. The thorax should be the shortest section.

Add large protruding eyes.

Draw legs extending from the body.

STAG BEETLE

BEETLE

CICADA

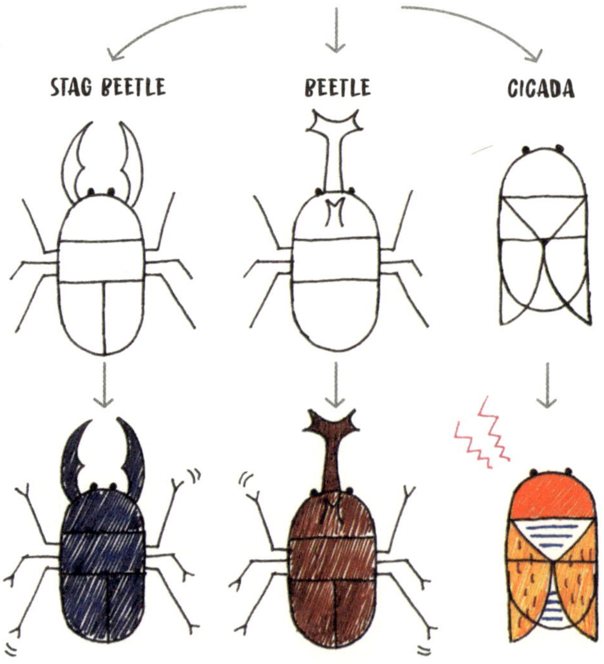

VARIATION

Draw the insects climbing up a tree for a summertime scene.

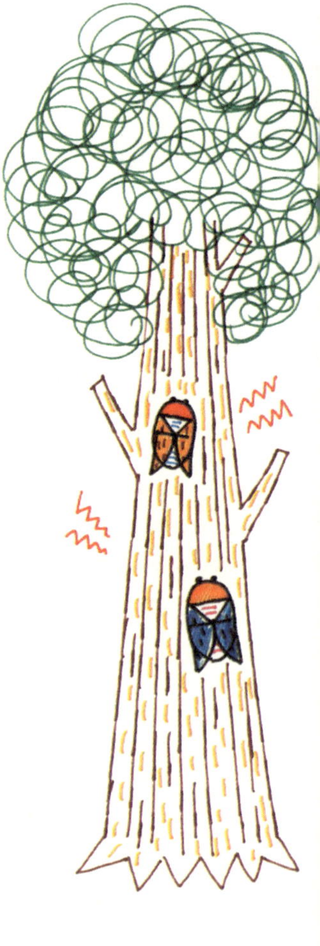

2 Draw the head and body (or wings) separately.

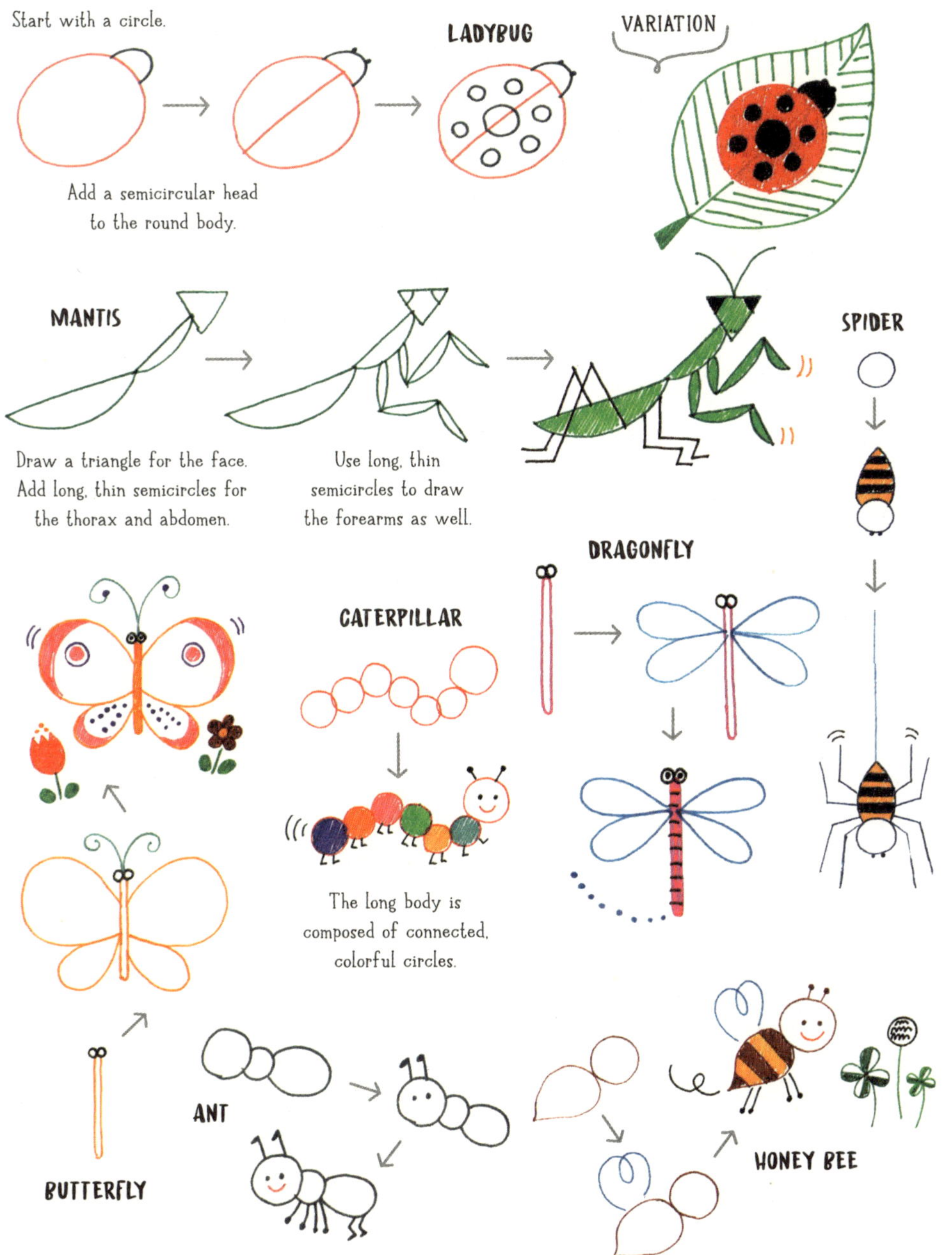

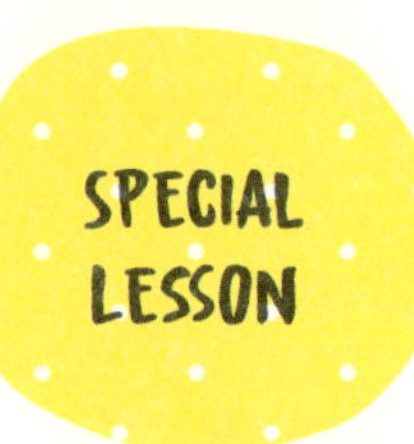

ANIMAL CHARACTERS

Draw funny facial expression and poses, or add outfits and accessories to make cute animals even cuter.

TECHNIQUE 1

Incorporate human facial expressions and actions.

WORRIED RABBIT

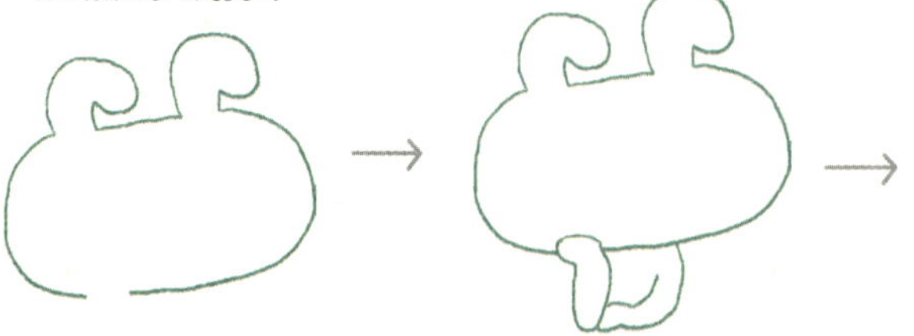

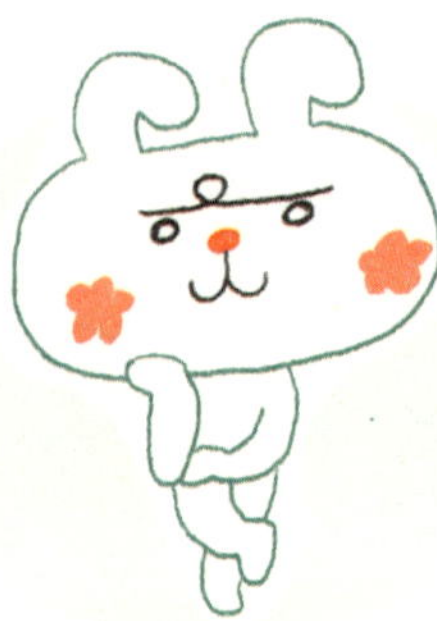

Draw his head supported by a hand and use a curly line to draw a furrowed brow.

WISE FOX

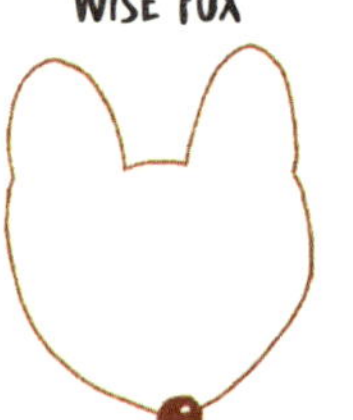

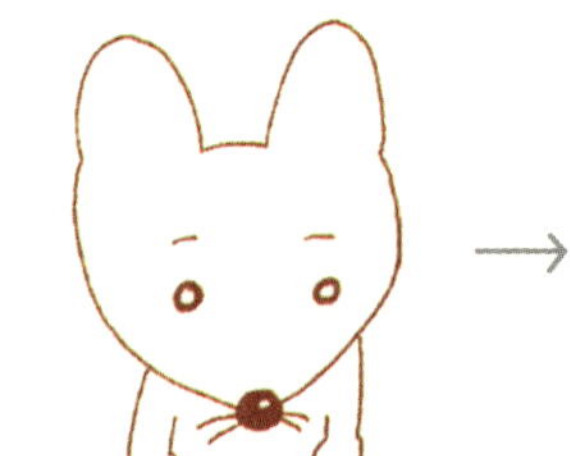

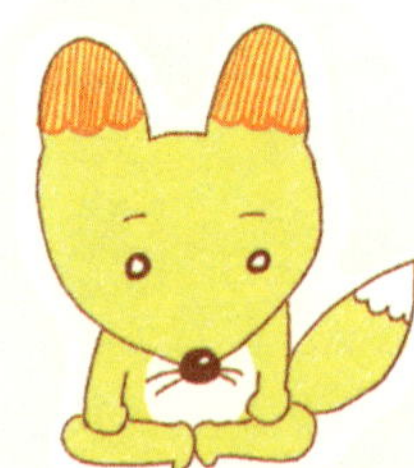

His legs are crossed and his hands are resting on his knees.

TAUNTING CAT

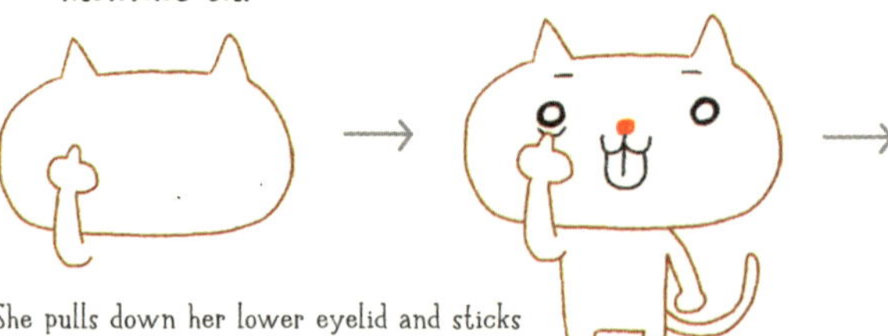

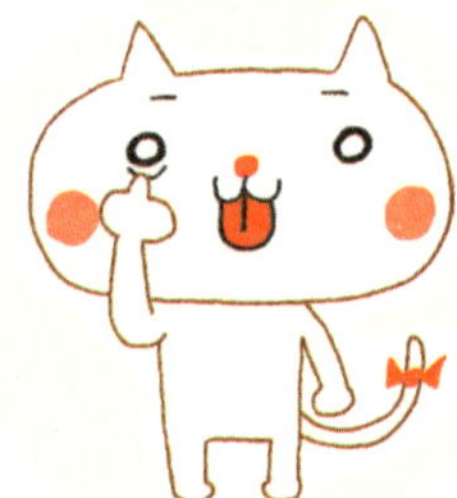

She pulls down her lower eyelid and sticks her tongue out—a taunting gesture in Japan.

CRYING DOG

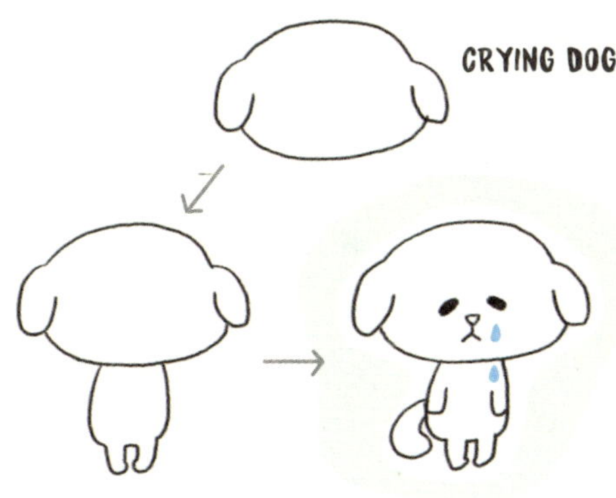

Tears stream down the face as he cries in disappointment.

BOUNCING PANDA

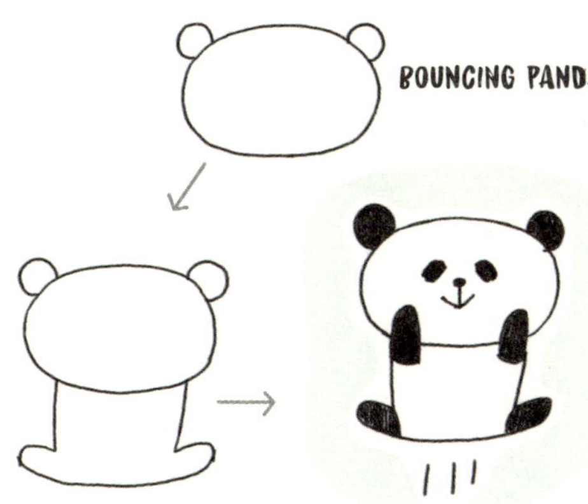

Draw the hands in the air. Draw three vertical lines underneath to show movement.

SCARED RACCOON DOG

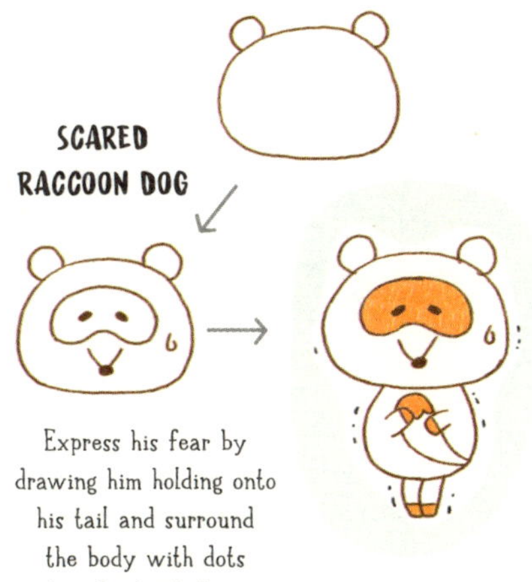

Express his fear by drawing him holding onto his tail and surround the body with dots to indicate shaking.

MISCHIEVOUS MONKEY

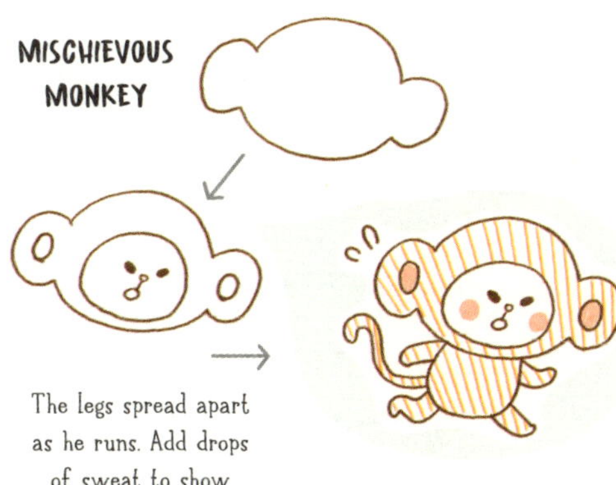

The legs spread apart as he runs. Add drops of sweat to show that he's in a hurry.

ANGRY PIG

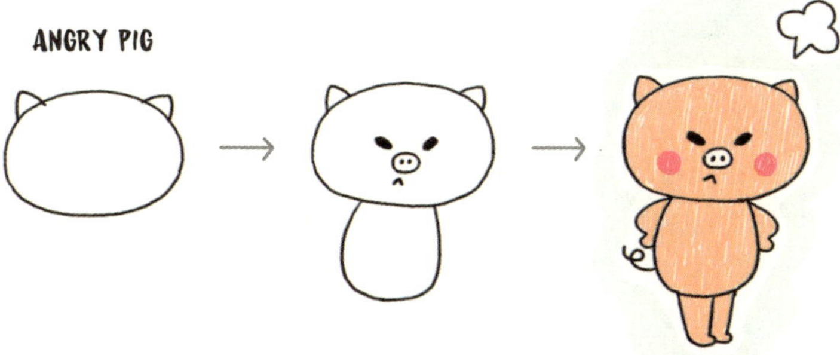

Place her hand on her hips and draw slanted eyes. Emphasize the anger with a puff of steam.

TECHNIQUE 2

Add clothes and accessories

BEAR & BALLOON

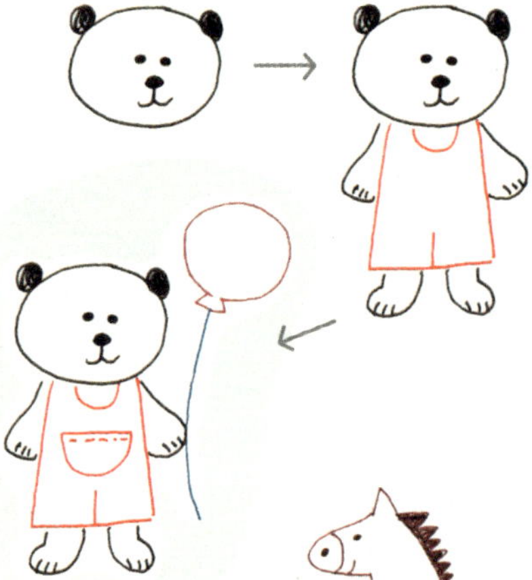

Add overalls and a balloon for a cute, childish look.

CAT & FLOWER

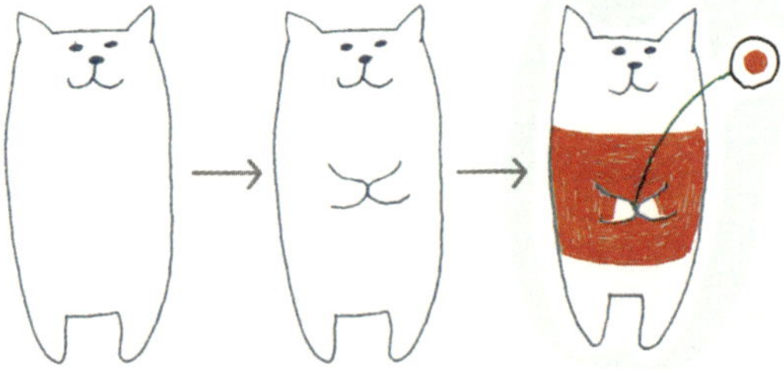

Match the color of the flower to the color of the shirt for a chic look.

HORSE & CARROT

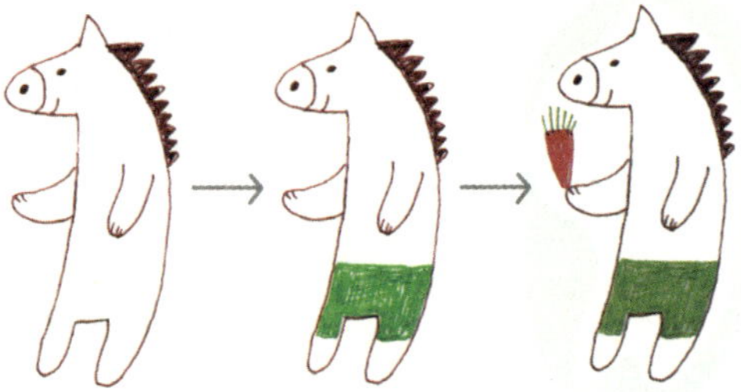

Draw the carrot in his outstretched hand.

DEER & DRESS

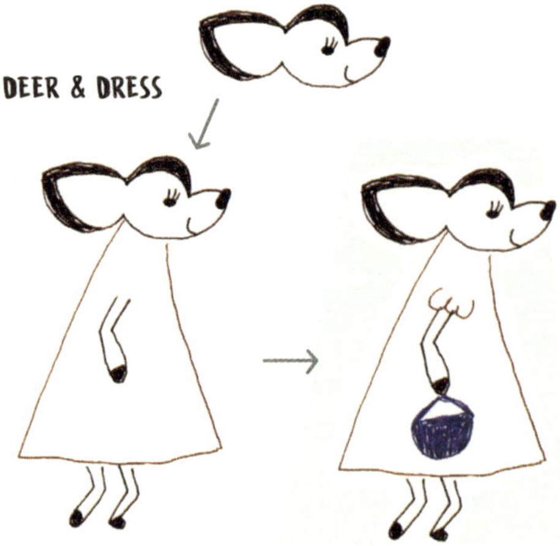

Draw a pretty dress and a coordinating purse for a fancy look.

LION & BASEBALL

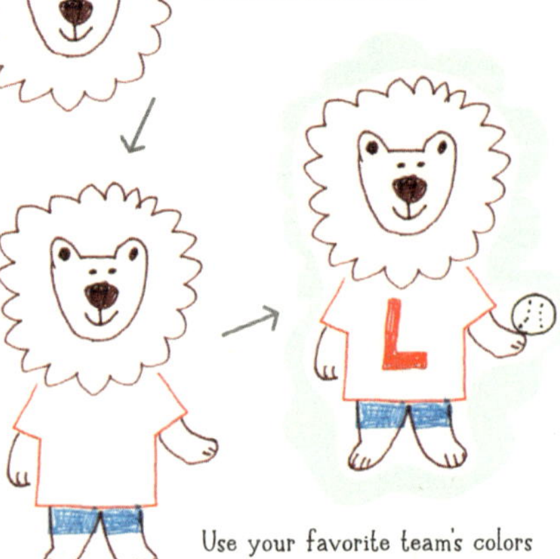

Use your favorite team's colors and logo for the uniform.

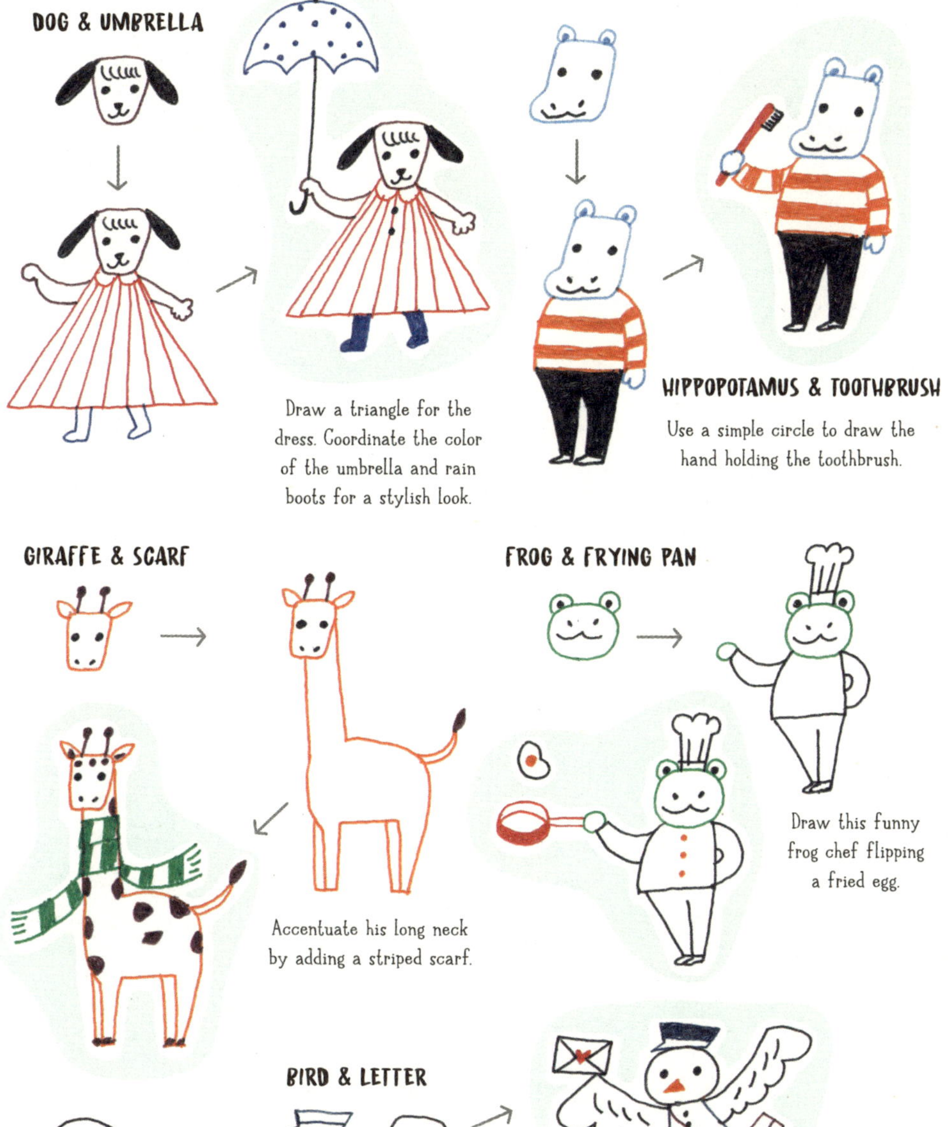

DOG & UMBRELLA

Draw a triangle for the dress. Coordinate the color of the umbrella and rain boots for a stylish look.

HIPPOPOTAMUS & TOOTHBRUSH

Use a simple circle to draw the hand holding the toothbrush.

GIRAFFE & SCARF

Accentuate his long neck by adding a striped scarf.

FROG & FRYING PAN

Draw this funny frog chef flipping a fried egg.

BIRD & LETTER

Draw a love letter balanced on the wing of a bird dressed in a mail carrier's uniform.

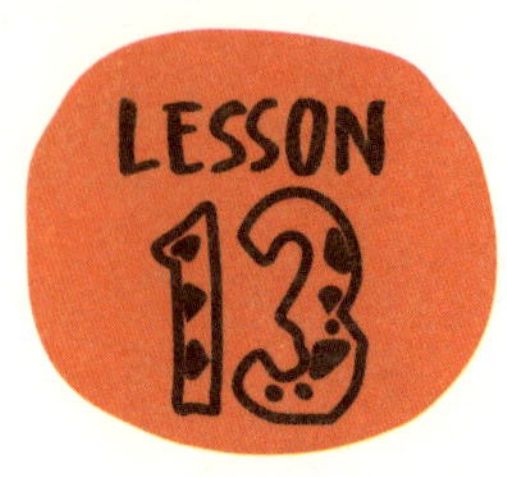

MYSTERIOUS CREATURES

Now let's draw some mysterious creatures, both from myths and legends and from ancient times.

1 Don't make these illustrations too scary, instead focus on cute expressions and gestures.

KAPPA

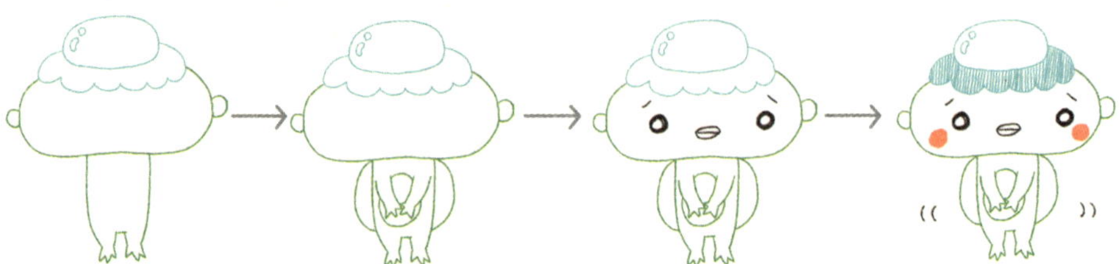

A kappa is a mythic creature of Japanese folklore that resides in ponds and rivers.

GHOST

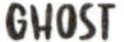

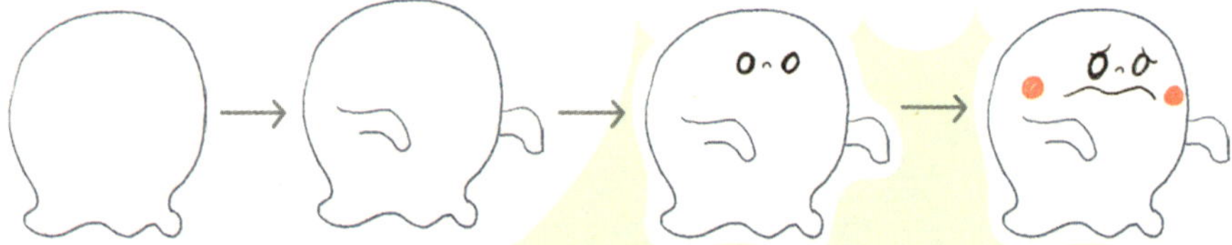

Inverted V-shaped eyebrows and a wavy mouth lend him a cute worried expression.

ALIEN

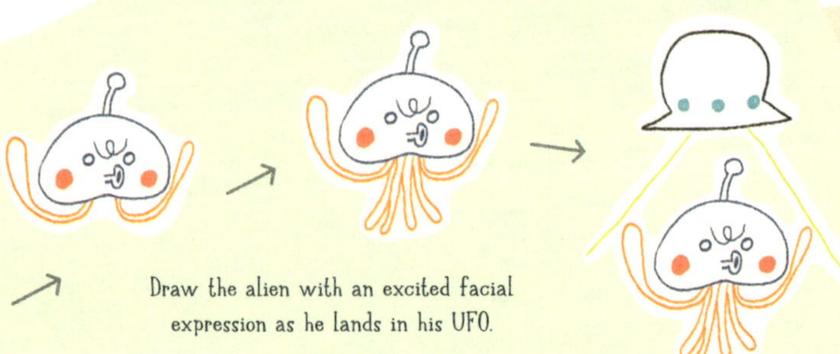

Draw the alien with an excited facial expression as he lands in his UFO.

2 Add objects for a human-like appearance.

MAMMOTH

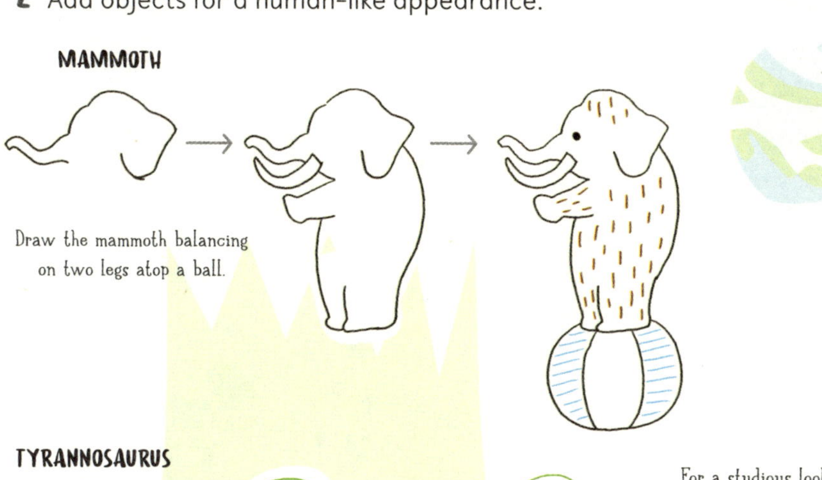

Draw the mammoth balancing on two legs atop a ball.

TYRANNOSAURUS

For a studious look, add glasses and a book.

STEGOSAURUS

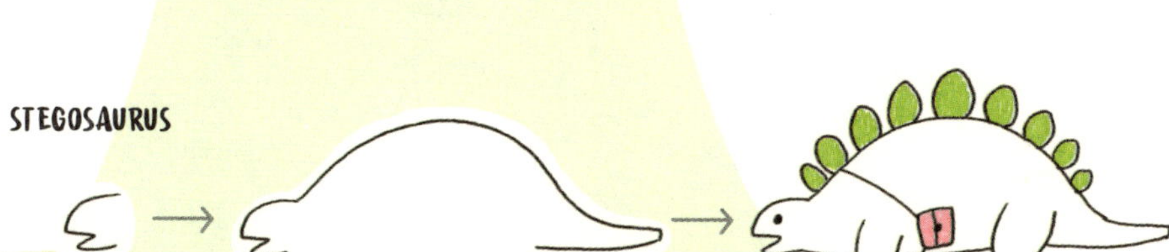

The contrast between the large body and the small purse is cute.

TRICERATOPS

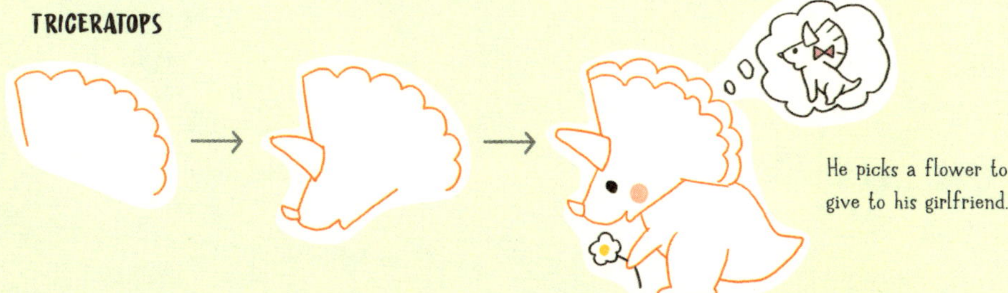

He picks a flower to give to his girlfriend.

ZODIAC ANIMALS

The Chinese zodiac uses animals to represent personality traits associated with birth year. You can adapt what you've learned about animal illustrations to draw zodiac animals, which are perfect for new year's cards.

1 Combine animal illustrations with popular lunar new year motifs.

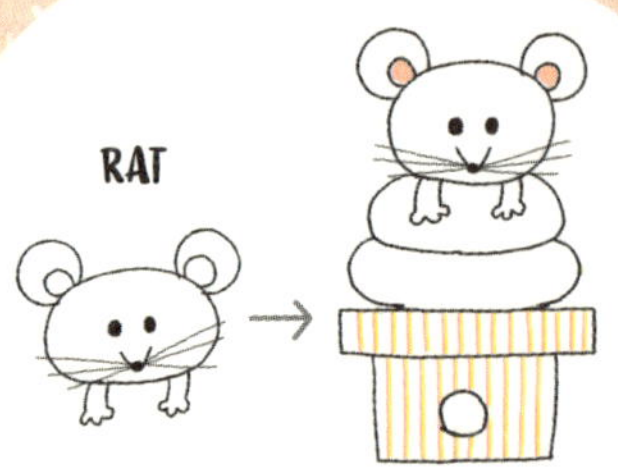

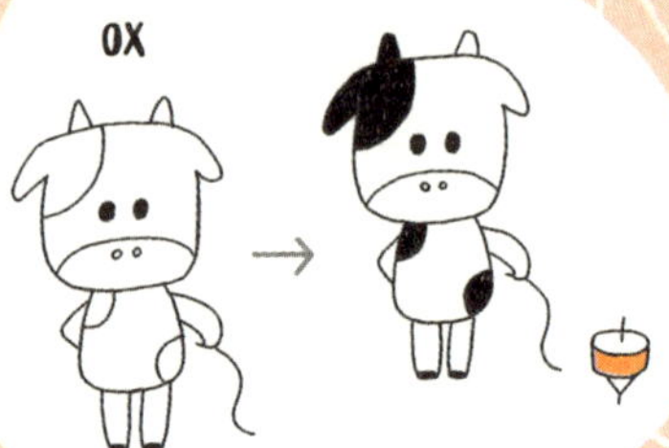

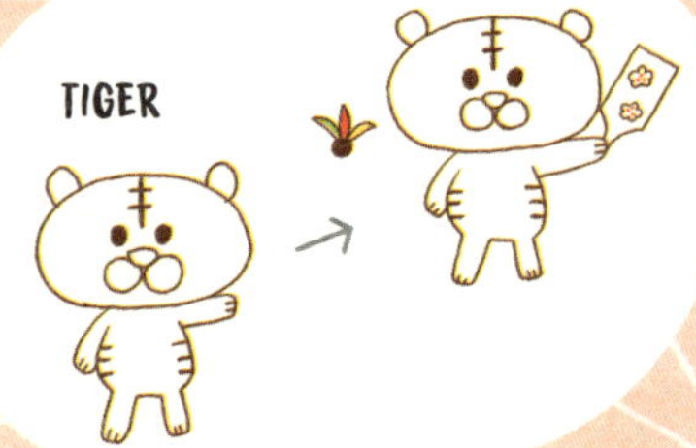

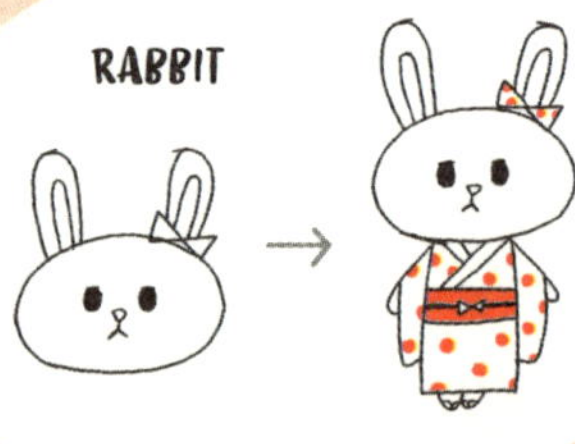

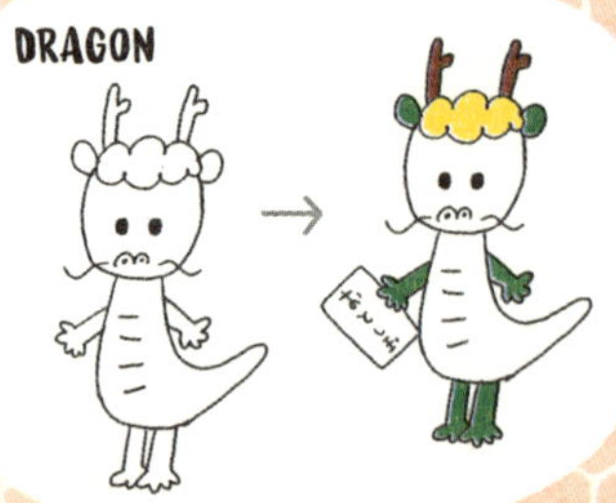

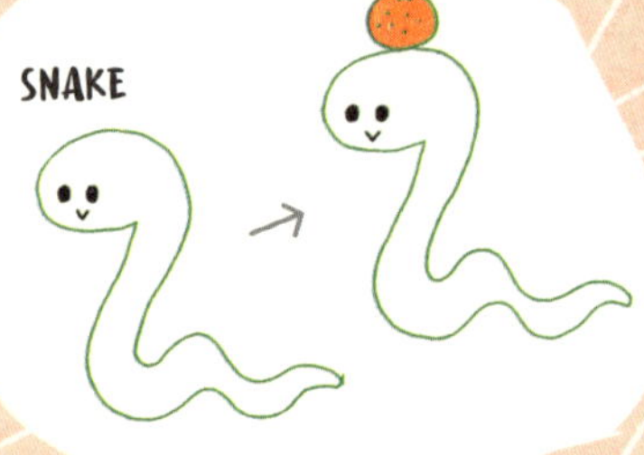

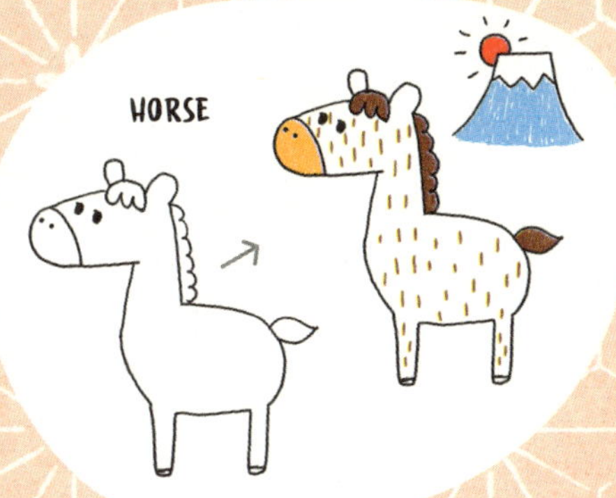
HORSE

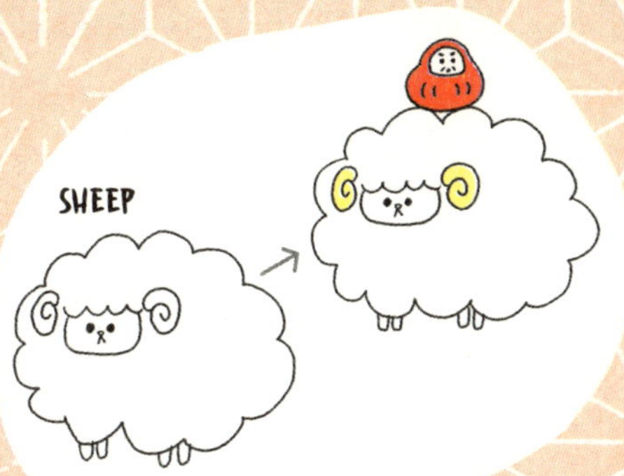
SHEEP

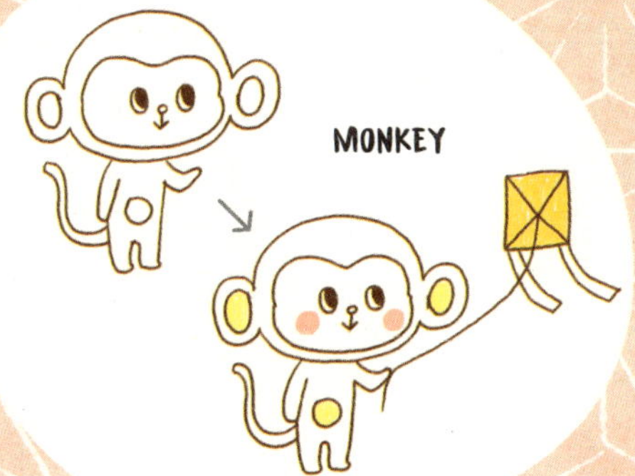
MONKEY

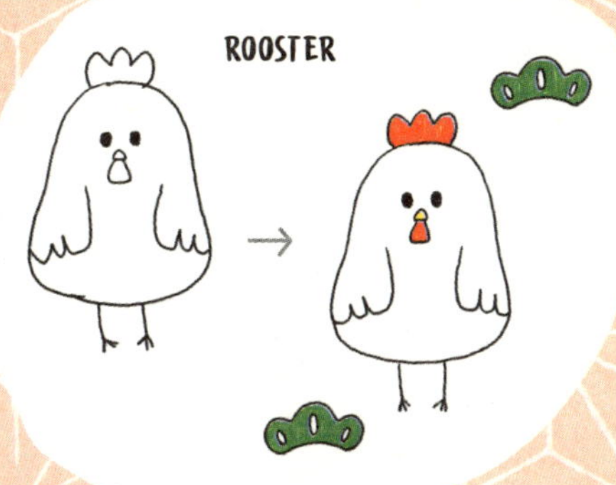
ROOSTER

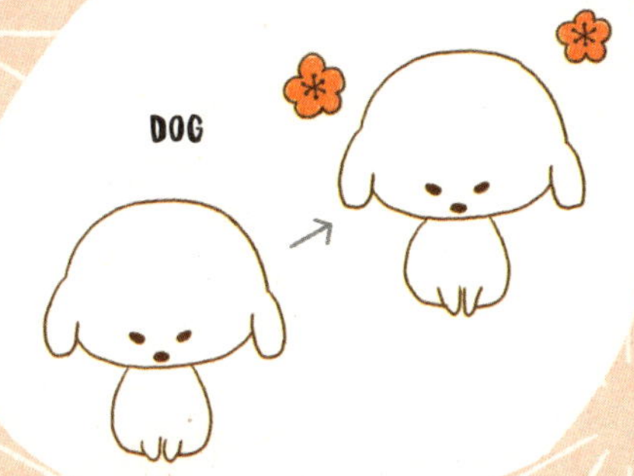
DOG

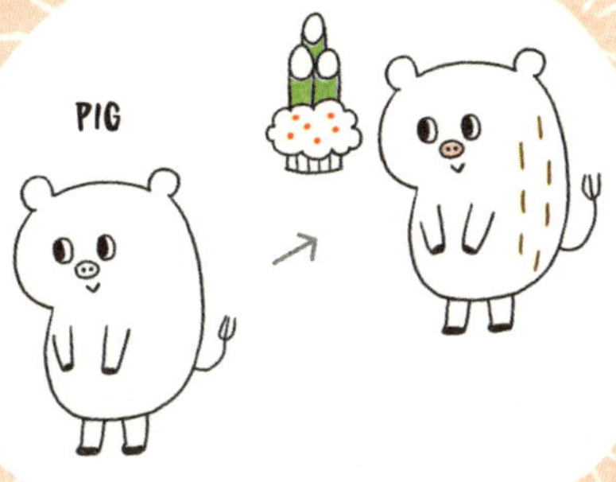
PIG

2 Use a single color, such as red, to draw animal symbols inspired by traditional seals.

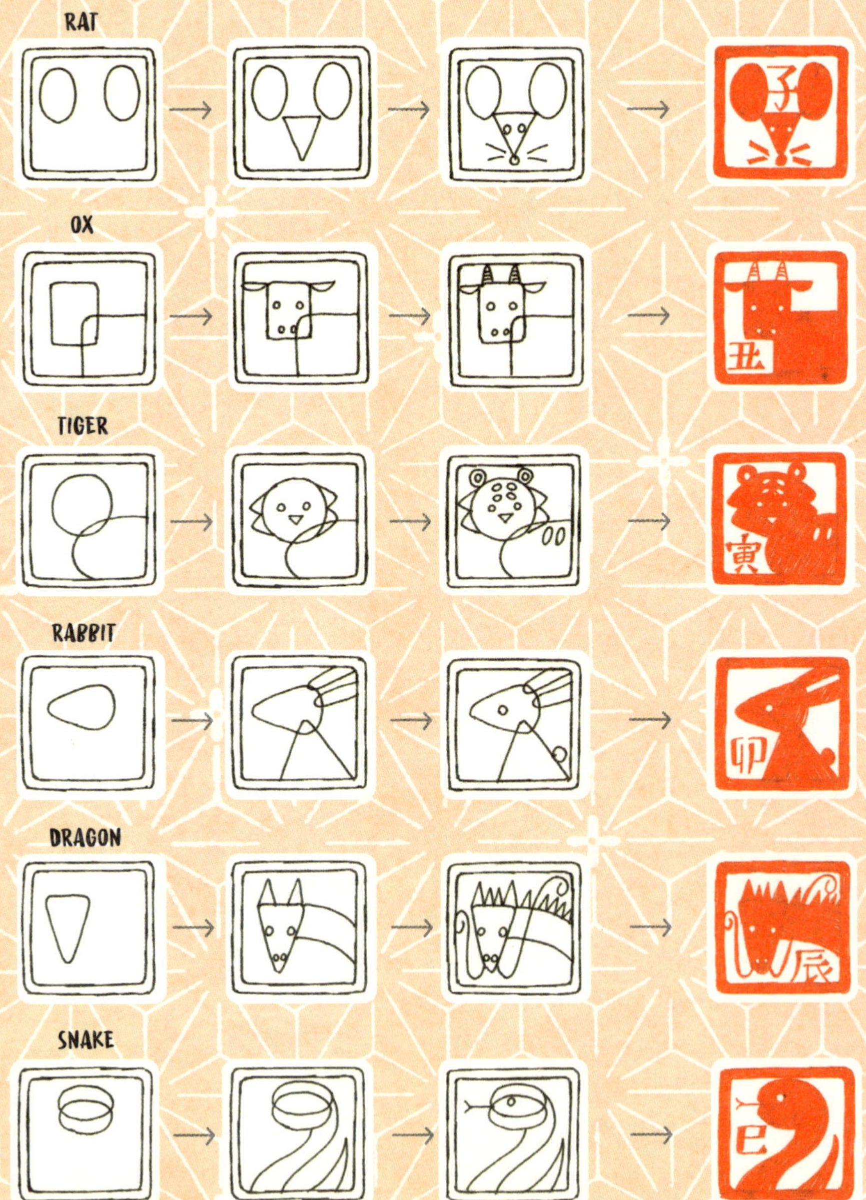

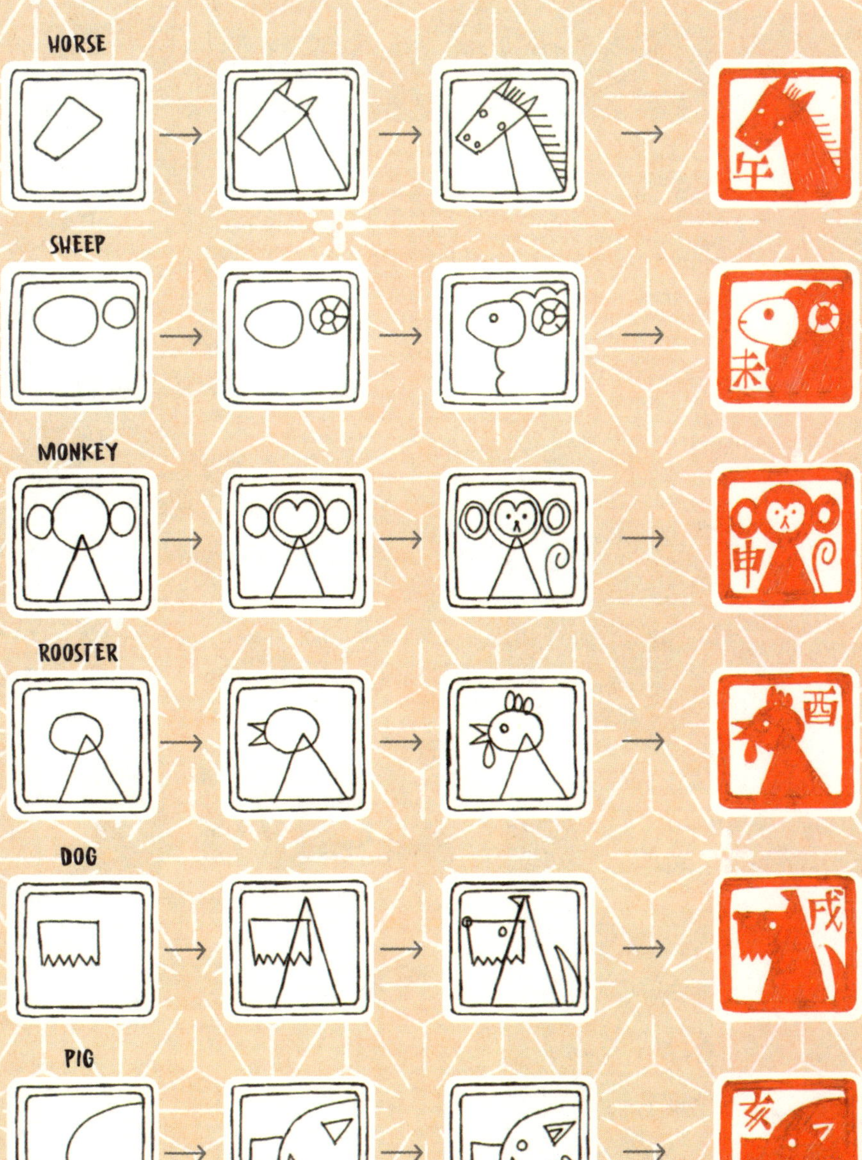
HORSE
午
SHEEP
未
MONKEY
申
ROOSTER
酉
DOG
戌
PIG
亥

VARIATION

NEW YEAR'S CARDS USING CHINESE ZODIAC ANIMAL ILLUSTRATIONS

Use Chinese zodiac animal illustrations to create new year's cards for your friends and family.

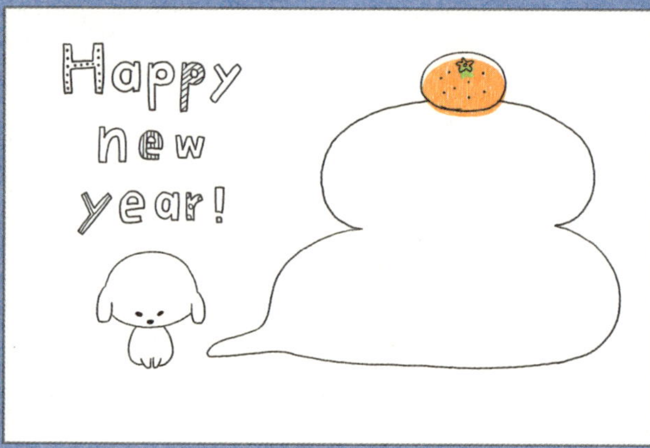

Dog illustration on page 69

The year 2018 was the year of the dog. Here, the dog welcomes the new year with a traditional Japanese rice cake. This design allows you to write a message inside.

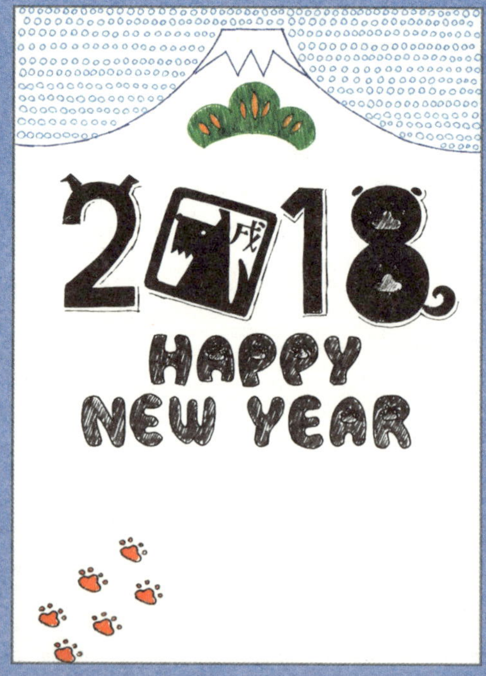

Dog illustration on page 71

Use the dog seal illustration in place of the 0 in 2018. Embellish the 8 with dog ears and a tail, then add paw prints to the corner of the card for a cute finish.

Chapter 2:

DRAWING PEOPLE

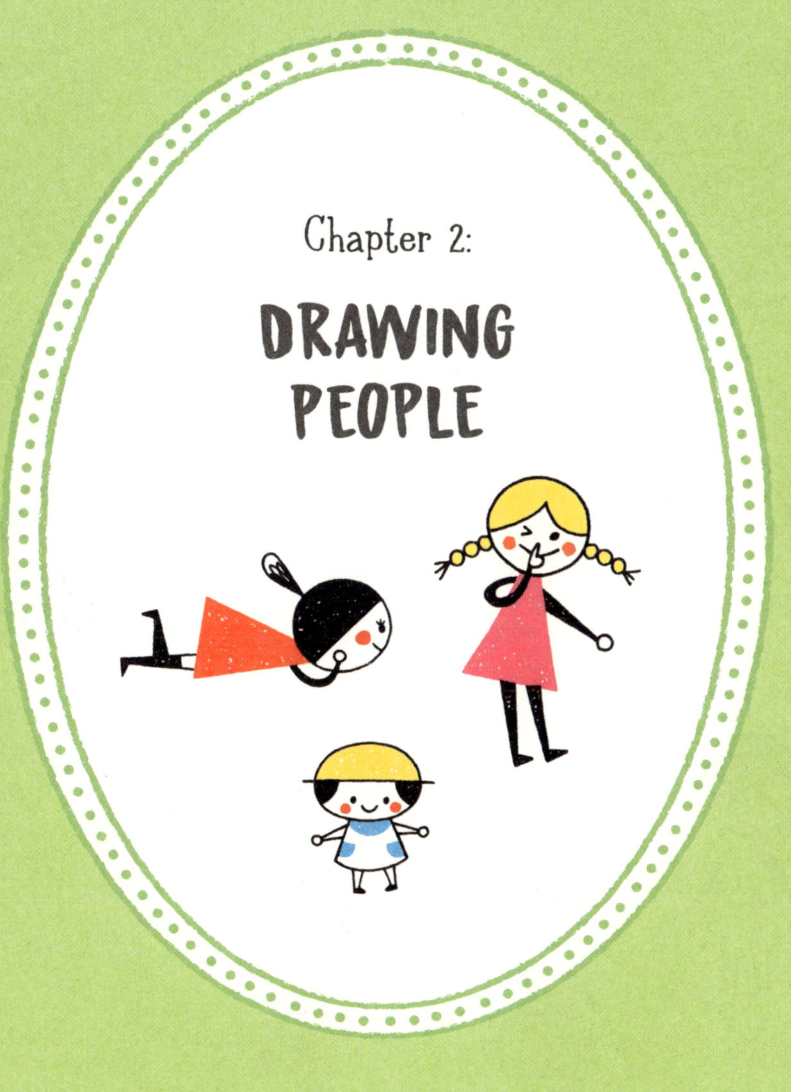

LESSON 1

DRAWING PEOPLE USING BASIC SHAPES

Let's start by learning how to draw a girl and a boy. You'll draw a circle for the head, then make the body the length of two heads.

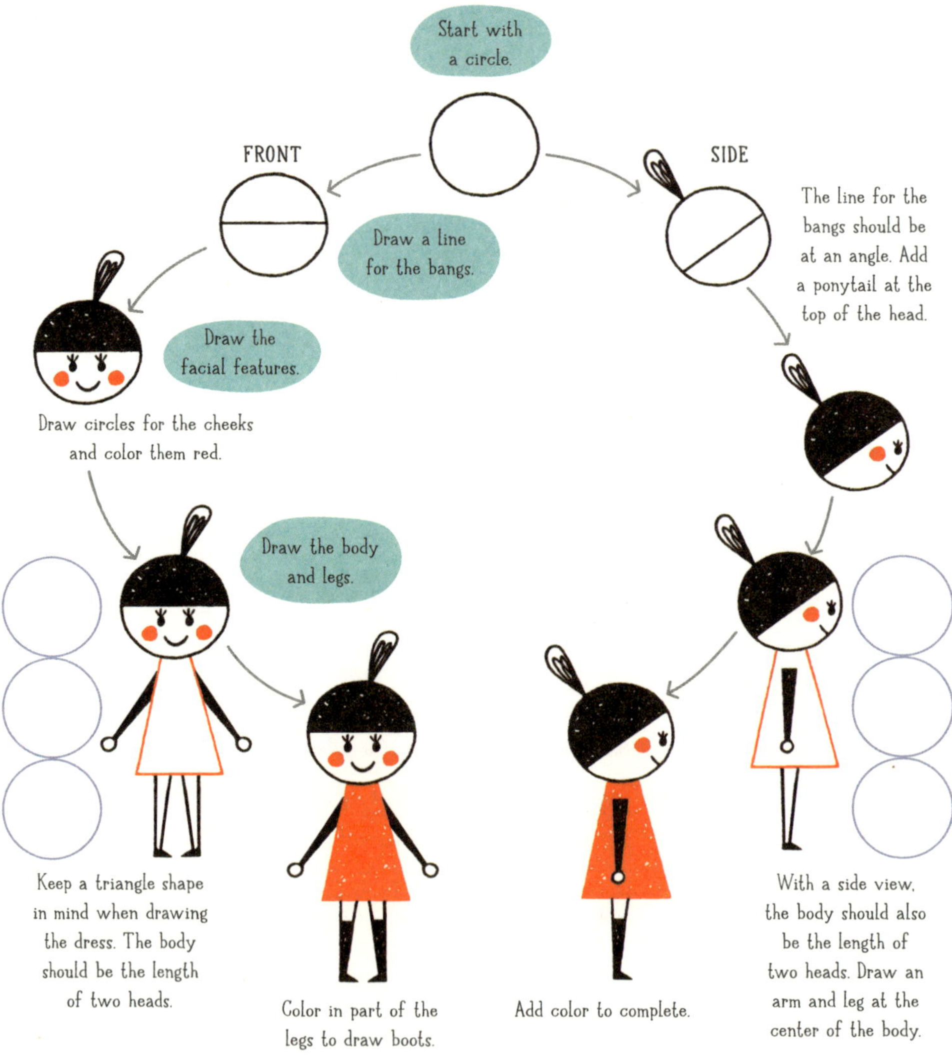

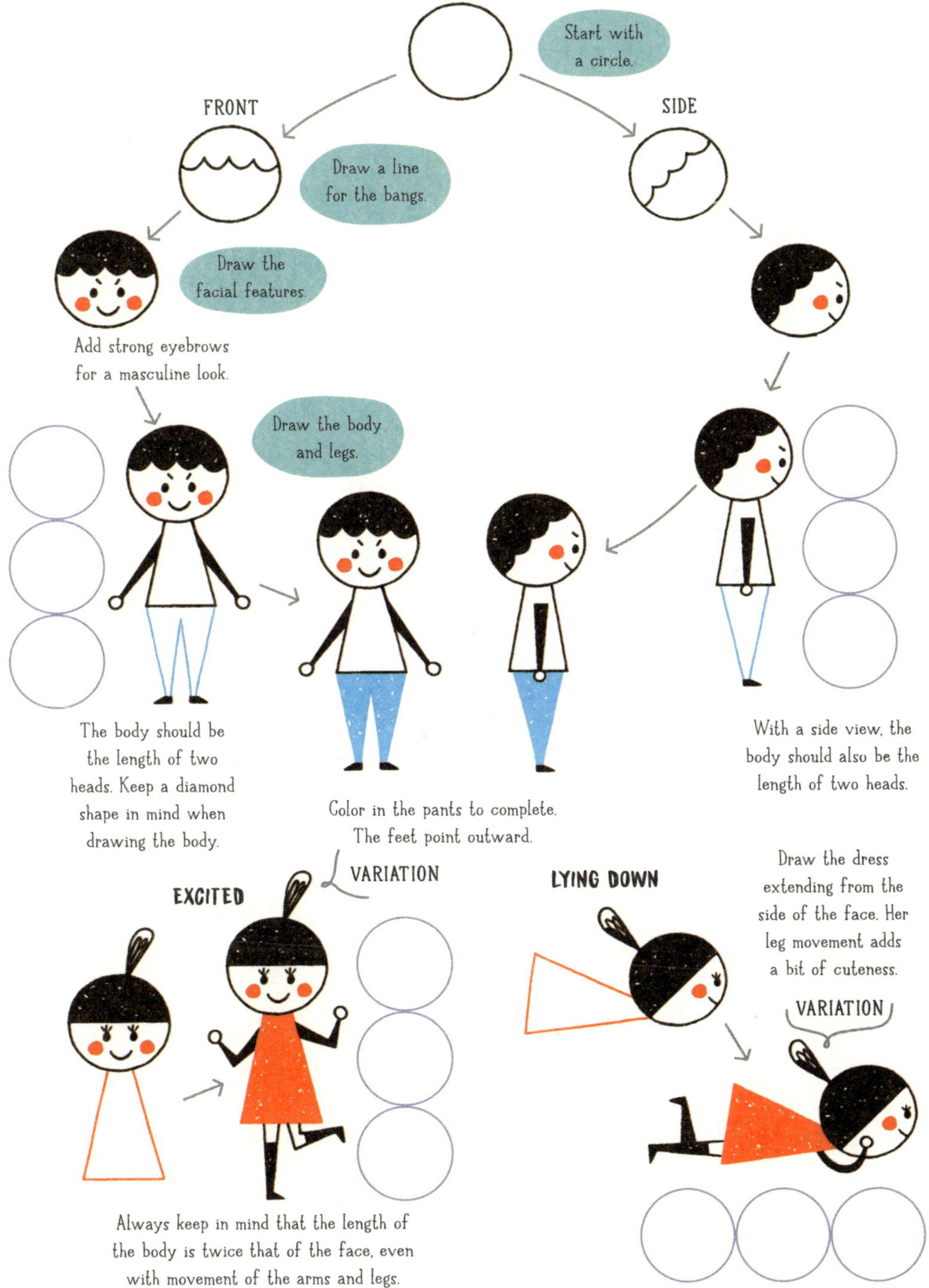
Start with a circle.
FRONT
SIDE
Draw a line for the bangs.
Draw the facial features.
Add strong eyebrows for a masculine look.
Draw the body and legs.
The body should be the length of two heads. Keep a diamond shape in mind when drawing the body.
Color in the pants to complete. The feet point outward.
With a side view, the body should also be the length of two heads.
VARIATION
EXCITED
LYING DOWN
Draw the dress extending from the side of the face. Her leg movement adds a bit of cuteness.
VARIATION
Always keep in mind that the length of the body is twice that of the face, even with movement of the arms and legs.

SPECIAL LESSON

DRAWING PEOPLE FROM DIFFERENT ANGLES

Now let's challenge ourselves to draw illustrations of people from more complex angles, such as from diagonally above or from diagonally below.

TECHNIQUE 1

Shift the position of the arms and facial features for a diagonal view.

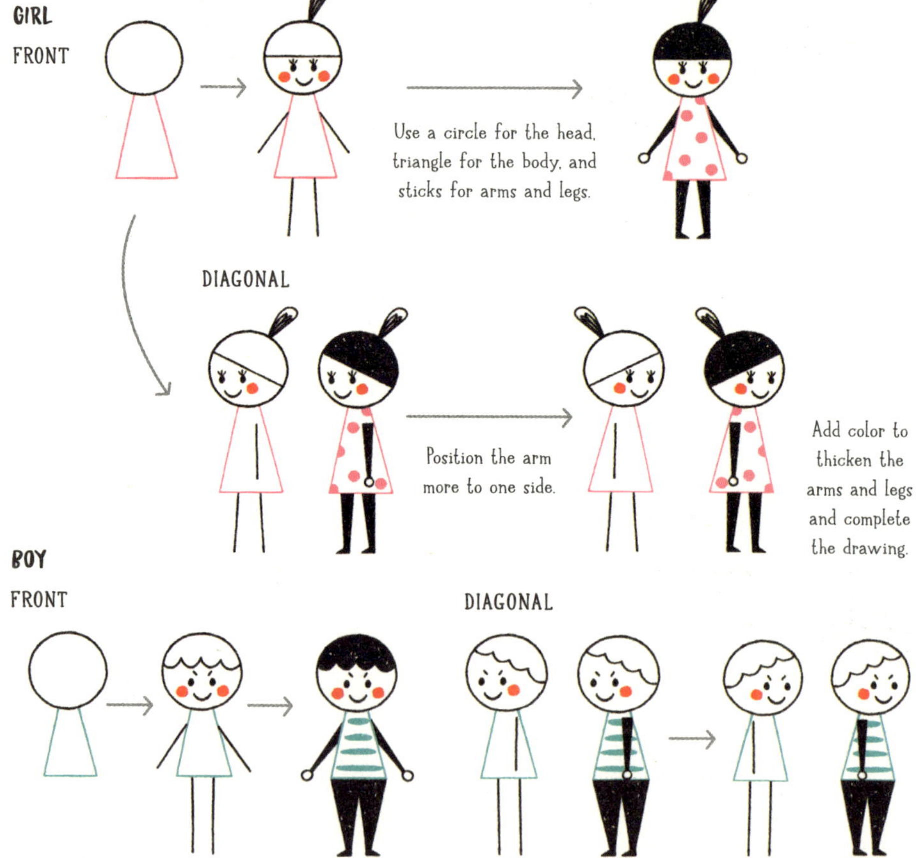

Draw the boy's legs slightly longer than the girl's.

TECHNIQUE 2

The body length becomes shorter when drawn from above or below.

GIRL

FROM ABOVE

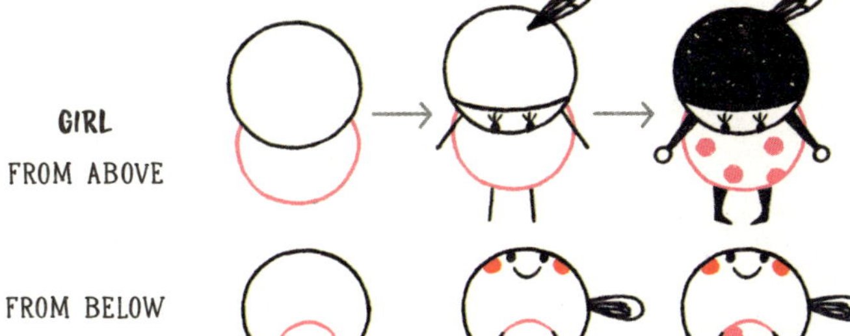

The hair takes up most of the head when drawn from above.

FROM BELOW

Draw a circle for the head. Make the dress shorter since the bottom of the body is visible.

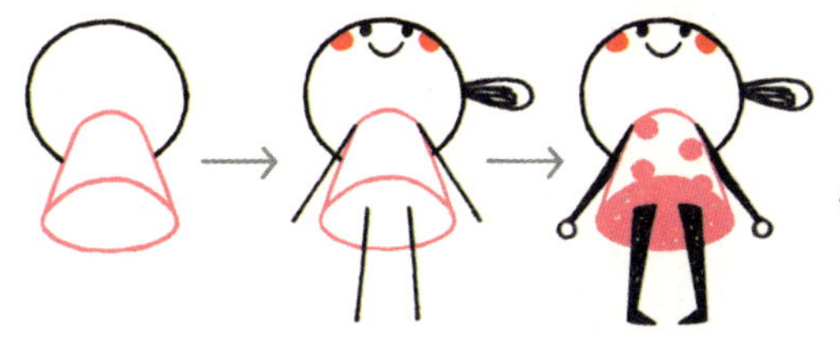

Color the bottom of the dress for a three-dimensional look.

The facial features are positioned at the top of the head. The length of the arms and legs is the same as with a frontal view.

BOY

FROM ABOVE

Draw a circle for the head. Add a trapezoid underneath.

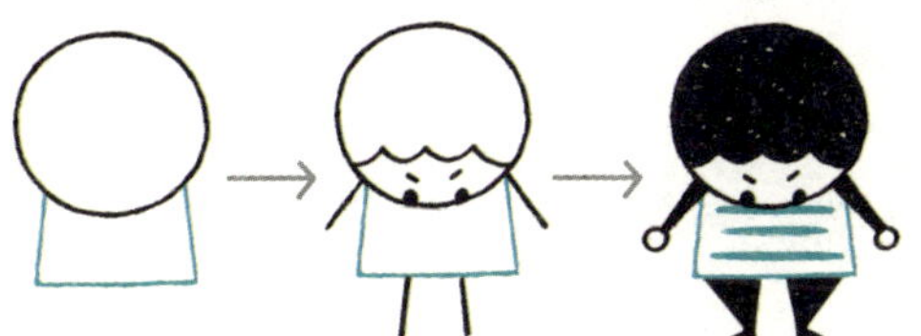

Do not draw the mouth since it is not visible from this angle.

Draw shorter arms and legs.

FROM BELOW

The drawing method of the face and the body is the same as the girl.

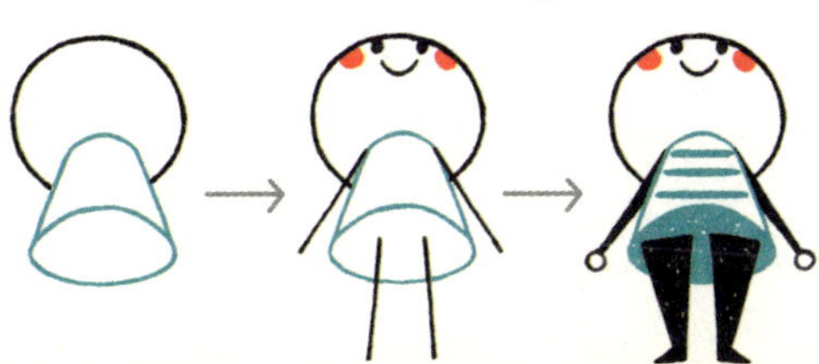

No need to draw any hair as it is not visible from this angle.

VARIATION

KNEELING

Bring the hands toward the center of the body. Bend the legs.

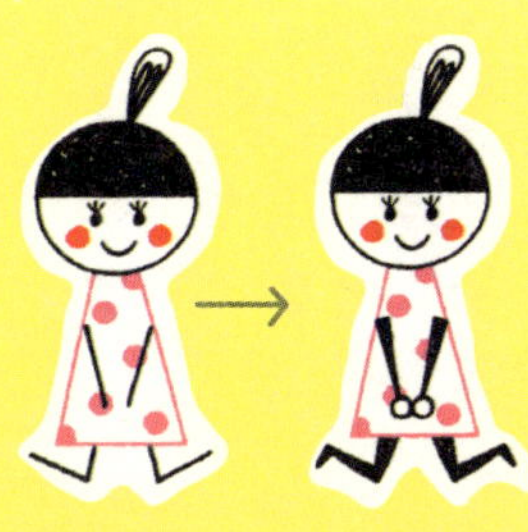

SITTING ON THE FLOOR

Draw a side view illustration and place the hand on the knee.

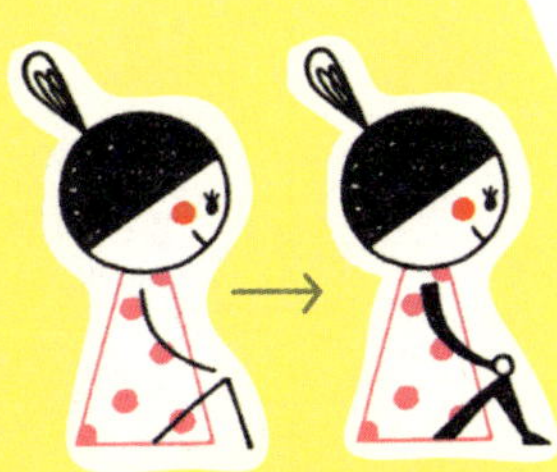

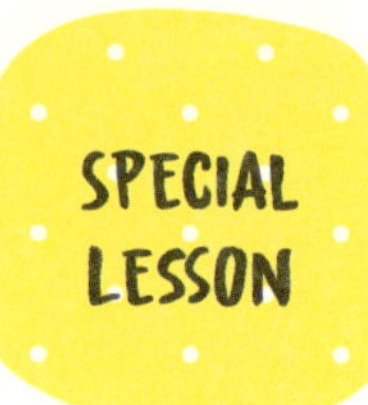

DRAWING PEOPLE OF DIFFERENT AGES

Now let' s draw illustrations of children, babies, and adults using the basics learned for drawing boys and girls.

TECHNIQUE 1

The faces of toddlers and babies are wide ovals. The position of the eyes is low and the body is short.

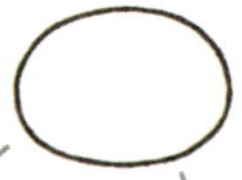

Start with a wide oval.

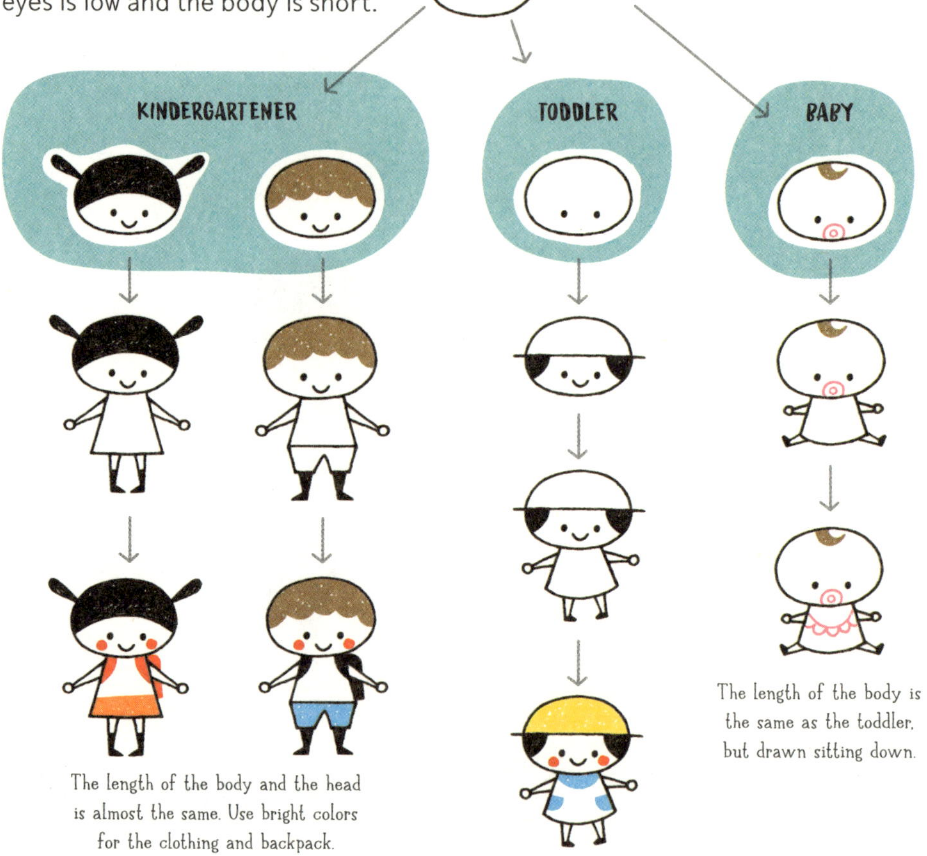

KINDERGARTENER

TODDLER

BABY

The length of the body and the head is almost the same. Use bright colors for the clothing and backpack.

The body is a little shorter than the head. Add a hat and cute clothing.

The length of the body is the same as the toddler, but drawn sitting down.

TECHNIQUE 2

Adults' faces are long ovals. The position of the eyes is higher and the body is longer.

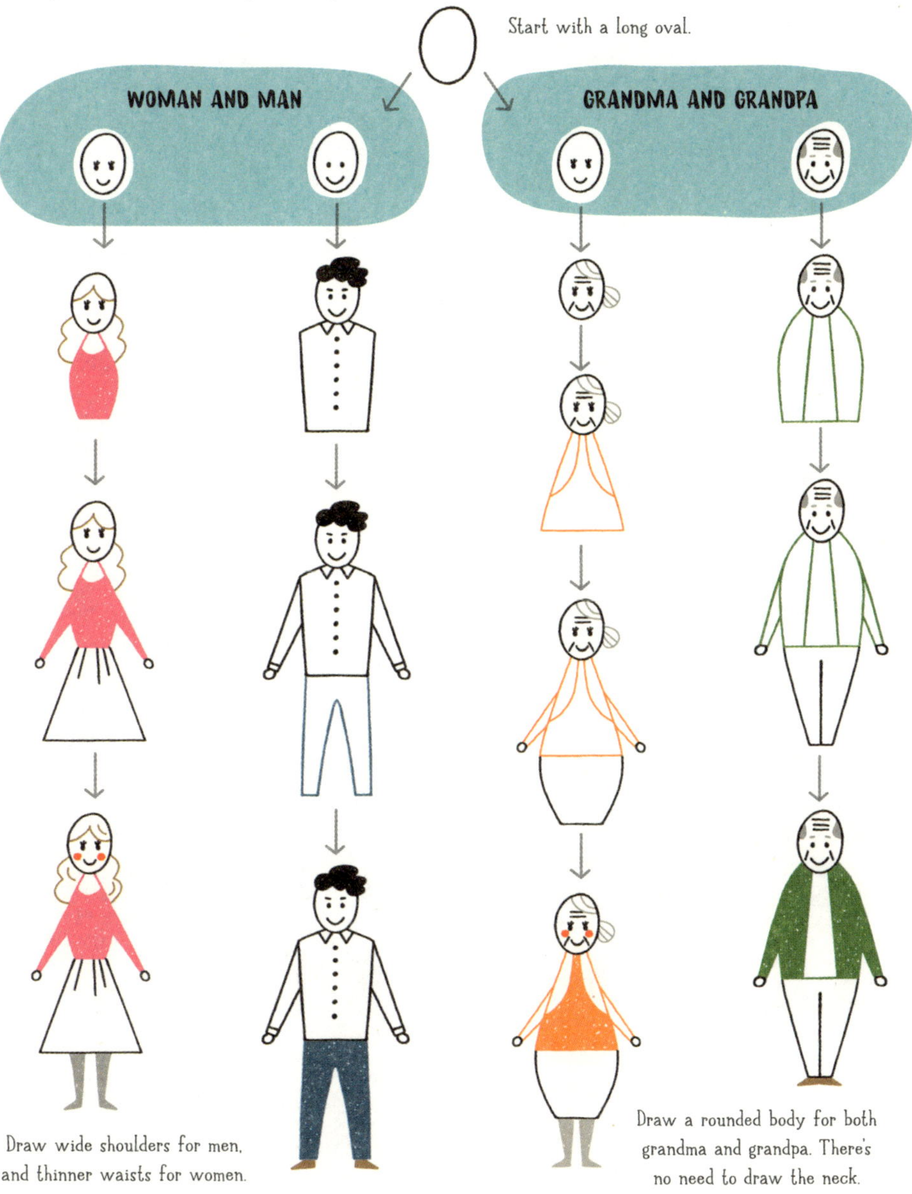

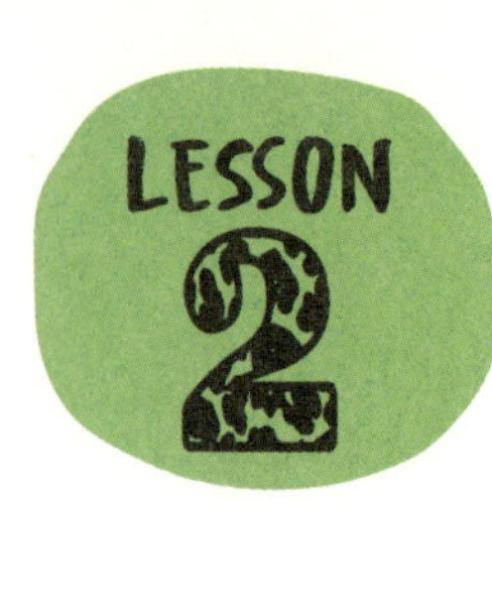

HAIRSTYLES

Even if the facial features are the same, changing the hairstyle can create a character with a unique impression. Try changing the bangs, hair length, and color.

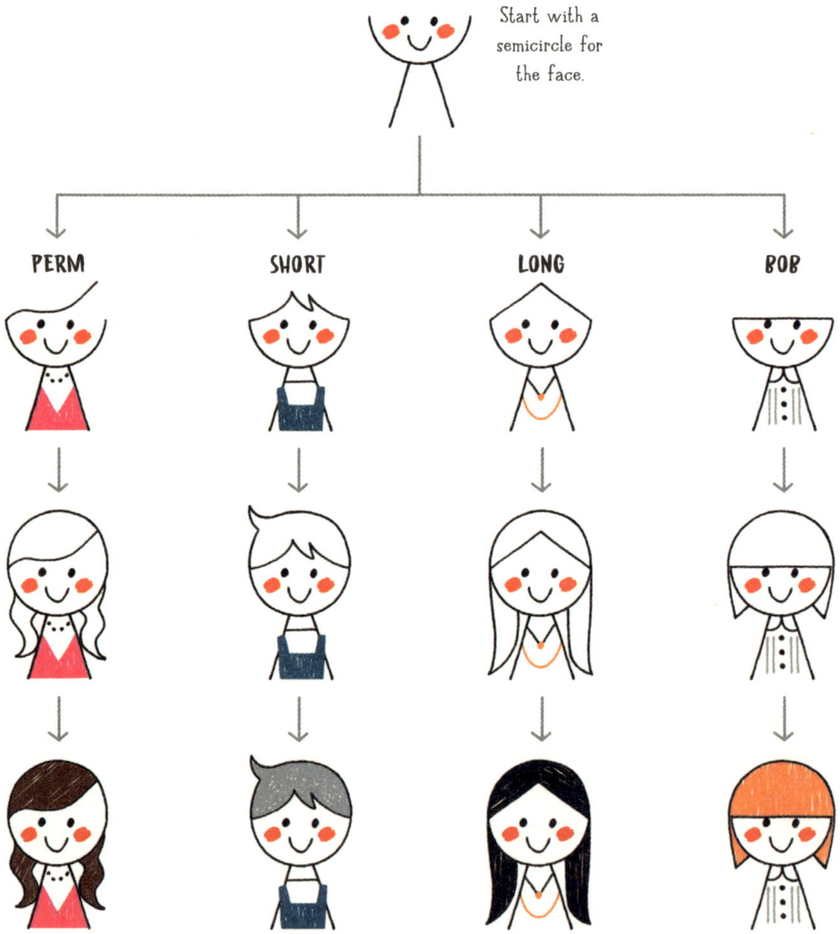

Start with a semicircle for the face.

PERM

Draw the bangs, then use softly curved lines for the back hair.

SHORT

Try spiked hair to create tomboy look.

LONG

Part the hair at the center and leave white spaces for highlights in shiny black hair.

BOB

Use a straight line for the bangs, just above the eyes, to create a distinctive look.

VARIATION

ADD HAIR ACCESSORIES FOR UNIQUE STYLE

Various hairstyles can be made by arranging the hair and adding accessories.

PONYTAIL & HAIR TIE

Draw a high ponytail. A pink hair tie is cute.

PIGTAILS & POMPOMS

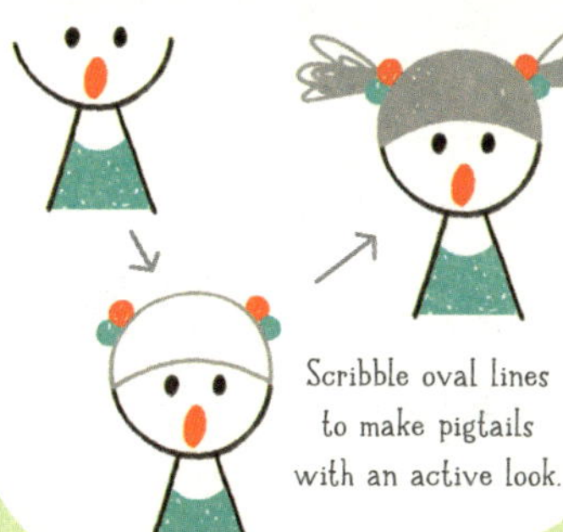

Scribble oval lines to make pigtails with an active look.

BRAID & BOW

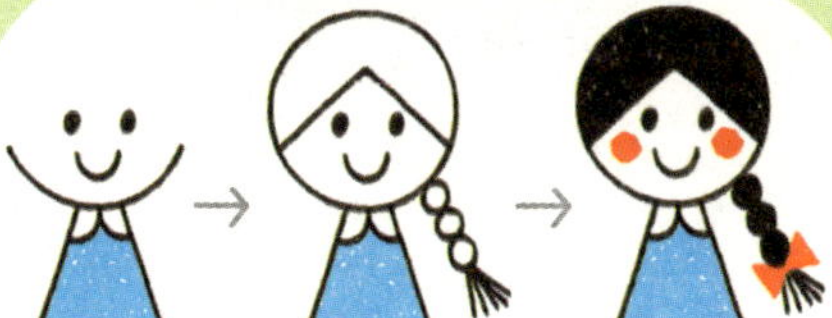

Part the bangs at the center and draw a low braid to create retro and cute look.

BOB & HEADBAND

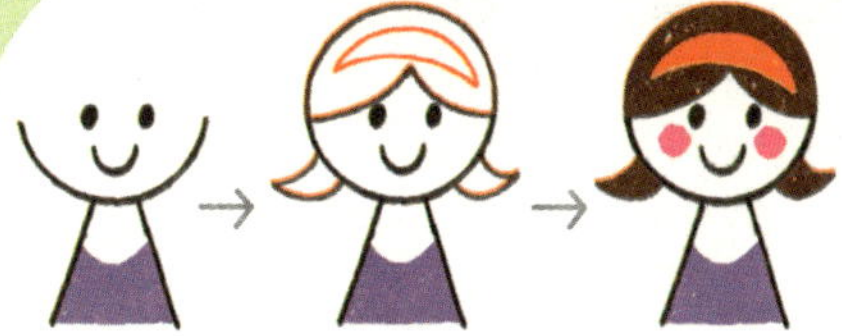

Add a thick headband using a curved line above the bangs.

BUN & SCRUNCHIE

Use fluffy lines to draw a scrunchie, and let the ends of the hair curl casually.

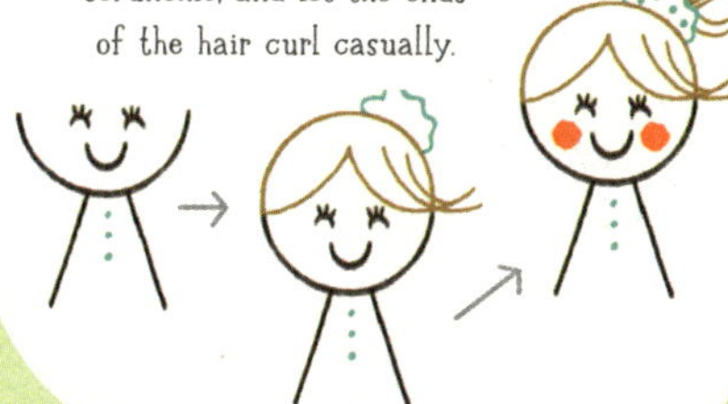

LONG & BARRETTE

Draw a teardrop-shaped barrette above the eyes. Try a diagonal part for a classic look.

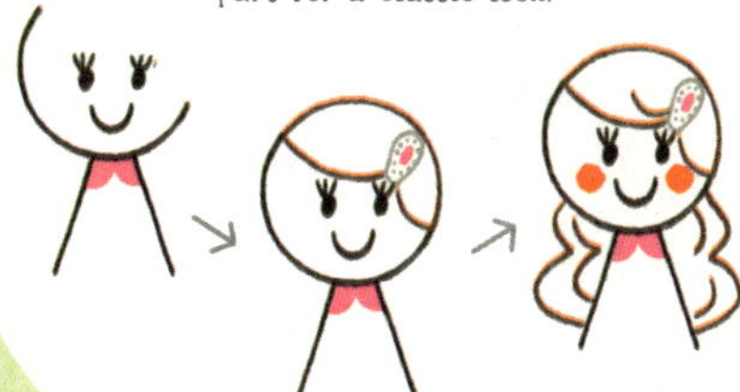

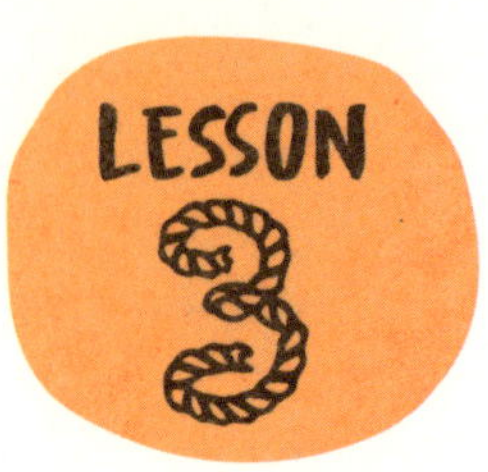

FACIAL EXPRESSIONS & EMOTIONS

Change the eyes, eyebrows, and mouth depending on the emotion of the character, such as joy, anger, sadness, or fun. You can even add captions.

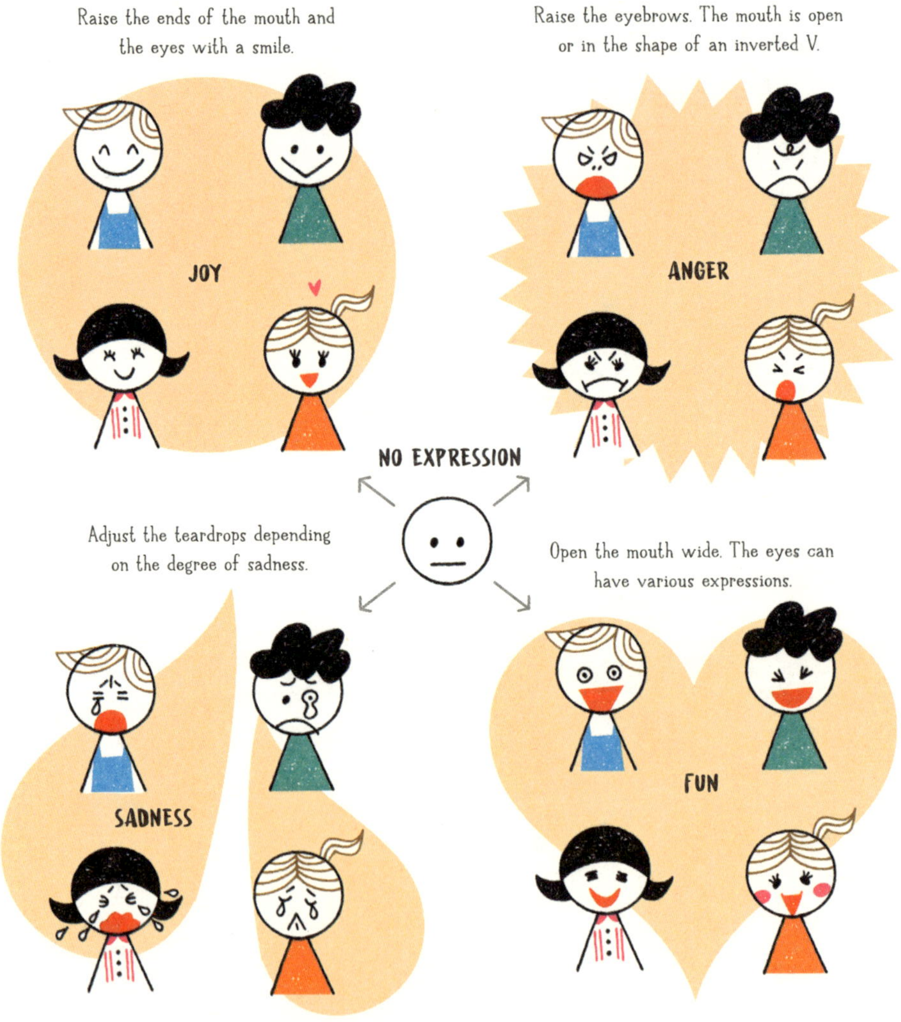

Raise the ends of the mouth and the eyes with a smile.

JOY

Raise the eyebrows. The mouth is open or in the shape of an inverted V.

ANGER

NO EXPRESSION

Adjust the teardrops depending on the degree of sadness.

SADNESS

Open the mouth wide. The eyes can have various expressions.

FUN

VARIATION

OTHER FACIAL EXPRESSIONS

Let's try drawing some more complex facial expressions. A little exaggeration can create a cute illustration.

SURPRISED

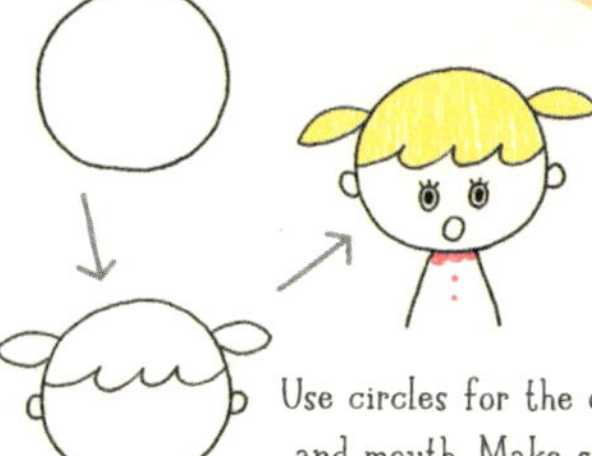

Use circles for the eyes and mouth. Make sure to open the eyes wide.

DEPRESSED

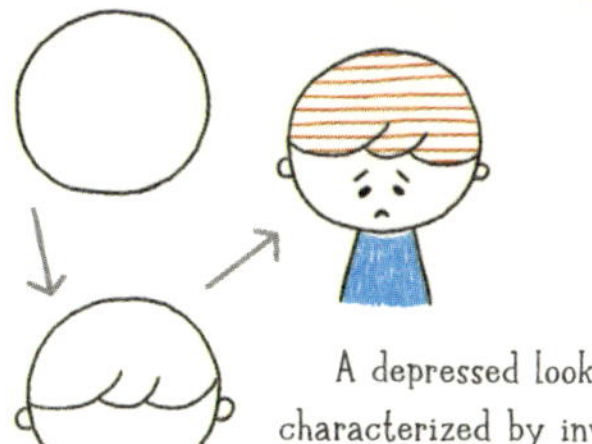

A depressed look is characterized by inverted V-shaped eyebrows, eyes, and mouth.

DROWSY

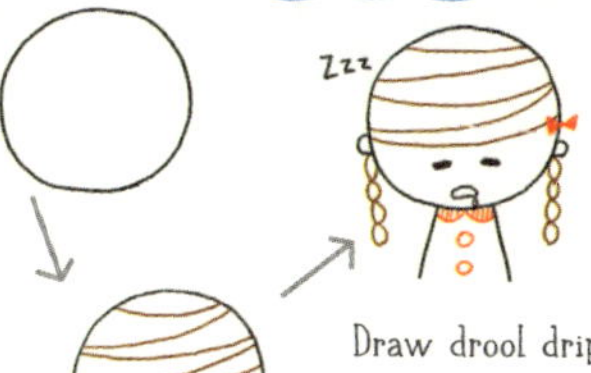

Draw drool dripping from the corner of the mouth. You can even add a few "ZZZs."

IMPATIENT

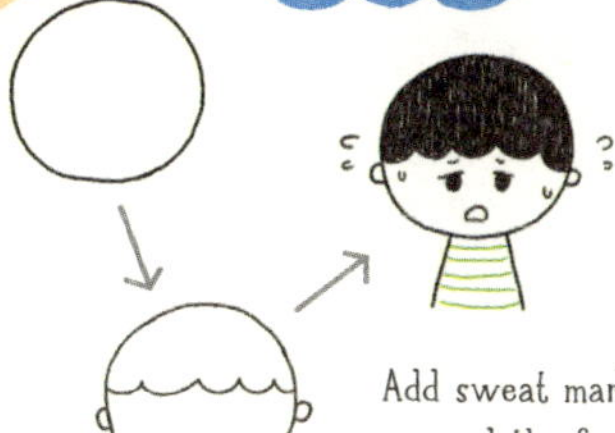

Add sweat marks around the face.

SHY

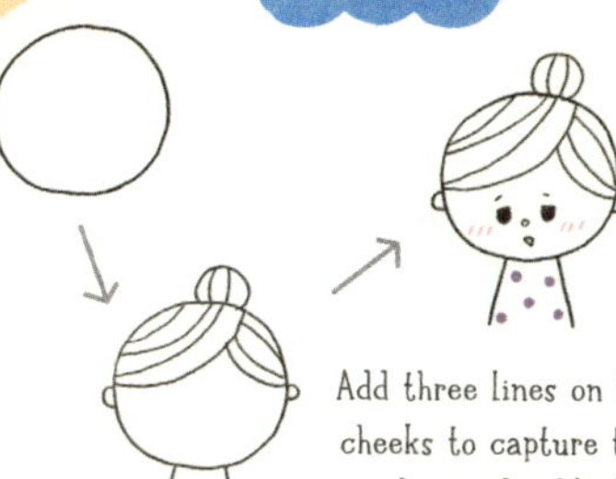

Add three lines on the cheeks to capture the redness of a blush.

WORRIED

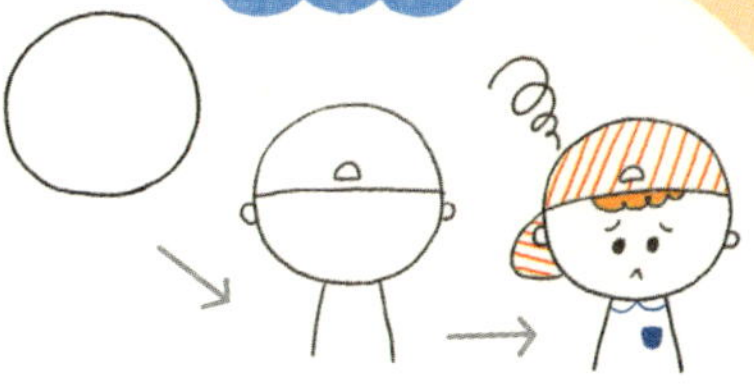

The eyebrows are lowered in an inverted V shape. Add a spiral above the head to represent his troubled thoughts.

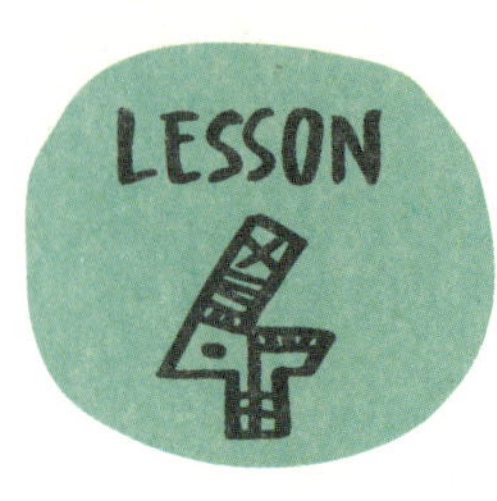

ACTIONS & MOVEMENTS

Now let's try drawing people on the move. Start by drawing the arms and legs as sticks, then thicken the lines. In addition to the movement of the arms and legs, it's important to express the action within the facial features.

WALK

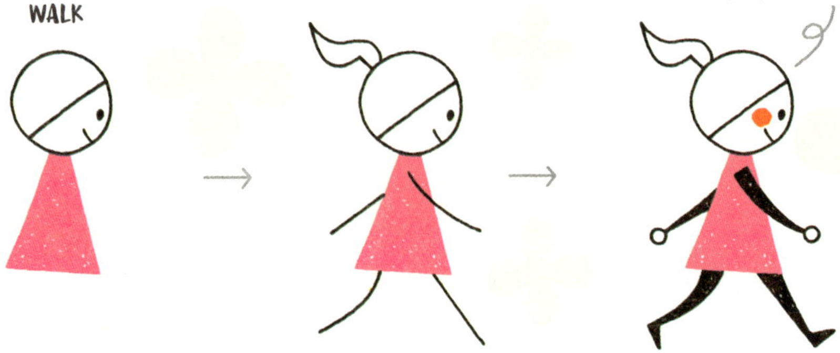

Start with a circle for the face and a triangle for the body.

For this side view pose, draw the arms and legs toward both the front and back of the body.

Draw a lively, smiling expression.

RUN

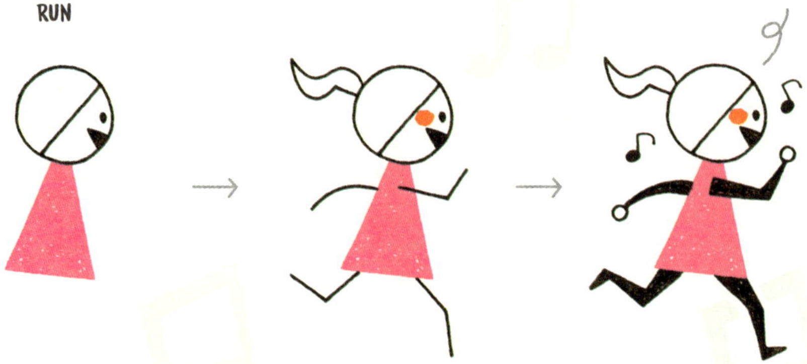

Bend the arms and legs more as she strides.

Open the mouth and add music notes for a fun look.

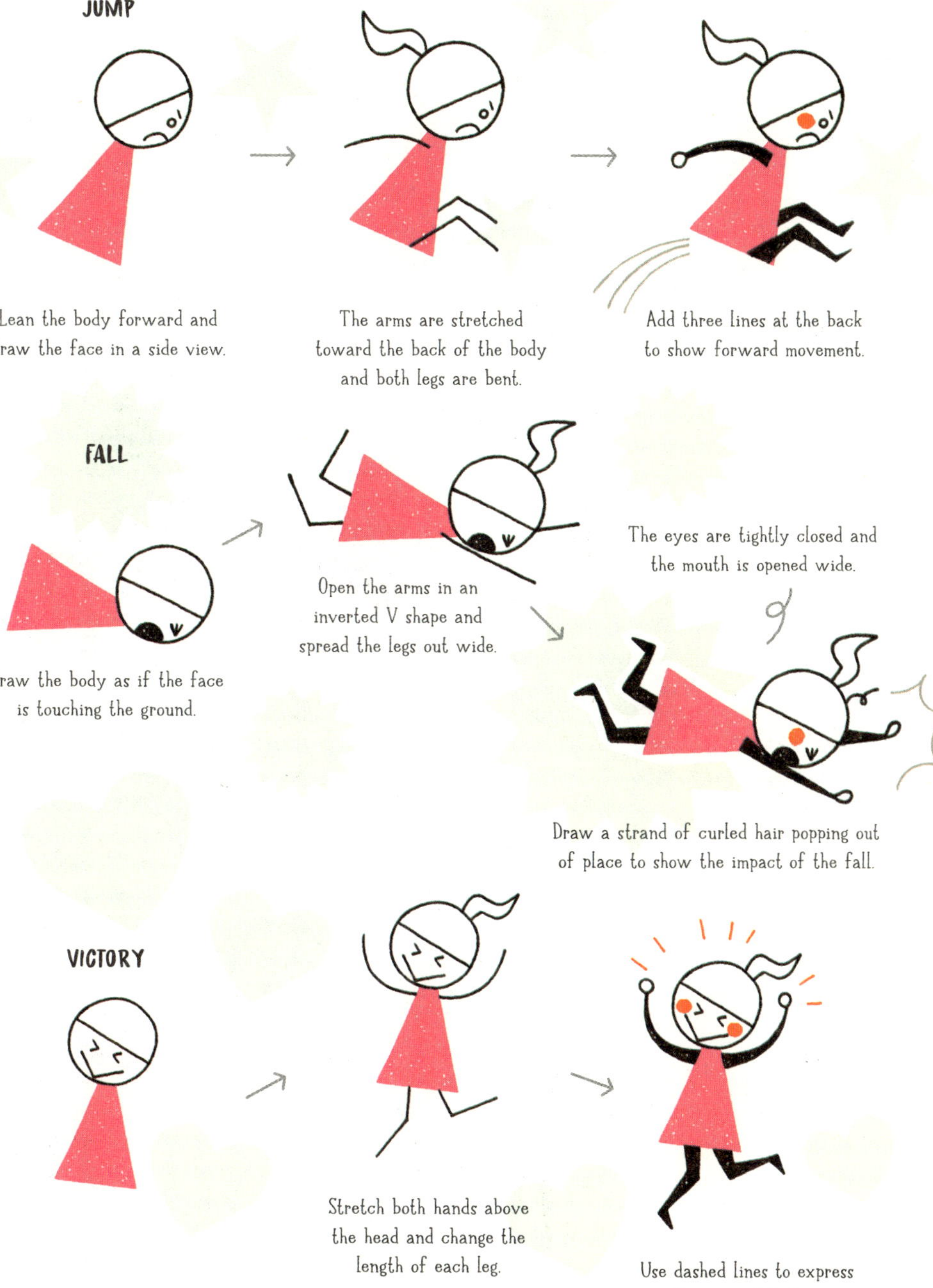

JUMP

Lean the body forward and draw the face in a side view.

The arms are stretched toward the back of the body and both legs are bent.

Add three lines at the back to show forward movement.

FALL

Draw the body as if the face is touching the ground.

Open the arms in an inverted V shape and spread the legs out wide.

The eyes are tightly closed and the mouth is opened wide.

Draw a strand of curled hair popping out of place to show the impact of the fall.

VICTORY

Stretch both hands above the head and change the length of each leg.

Use dashed lines to express the excited feeling.

VARIATION

ADD CAPTIONS

Add captions to your illustrations to help convey a message.

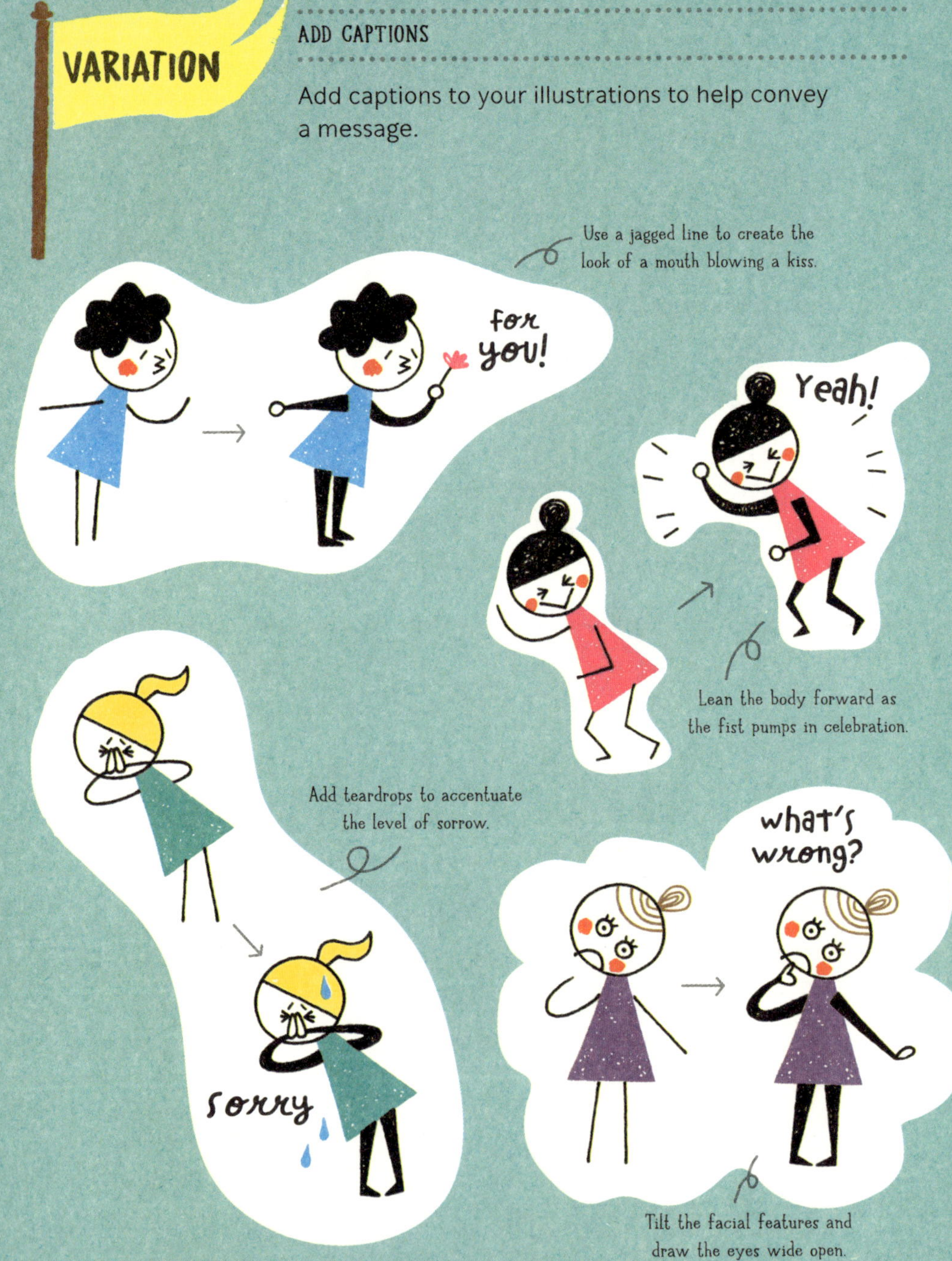

Use a jagged line to create the look of a mouth blowing a kiss.

Lean the body forward as the fist pumps in celebration.

Add teardrops to accentuate the level of sorrow.

Tilt the facial features and draw the eyes wide open.

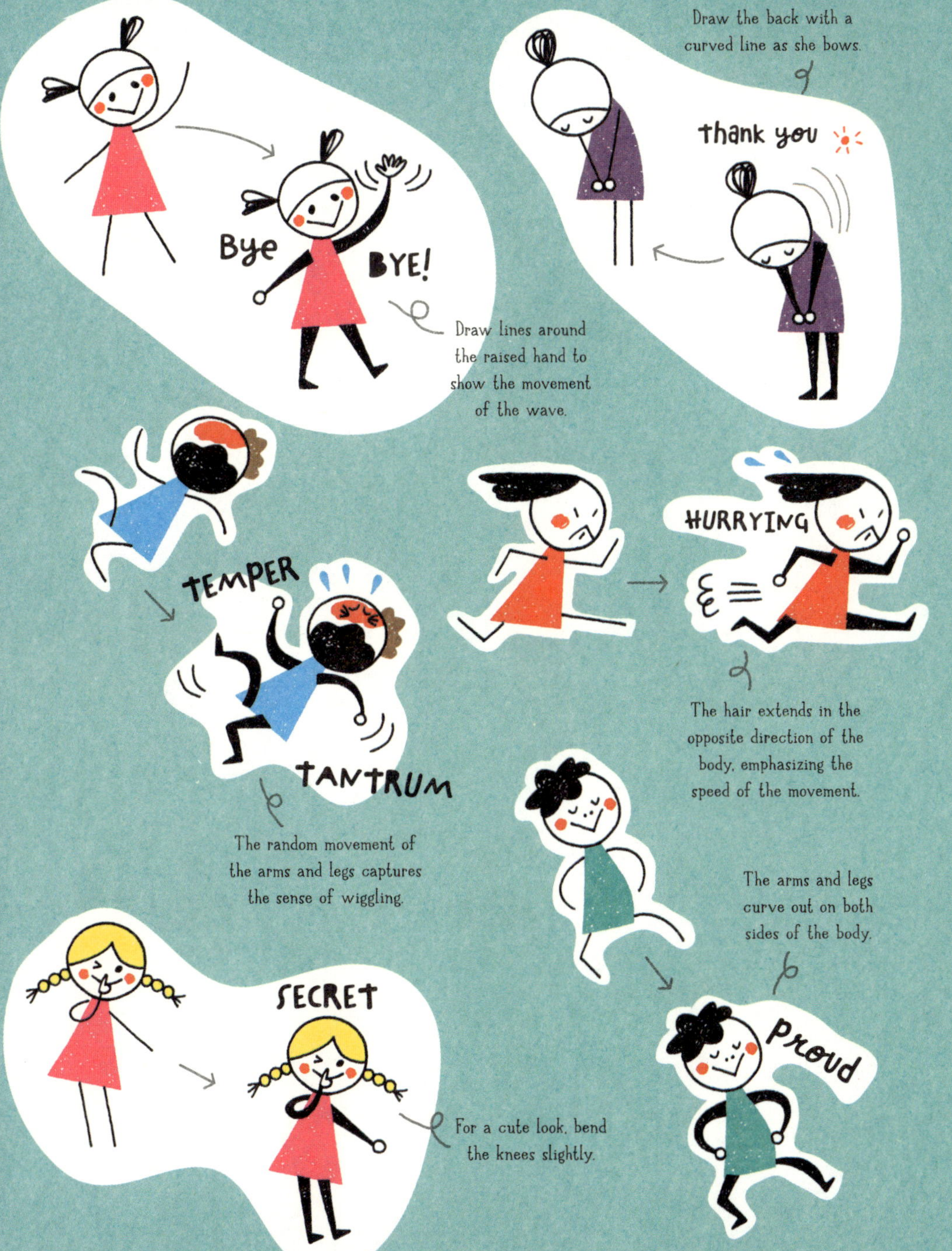
Bye
BYE!
Draw lines around the raised hand to show the movement of the wave.
Draw the back with a curved line as she bows.
thank you
TEMPER
TANTRUM
The random movement of the arms and legs captures the sense of wiggling.
HURRYING
The hair extends in the opposite direction of the body, emphasizing the speed of the movement.
The arms and legs curve out on both sides of the body.
Proud
SECRET
For a cute look, bend the knees slightly.

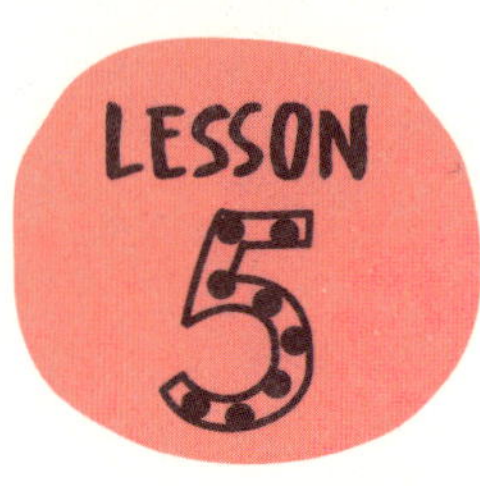

CLOTHING & ACCESSORIES

Incorporating a variety of clothing and accessories into your illustrations will allow you to create unique characters with distinct personalities.

LOOSE CLOTHING

Start with a circle for the face and a triangle for the body.

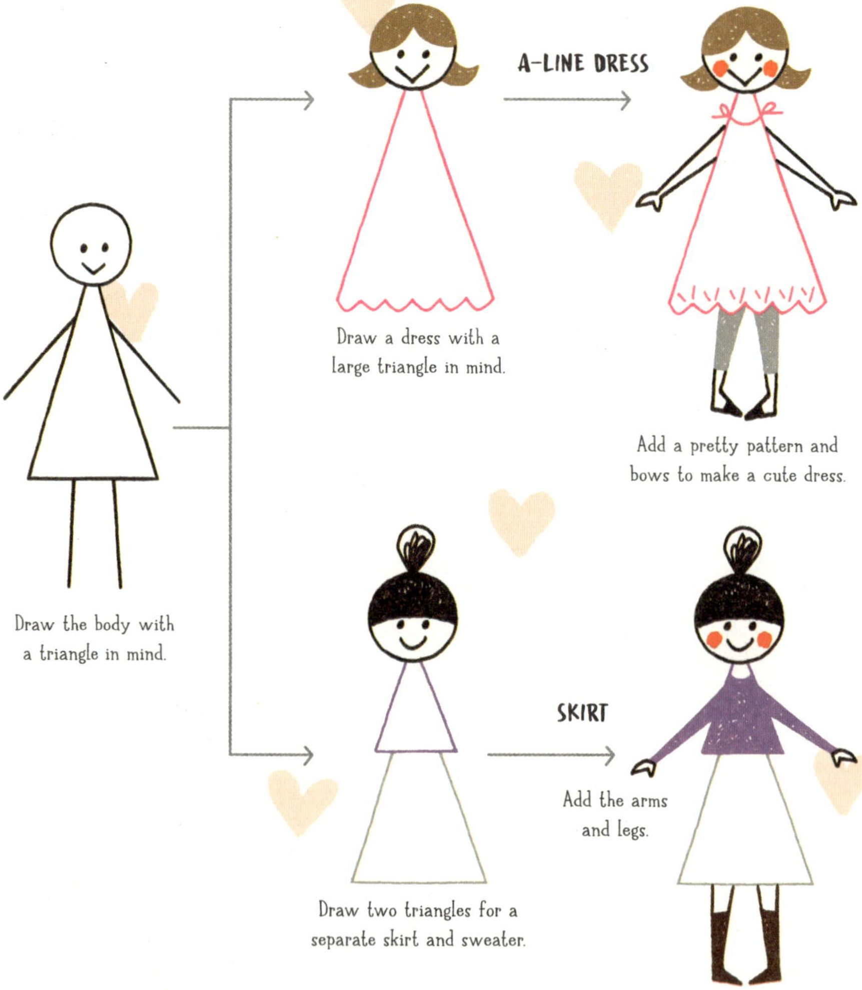

Draw the body with a triangle in mind.

Draw a dress with a large triangle in mind.

A-LINE DRESS

Add a pretty pattern and bows to make a cute dress.

Draw two triangles for a separate skirt and sweater.

SKIRT

Add the arms and legs.

TIGHT CLOTHING

Start with a circle for the face and a thin circle for the body.

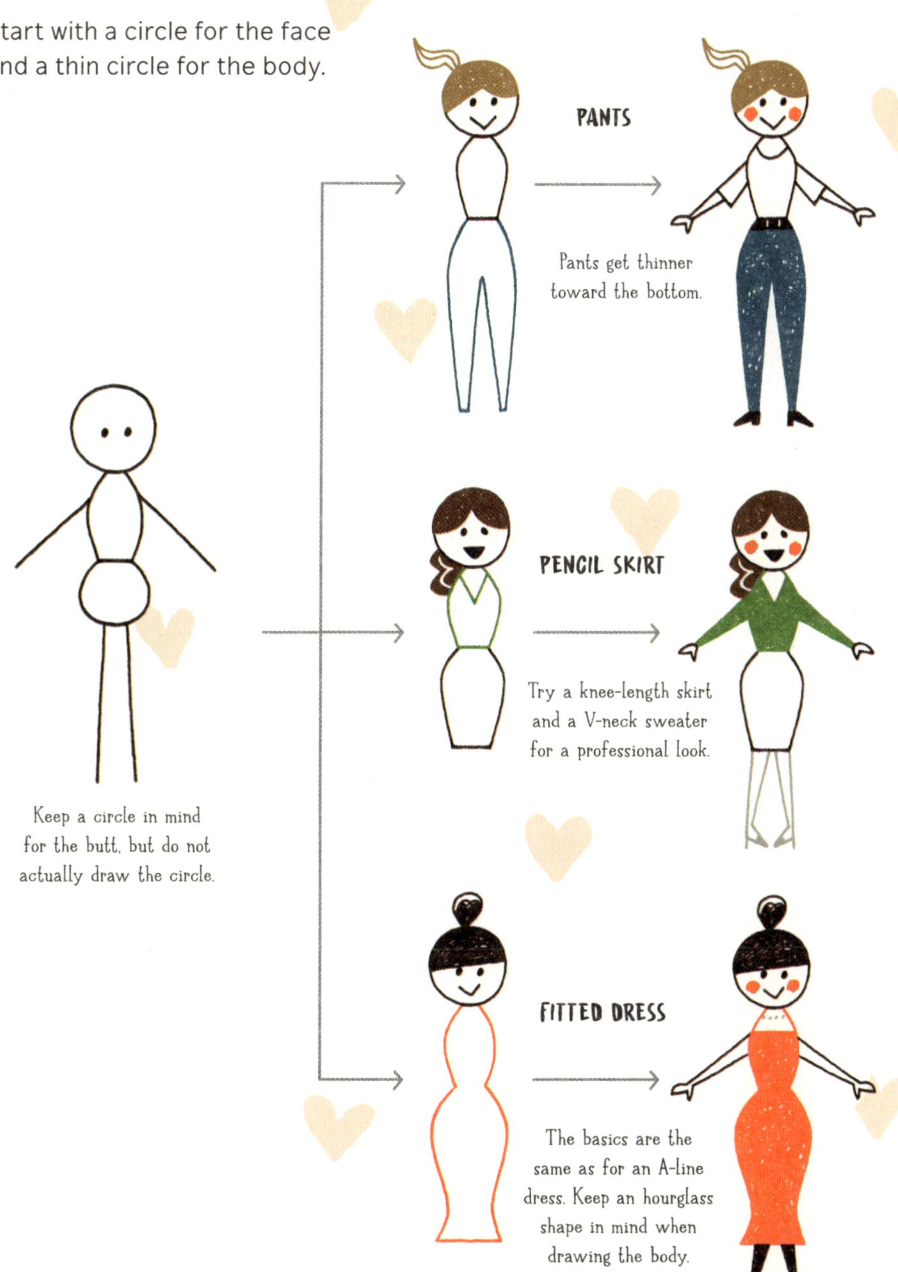

VARIATION

DRAW CLOTHES FOR EVERY SEASON

Let's try drawing outfits for each season. Incorporate accessories, such as bags, shoes, and jewelry for unique styles.

SPRING

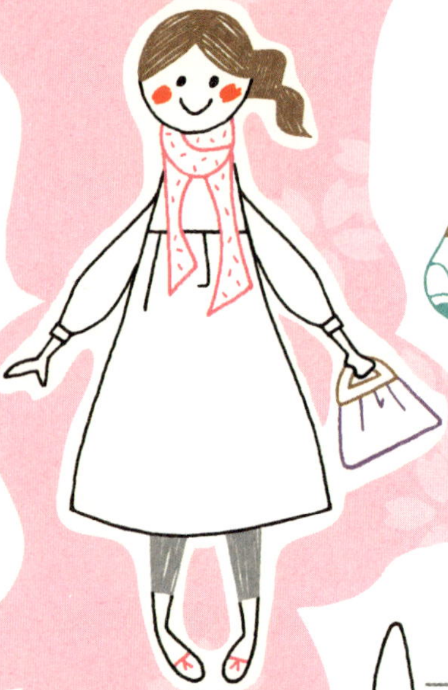

DRESS

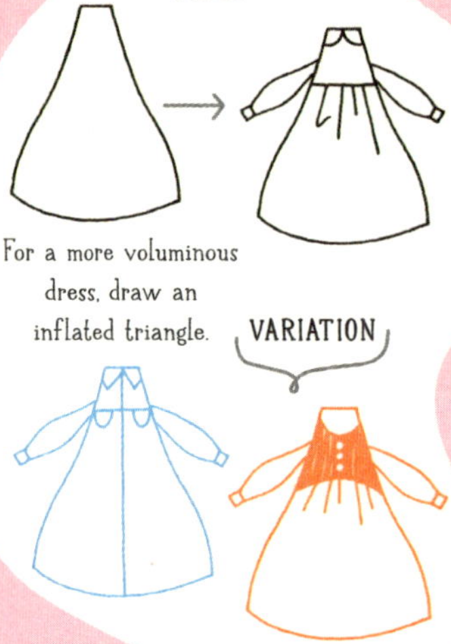

For a more voluminous dress, draw an inflated triangle.

VARIATION

BAG

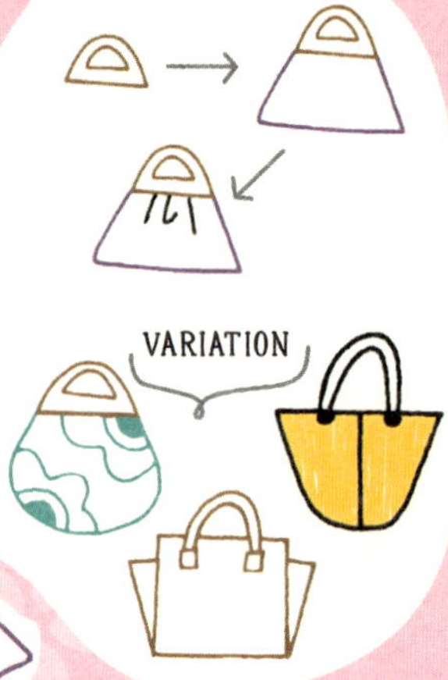

VARIATION

For a feminine look, try drawing a simple dress with leggings and a scarf.

SCARF

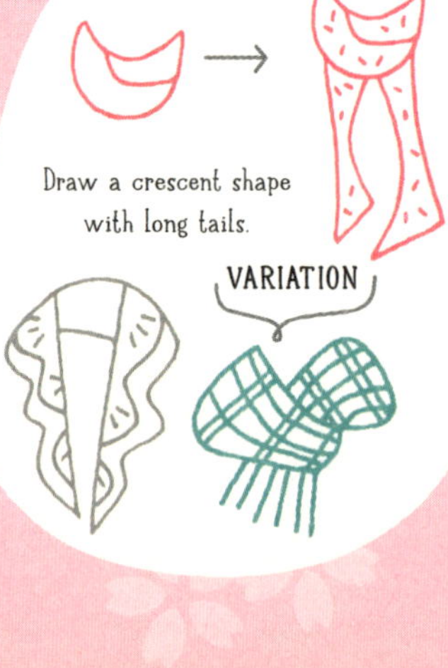

Draw a crescent shape with long tails.

VARIATION

SHOES

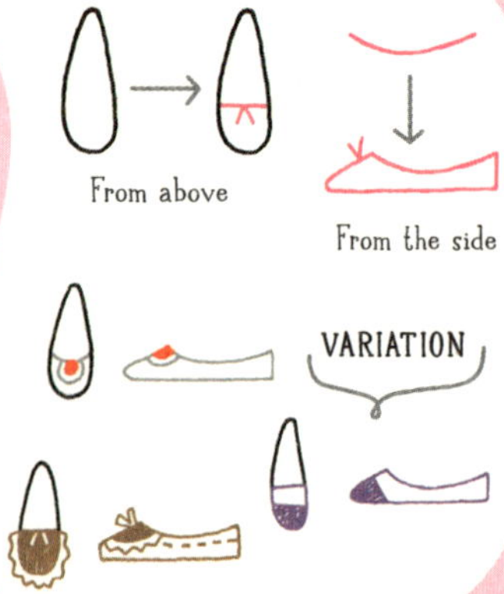

From above

From the side

VARIATION

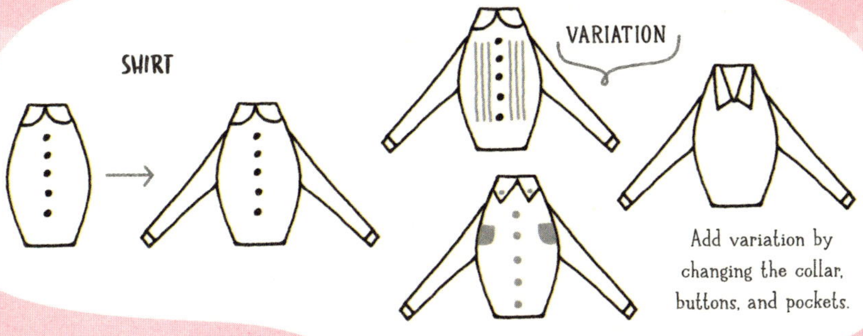

SWEATER

VARIATION

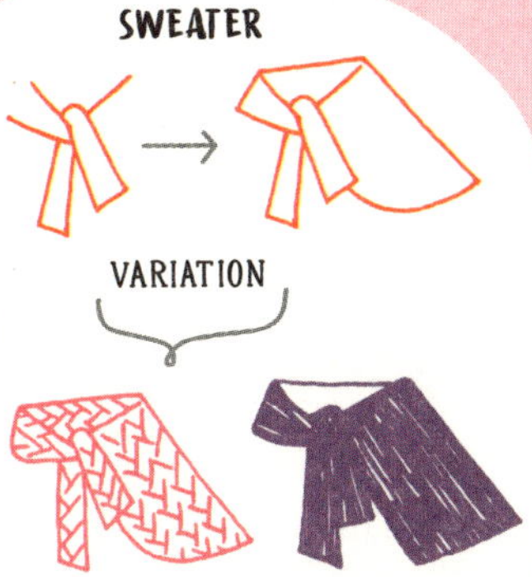

Use pattern to describe the texture of the fabric.

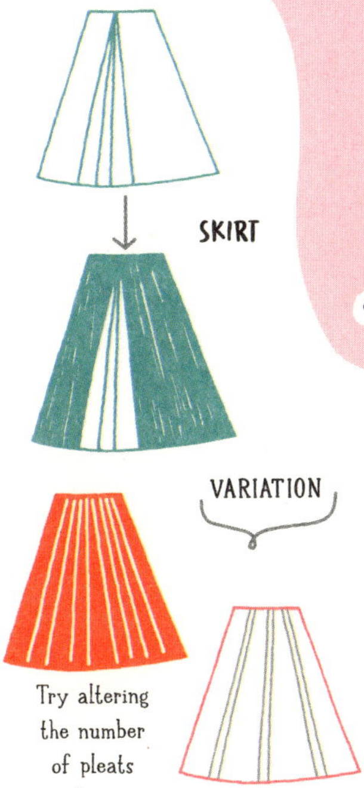

SKIRT

VARIATION

Try altering the number of pleats or changing the color.

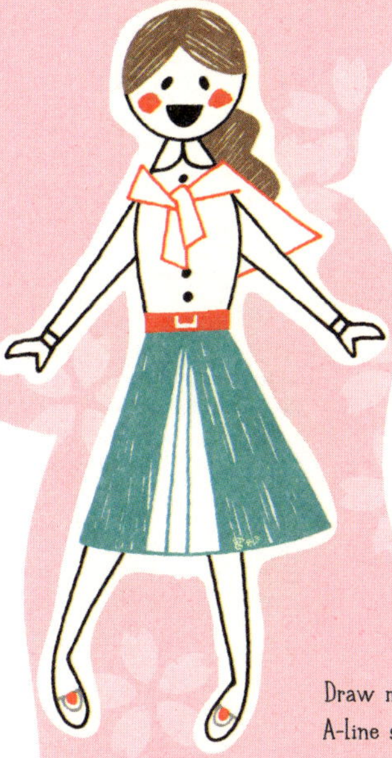

Draw more fitted clothes for a dressier look. An A-line skirt does not show the hip line so there's no need to create roundness through the body.

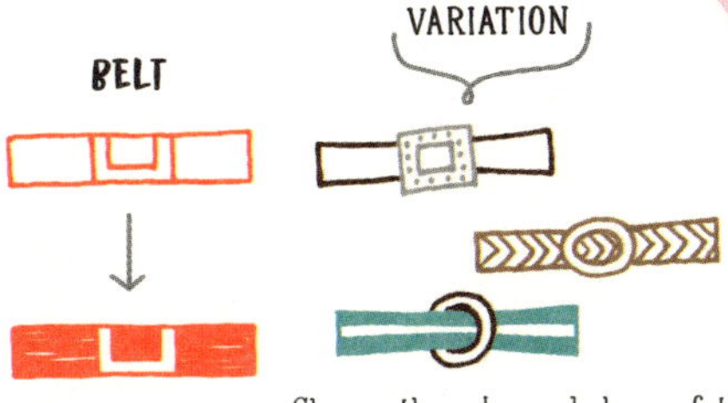

BELT

VARIATION

Change the color and shape of the buckle to accent the outfit.

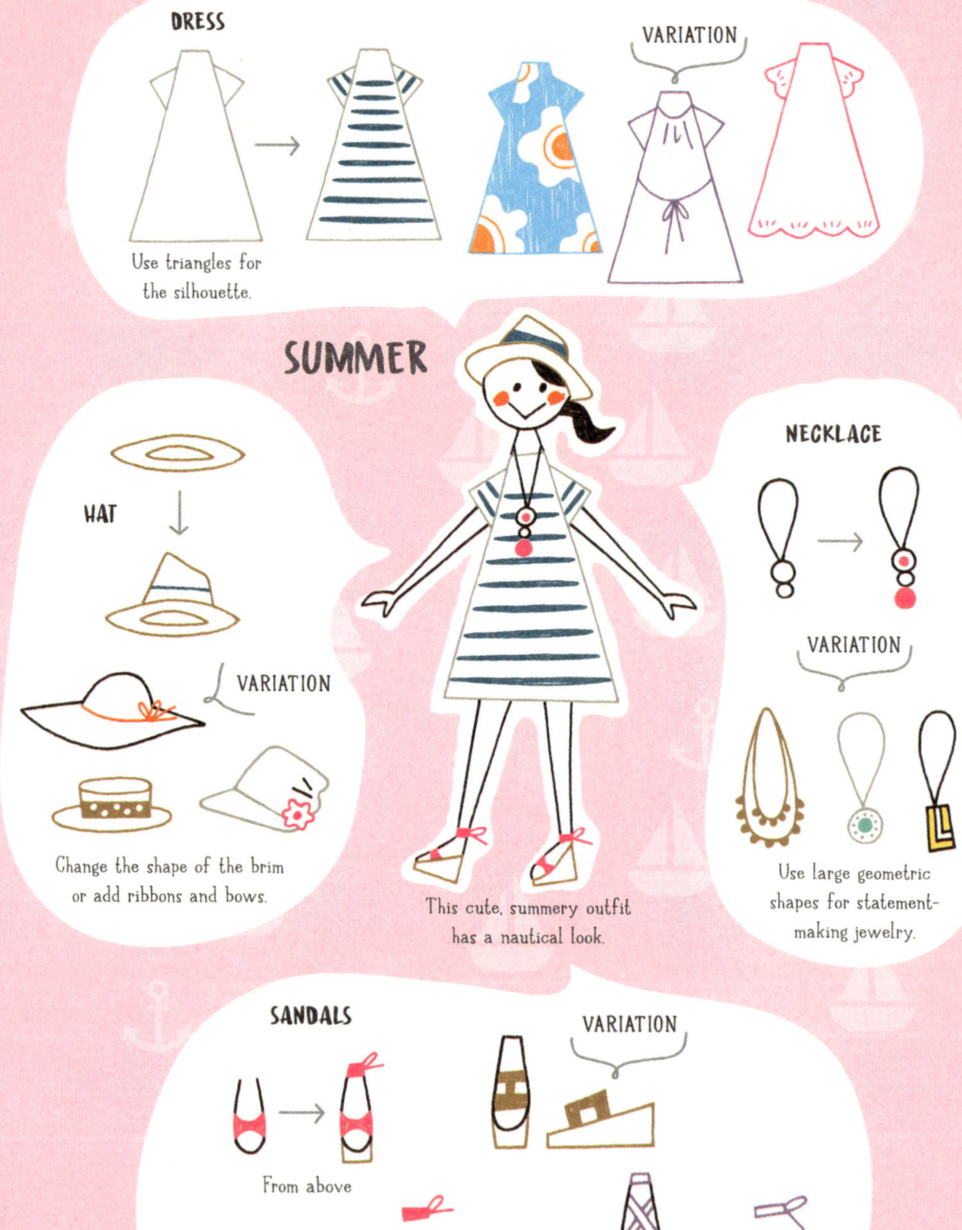
DRESS
VARIATION
Use triangles for the silhouette.
SUMMER
HAT
VARIATION
Change the shape of the brim or add ribbons and bows.
This cute, summery outfit has a nautical look.
NECKLACE
VARIATION
Use large geometric shapes for statement-making jewelry.
SANDALS
VARIATION
From above
From the side

TANK TOP

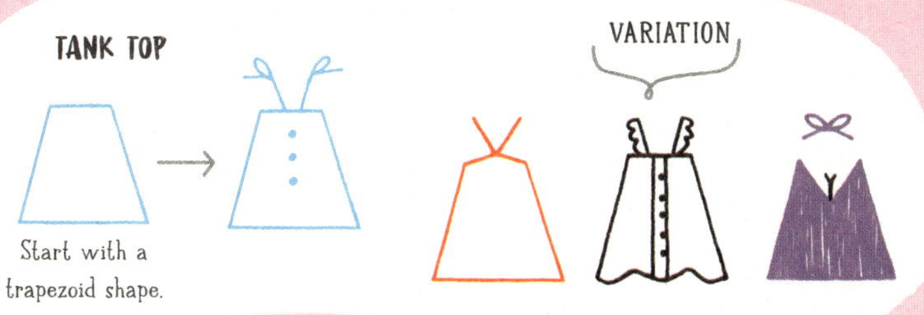

Start with a trapezoid shape.

PURSE

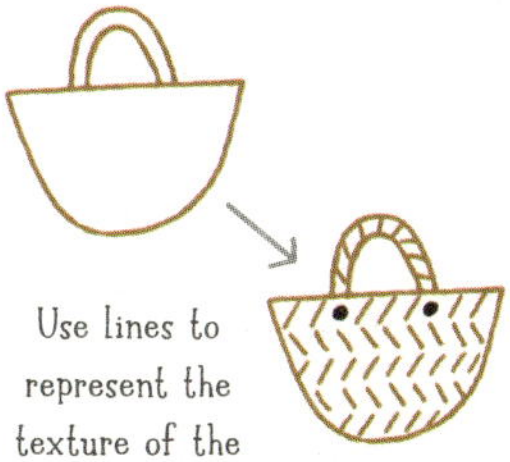

Use lines to represent the texture of the straw bag.

VARIATION

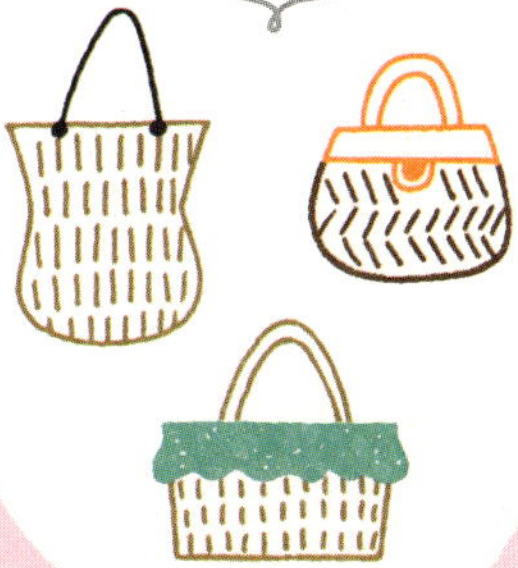

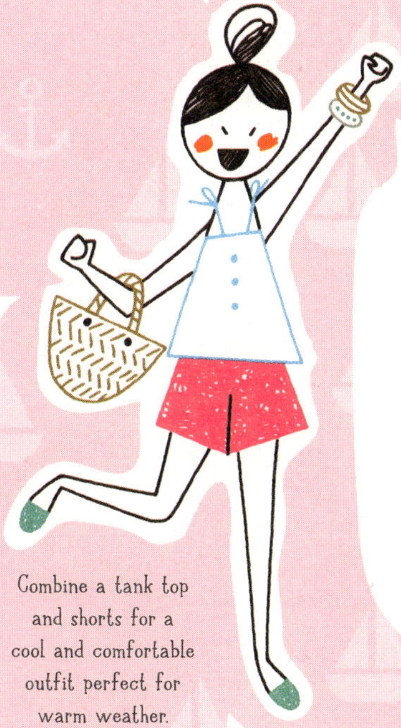

Combine a tank top and shorts for a cool and comfortable outfit perfect for warm weather.

BRACELET

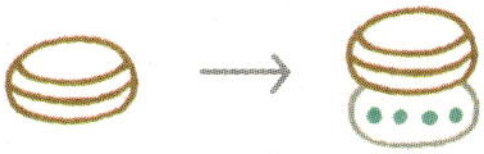

VARIATION

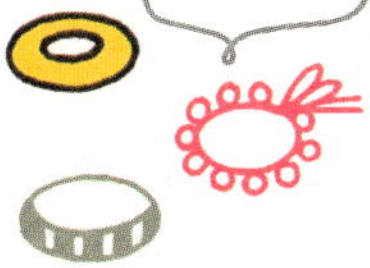

Use color, line, and shape to add detail to the bracelet design.

SHORTS

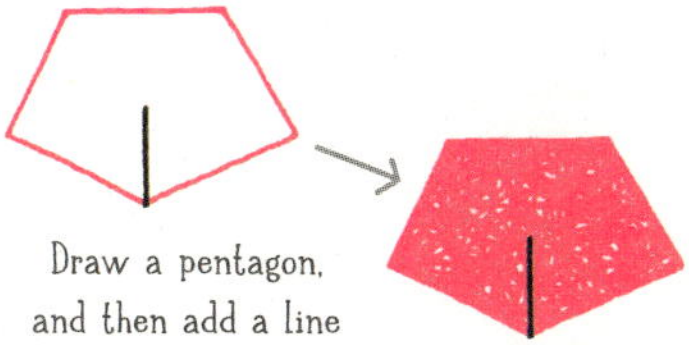

VARIATION

Draw a pentagon, and then add a line at the center.

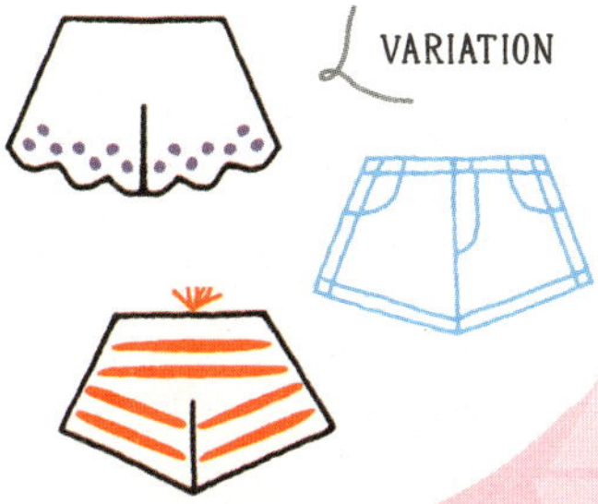

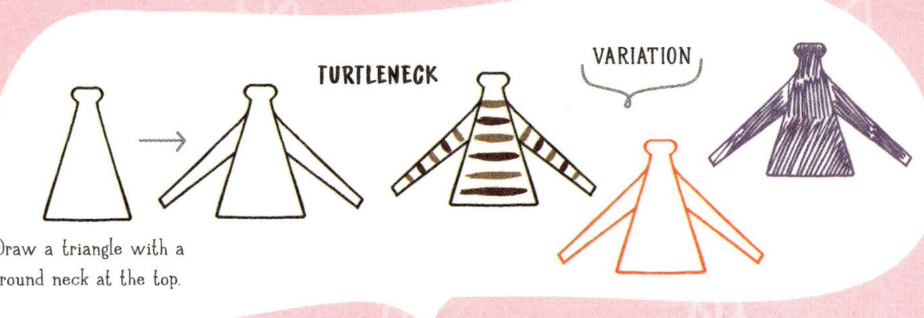

Draw a triangle with a round neck at the top.

AUTUMN

OVERALLS

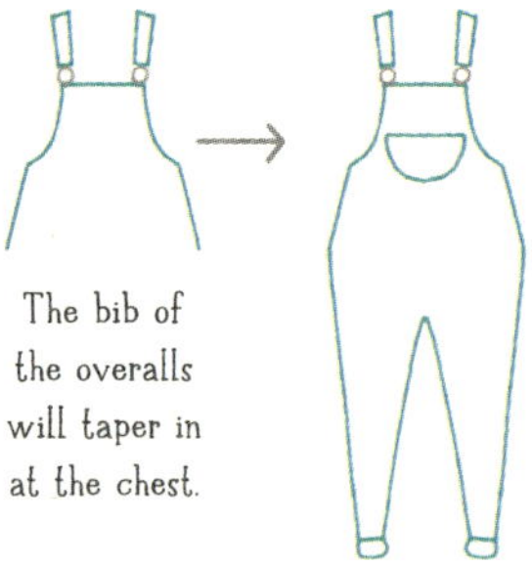

The bib of the overalls will taper in at the chest.

VARIATION

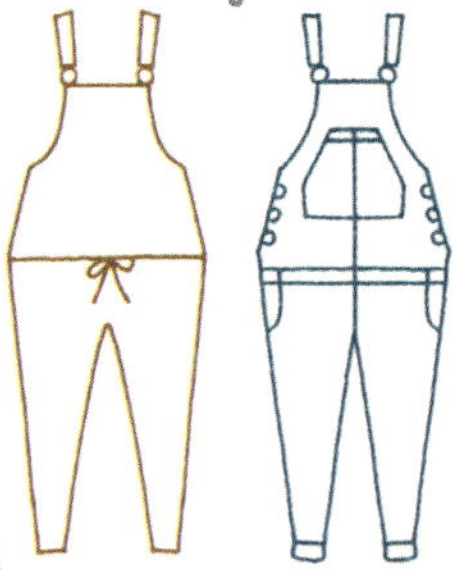

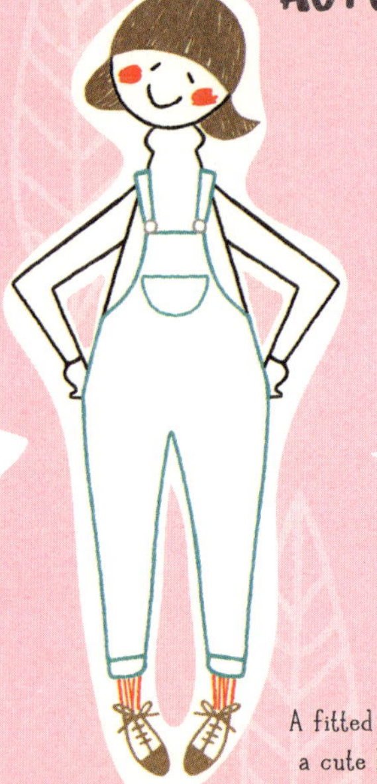

SOCKS

VARIATION

A fitted turtleneck and overalls create a cute layered look for fall. Give the overalls a rounded shape at the hip.

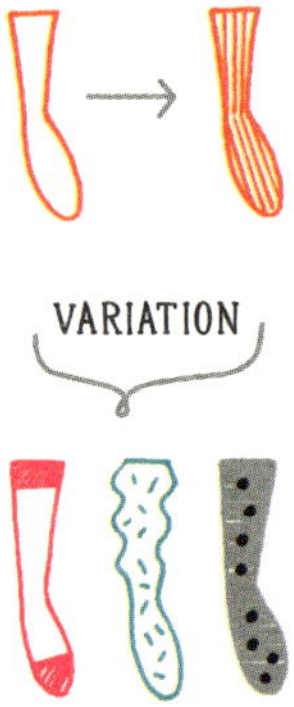

SHOES

VARIATION

From above

From the side

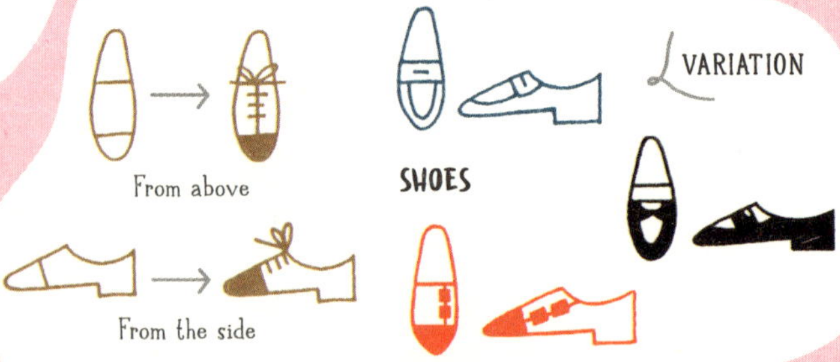

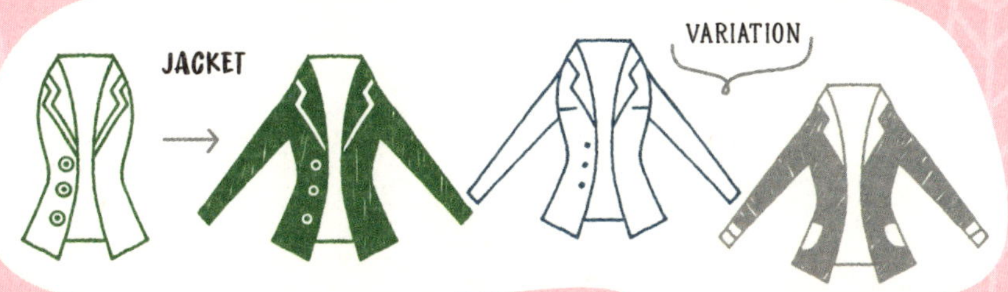

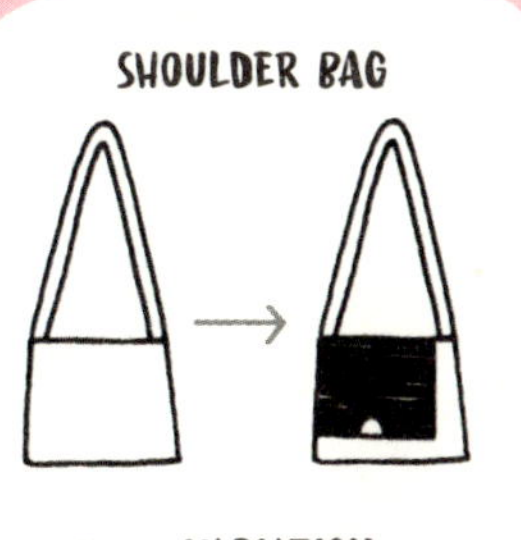

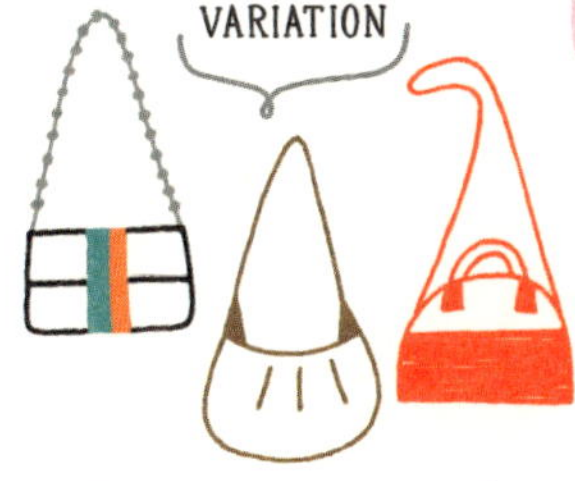

Try changing the strap of the bag—a chain or thin strap creates a feminine look.

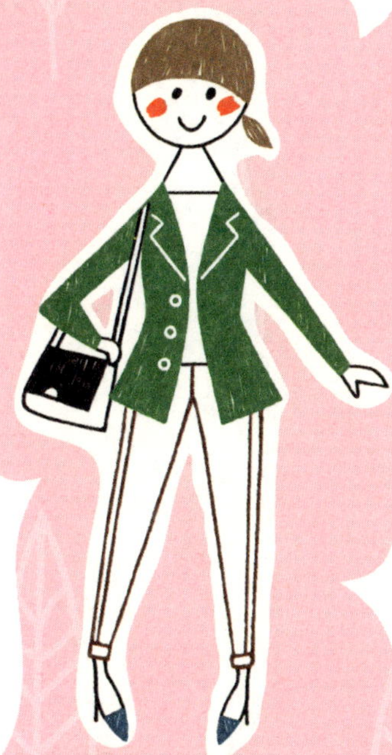

The jacket is the main element of this outfit. The fitted silhouette flares out at the waist for a stylish look.

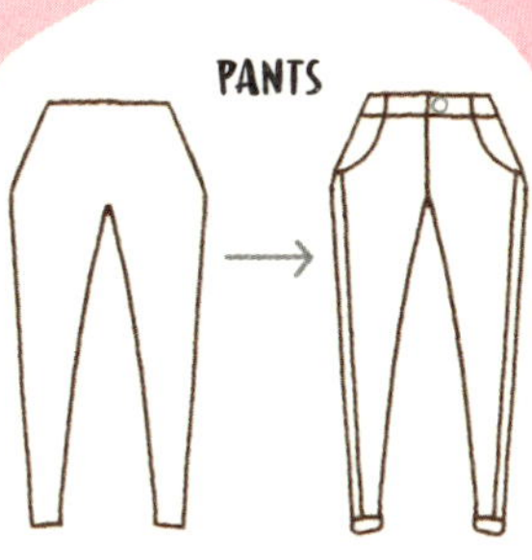

Add seams to the pants for a realistic look.

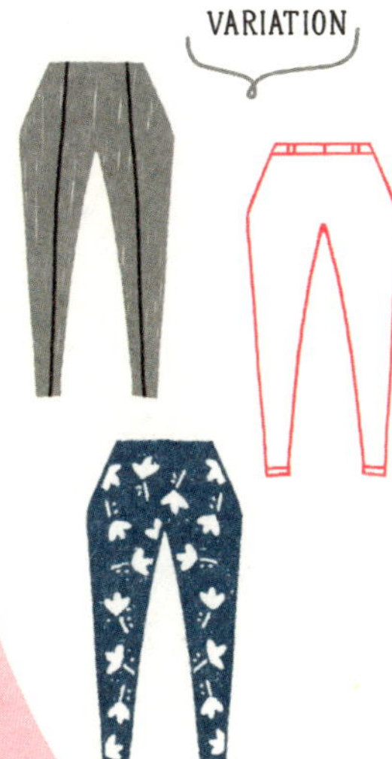

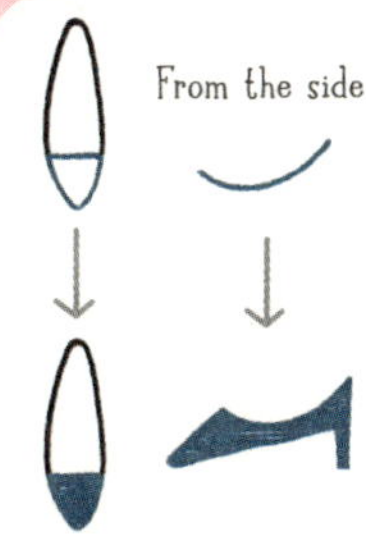

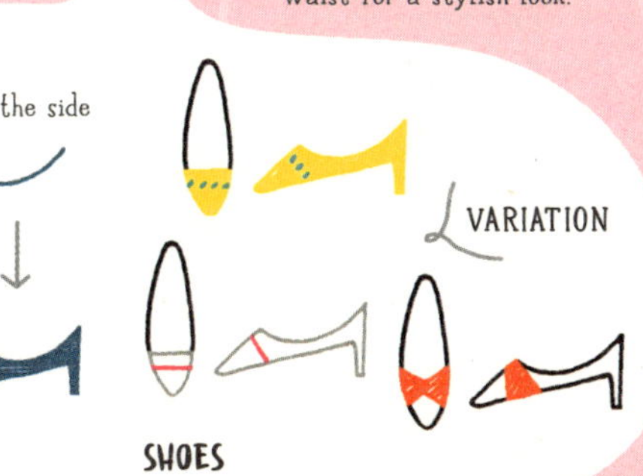

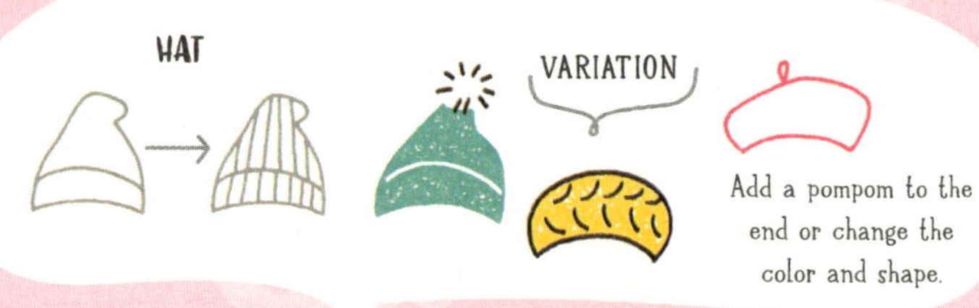

Add a pompom to the end or change the color and shape.

WINTER

COAT

VARIATION

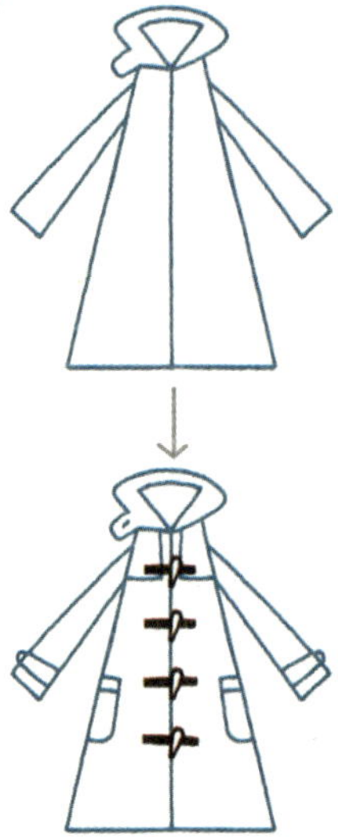

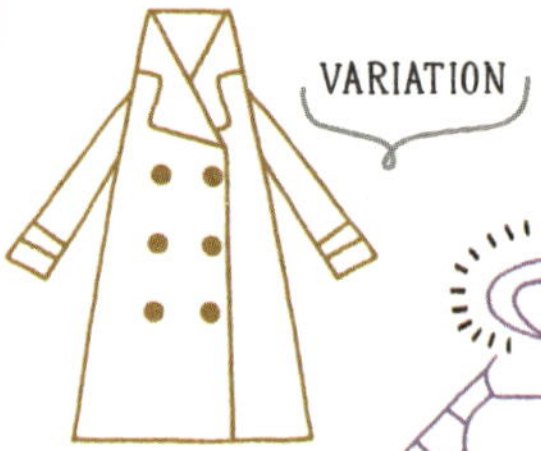

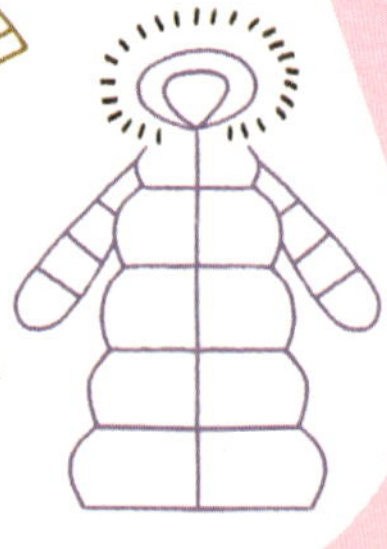

Align two rows of buttons for a trench style coat. Or draw with fluffy lines to create down coat.

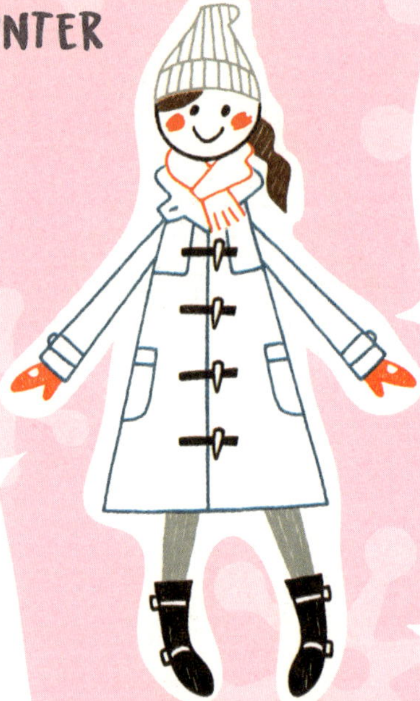

Use a large triangle to draw the coat, just like drawing a dress. Add details, such as buttons and a hood.

GLOVES

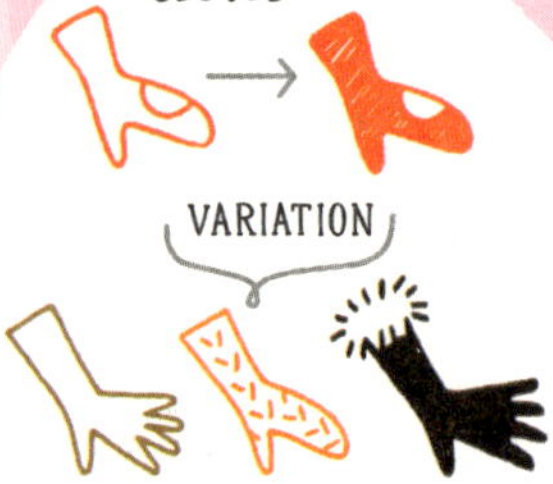

VARIATION

Extend the length of the wrist for a more elegant look.

BOOTS

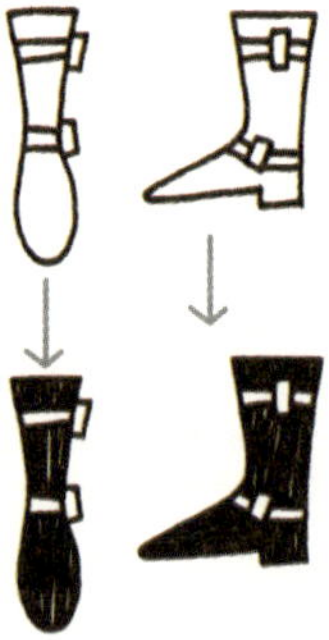

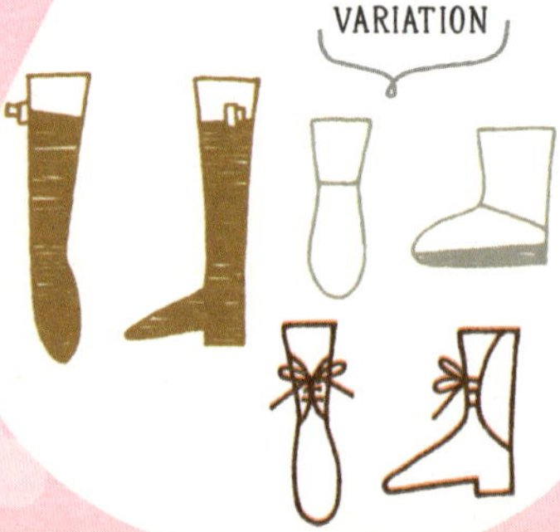

VARIATION

SWEATER

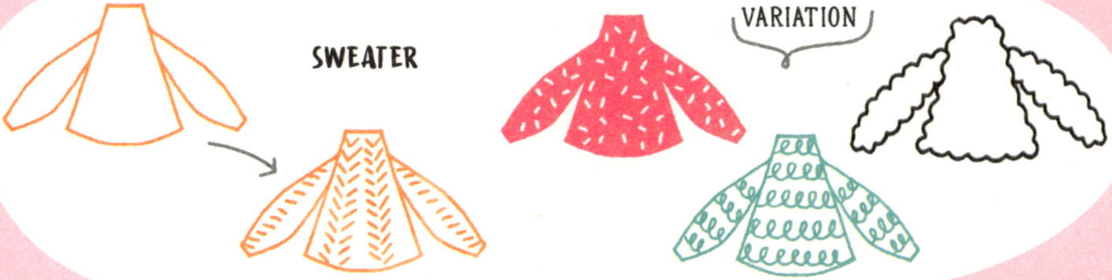

VARIATION

CLUTCH BAG

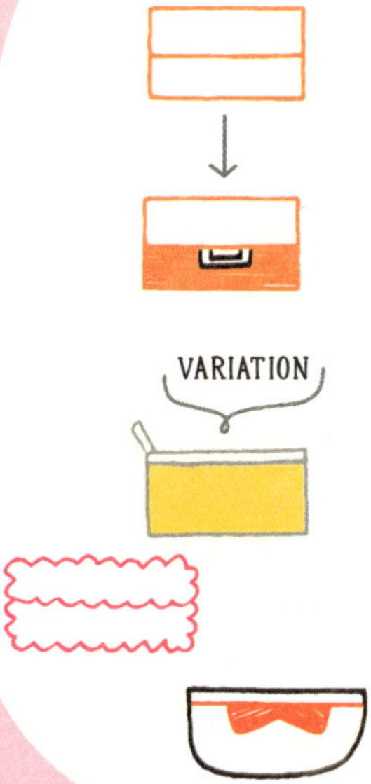

VARIATION

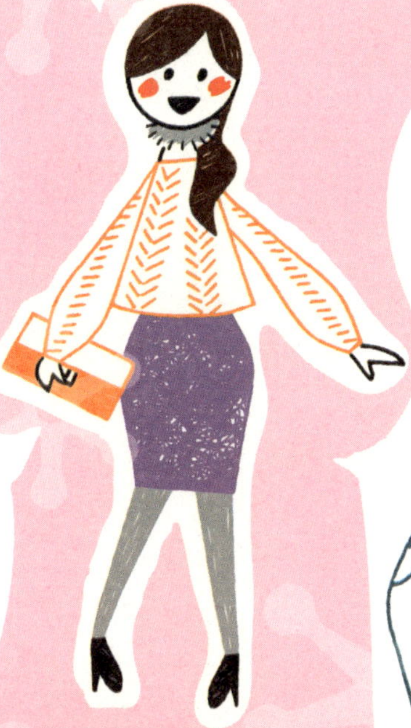

A pretty sweater and a fitted skirt combine for a feminine look. Add some style with fuller sleeves and a textured pattern for the sweater.

SKIRT

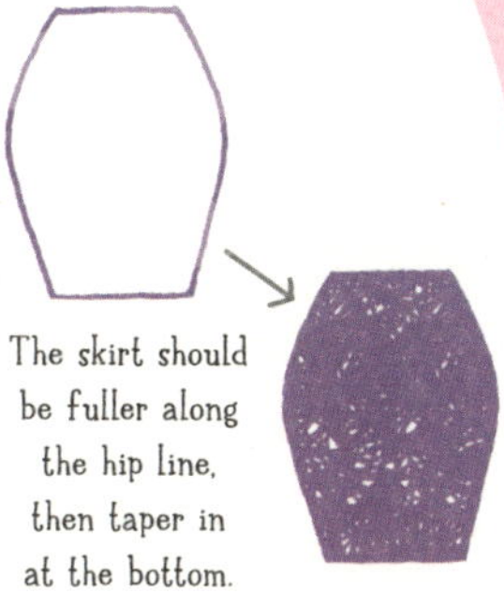

The skirt should be fuller along the hip line, then taper in at the bottom.

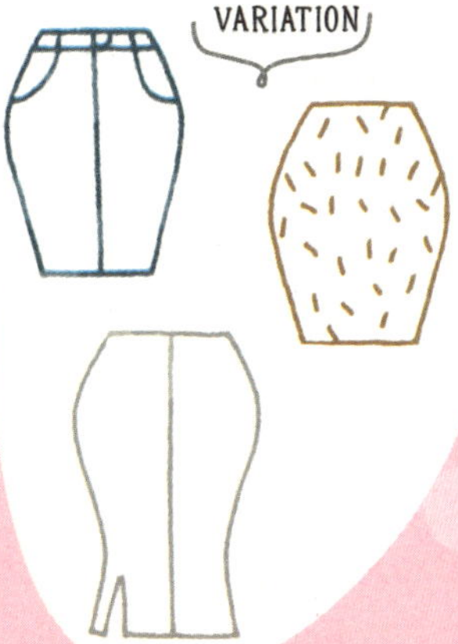

VARIATION

FUR SCARF

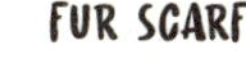
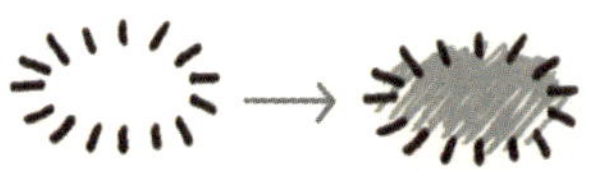
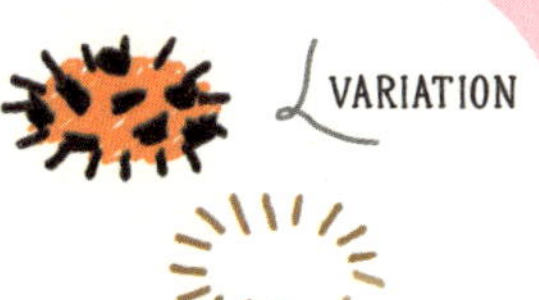

VARIATION

Use dotted lines to represent the fluffy texture.

SPECIAL LESSON

HOW TO DRAW UNIQUE CHARACTERS

Give your character a signature look through the use of accessories, hairstyles, or clothing.

TECHNIQUE 1

Emphasize a character's unique trademark.

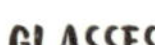

GLASSES

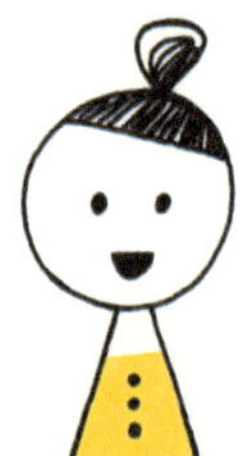

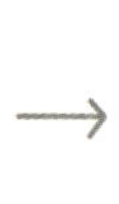

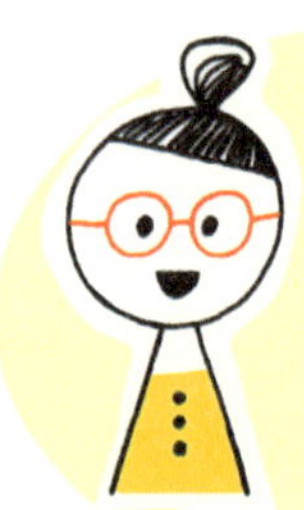

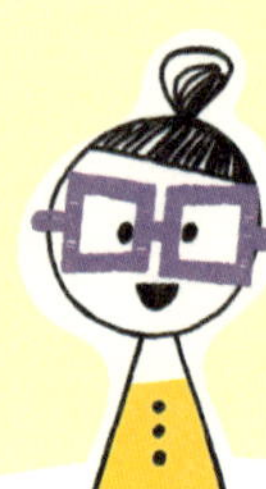

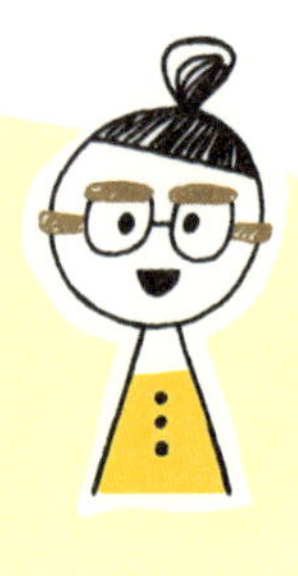

HATS

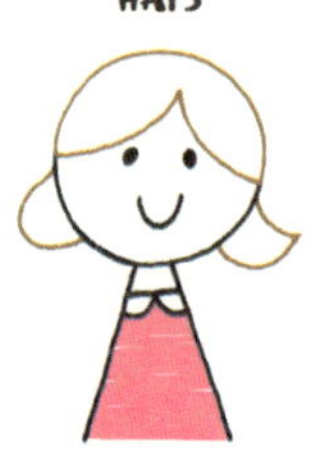

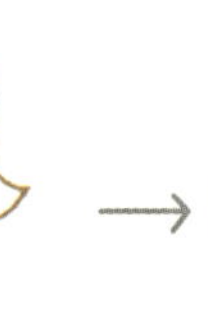

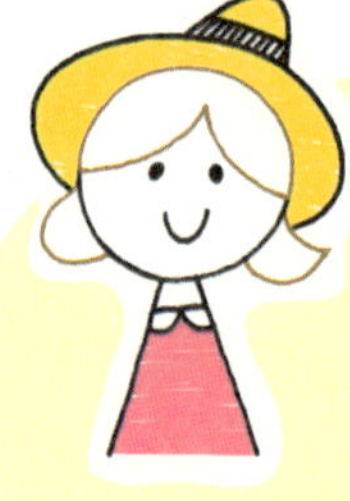

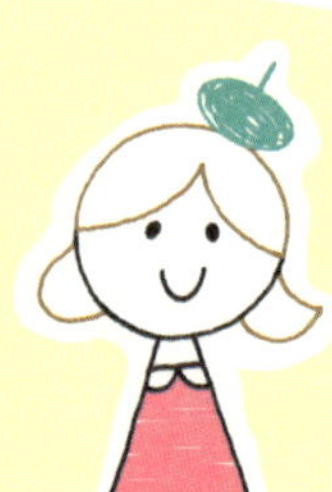

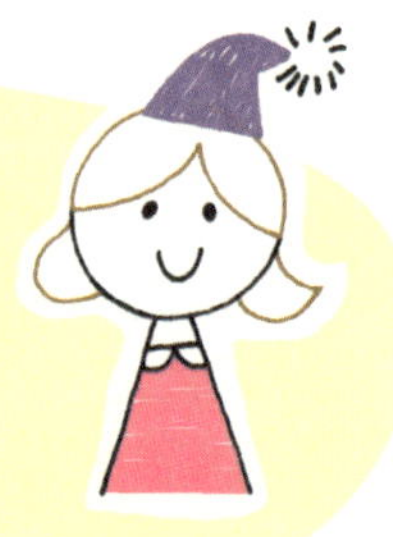

BOBBED HAIR

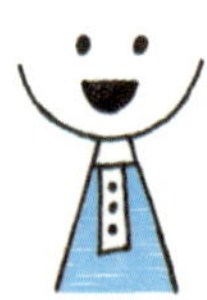

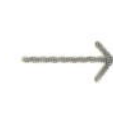

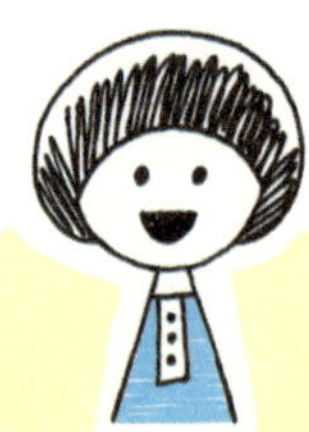

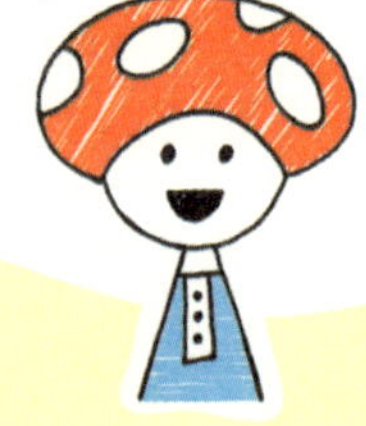

This type of mushroom is cute for a fairytale character.

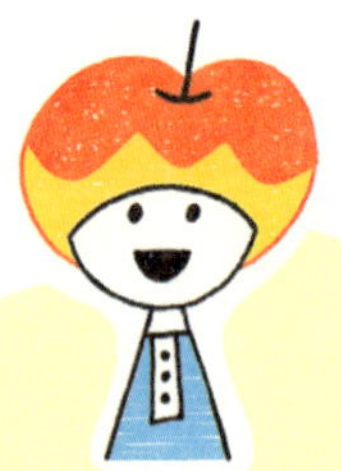

Apples are also a fun option.

TECHNIQUE 2

Give animal characters human personality traits and hobbies.

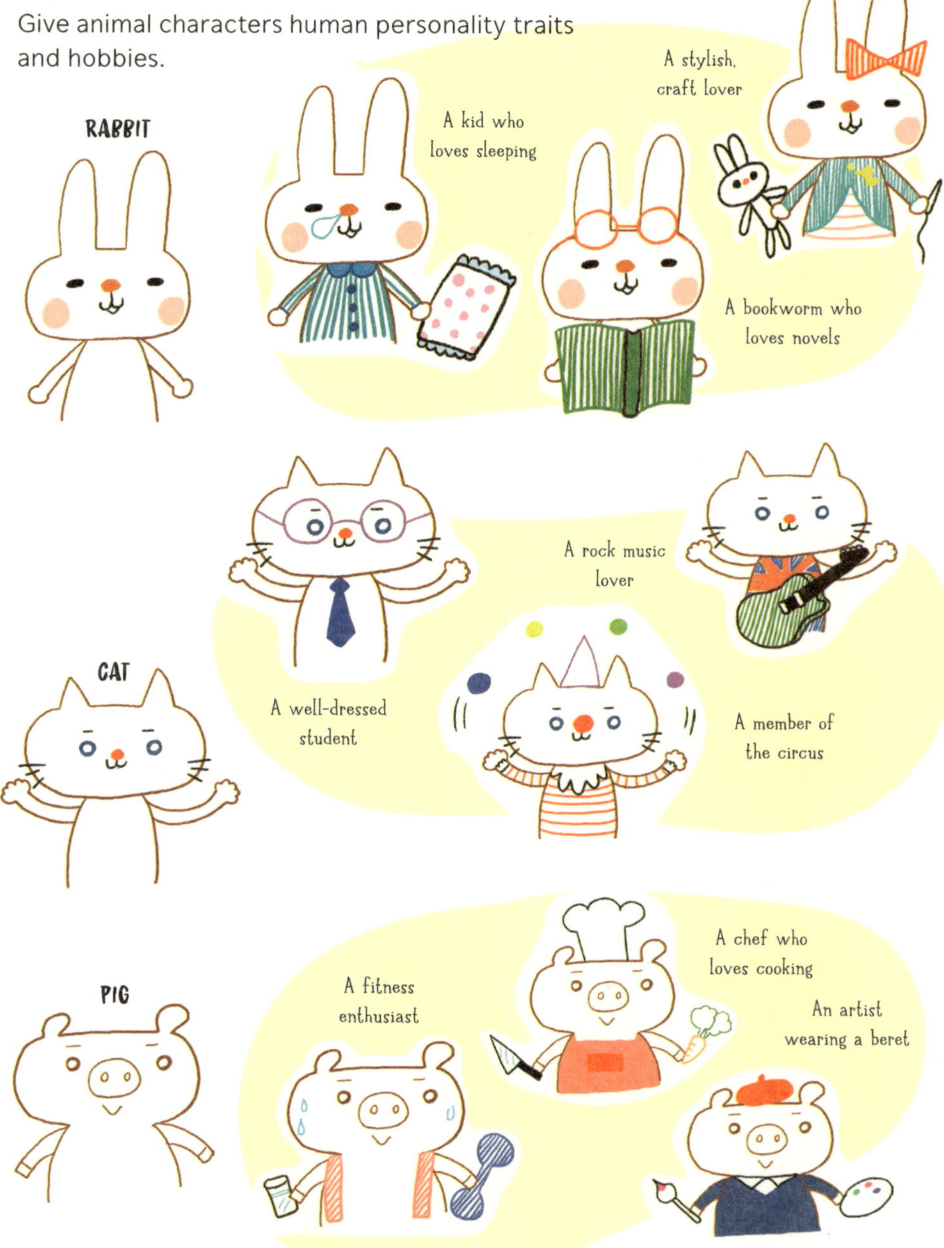

SPECIAL LESSON

FAIRYTALE CHARACTERS

These fairytale characters appear in fantasy stories. Don't forget to incorporate cute facial expressions and gestures!

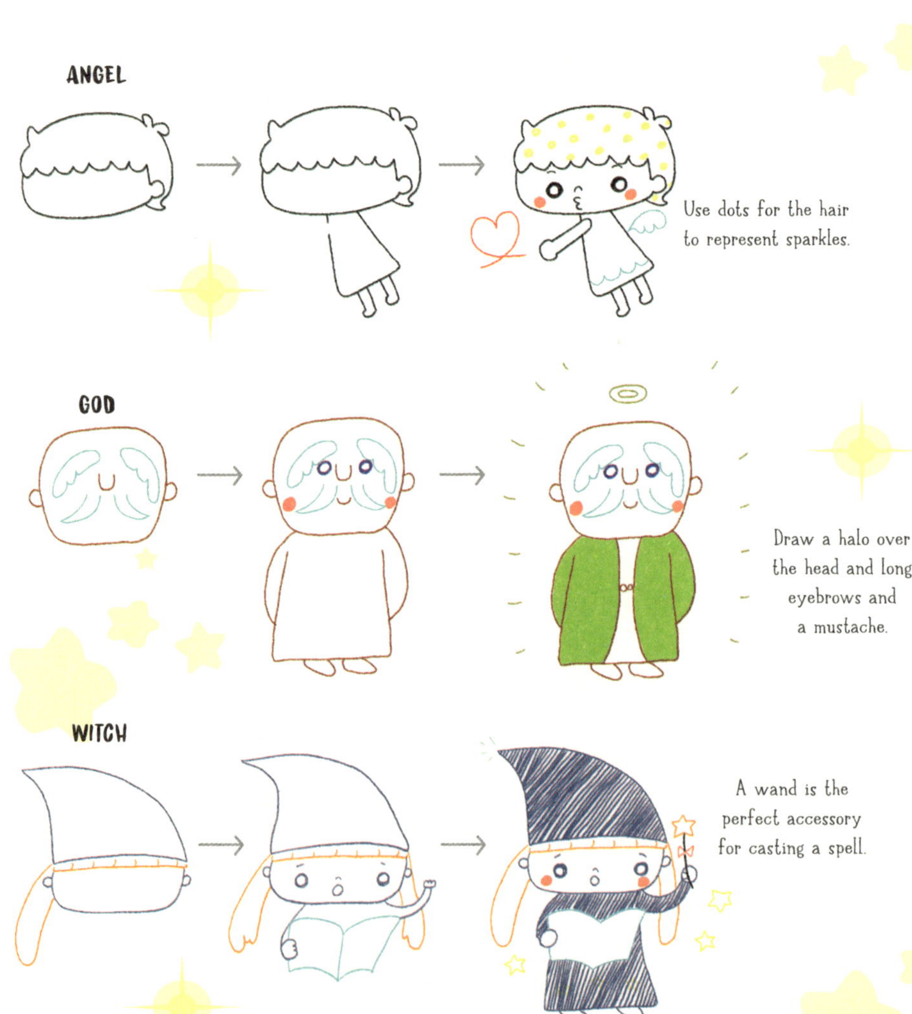

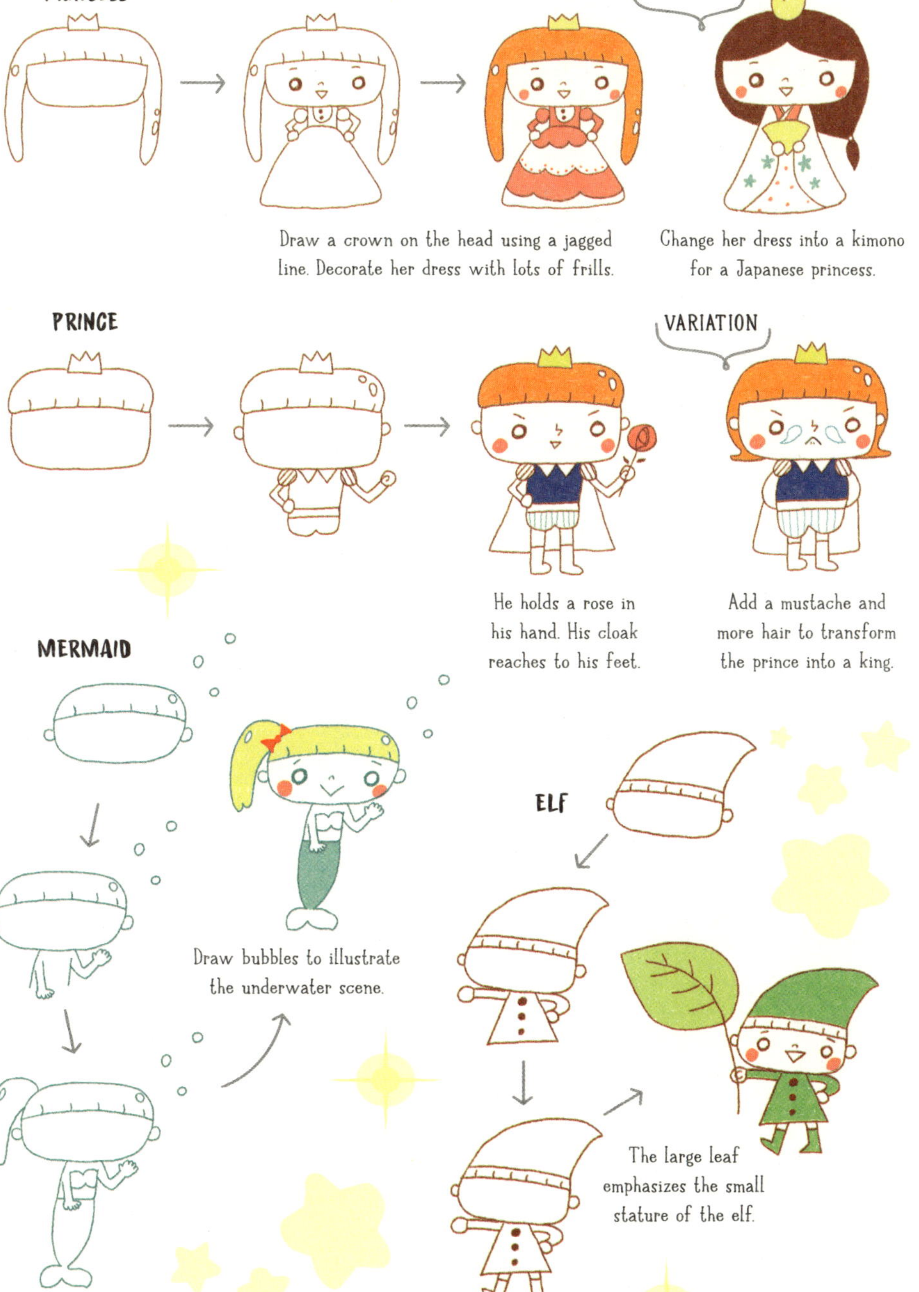
PRINCESS
VARIATION
Draw a crown on the head using a jagged line. Decorate her dress with lots of frills.
Change her dress into a kimono for a Japanese princess.
PRINCE
VARIATION
He holds a rose in his hand. His cloak reaches to his feet.
Add a mustache and more hair to transform the prince into a king.
MERMAID
Draw bubbles to illustrate the underwater scene.
ELF
The large leaf emphasizes the small stature of the elf.

SPECIAL LESSON

HOROSCOPE CHARACTERS

Combine human features with items or animals from each constellation to create original horoscope-inspired illustrations.

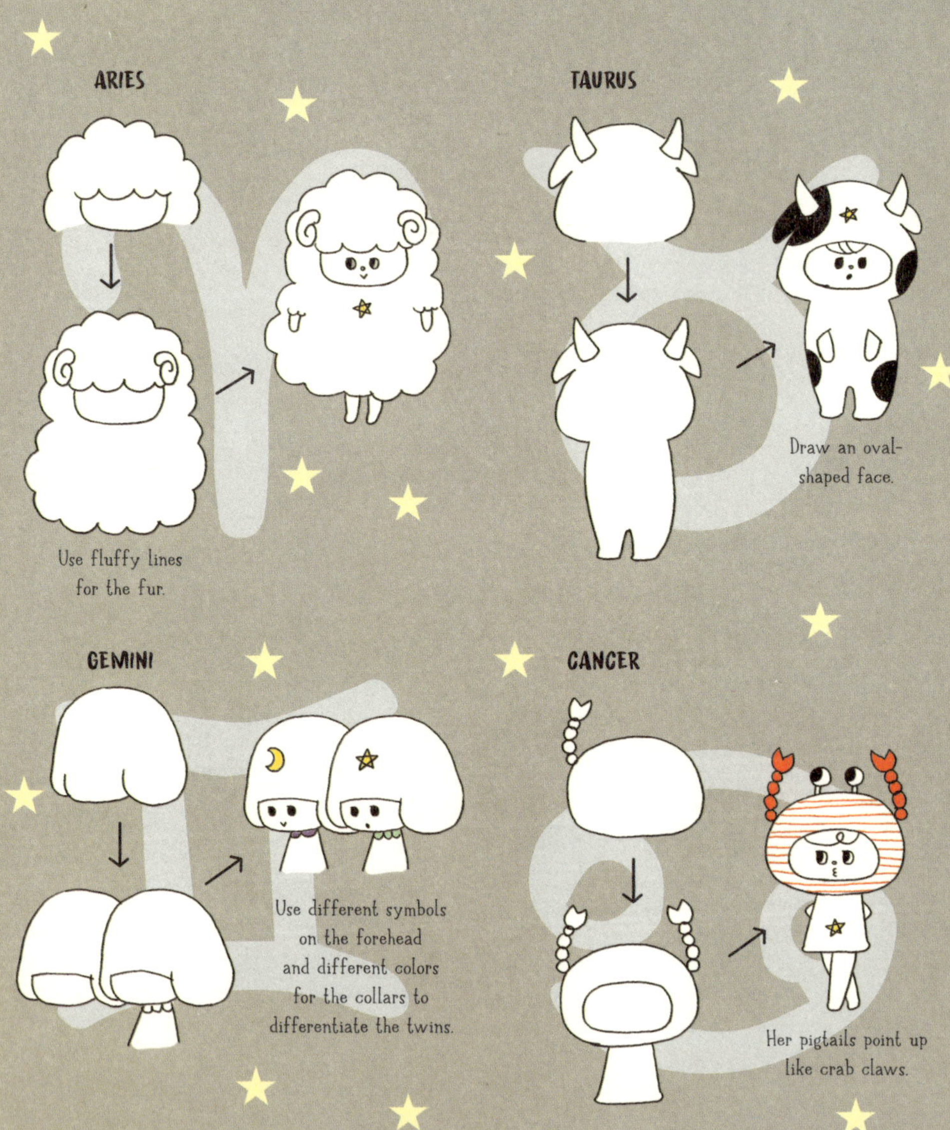

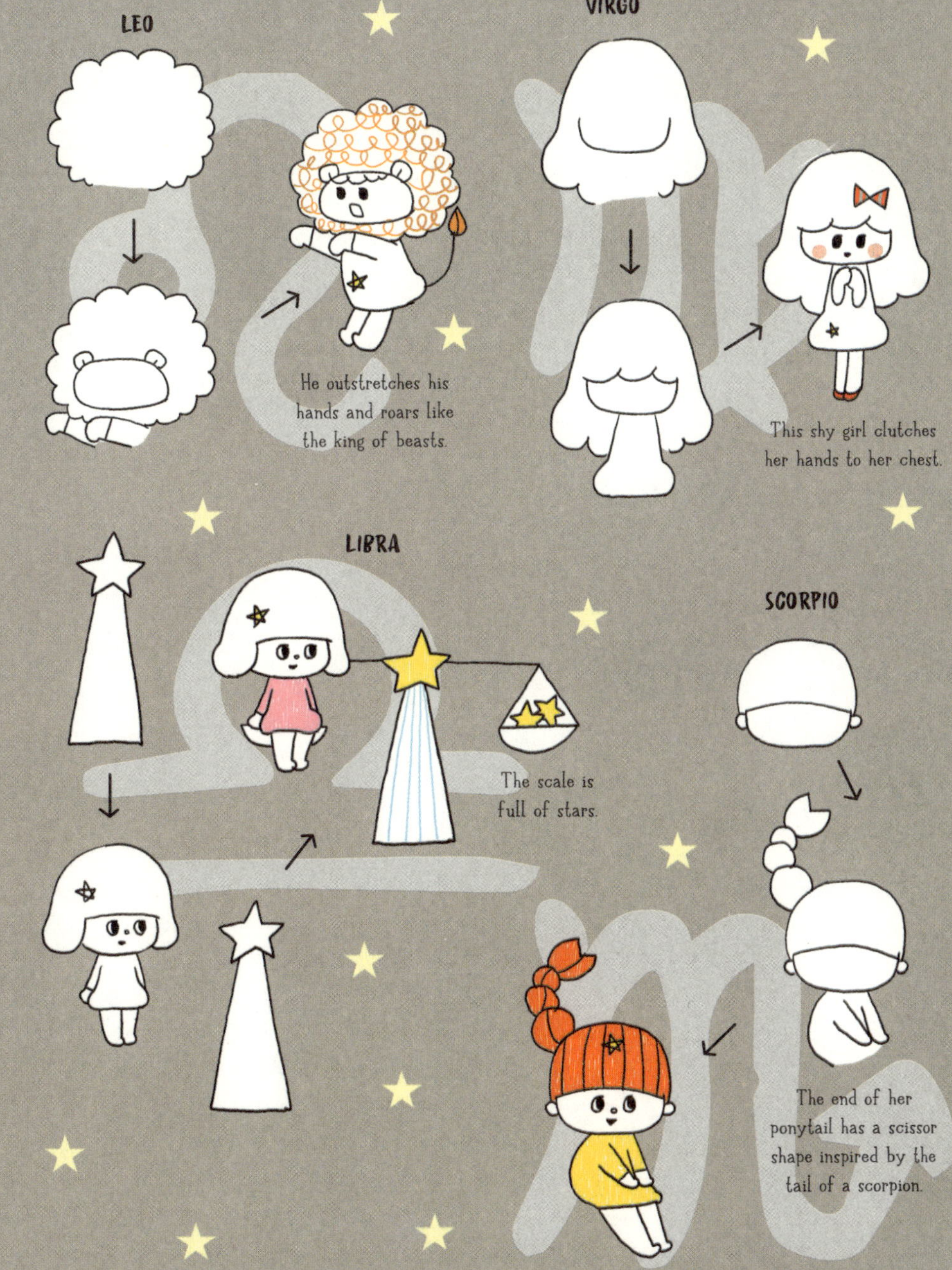
LEO
He outstretches his hands and roars like the king of beasts.
VIRGO
This shy girl clutches her hands to her chest.
LIBRA
The scale is full of stars.
SCORPIO
The end of her ponytail has a scissor shape inspired by the tail of a scorpion.

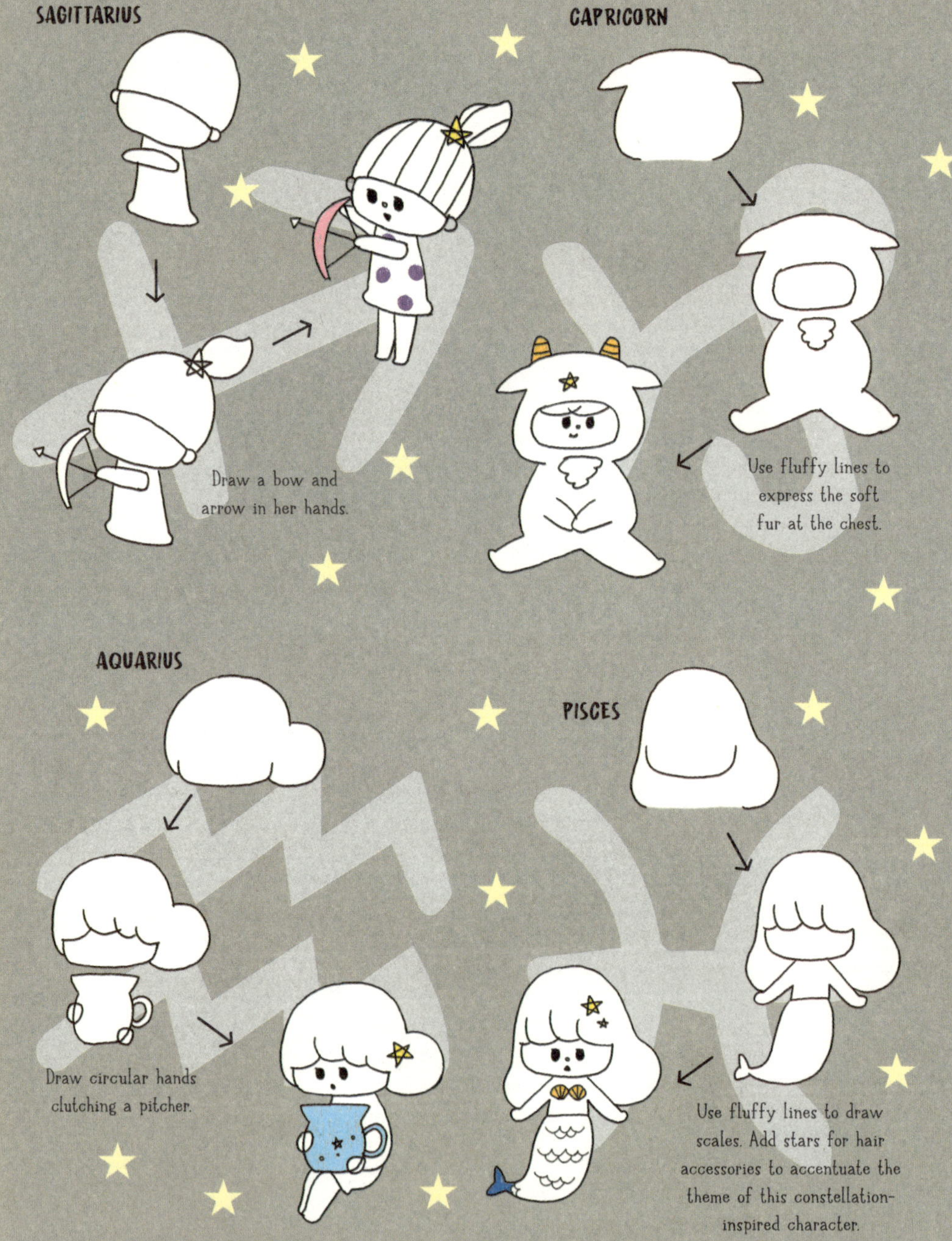
SAGITTARIUS
Draw a bow and arrow in her hands.
CAPRICORN
Use fluffy lines to express the soft fur at the chest.
AQUARIUS
Draw circular hands clutching a pitcher.
PISCES
Use fluffy lines to draw scales. Add stars for hair accessories to accentuate the theme of this constellation-inspired character.

Chapter 3:

DRAWING EVERYDAY OBJECTS

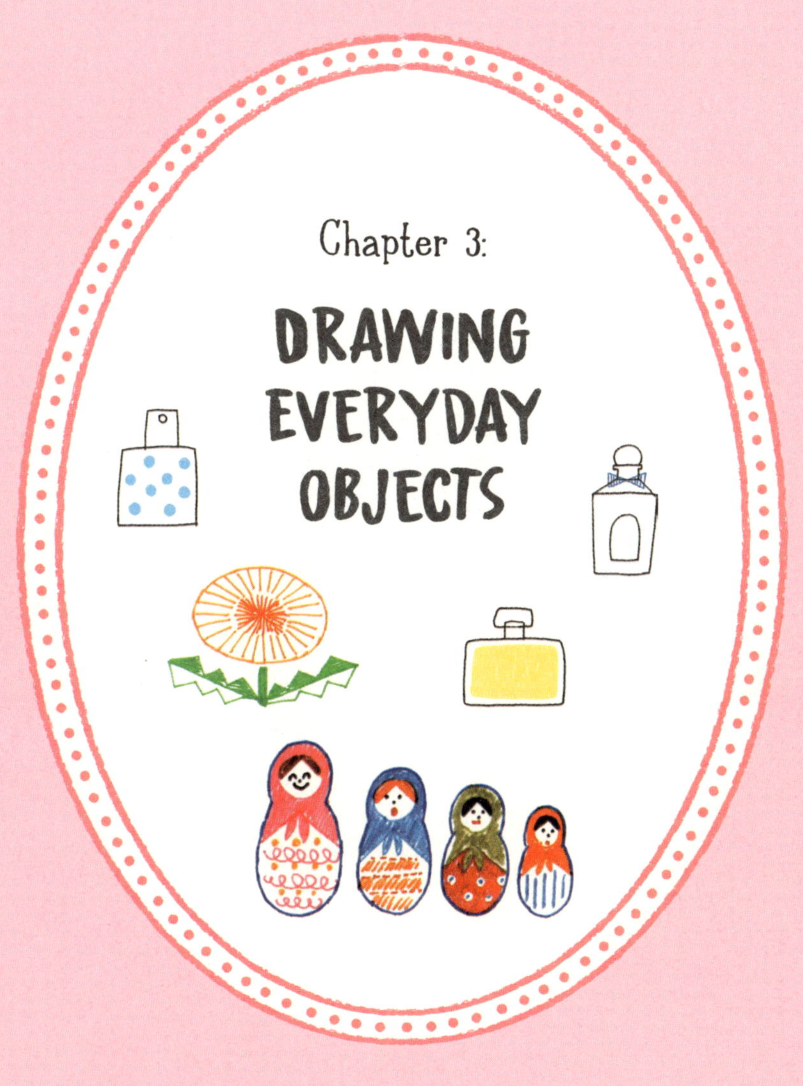

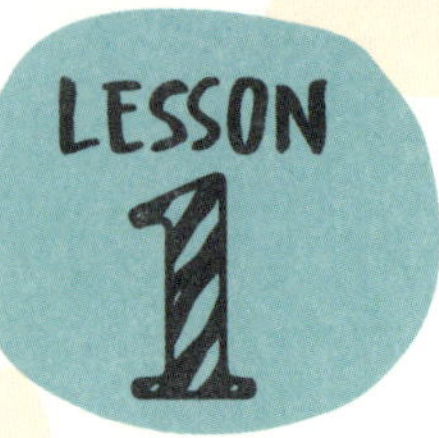

FLOWERS & TREES

Once you master the basics of drawing flowers and trees, the possibilities are endless! You can create lots of cute, unique illustrations just by changing the colors and shapes.

FLOWERS

1 For flowers with individual petals, start with the center and then add the petals.

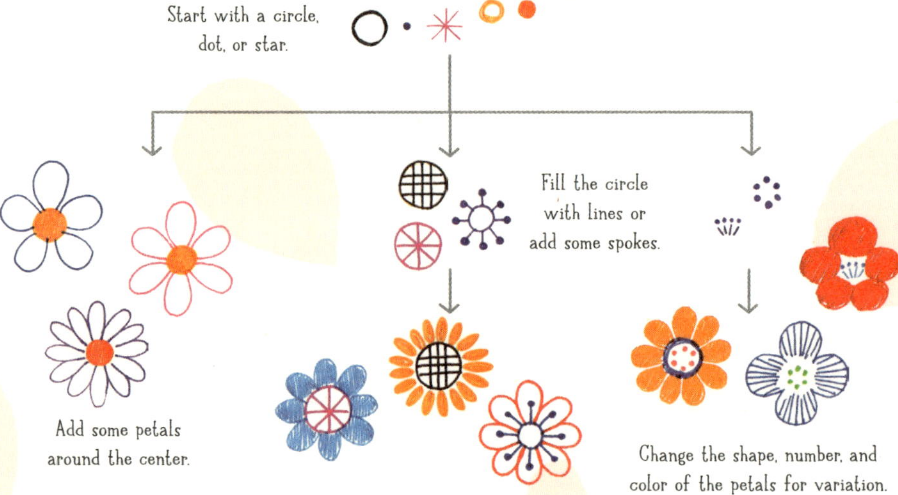

2 For flowers with connected petals, draw the outline of the petals, and then add the center.

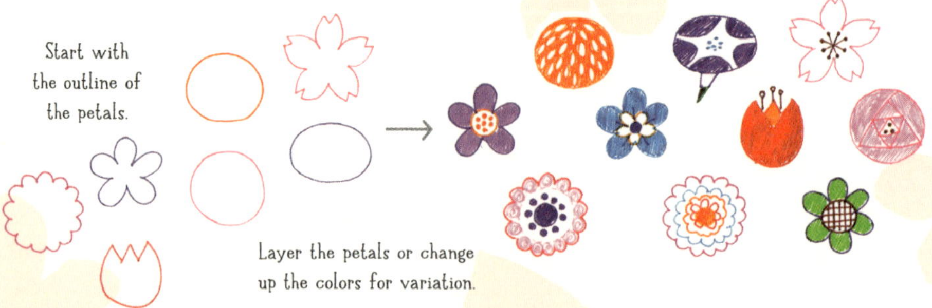

3 Draw a few simple flowers to make a bouquet or a flower arrangement.

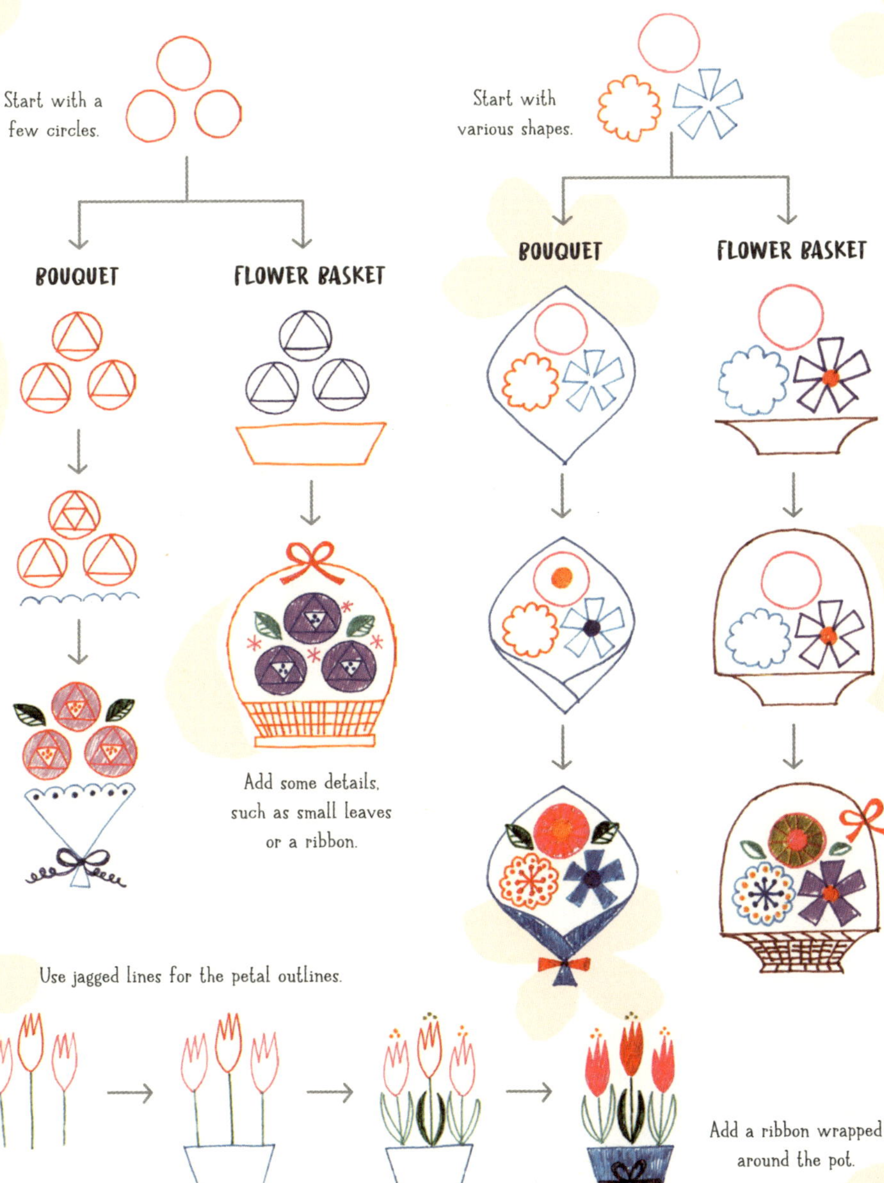

Use jagged lines for the petal outlines.

Add a ribbon wrapped around the pot.

LEAVES

1 Start at the center by drawing the leaf vein or vine.

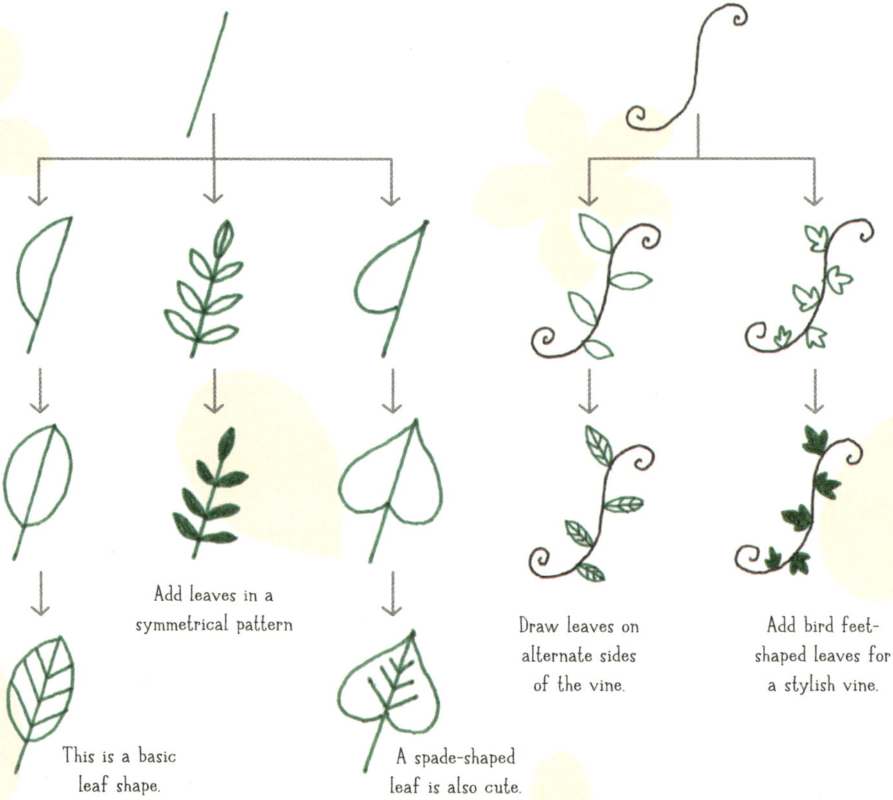

Add leaves in a symmetrical pattern

Draw leaves on alternate sides of the vine.

Add bird feet-shaped leaves for a stylish vine.

This is a basic leaf shape.

A spade-shaped leaf is also cute.

2 Or start with the leaf outline and then add the vein.

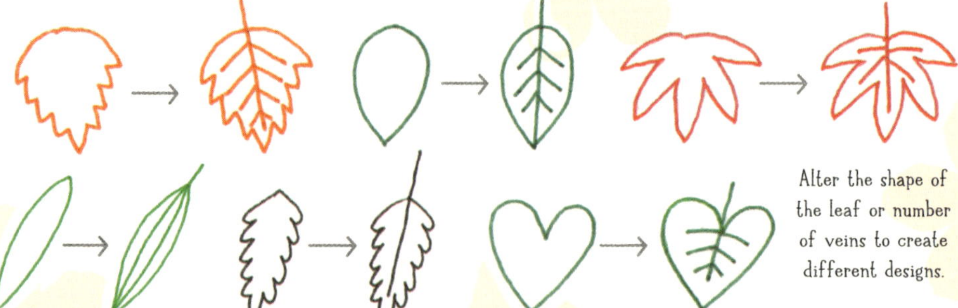

Alter the shape of the leaf or number of veins to create different designs.

TREES

Trees can be intimidating to draw, but they are composed of just two basic elements: the trunk and the leaves.

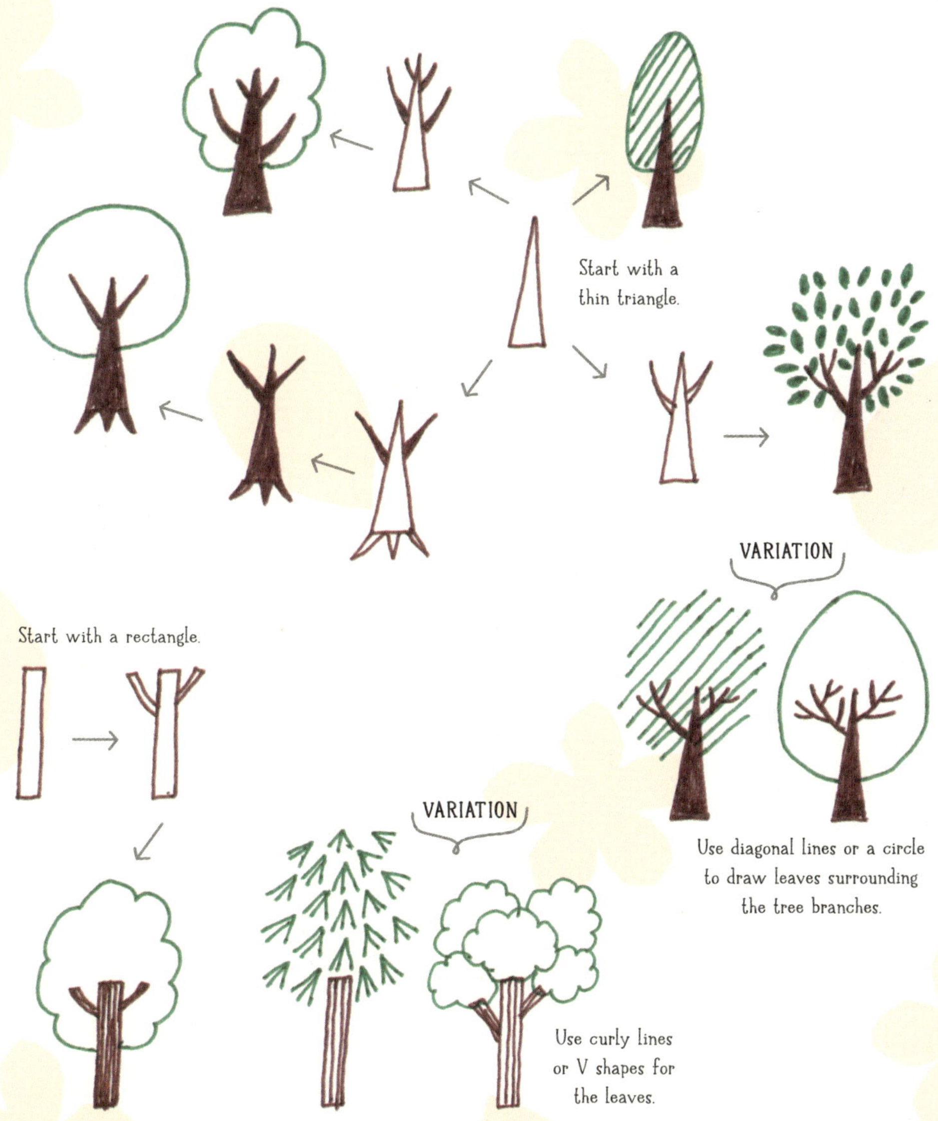

VARIATION

LET'S DRAW SEASONAL PLANTS

Now let's try drawing some specific flower types based on seasons. These illustrations are perfect for greeting cards and postcards.

SPRING

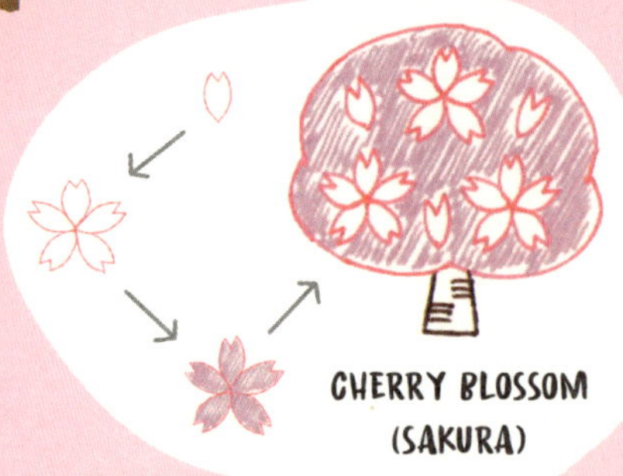

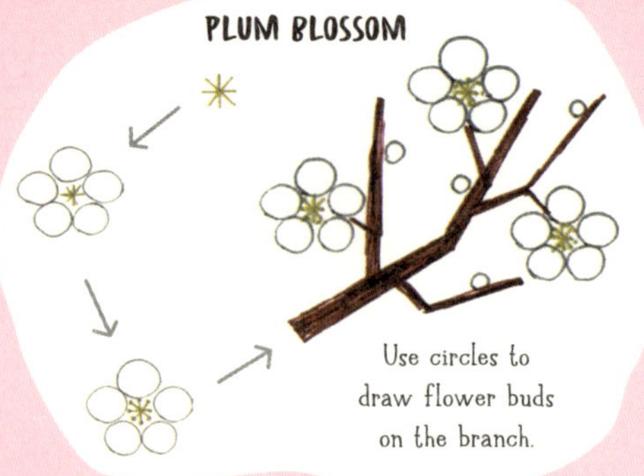

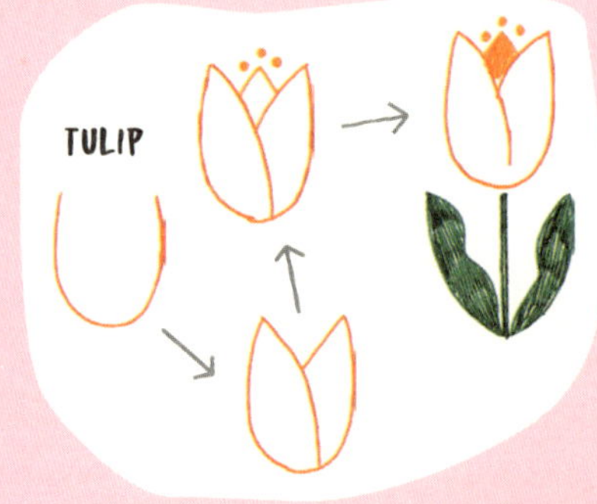

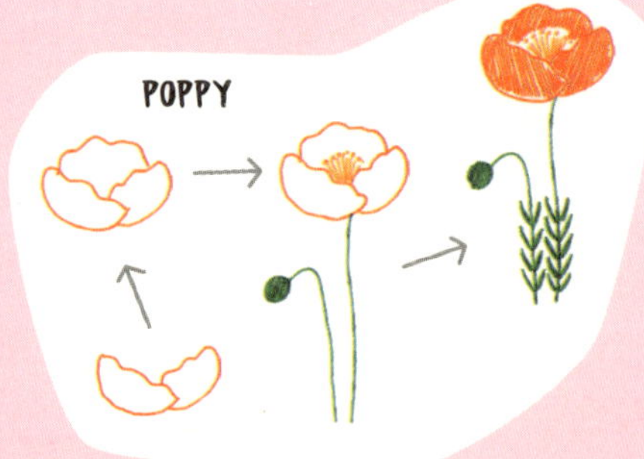

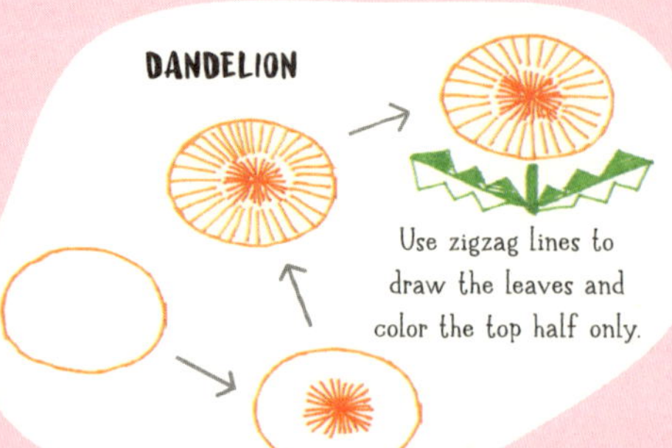

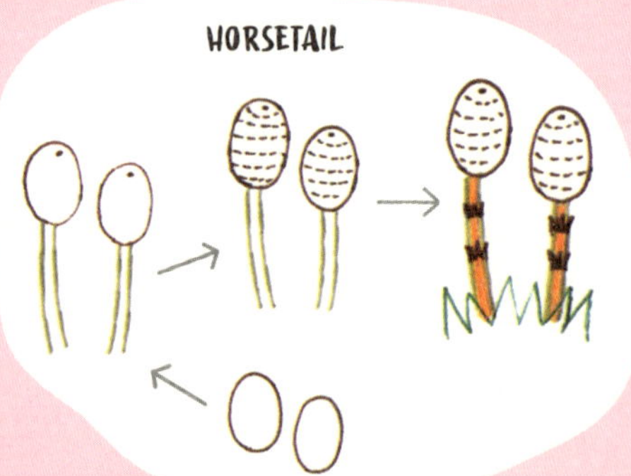

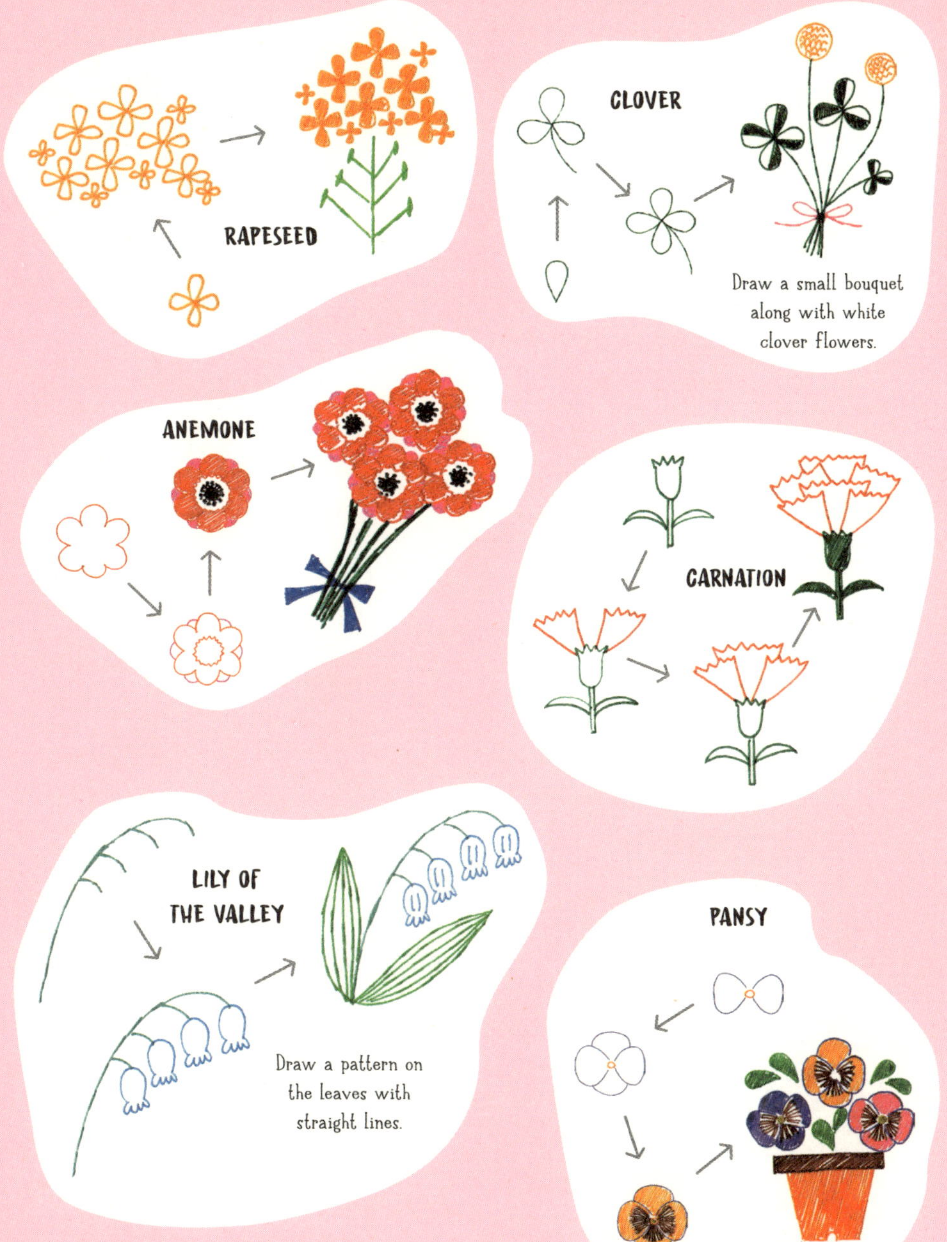
RAPESEED
CLOVER
Draw a small bouquet along with white clover flowers.
ANEMONE
CARNATION
LILY OF THE VALLEY
Draw a pattern on the leaves with straight lines.
PANSY

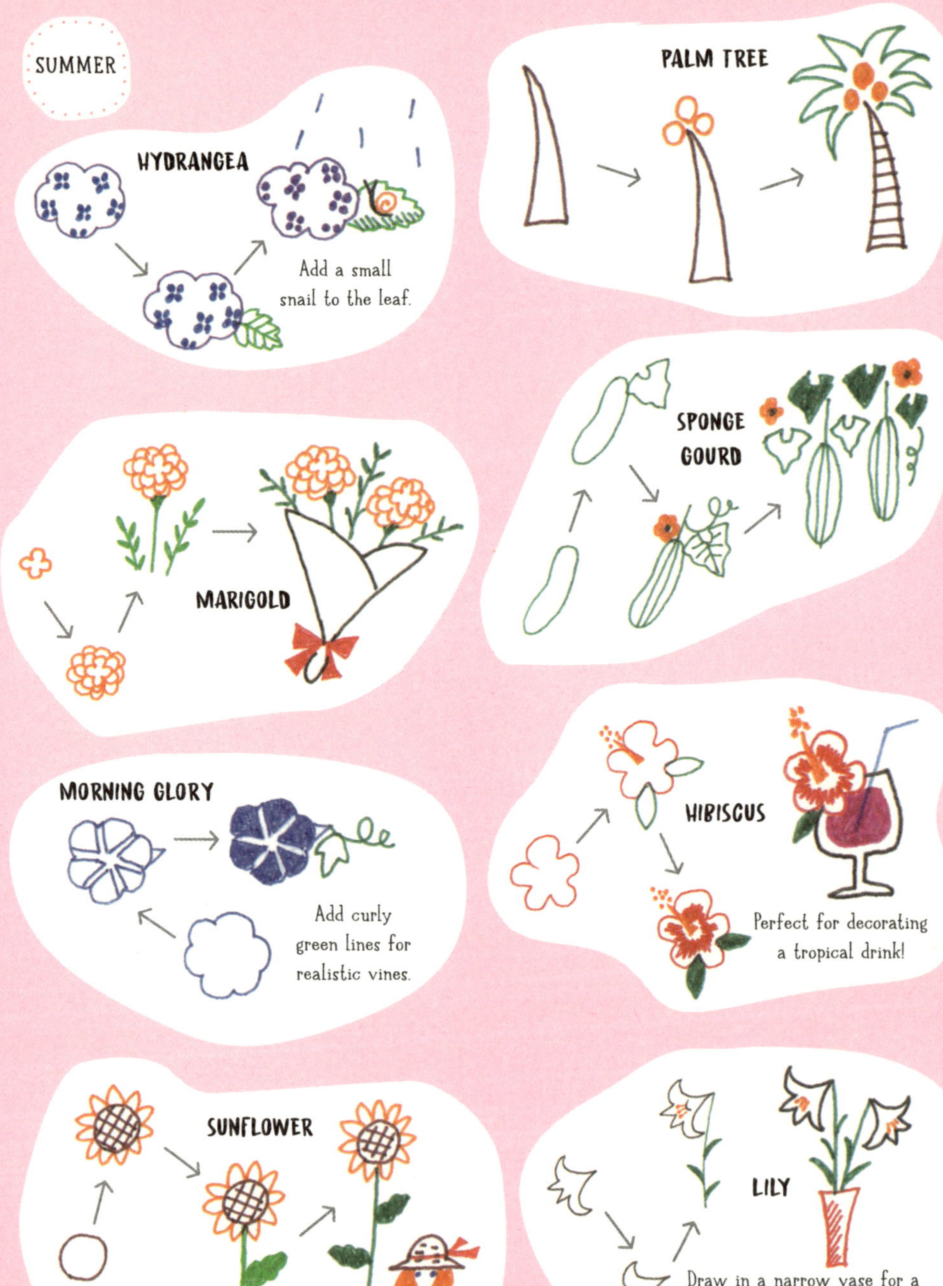
SUMMER
HYDRANGEA
Add a small snail to the leaf.
PALM TREE
MARIGOLD
SPONGE GOURD
MORNING GLORY
Add curly green lines for realistic vines.
HIBISCUS
Perfect for decorating a tropical drink!
SUNFLOWER
LILY
Draw in a narrow vase for a sophisticated floral arrangement.

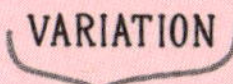

Use summer flowers for seasonal greeting cards!

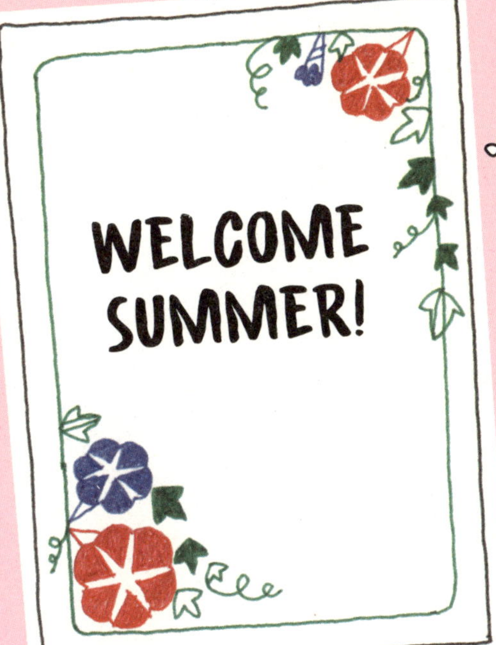

Morning glory illustration on page 112.

The vines of the morning glory form a decorative frame. Draw the flowers on two opposite corners of the card to create a well-balanced illustration.

Palm tree illustration on page 112.

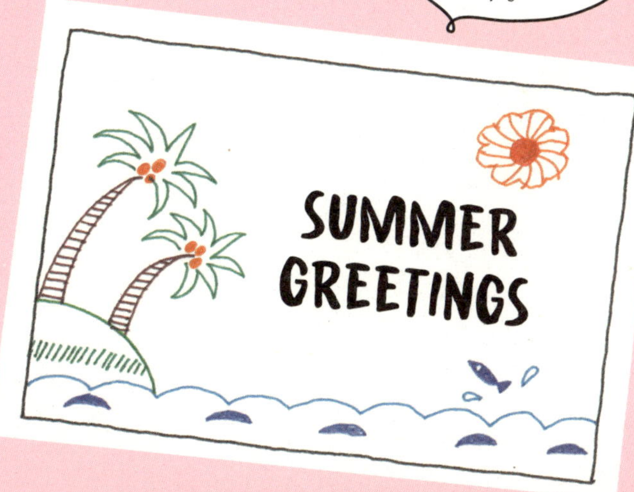

Add waves to create a summer scene.

COSMOS

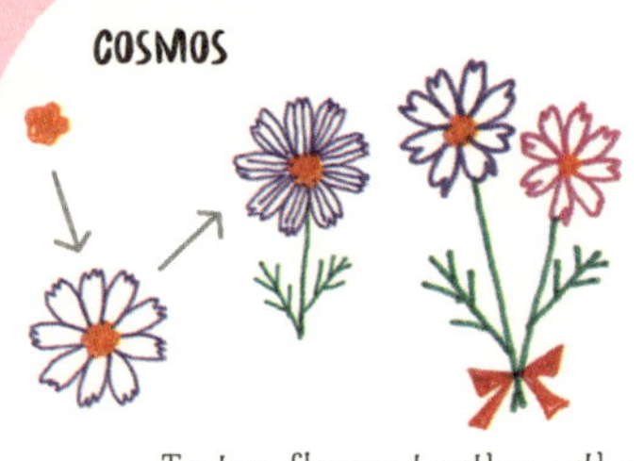

Tie two flowers together with a ribbon to make a petite bouquet.

CHRYSANTHEMUM

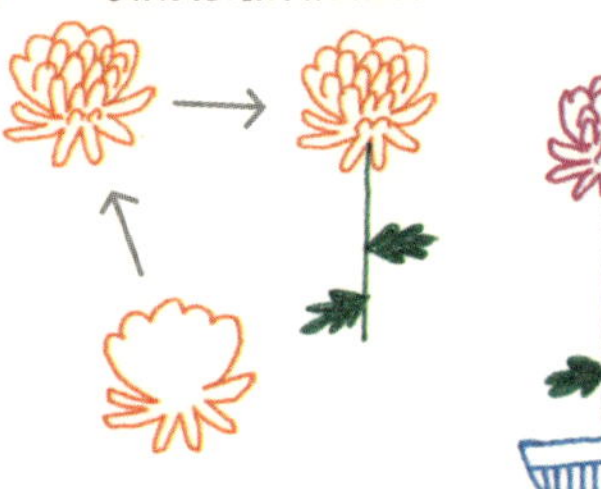

Arrange a single flower in a shallow pot for a chic, minimalist look.

JAPANESE MAPLE

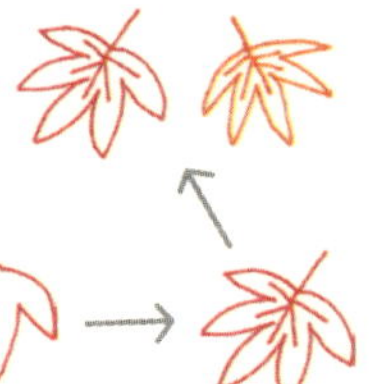

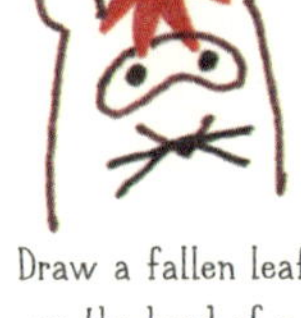

Draw a fallen leaf on the head of a cute animal for a seasonal look.

OSMANTHUS

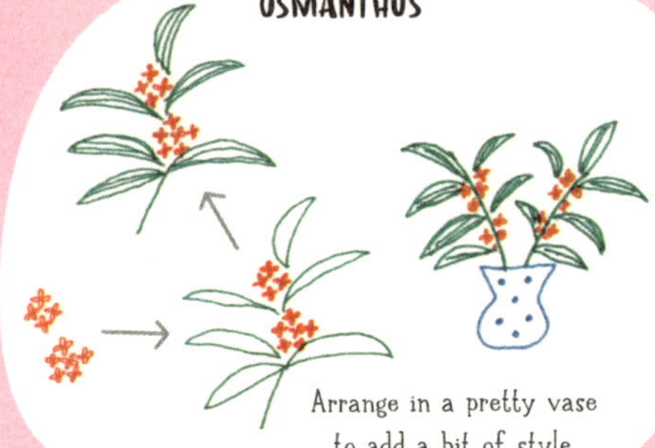

Arrange in a pretty vase to add a bit of style.

GINKGO

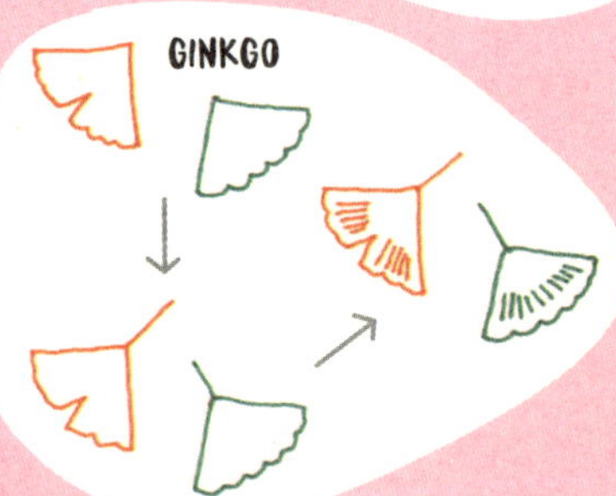

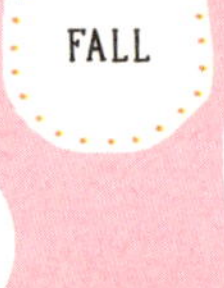

RED SPIDER LILY

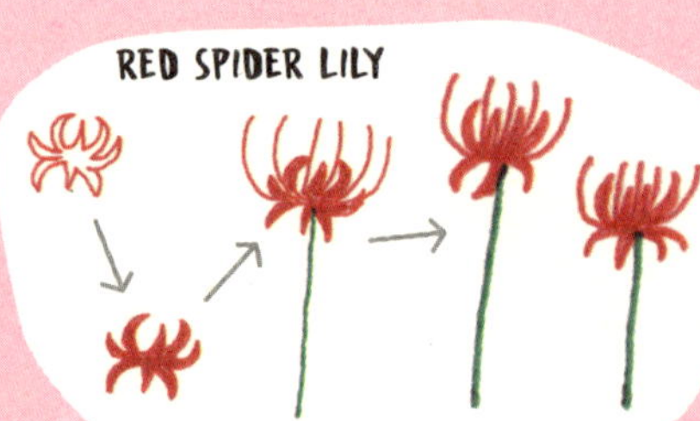

Chestnut

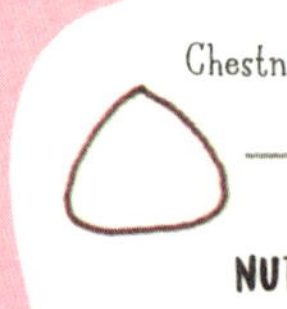

Acorn

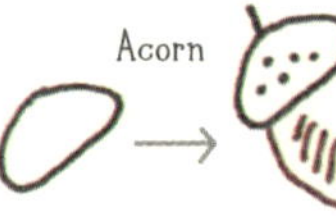

Sawtooth acorn

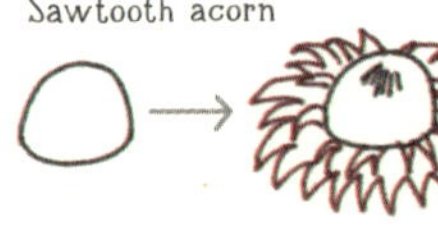

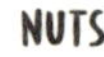

NUTS

Walnut

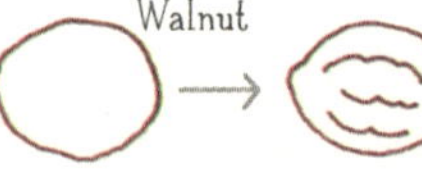

Pine cone

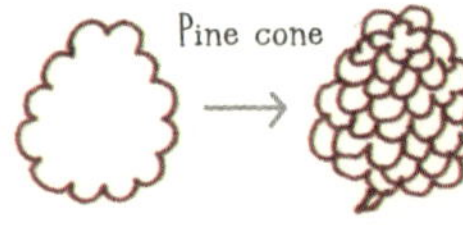

WINTER

CAMELLIA

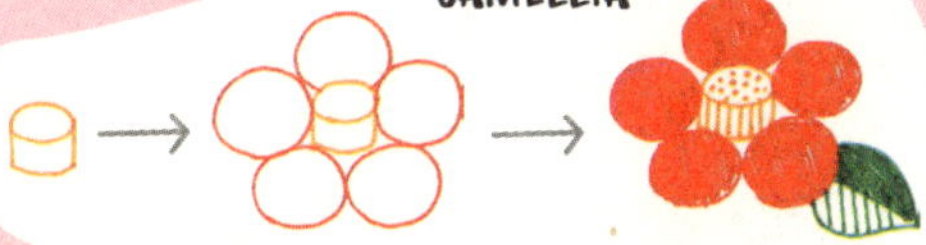

POINSETTIA

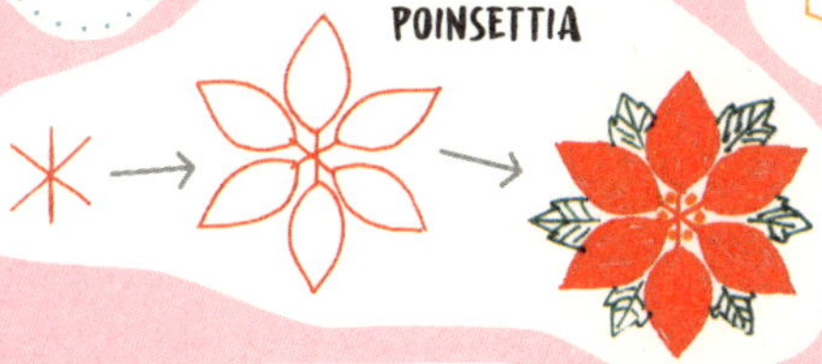

BONSAI

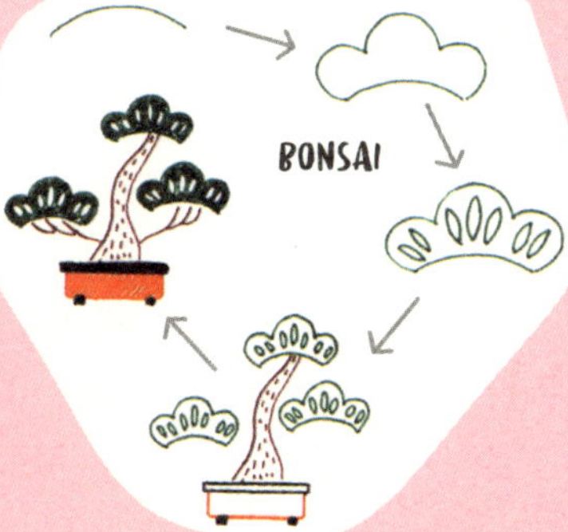

HOLLY

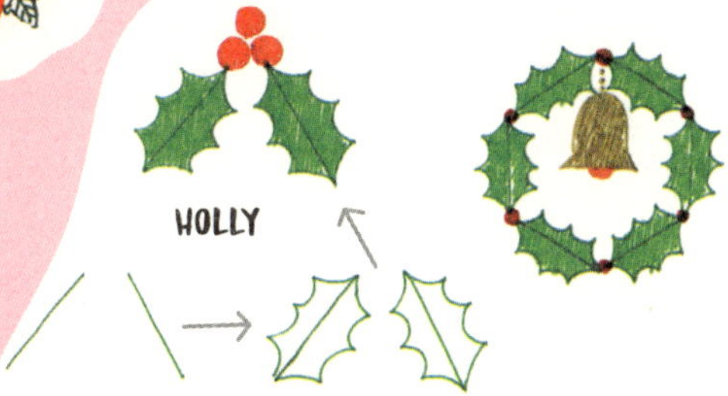

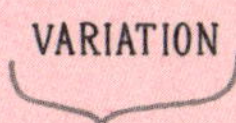

Draw several leaves in a circle to create a Christmas wreath.

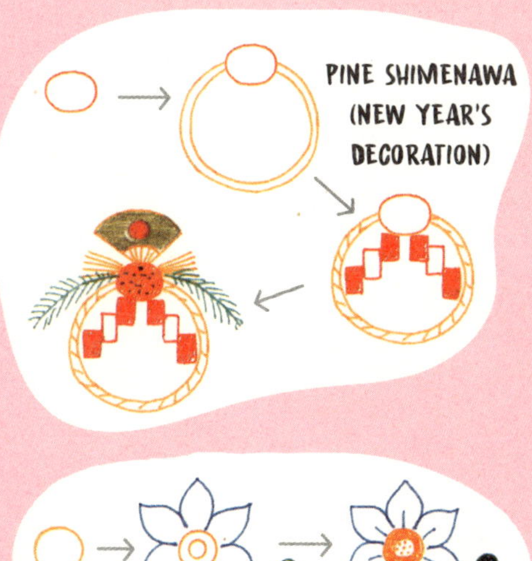

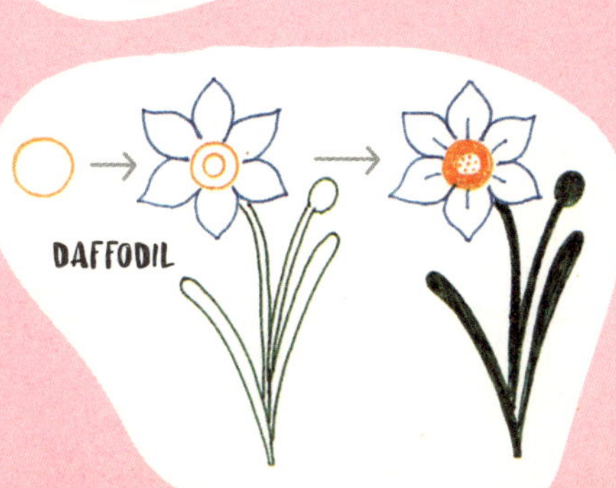

VARIATION

Use winter plants for a holiday greeting card!

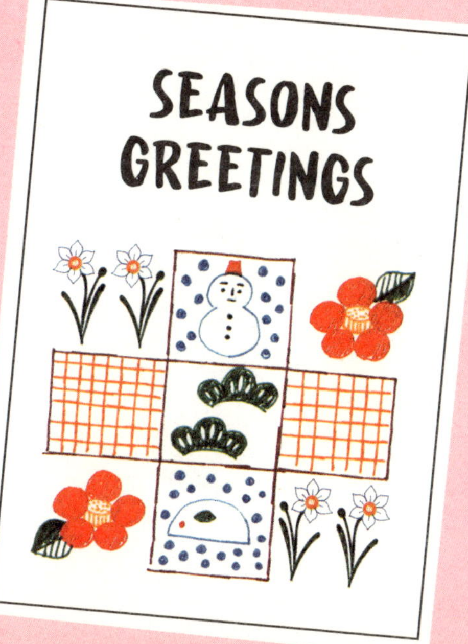

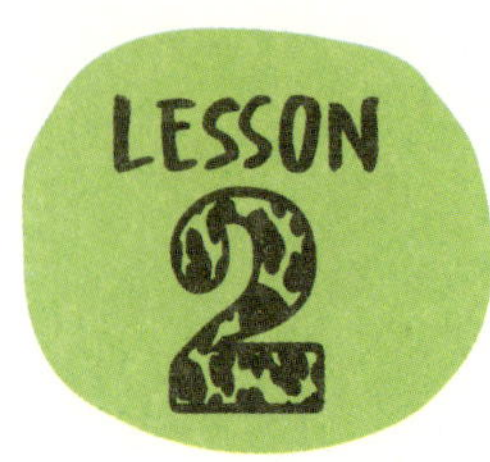

FRUIT

Fruit is easy to draw as most varieties have a simple circle or oval shape. Change the color or pattern to illustrate various kinds of fruits.

1 Fill a circle with color and pattern and then add a stem.

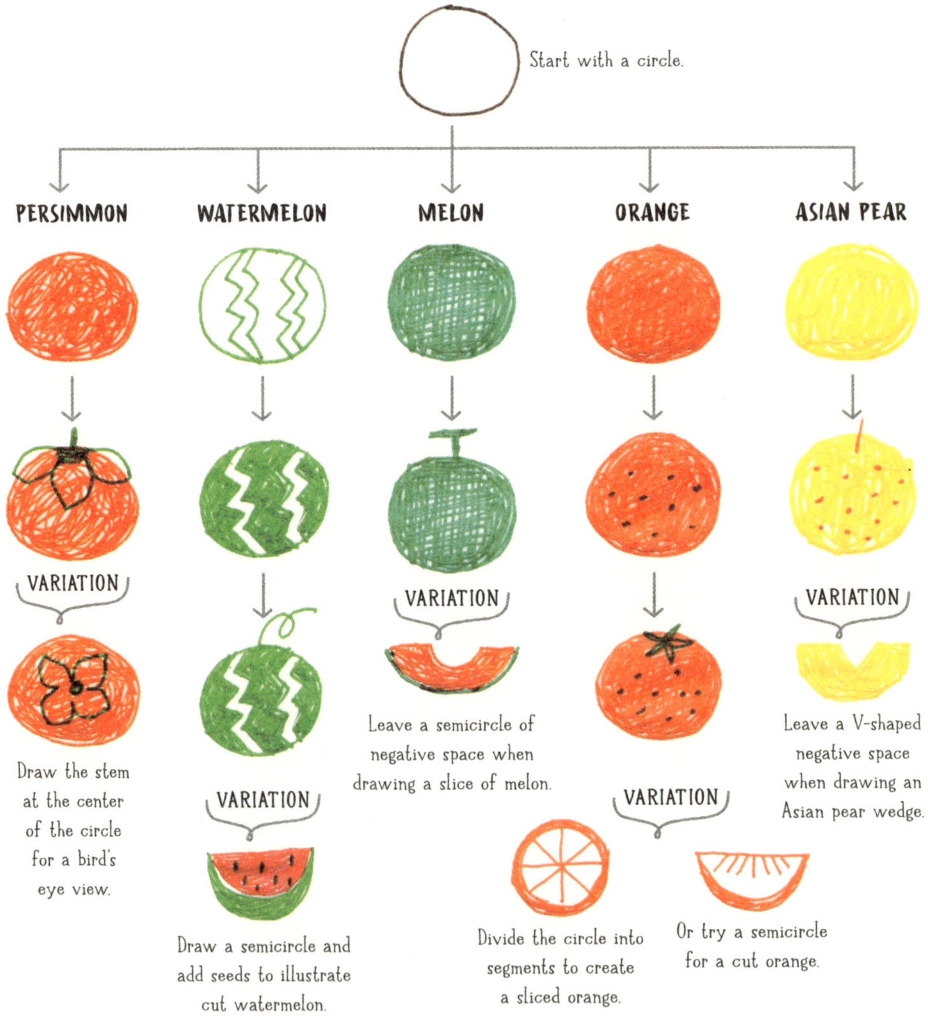

Start with a circle.

PERSIMMON

VARIATION

Draw the stem at the center of the circle for a bird's eye view.

WATERMELON

VARIATION

Draw a semicircle and add seeds to illustrate cut watermelon.

MELON

VARIATION

Leave a semicircle of negative space when drawing a slice of melon.

ORANGE

VARIATION

Divide the circle into segments to create a sliced orange.

Or try a semicircle for a cut orange.

ASIAN PEAR

VARIATION

Leave a V-shaped negative space when drawing an Asian pear wedge.

2 Other fruits can be drawn with a combination of a few circles and ovals.

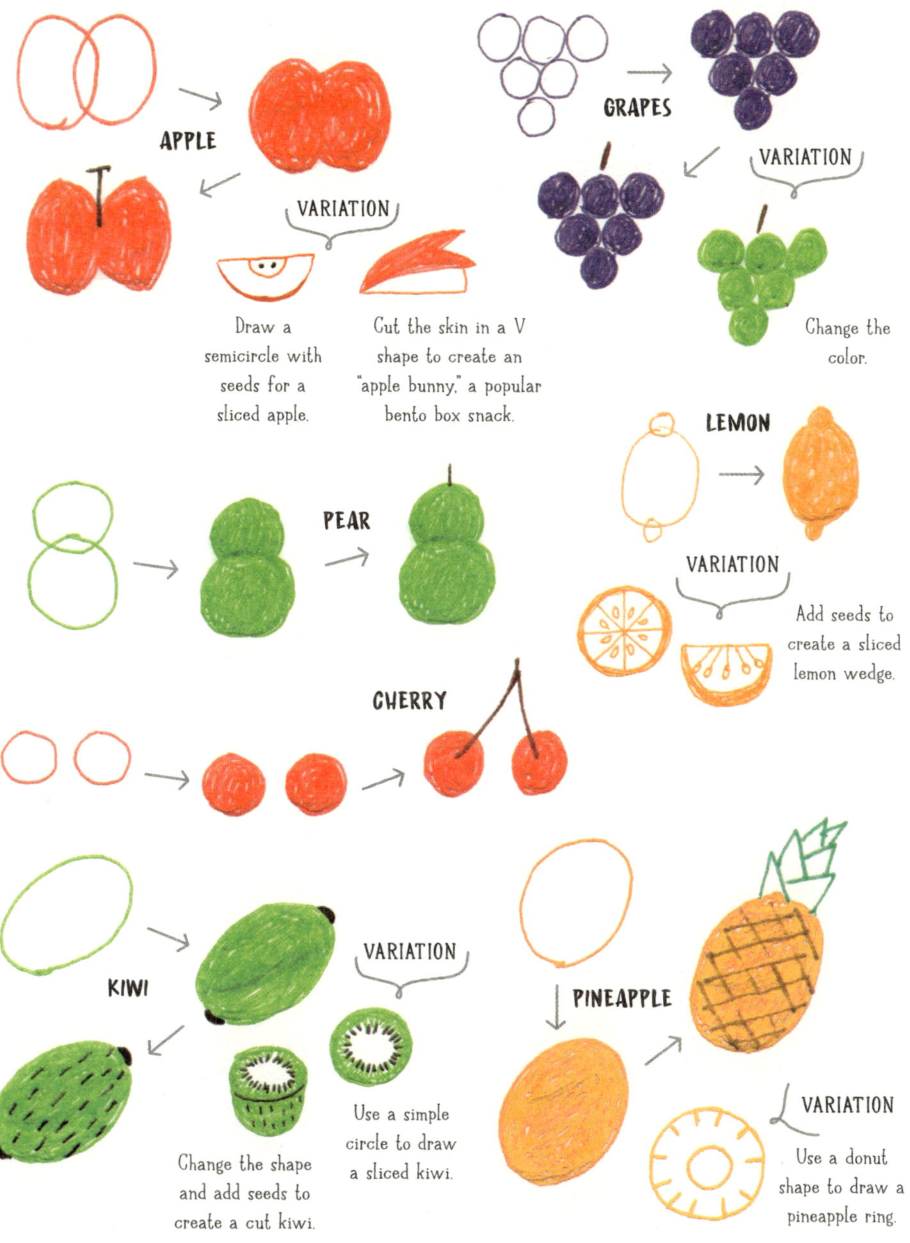

VARIATION

UNIQUELY SHAPED FRUITS

Now let's try drawing fruit with slightly more complex shapes. The process is the same—first draw the outline, then add color.

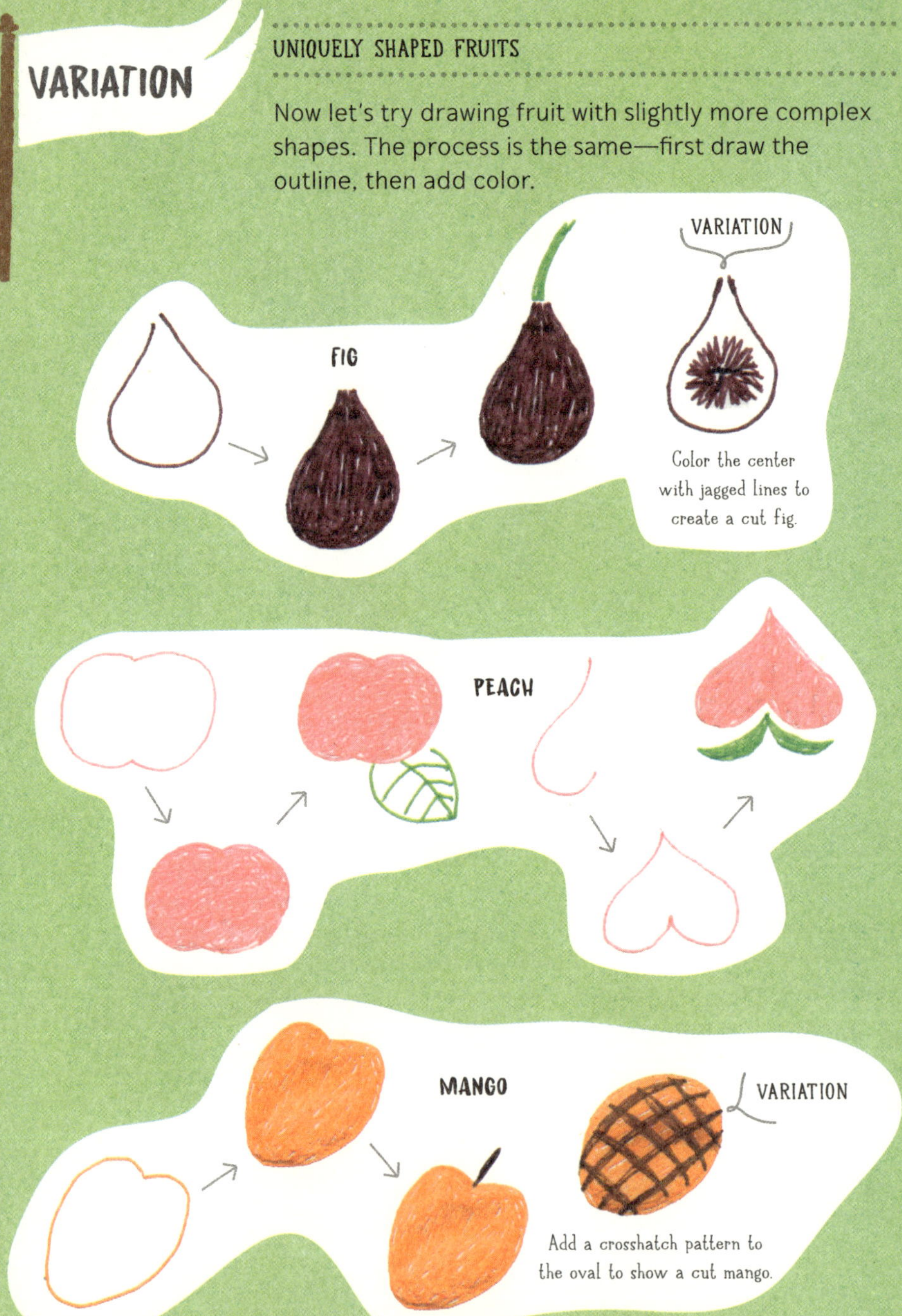

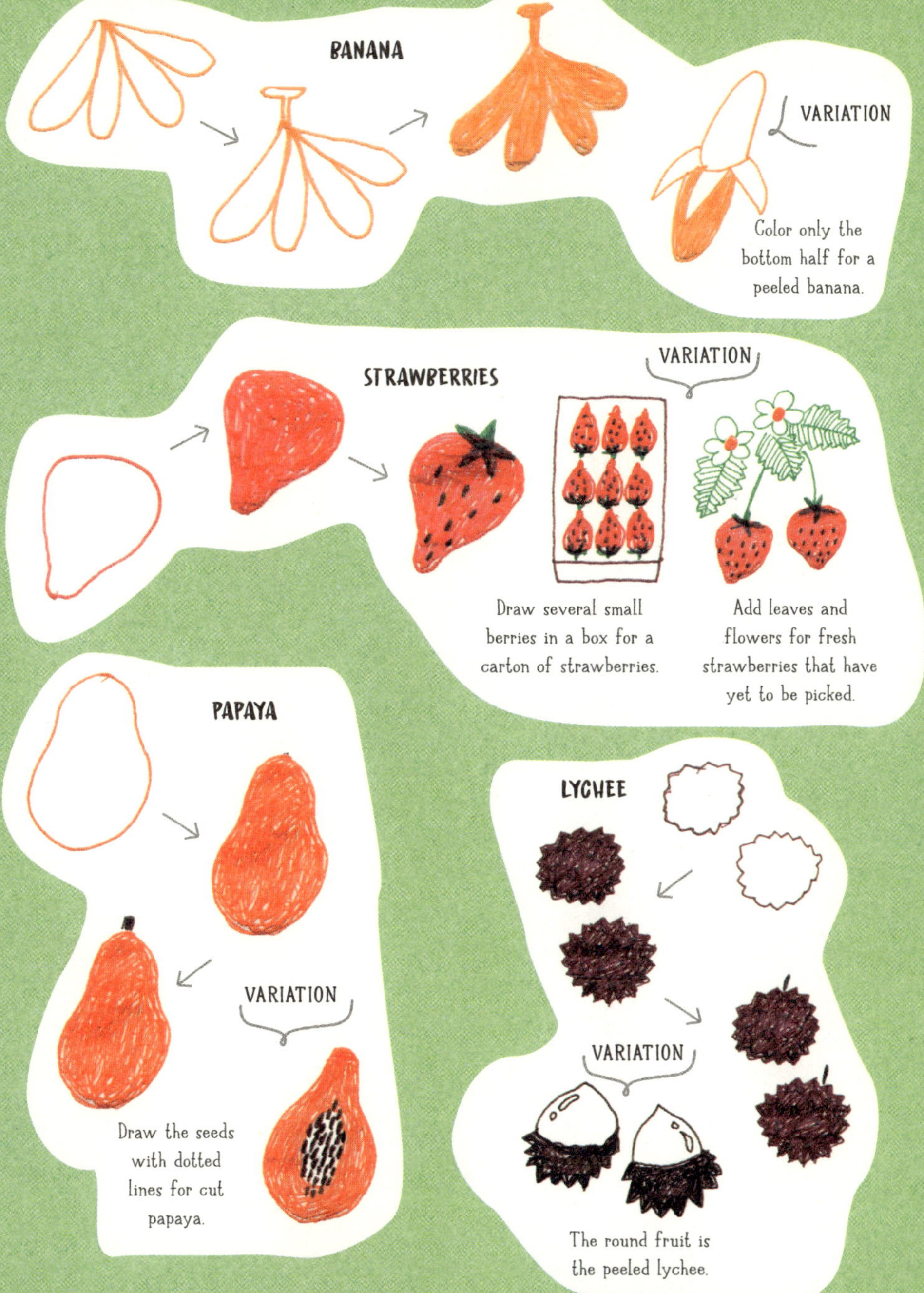
BANANA
VARIATION
Color only the bottom half for a peeled banana.
STRAWBERRIES
VARIATION
Draw several small berries in a box for a carton of strawberries.
Add leaves and flowers for fresh strawberries that have yet to be picked.
PAPAYA
VARIATION
Draw the seeds with dotted lines for cut papaya.
LYCHEE
VARIATION
The round fruit is the peeled lychee.

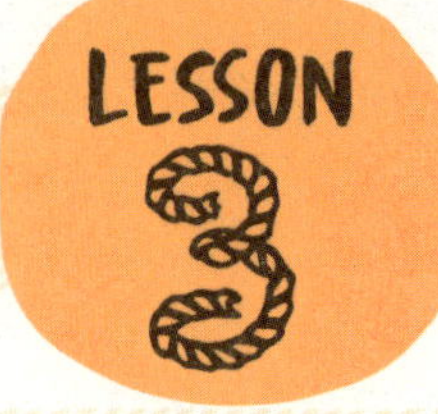

VEGETABLES

Start with the basic outline, and then add color and texture to capture the unique look of each vegetable.

DAIKON

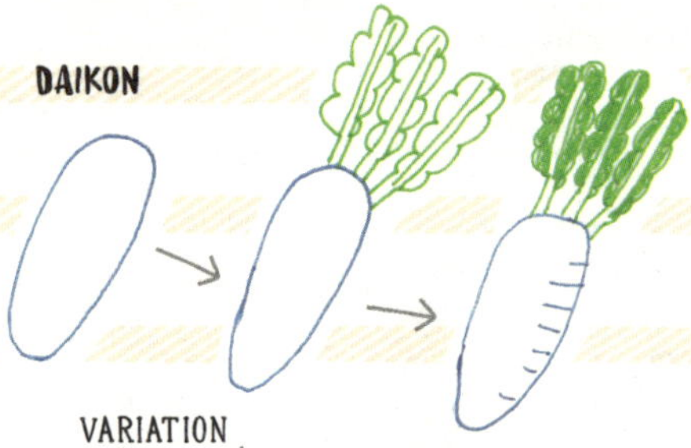

Use a classic green and white color scheme.

VARIATION

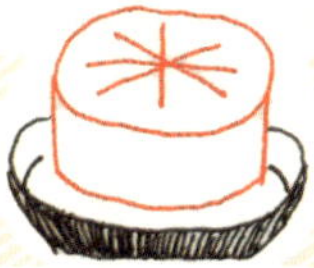

Use brown or red pen to represent a cooked daikon radish.

TURNIP

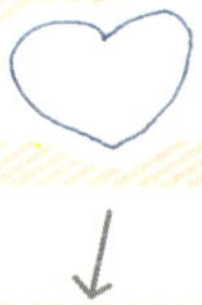

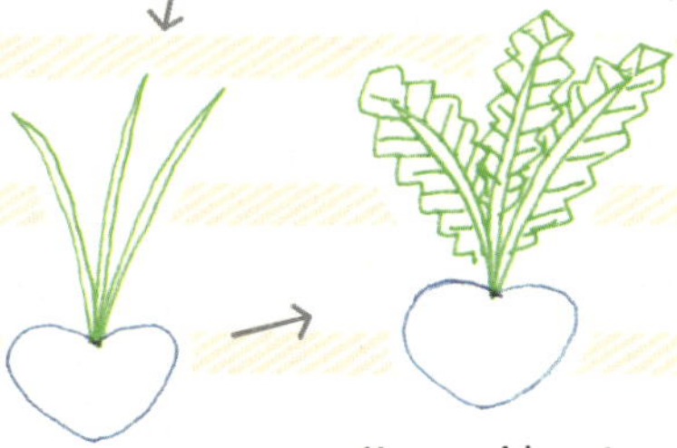

Use jagged lines to draw the leaves.

VARIATION

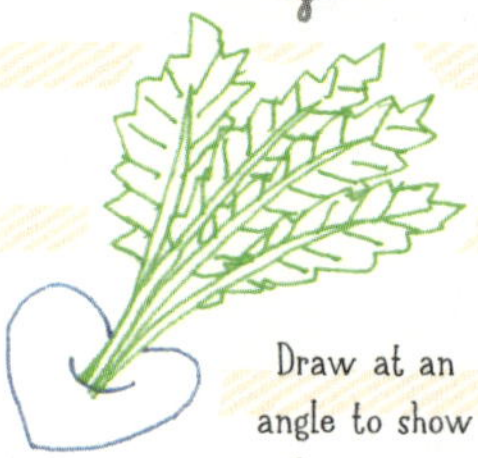

Draw at an angle to show dimension.

CARROT

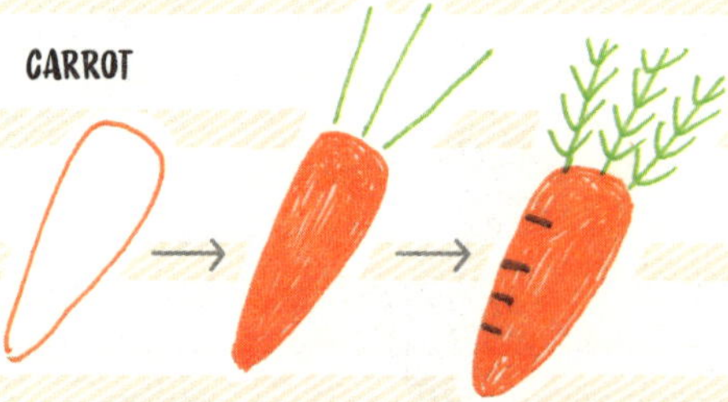

Add some short horizontal lines.

VARIATION

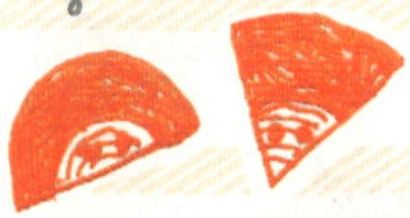

When drawing chopped carrots, leave some white space at the center.

TOMATO

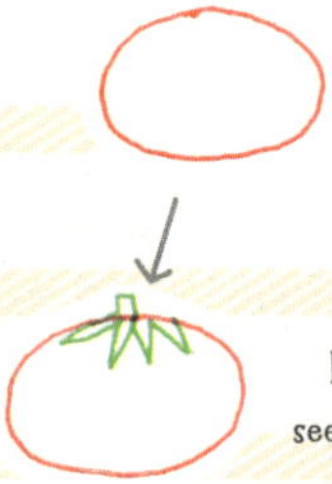

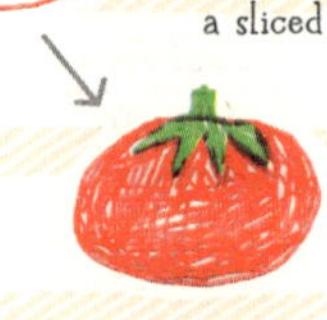

Fill with bold red pen to capture the ripeness of the tomato.

VARIATION

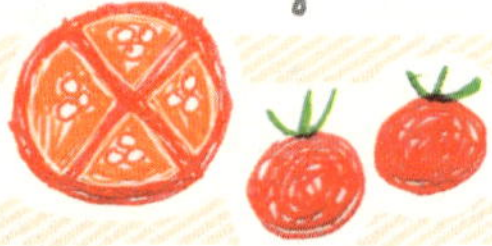

Don't forget the seeds when drawing a sliced tomato.

Try drawing cute little cherry tomatoes.

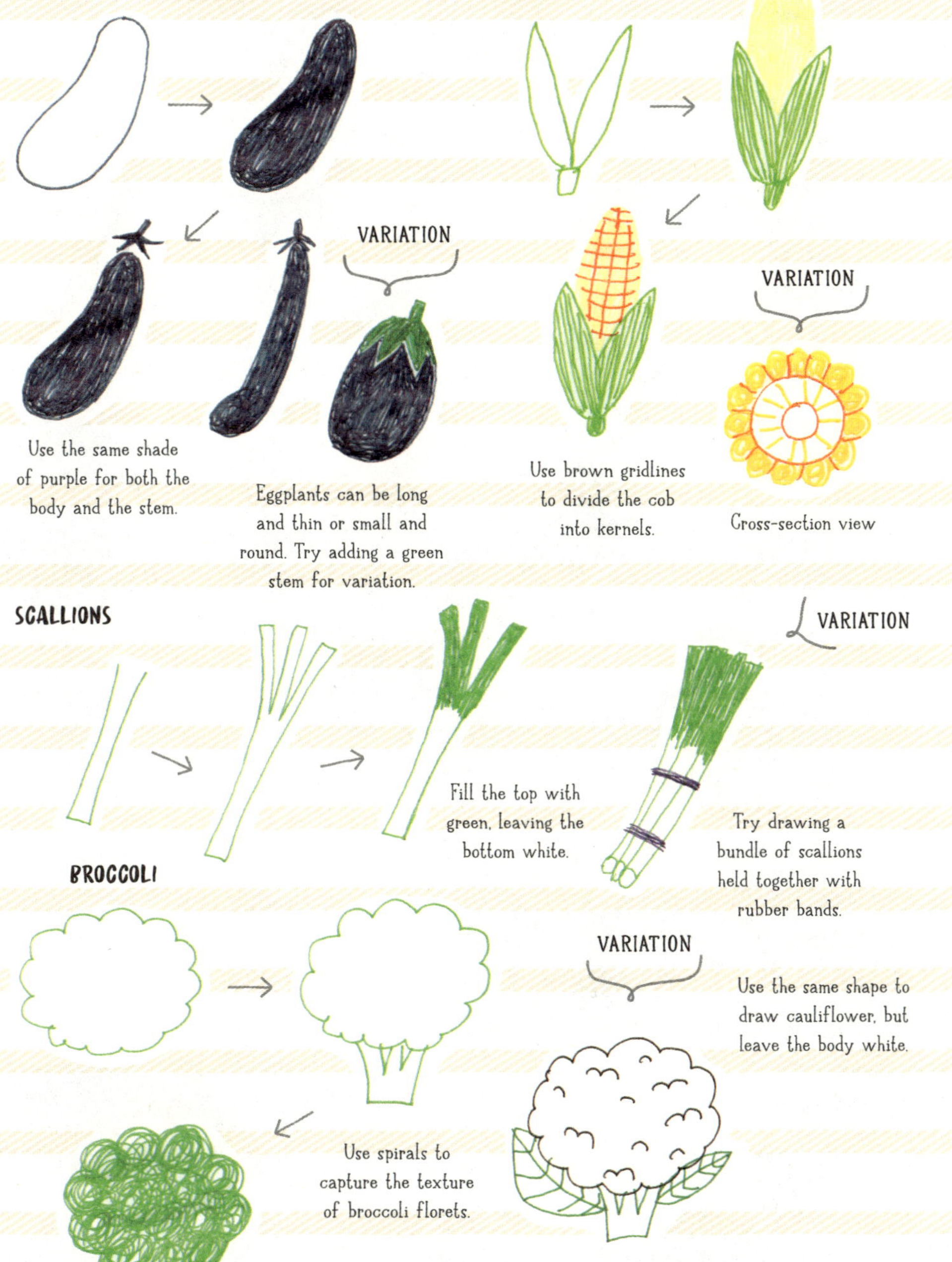
EGGPLANT
VARIATION
Use the same shade of purple for both the body and the stem.
Eggplants can be long and thin or small and round. Try adding a green stem for variation.
CORN
VARIATION
Use brown gridlines to divide the cob into kernels.
Cross-section view
SCALLIONS
Fill the top with green, leaving the bottom white.
VARIATION
Try drawing a bundle of scallions held together with rubber bands.
BROCCOLI
VARIATION
Use the same shape to draw cauliflower, but leave the body white.
Use spirals to capture the texture of broccoli florets.

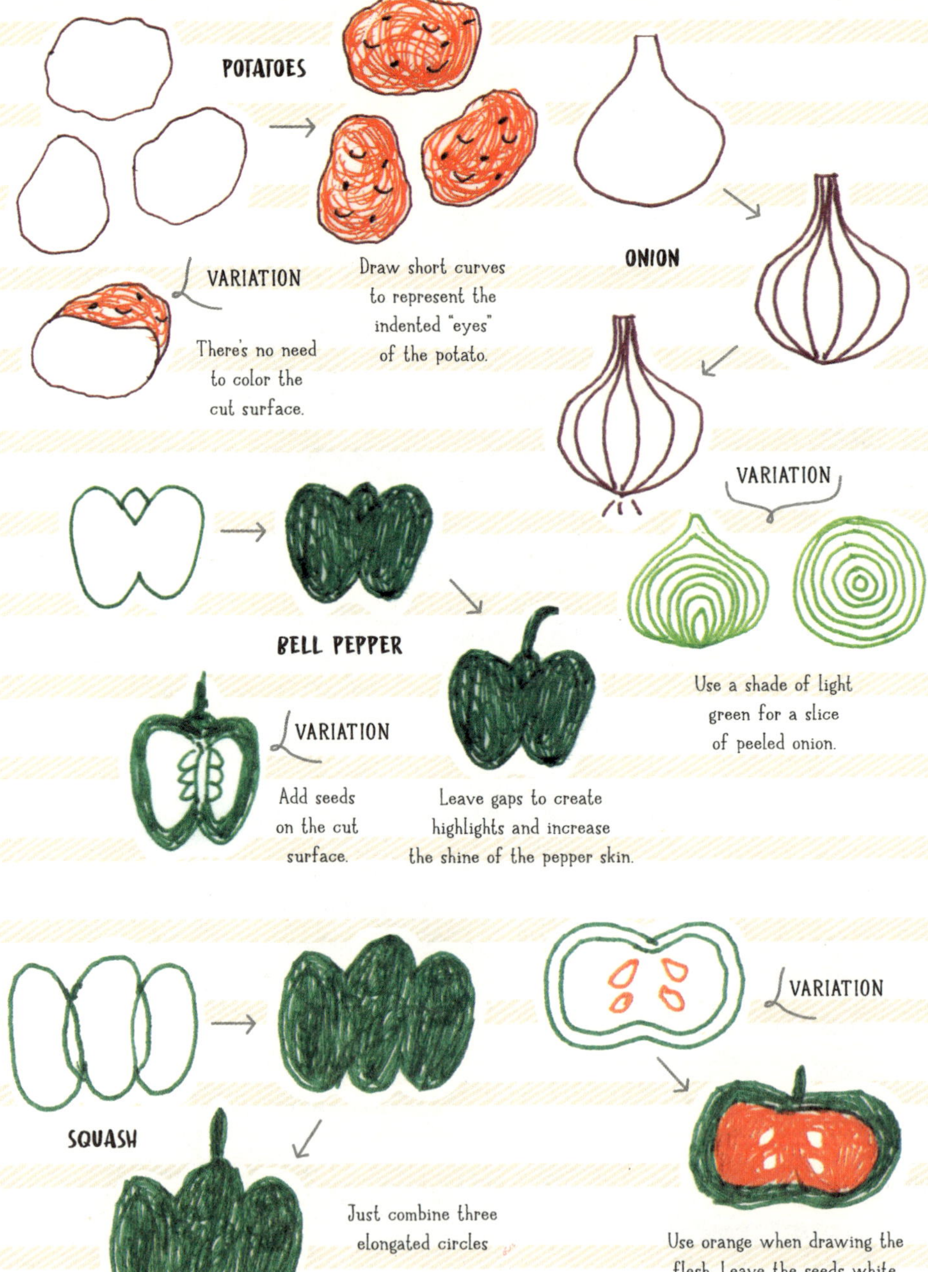
POTATOES
Draw short curves to represent the indented "eyes" of the potato.
VARIATION
There's no need to color the cut surface.
ONION
VARIATION
Use a shade of light green for a slice of peeled onion.
BELL PEPPER
VARIATION
Add seeds on the cut surface.
Leave gaps to create highlights and increase the shine of the pepper skin.
SQUASH
Just combine three elongated circles
VARIATION
Use orange when drawing the flesh. Leave the seeds white.

SHIITAKE MUSHROOM

Color to fill in the cap of the mushroom.

VARIATION

When drawing the view from below, use radial lines for the underside of the cap.

MATSUTAKE MUSHROOM

Add patterns on the stem with dotted lines.

VARIATION

Draw only the outline for a sliced matsutake.

CHINESE CABBAGE

Leave the core white.

VARIATION

Do not color the surface—instead use lines to create the individual leaves.

For lettuce, color the surface and use jagged lines to draw the leaf edge.

LOTUS ROOT

Draw dotted lines on the side to represent the rough texture.

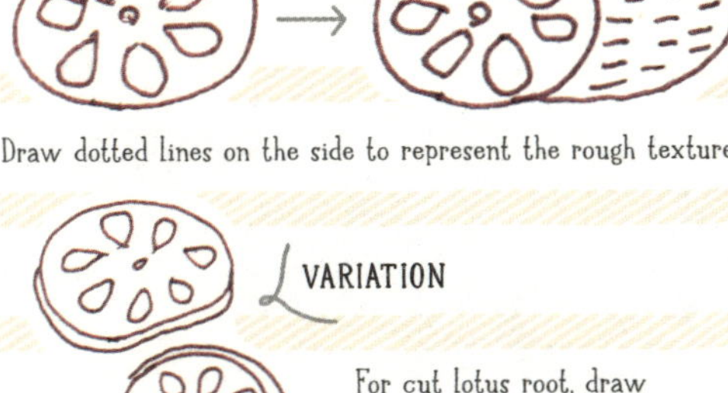

For cut lotus root, draw thin slices and add large, teardrop-shaped holes.

BROAD BEANS

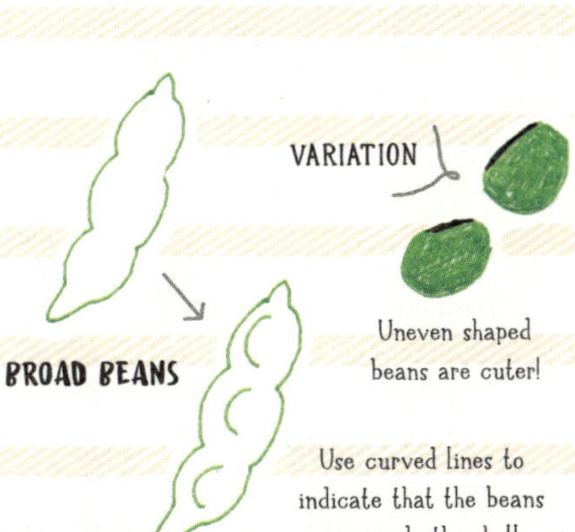

Uneven shaped beans are cuter!

Use curved lines to indicate that the beans are inside the shell.

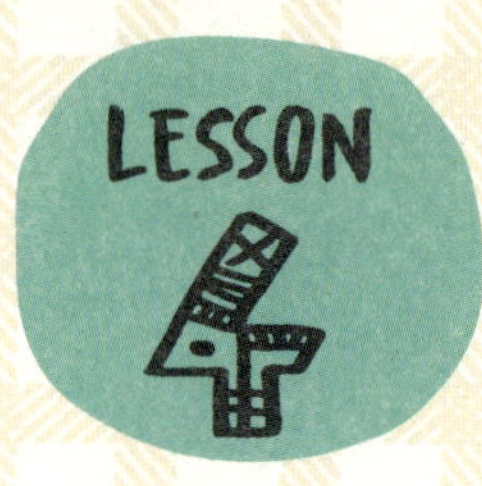

BREAD

When drawing bread, the key is to use curved lines to give it a soft, three-dimensional shape. Add details, such as score marks on the top, for a realistic look.

1 Incorporate depth when drawing sliced bread to give it a three-dimensional look.

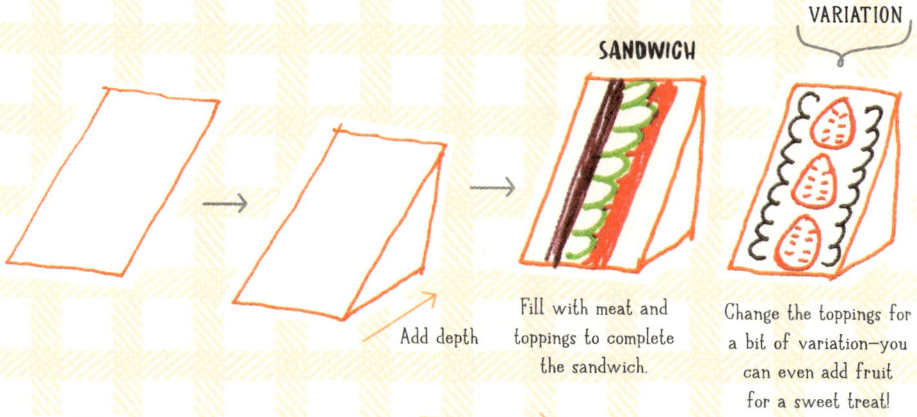

SANDWICH

VARIATION

Add depth

Fill with meat and toppings to complete the sandwich.

Change the toppings for a bit of variation—you can even add fruit for a sweet treat!

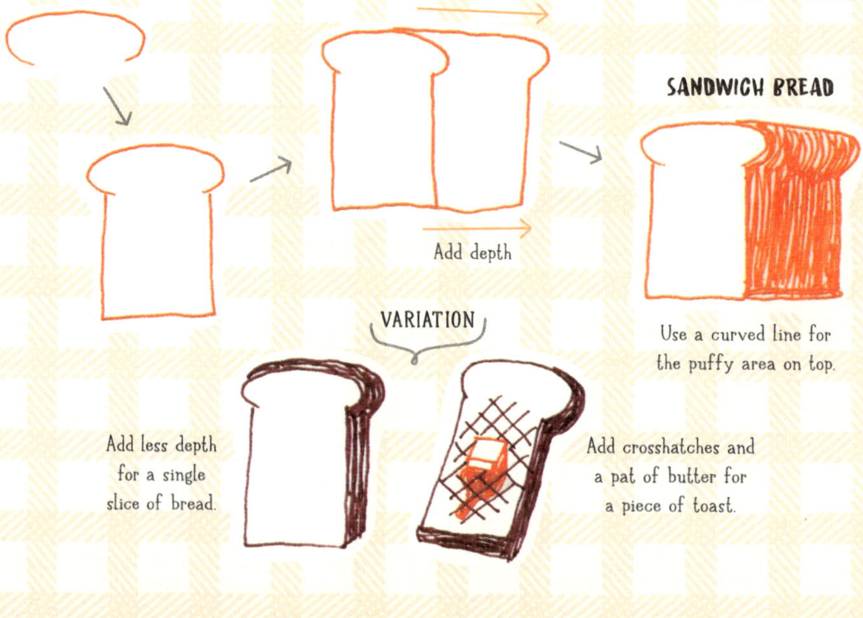

SANDWICH BREAD

Add depth

Use a curved line for the puffy area on top.

VARIATION

Add less depth for a single slice of bread.

Add crosshatches and a pat of butter for a piece of toast.

2 Consider the shape when adding color to illustrations of round bread to give it a three-dimensional look.

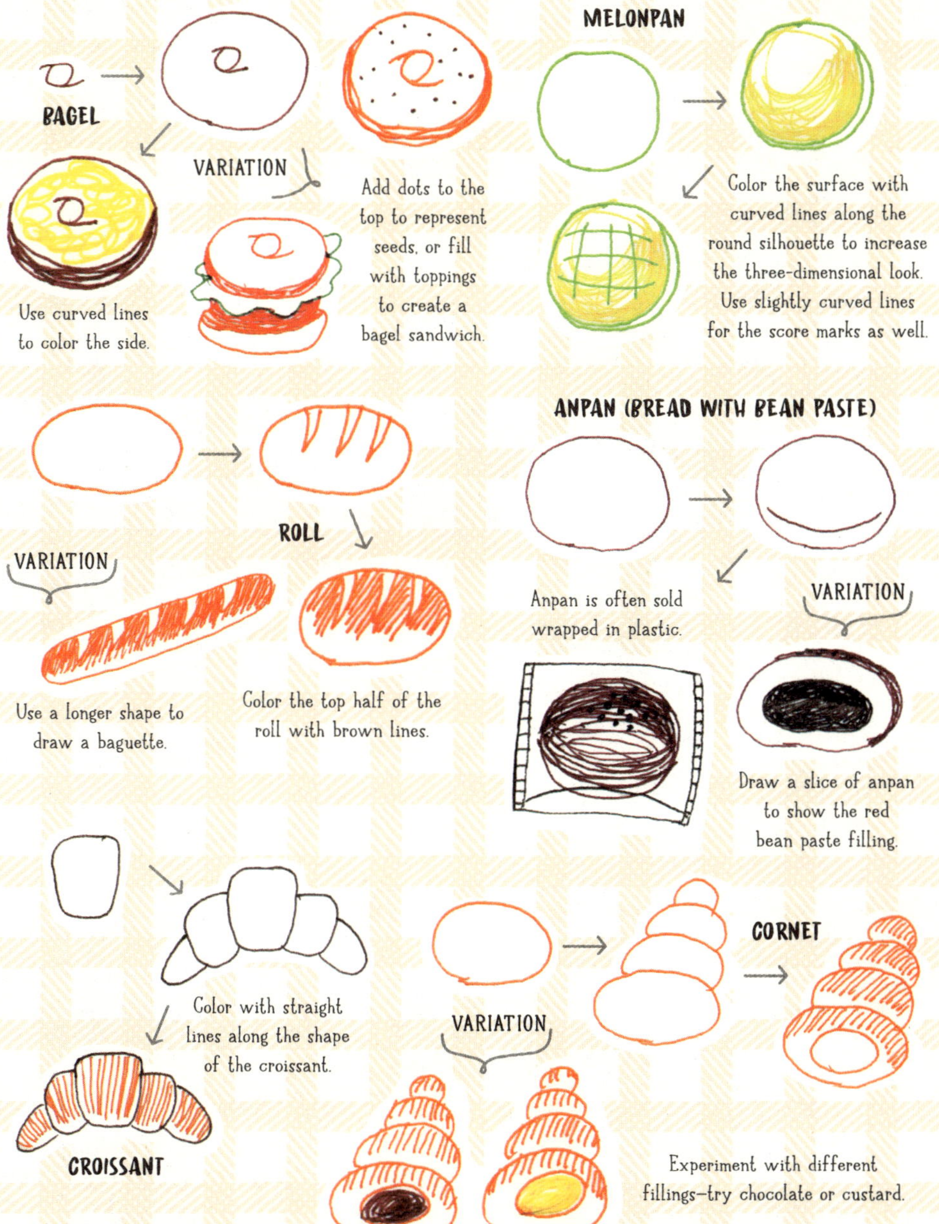

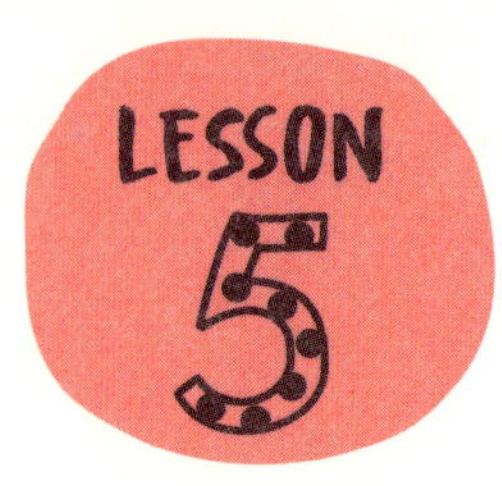

SWEETS

Sweets are fun to draw as they come in a variety of bright colors and unique shapes.

1 Incorporate lots of color for fun, festive illustrations.

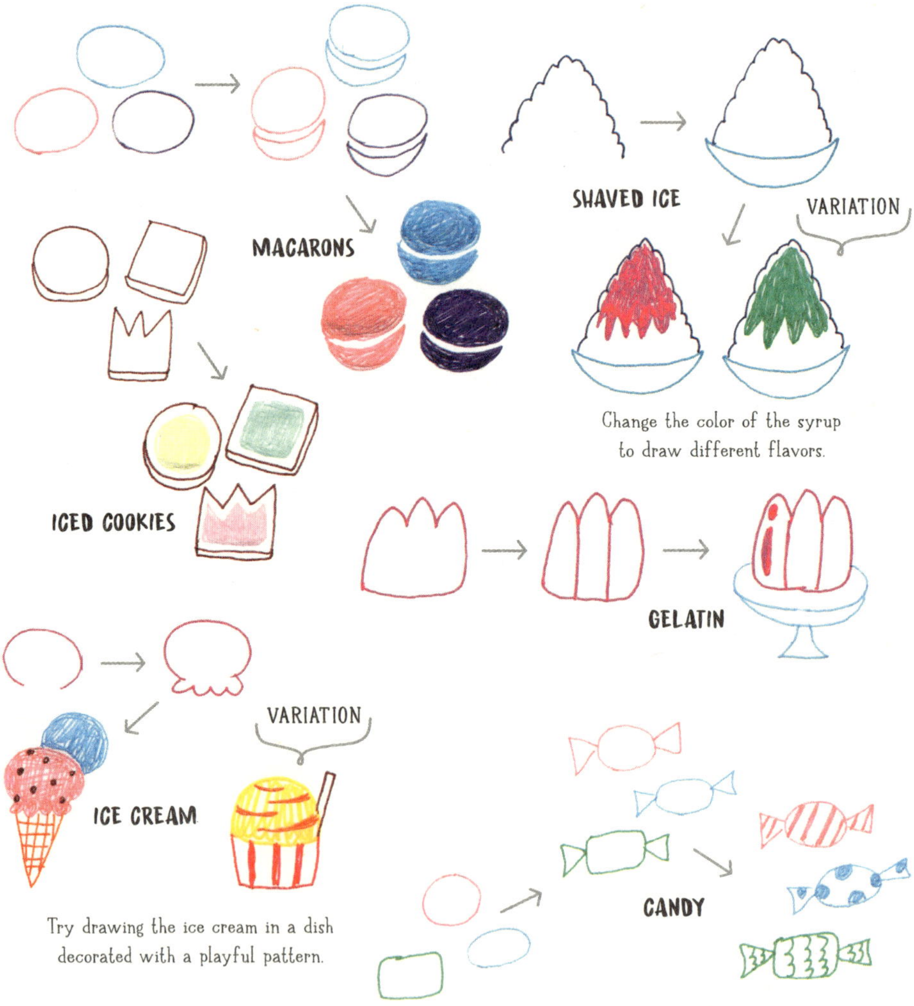

MACARONS

SHAVED ICE

VARIATION

Change the color of the syrup to draw different flavors.

ICED COOKIES

GELATIN

VARIATION

ICE CREAM

Try drawing the ice cream in a dish decorated with a playful pattern.

CANDY

2 For desserts that are predominantly brown, incorporate color through the toppings, garnishes, and plates.

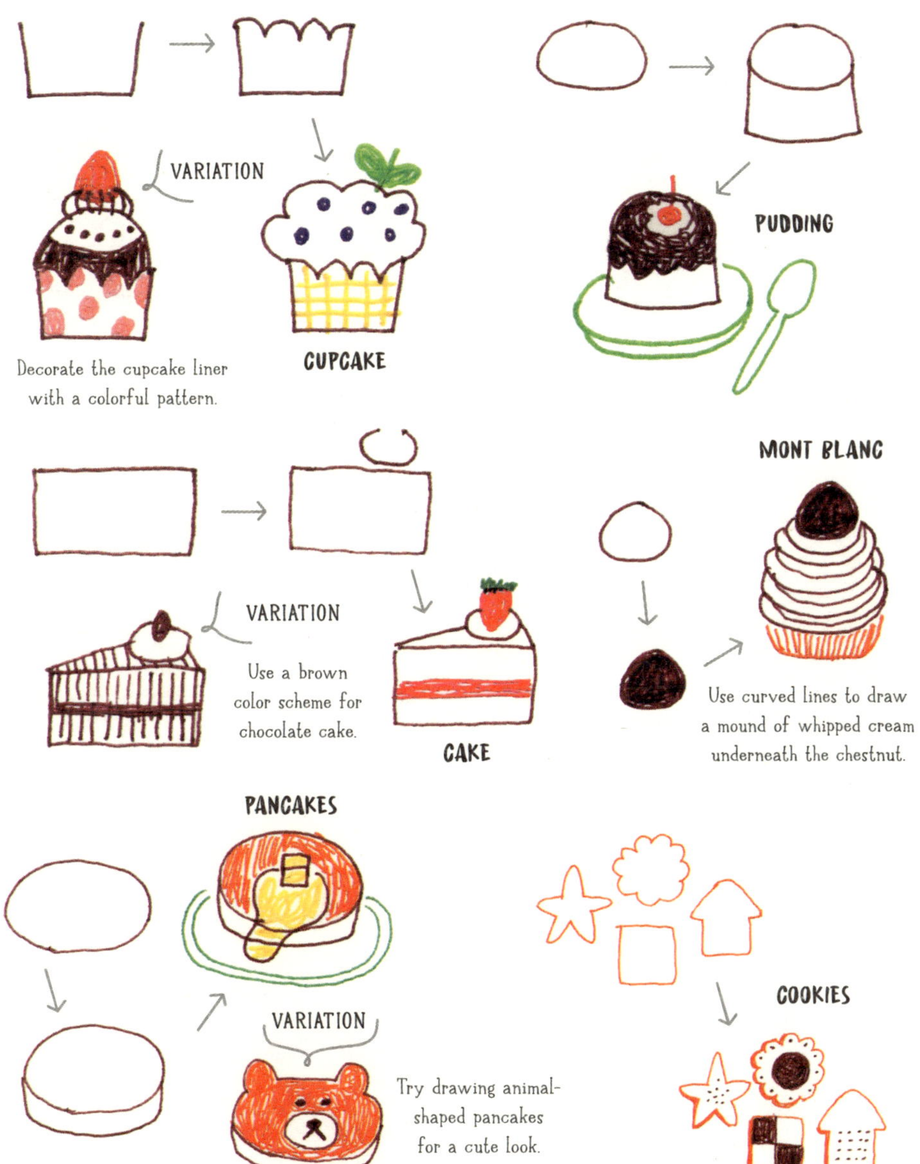

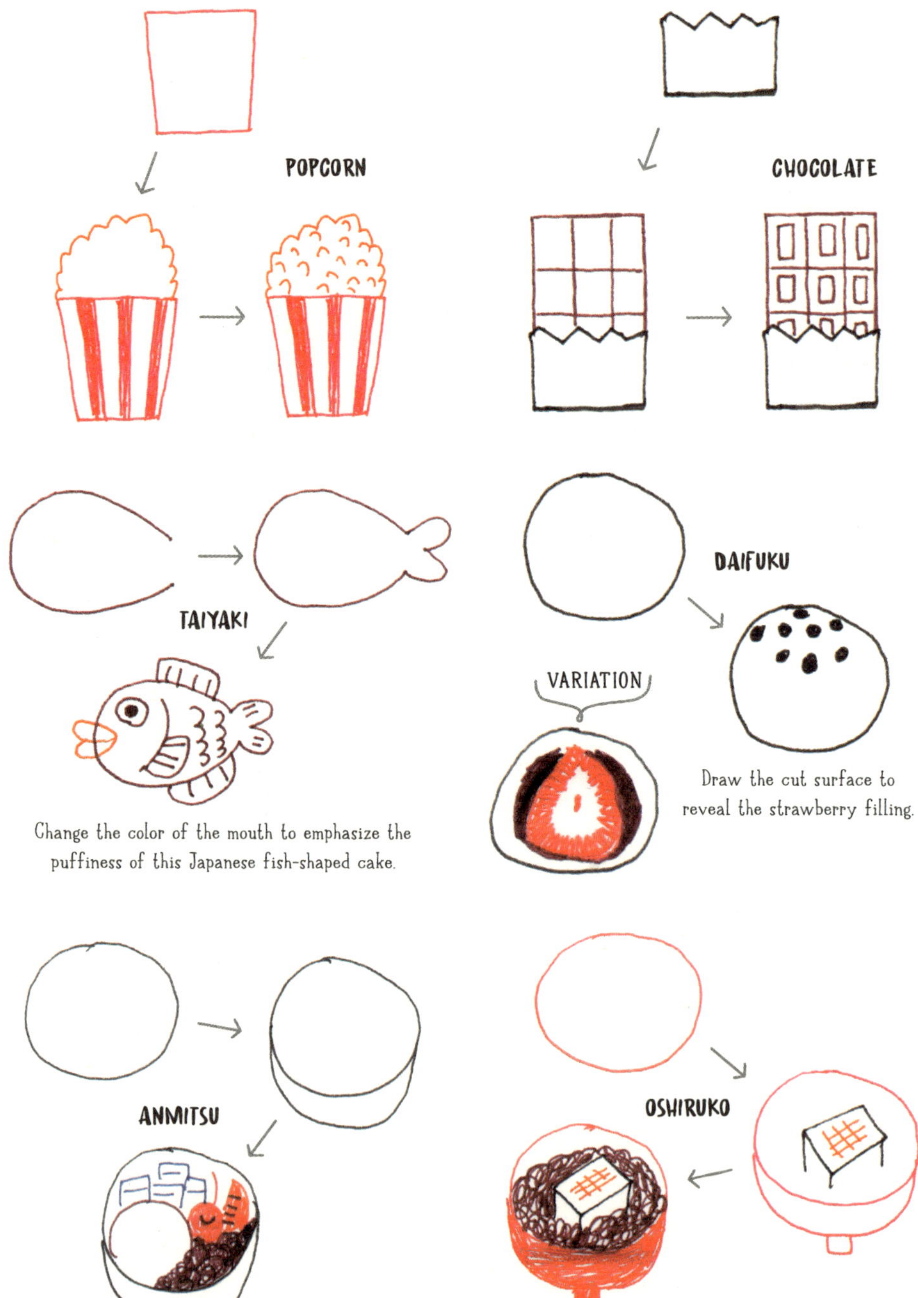

Change the color of the mouth to emphasize the puffiness of this Japanese fish-shaped cake.

Draw the cut surface to reveal the strawberry filling.

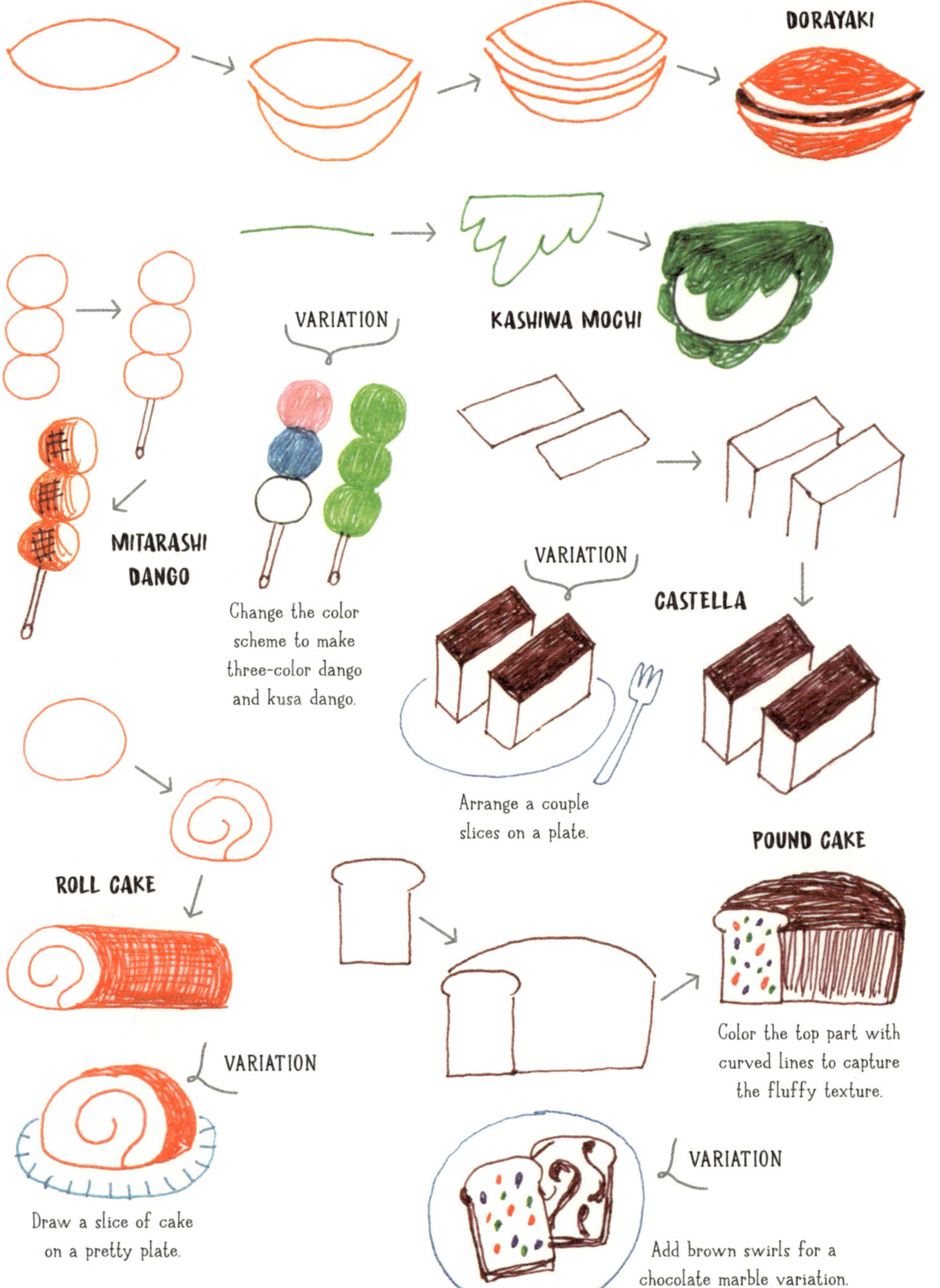
DORAYAKI
KASHIWA MOCHI
VARIATION
MITARASHI DANGO
Change the color scheme to make three-color dango and kusa dango.
VARIATION
CASTELLA
Arrange a couple slices on a plate.
ROLL CAKE
POUND CAKE
VARIATION
Draw a slice of cake on a pretty plate.
Color the top part with curved lines to capture the fluffy texture.
VARIATION
Add brown swirls for a chocolate marble variation.

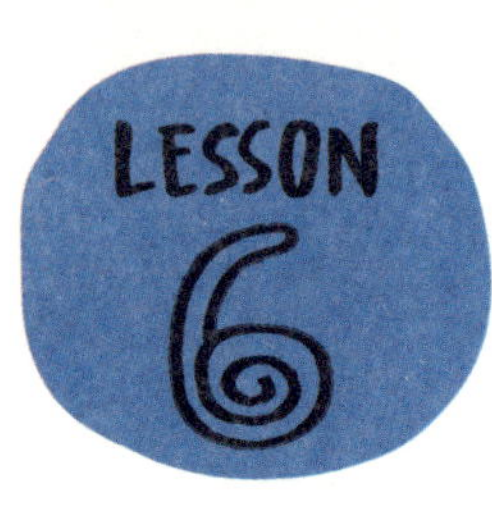

MEALS

It may seem difficult to draw food arranged on a plate or in a bowl, but once you understand the process, you'll be able to draw well-balanced illustrations. Make sure to incorporate details to help identify the food.

1 Start by drawing the food, then add the plate.

OMELET

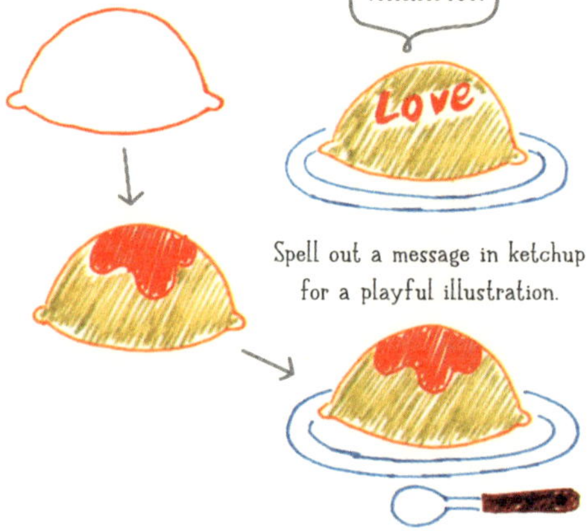

VARIATION

Love

Spell out a message in ketchup for a playful illustration.

CHEESEBURGER

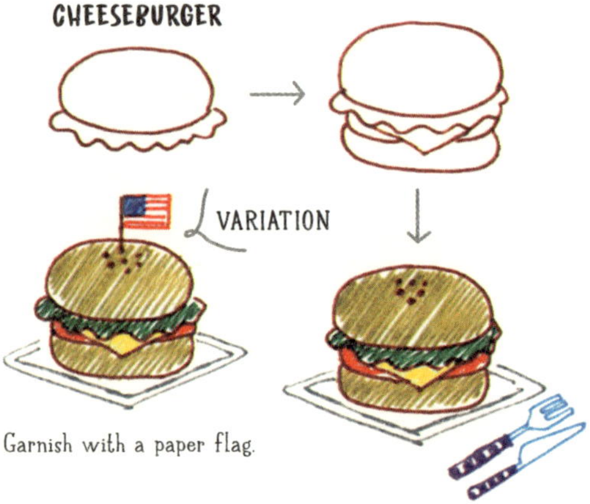

VARIATION

Garnish with a paper flag.

TEMPURA

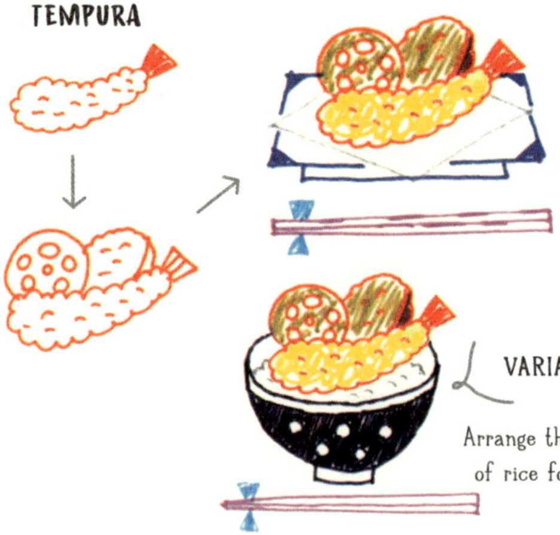

VARIATION

Arrange the tempura on a bed of rice for a complete meal.

RICE

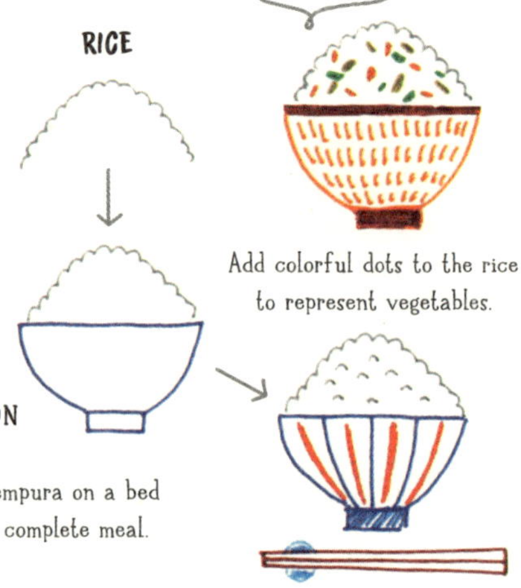

VARIATION

Add colorful dots to the rice to represent vegetables.

2 You can also start by drawing the plate or dish, and then fill in with food.

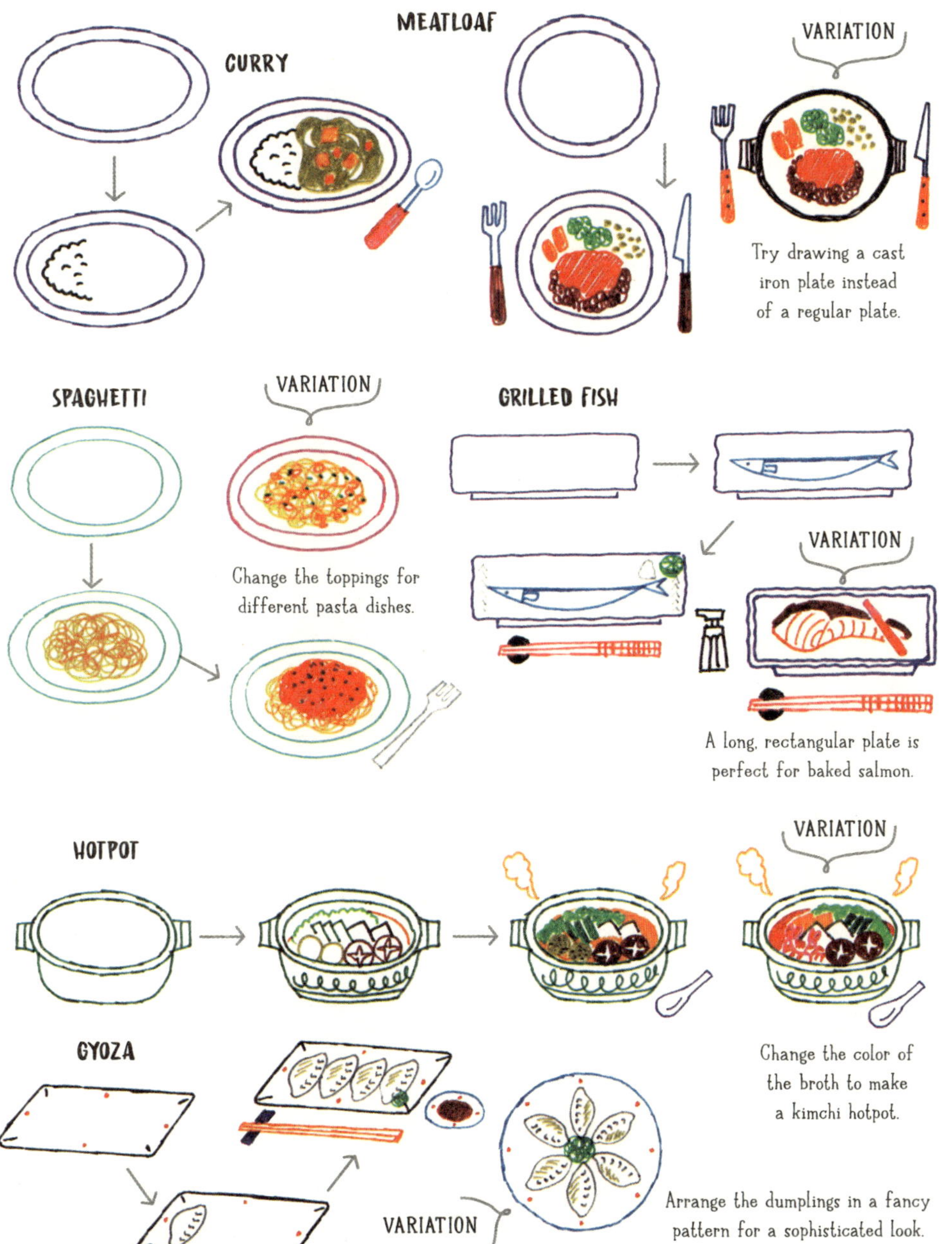

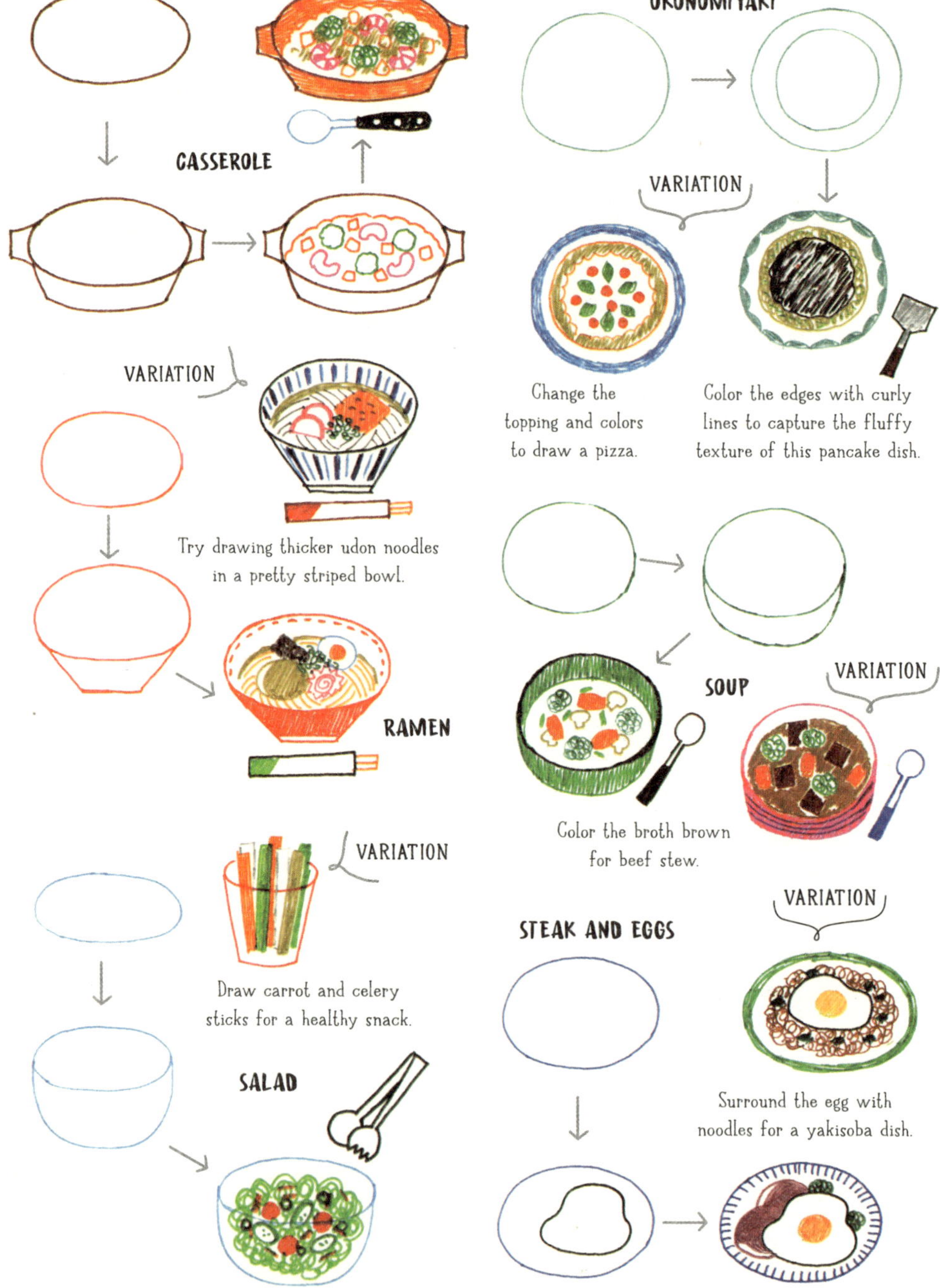
CASSEROLE
VARIATION
Try drawing thicker udon noodles in a pretty striped bowl.
RAMEN
VARIATION
Draw carrot and celery sticks for a healthy snack.
SALAD
OKONOMIYAKI
VARIATION
Change the topping and colors to draw a pizza.
Color the edges with curly lines to capture the fluffy texture of this pancake dish.
SOUP
VARIATION
Color the broth brown for beef stew.
STEAK AND EGGS
VARIATION
Surround the egg with noodles for a yakisoba dish.

VARIATION

RECIPE ILLUSTRATIONS

Use the illustrations on pages 130–132 to illustrate recipes, make meal plans, or create menus.

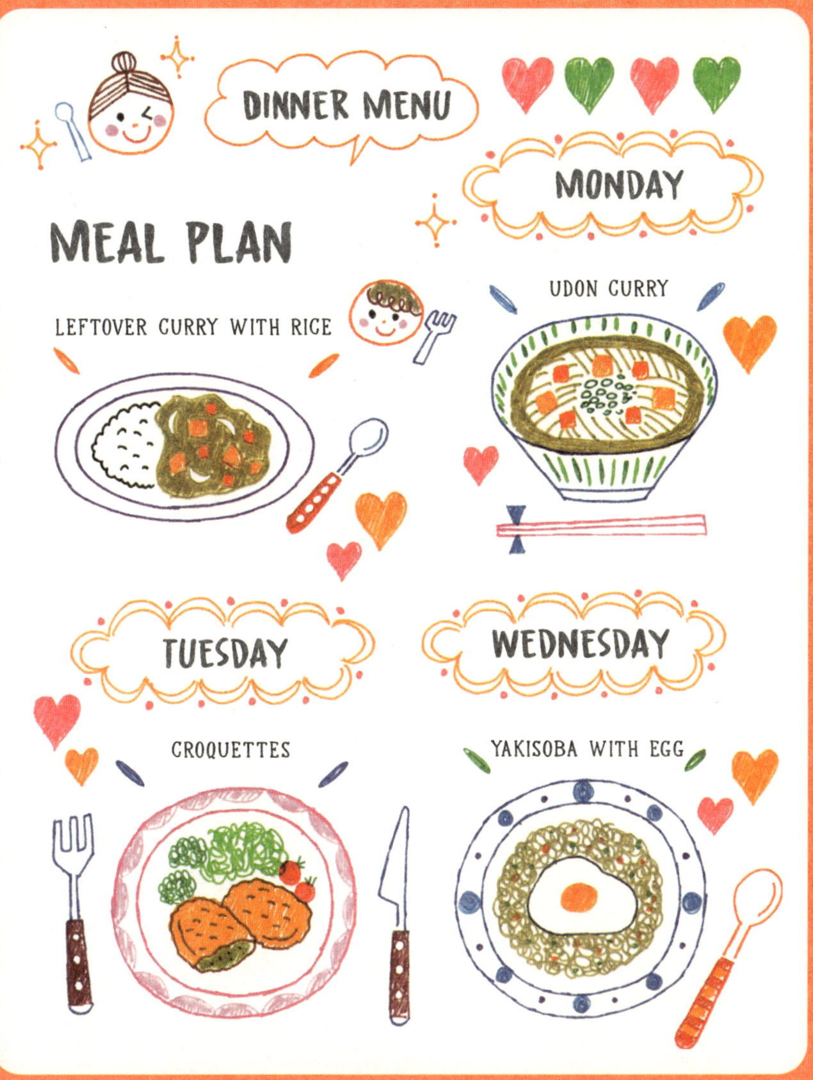

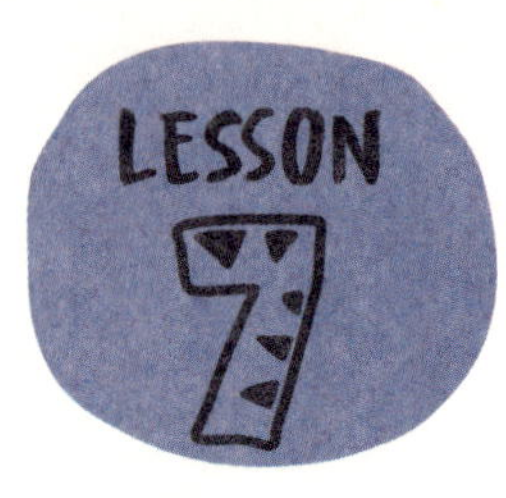

DRINKS

The key to drawing recognizable drinks is mastering the shape of the glass or cup. You can also use color to help make the beverage identifiable.

1 You can use different colors to create variation, even when the drink is served in the same glass or cup.

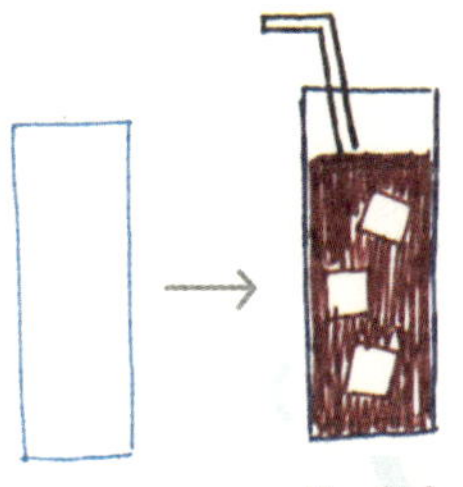

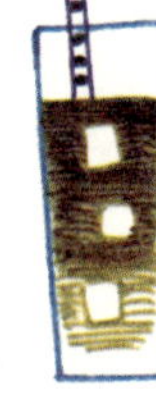

Use dark brown for iced coffee.

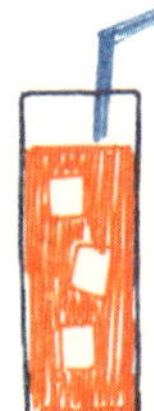

Use different shades of brown for an iced latte.

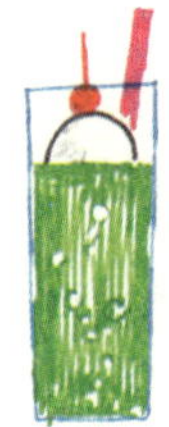

Of course orange is used for orange juice.

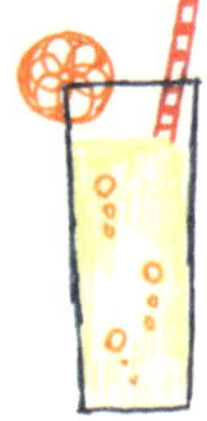

Add a scoop of ice cream for an ice cream soda.

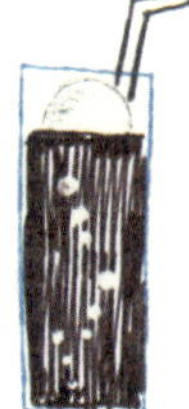

Garnish a glass of lemonade with a slice of lemon.

Add a scoop of vanilla on top of brown soda for a root beer float.

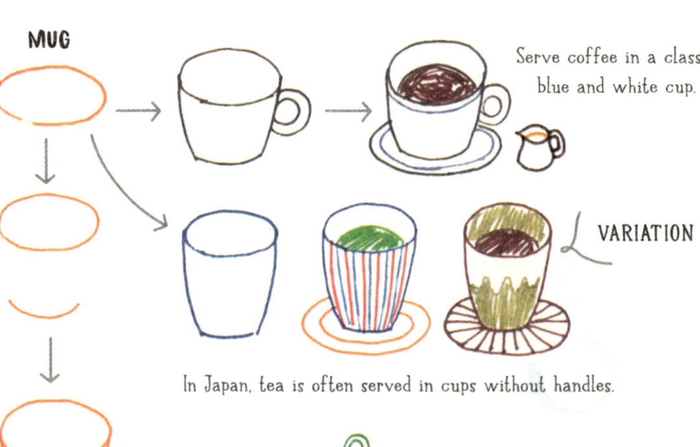

Serve coffee in a classic blue and white cup.

In Japan, tea is often served in cups without handles.

Add a teapot to complete the set.

VARIATION

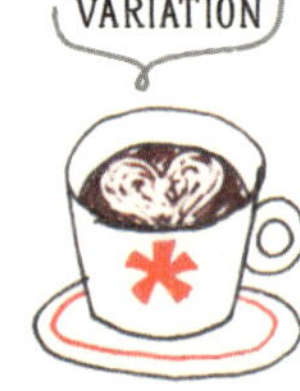

Leave a bit of white space for fancy latte art!

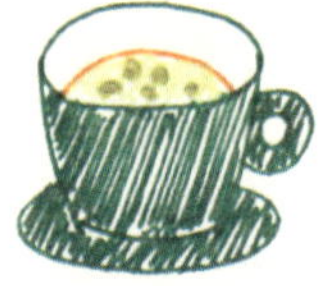

Color the liquid yellow and add dots for corn chowder served in a mug.

2 Alcoholic beverages are often served in specific glasses.

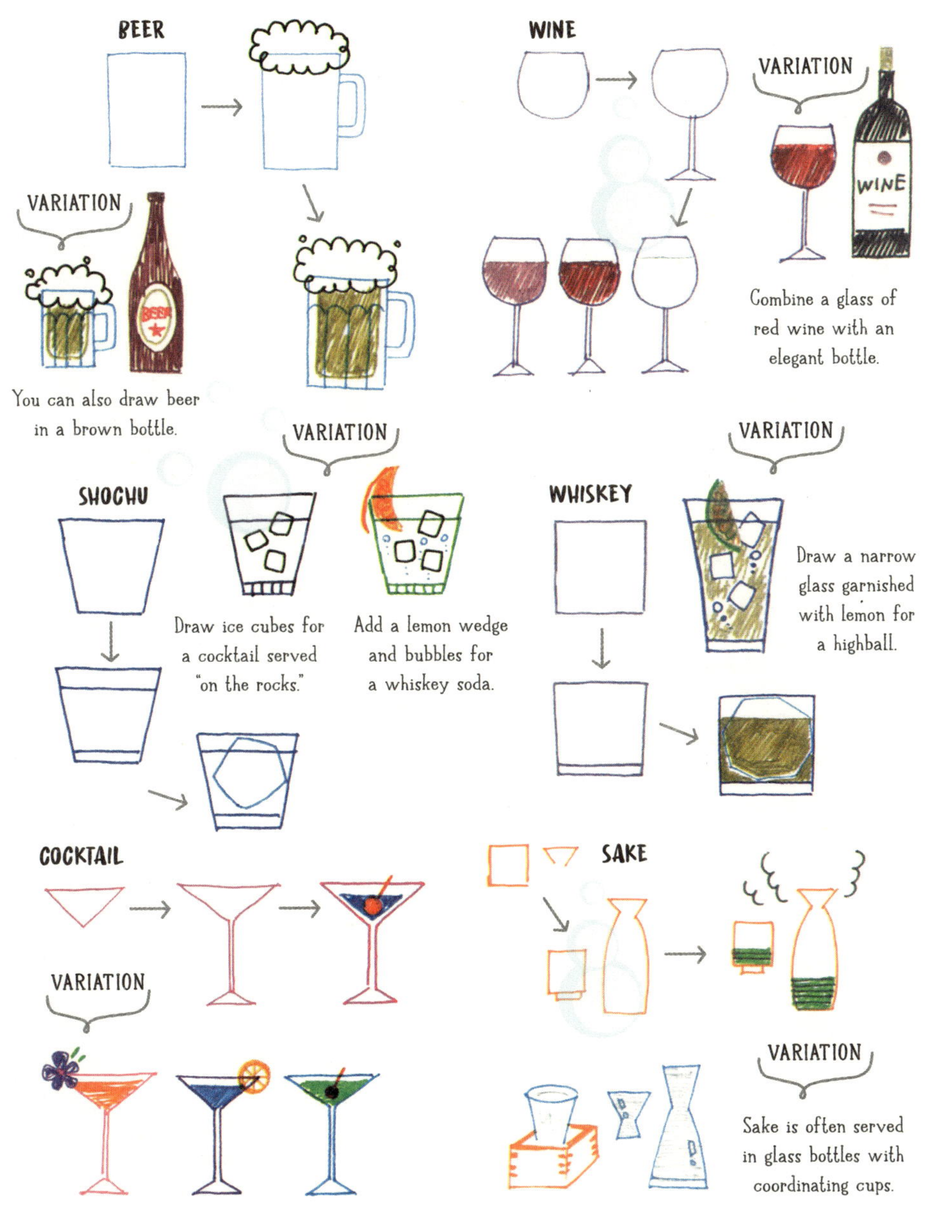

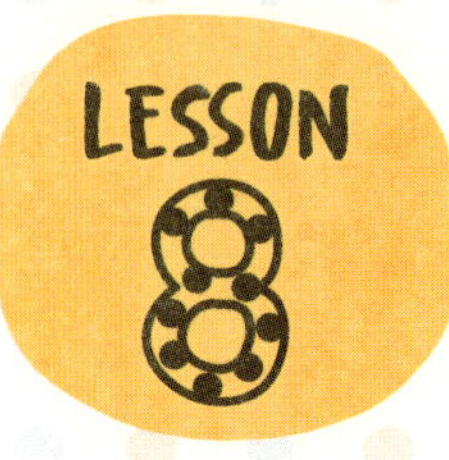

DISHES & KITCHENWARE

Incorporate bright colors and fun patterns when drawing dishes and other kitchenware.

PLATES

Start with a circle.

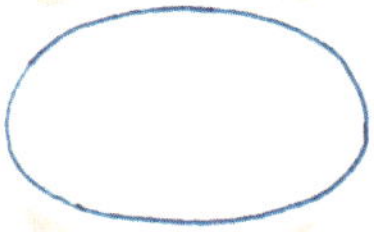

View from above

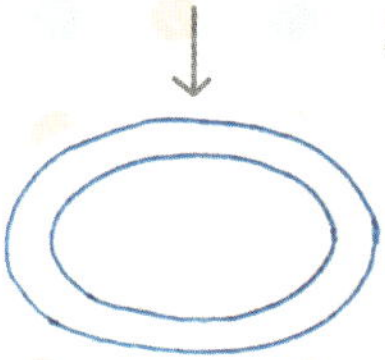

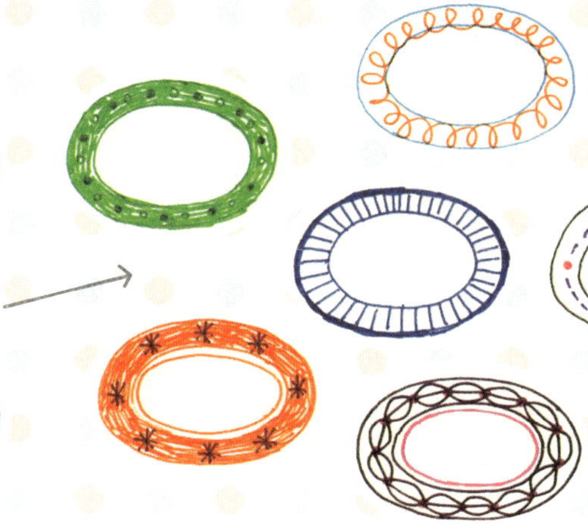

Add a pattern along the edge of the plates.

Start with two lines.

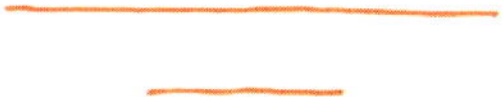

View from the side

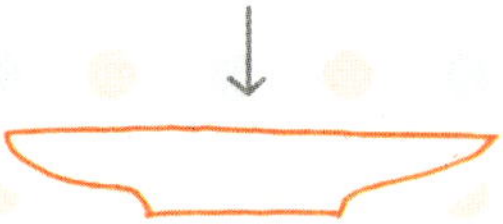

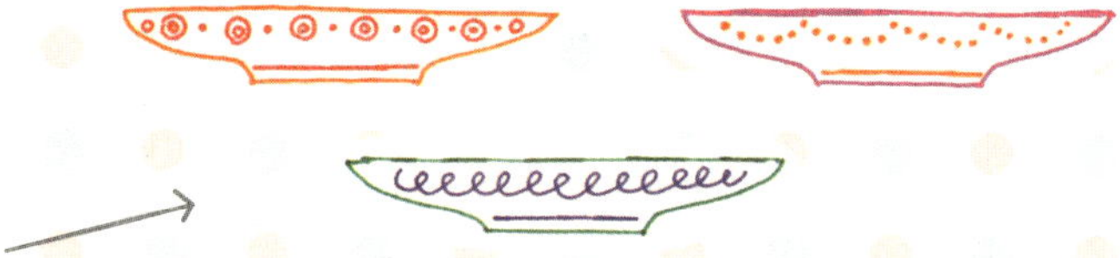

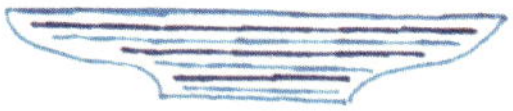

Dotted lines, curly lines, and straight lines work well for decorating the small surface area of the plates.

BOWL

Start with a semicircle.

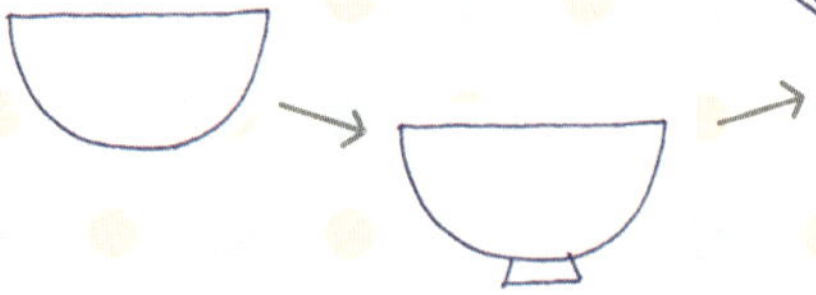

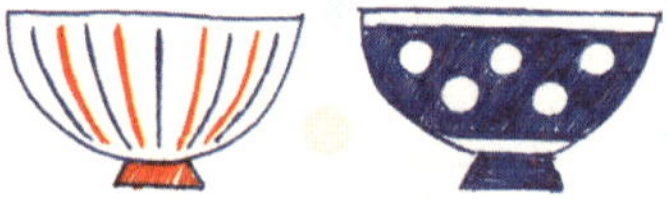

Use a blue and white pattern for a traditional Japanese rice bowl.

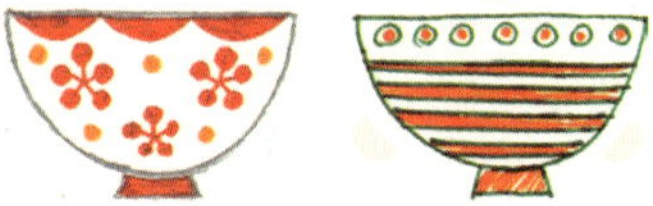

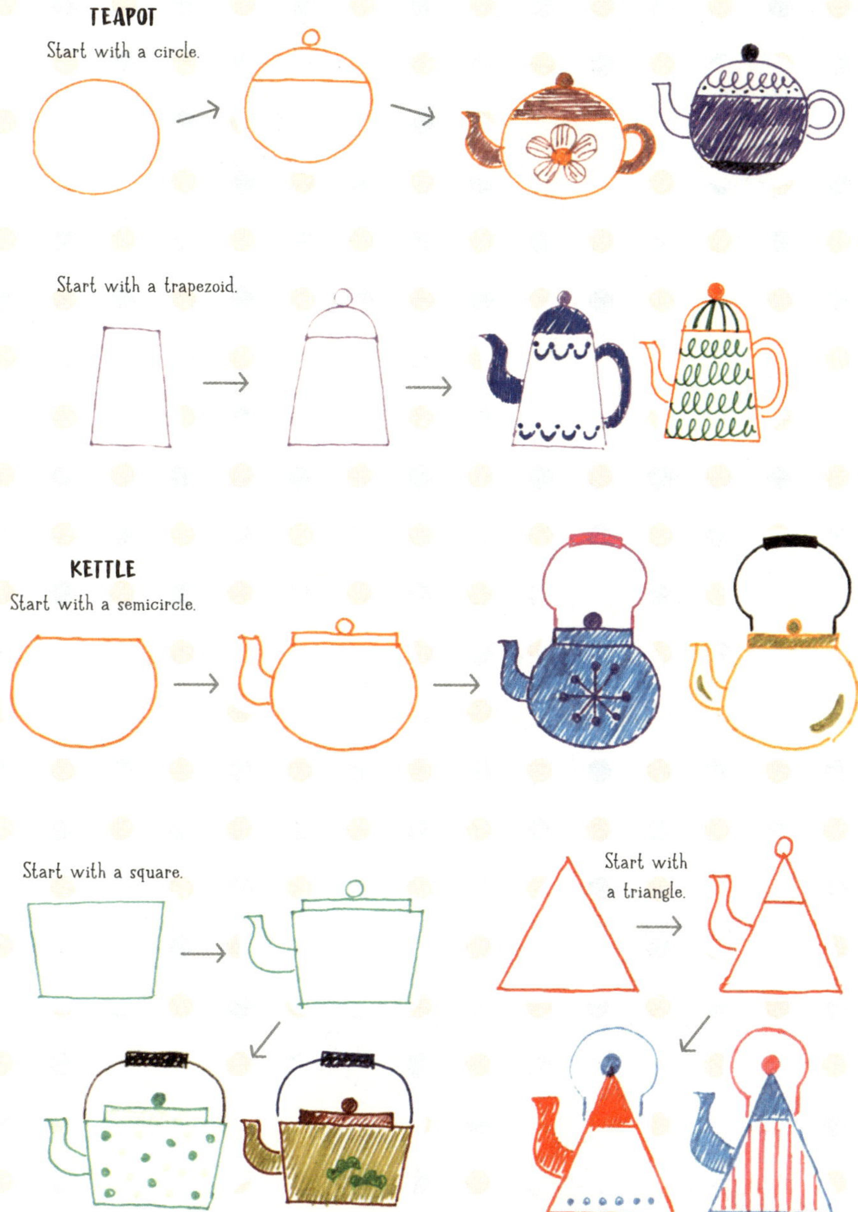

A retro pattern is perfect for a tea kettle.

For a modern-shaped kettle, finish with stripes or dots.

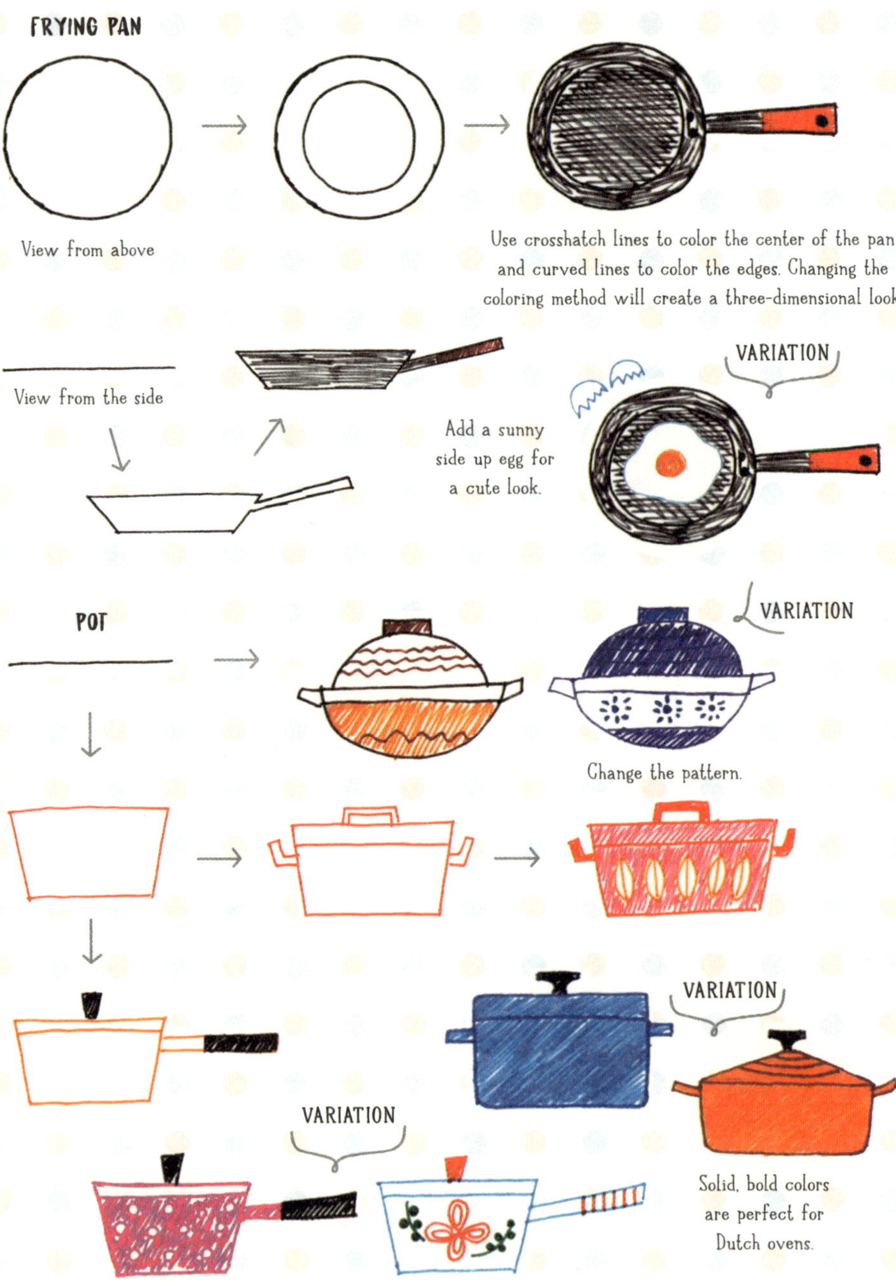
FRYING PAN
View from above
Use crosshatch lines to color the center of the pan and curved lines to color the edges. Changing the coloring method will create a three-dimensional look.
View from the side
VARIATION
Add a sunny side up egg for a cute look.
POT
VARIATION
Change the pattern.
VARIATION
VARIATION
Solid, bold colors are perfect for Dutch ovens.
Use different patterns or color schemes to create different styles of kitchenware.

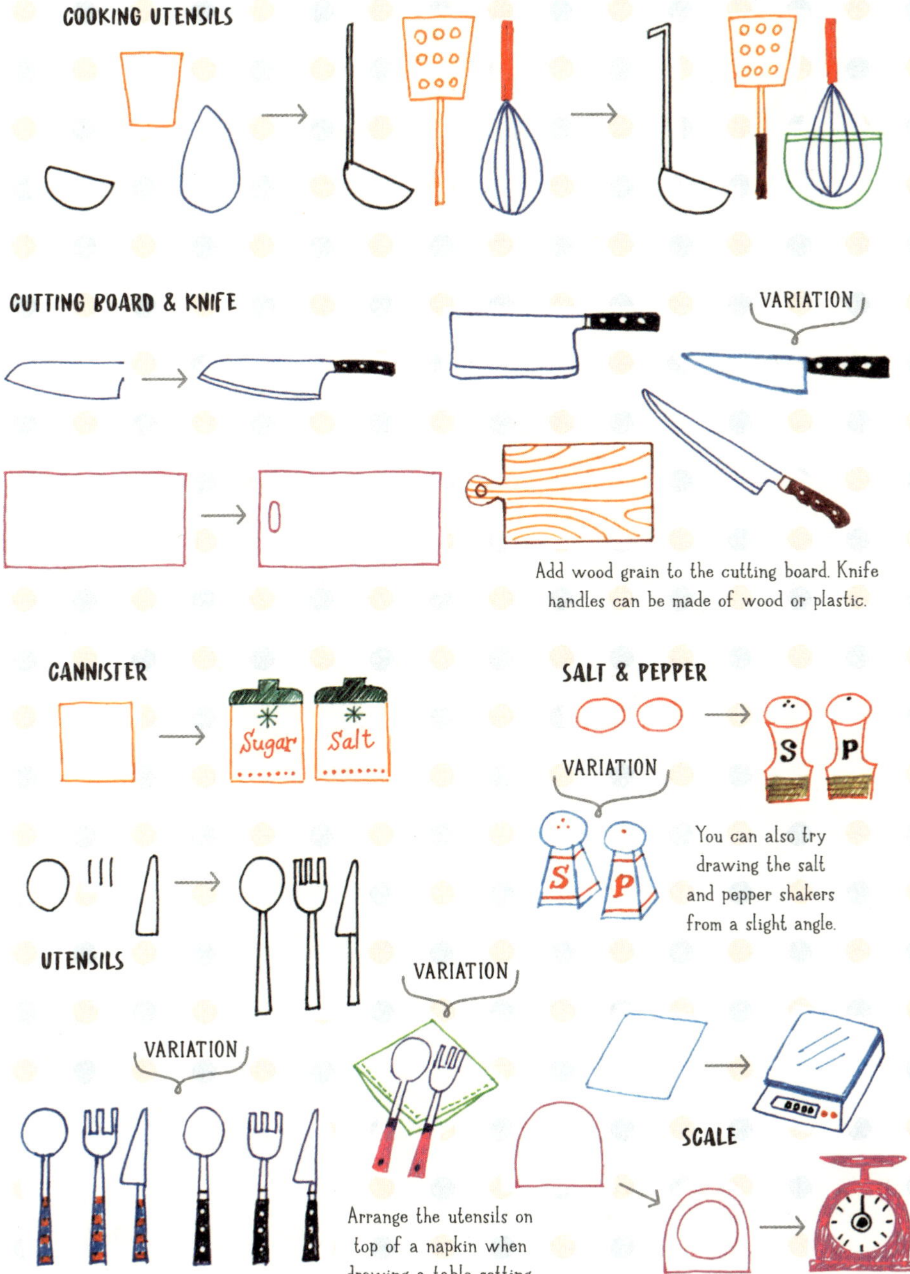

Add wood grain to the cutting board. Knife handles can be made of wood or plastic.

You can also try drawing the salt and pepper shakers from a slight angle.

Arrange the utensils on top of a napkin when drawing a table setting.

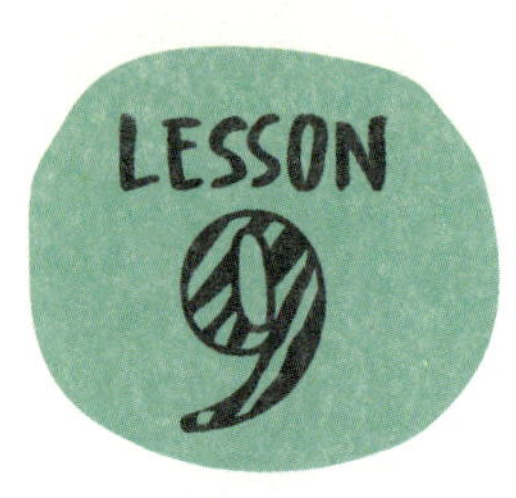

HOUSEHOLD OBJECTS

You see these objects every day, but you can draw them? Start with simple shapes, then add variation with colors and patterns.

SEWING THREAD

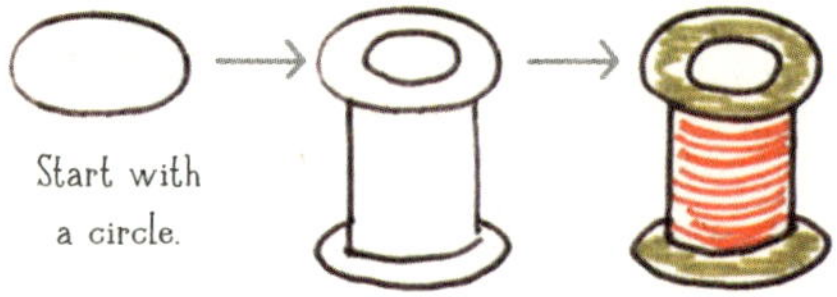

Start with a circle.

ROUND BUTTON

Start with a circle.

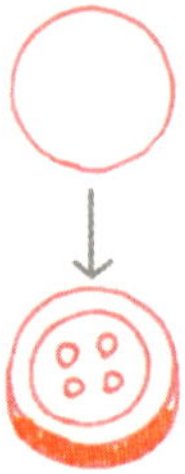

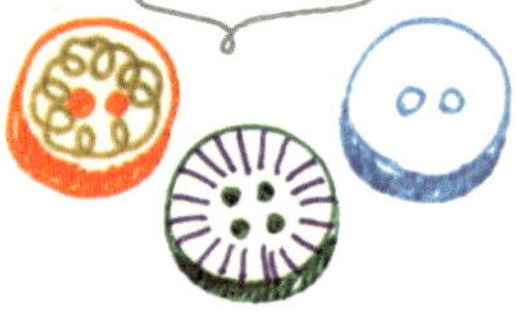

SHANK BUTTON

Start with a semicircle.

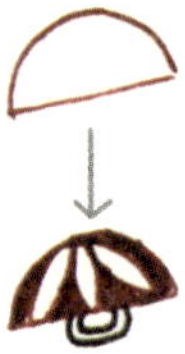

BOBBIN THREAD

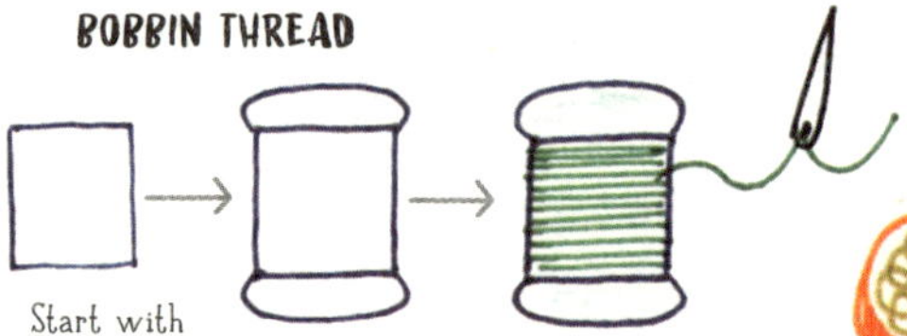

Start with a square.

VARIATION

SQUARE BUTTON

Start with a square.

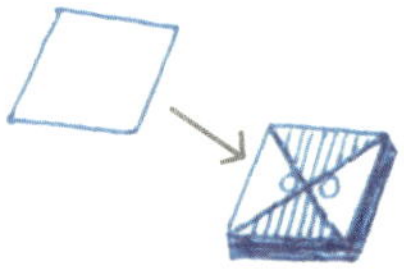

EMBROIDERY FLOSS

Start with a rectangle.

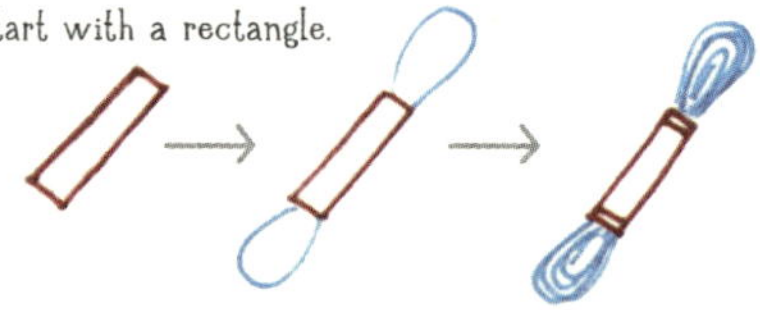

IRON

Start with a triangle.

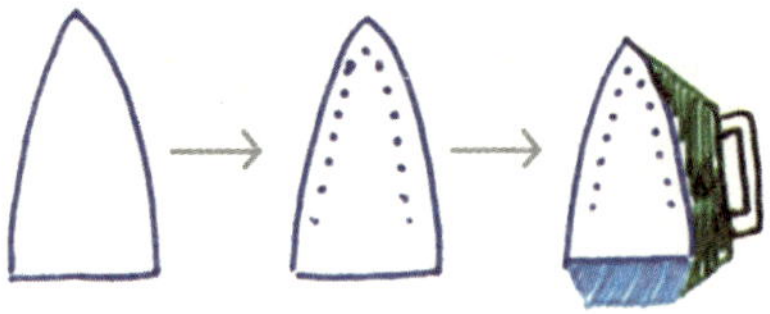

THREAD SCISSORS

Start with a semicircle.

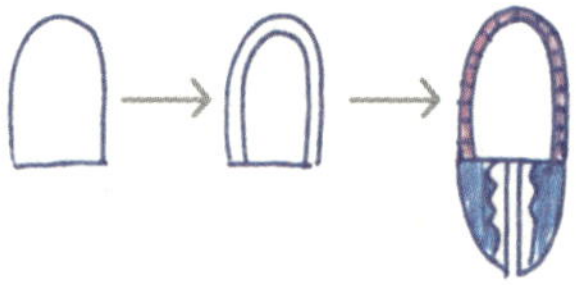

FABRIC SCISSORS

Start with a semicircle.

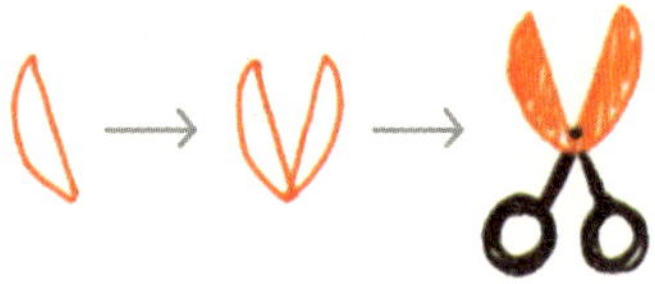

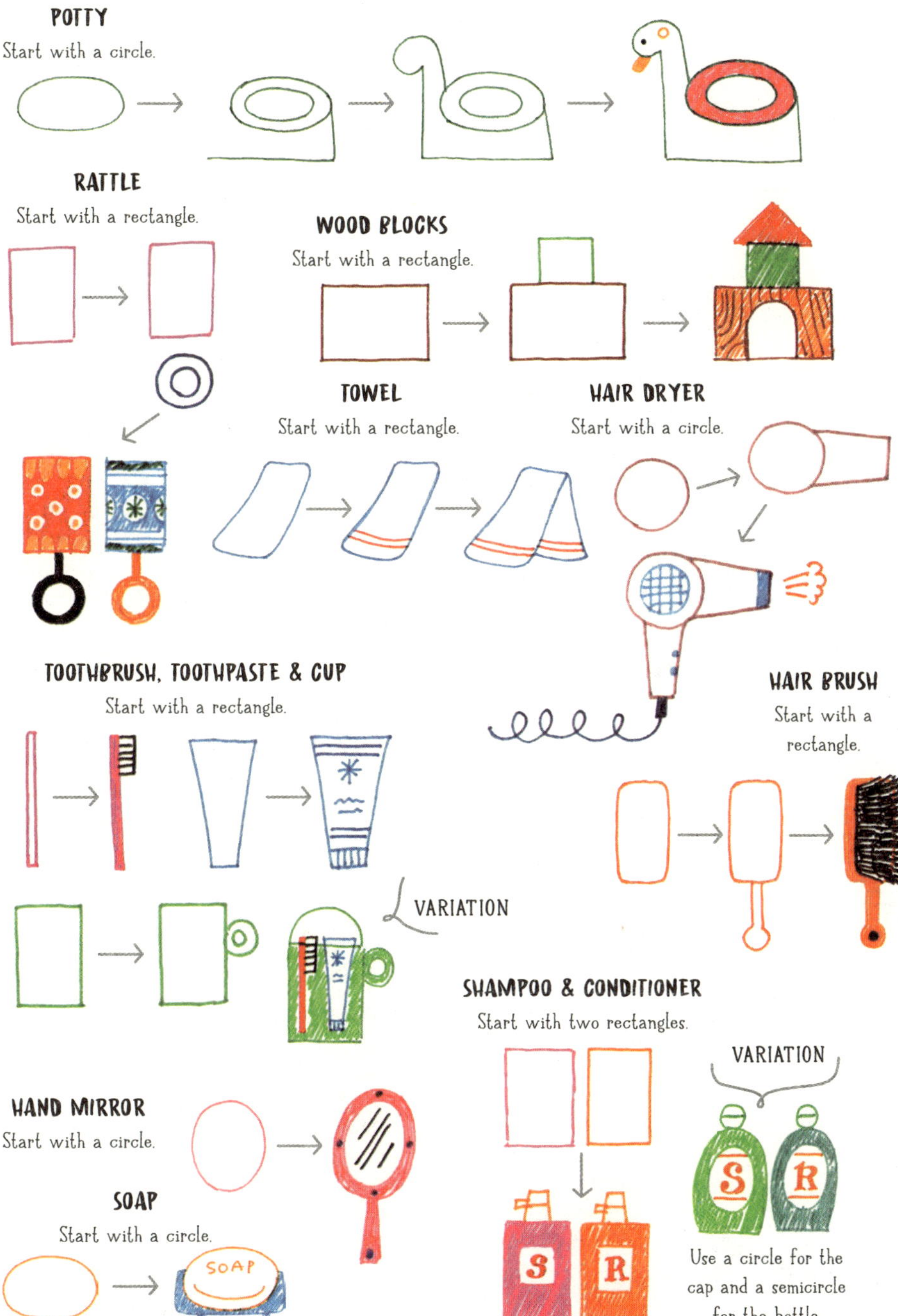
POTTY
Start with a circle.
RATTLE
Start with a rectangle.
WOOD BLOCKS
Start with a rectangle.
TOWEL
Start with a rectangle.
HAIR DRYER
Start with a circle.
TOOTHBRUSH, TOOTHPASTE & CUP
Start with a rectangle.
VARIATION
HAIR BRUSH
Start with a rectangle.
SHAMPOO & CONDITIONER
Start with two rectangles.
VARIATION
S
R
S
R
Use a circle for the cap and a semicircle for the bottle.
HAND MIRROR
Start with a circle.
SOAP
Start with a circle.
SOAP

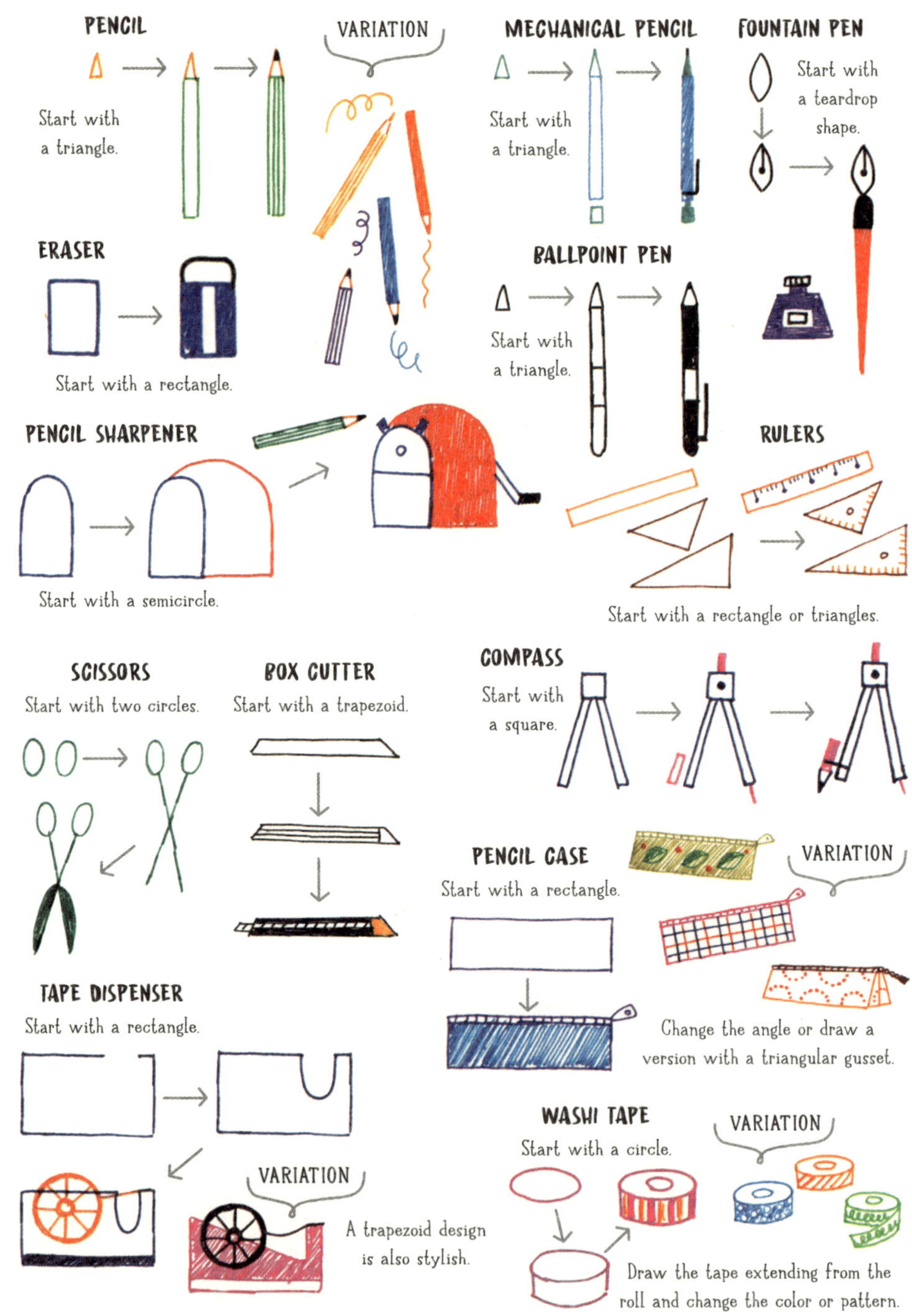
PENCIL
Start with a triangle.
VARIATION
MECHANICAL PENCIL
Start with a triangle.
FOUNTAIN PEN
Start with a teardrop shape.
ERASER
Start with a rectangle.
BALLPOINT PEN
Start with a triangle.
PENCIL SHARPENER
Start with a semicircle.
RULERS
Start with a rectangle or triangles.
SCISSORS
Start with two circles.
BOX CUTTER
Start with a trapezoid.
COMPASS
Start with a square.
PENCIL CASE
Start with a rectangle.
VARIATION
Change the angle or draw a version with a triangular gusset.
TAPE DISPENSER
Start with a rectangle.
VARIATION
A trapezoid design is also stylish.
WASHI TAPE
Start with a circle.
VARIATION
Draw the tape extending from the roll and change the color or pattern.

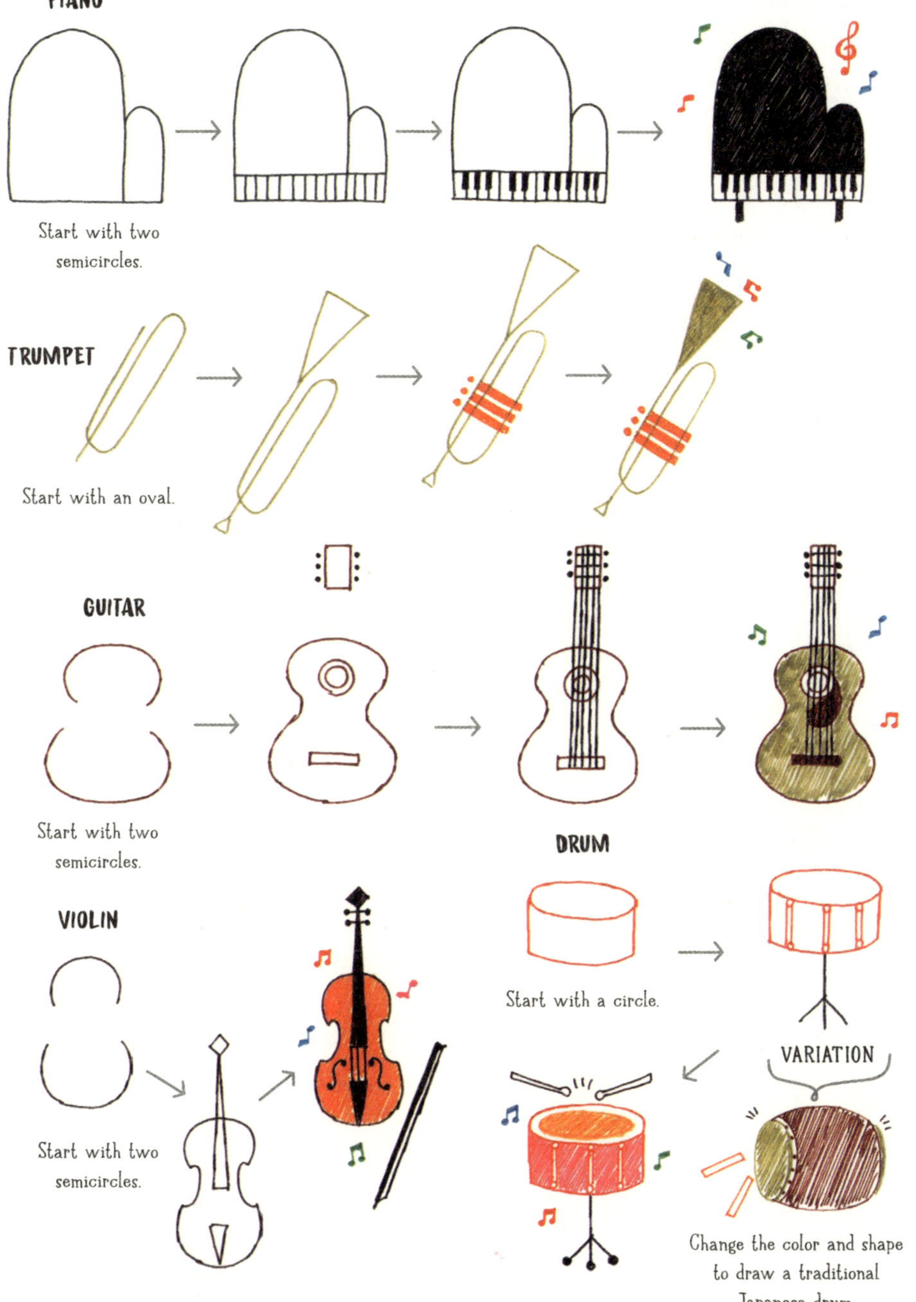
PIANO
Start with two semicircles.
TRUMPET
Start with an oval.
GUITAR
Start with two semicircles.
DRUM
Start with a circle.
VIOLIN
Start with two semicircles.
VARIATION
Change the color and shape to draw a traditional Japanese drum.

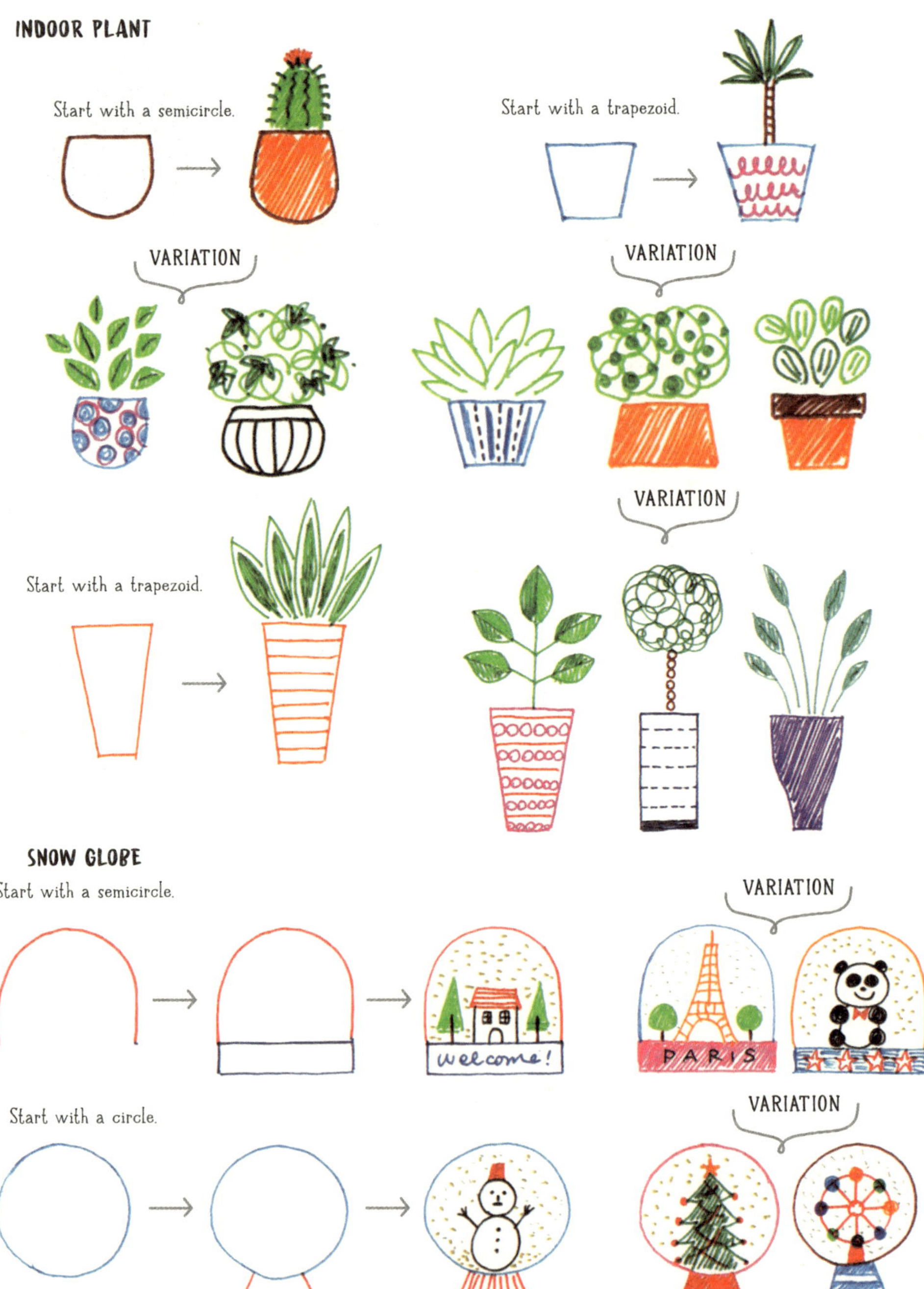
INDOOR PLANT
Start with a semicircle.
Start with a trapezoid.
VARIATION
VARIATION
VARIATION
Start with a trapezoid.
SNOW GLOBE
Start with a semicircle.
VARIATION
welcome!
PARIS
Start with a circle.
VARIATION

MATRYOSHKA DOLLS

Start with a gourd shape.

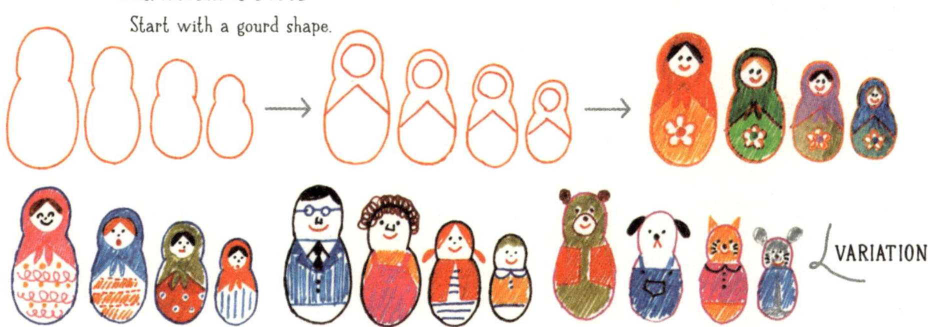

Change the clothing, face, or hairstyle to design your own original matryoshka dolls.

KOKESHI DOLL

Start with a circle.

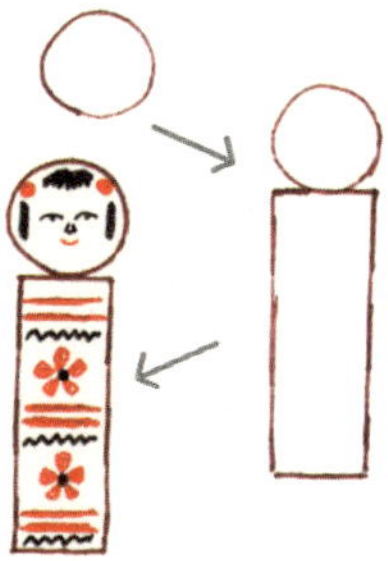

CANDLE

VARIATION

Start with a square.

Start with a circle.

Start with a trapezoid.

Start with a circle.

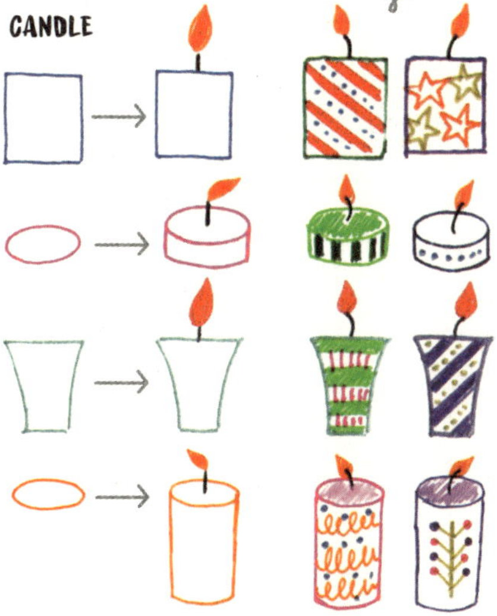

CLOCK

Start with a circle.

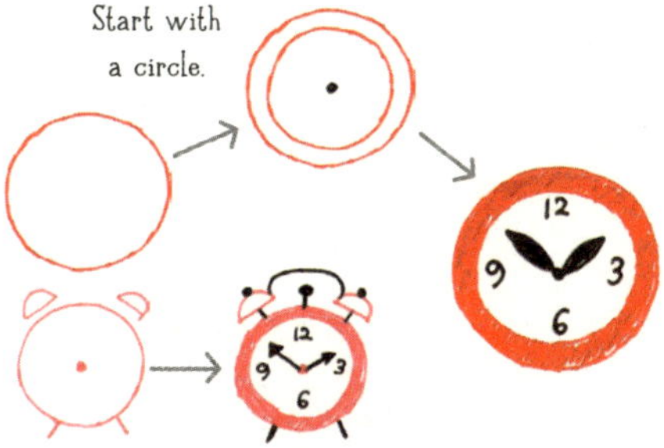

Start with a square.

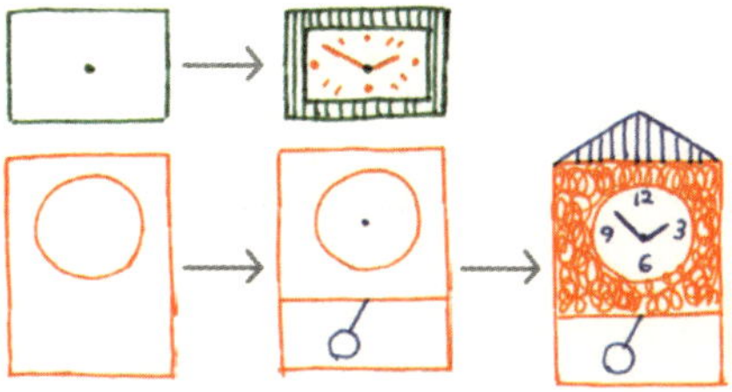

Start with a semicircle.

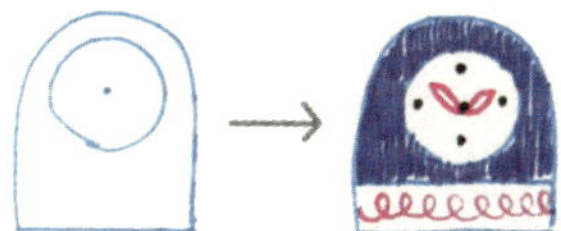

Start with a long, thin oval.

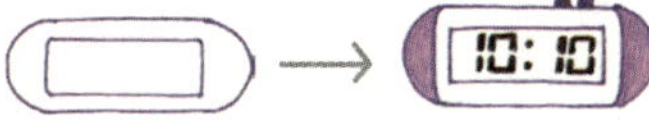

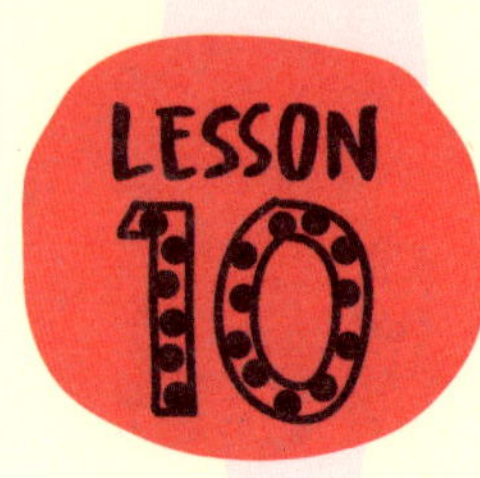

FURNITURE

Use simple shapes to draw furniture, such as sofas, tables, and beds. Adding details like fabric patterns and texture can create cute illustrations.

SOFAS & CHAIRS

Use simple circles and ovals to draw the furniture, then add colorful patterns and textures.

SOFA

Start with two semicircles.

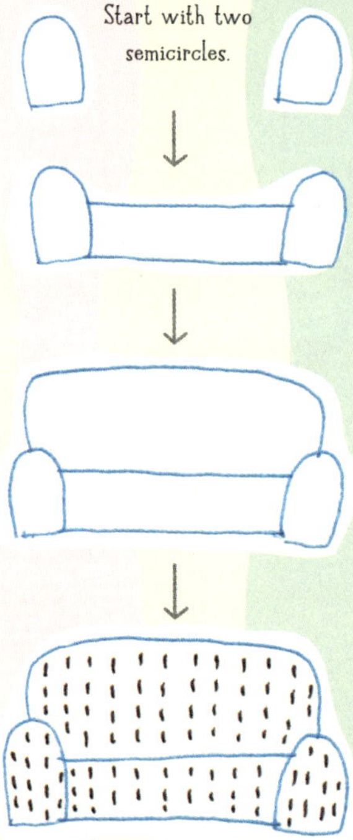

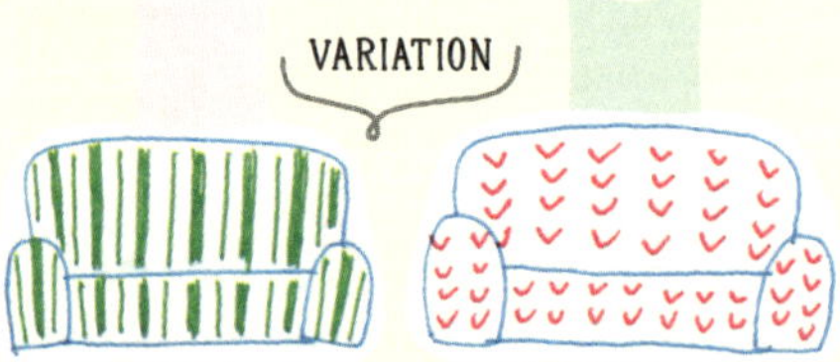

VARIATION

Try alternating thick and thin stripes or use a V-shaped pattern to add texture.

CHAIR

FRONT

Start with a circle.

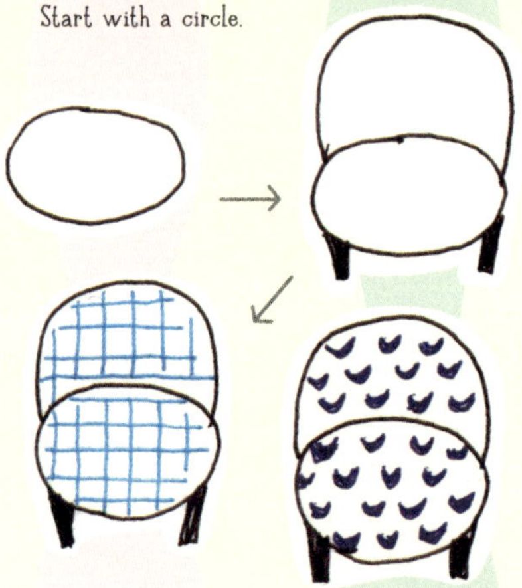

SIDE

Start with a semicircle.

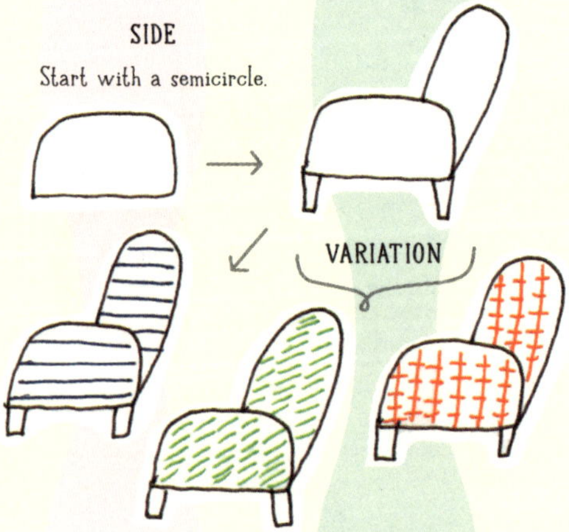

VARIATION

Change the angle of the lines to replicate the texture of different fabrics.

TABLES

Decide whether your table will have wood grain or will be covered with a cloth.

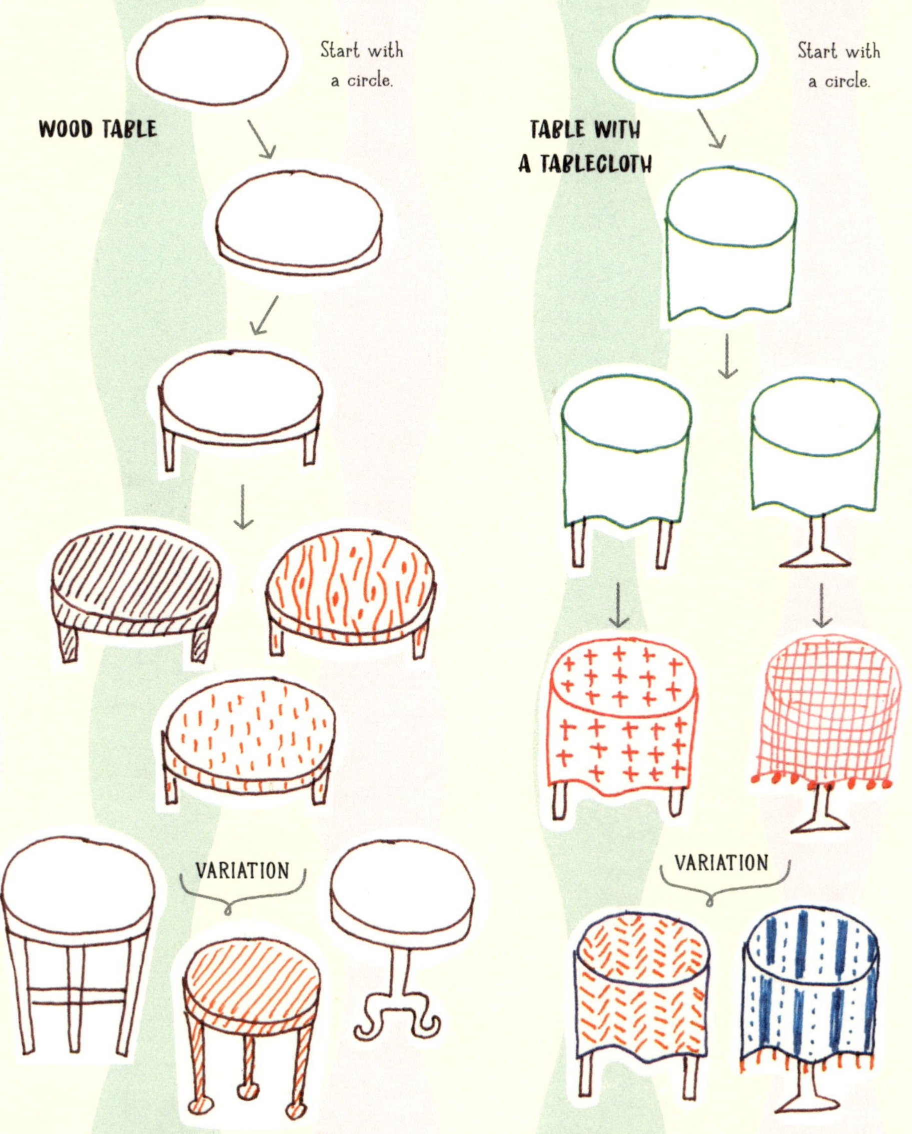

Change the style of the table by altering the design of the legs.

Use wavy lines to capture the flowy texture of the fabric. Embellish with fringe or pompoms for added style.

LAMPS

Try drawing both Japanese and Western style lamps.

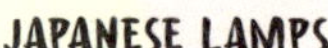

JAPANESE LAMPS

Start with a circle.

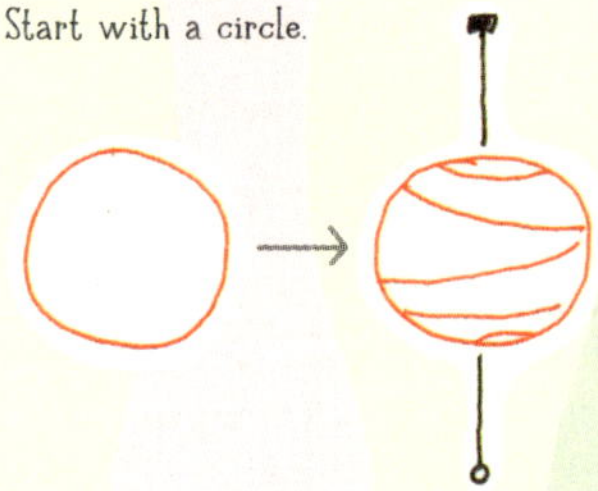

Start with a rectangle.

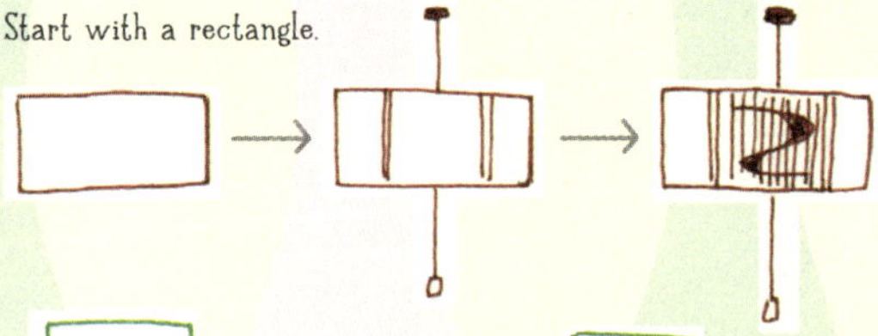

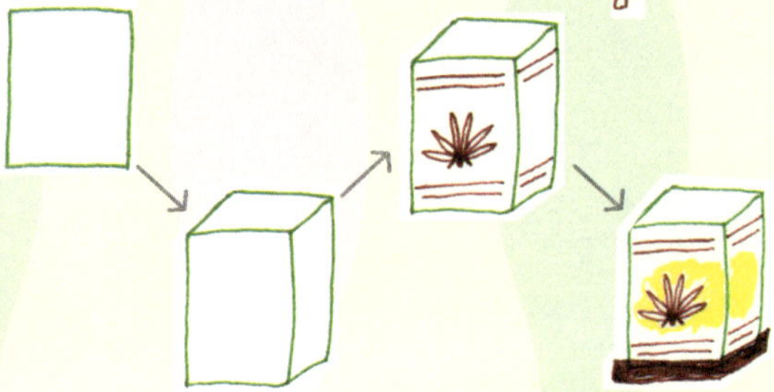

Start with a semicircle.

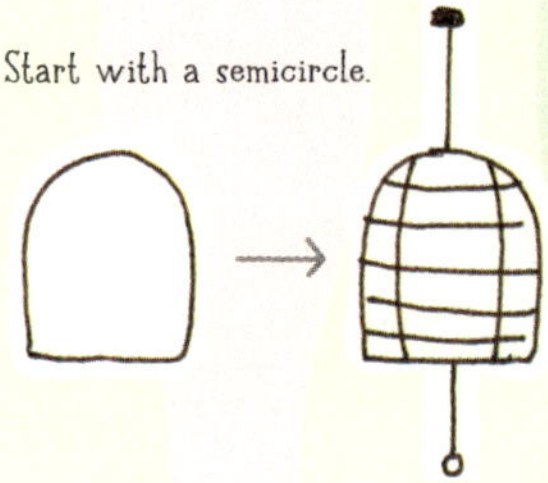

WESTERN LAMPS

Start with a circle.

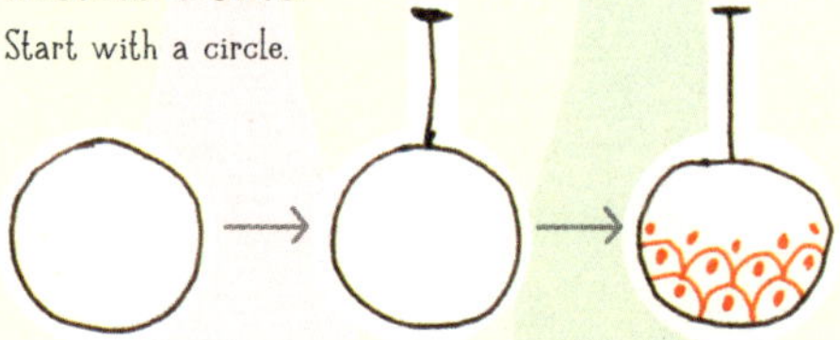

Start with a triangle.

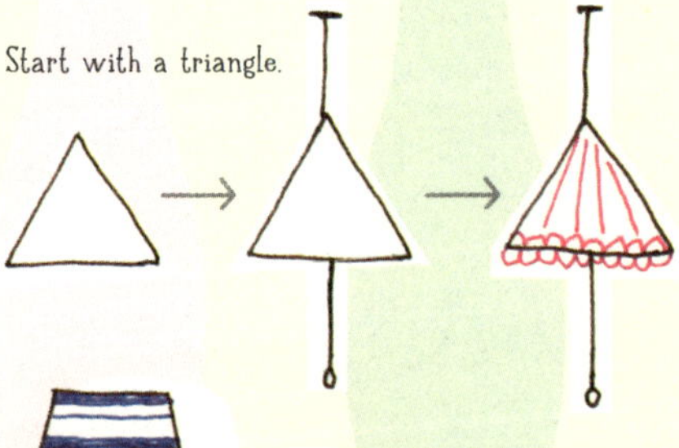

Start with a trapezoid.

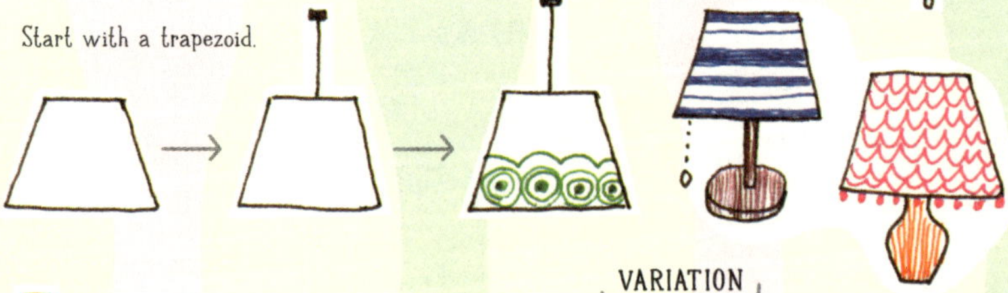

VARIATION

Add a base to the lampshade to transform into a table lamp.

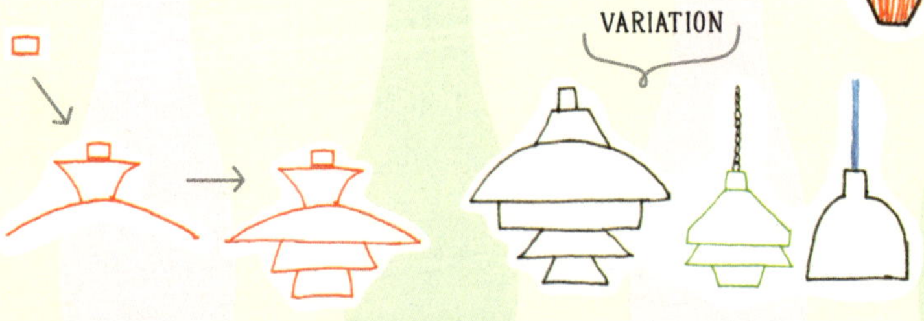

VARIATION

Draw a layered shade for a stylish Scandinavian-style pendant light.

BEDS

Start with a simple rectangle, then add a frame and linens for a comfortable bed.

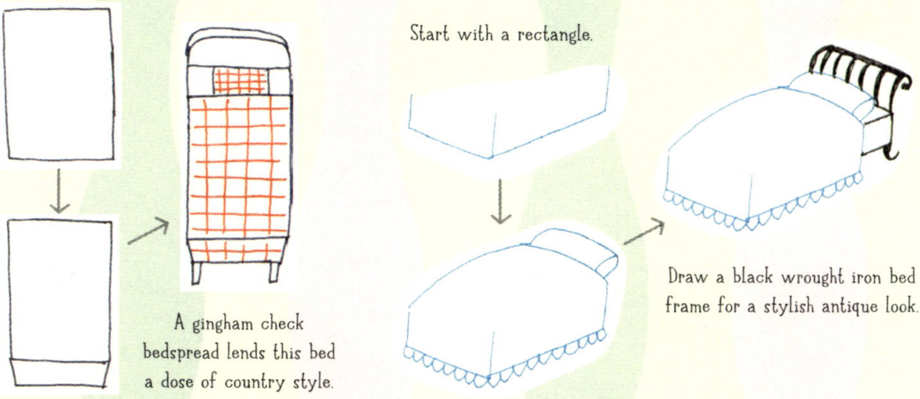

VASES

Draw patterns by combining simple shapes and lines, such as circles, triangles, curly lines, and jagged lines.

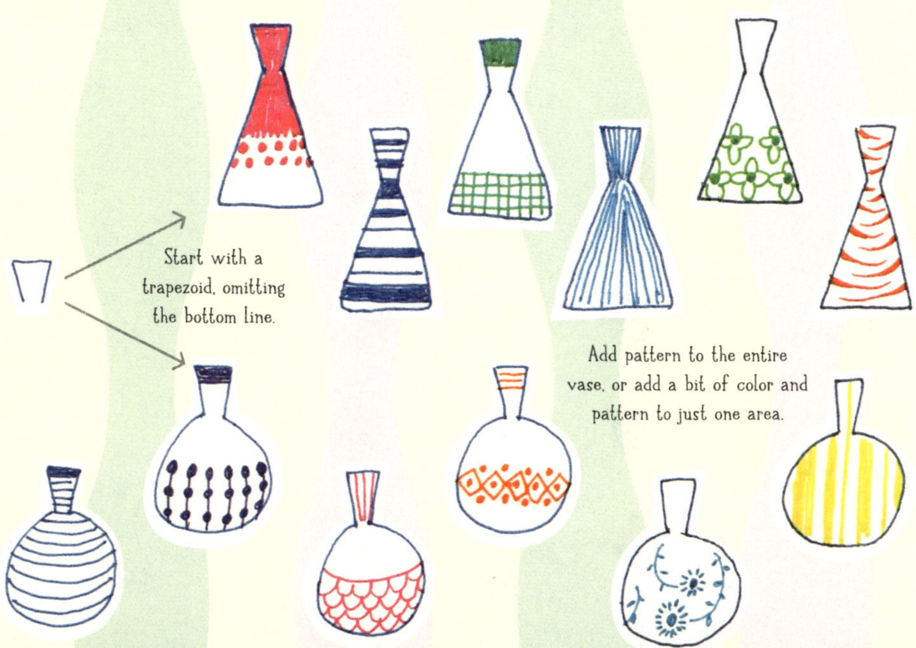

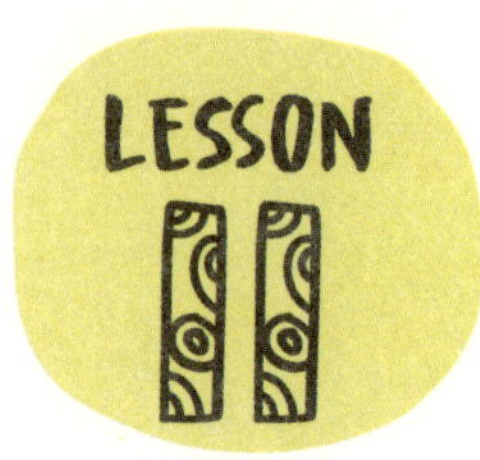

COSMETICS

Cosmetics are known for their pretty, feminine packaging. Use bright colors and chic patterns to decorate the bottles and tubes.

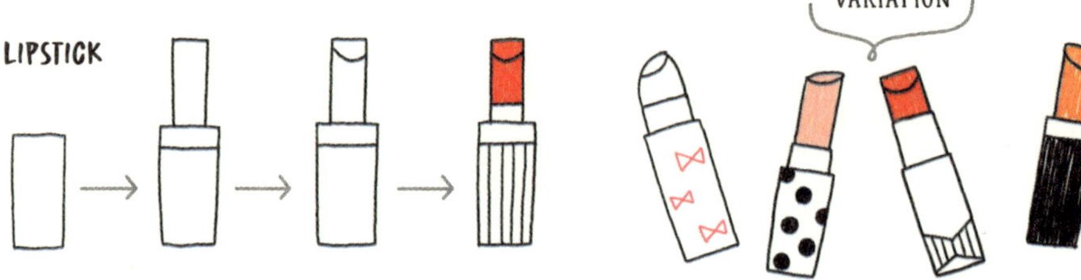

Draw several shades of lipstick, each with a tube design.

BRUSH

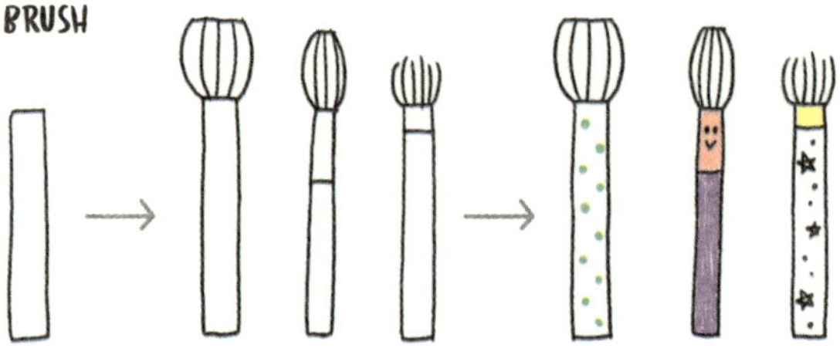

COMPACT PUFF

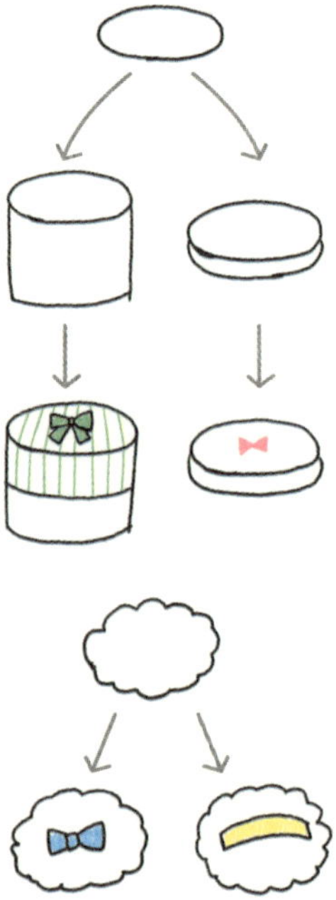

VARIATION

NAIL POLISH

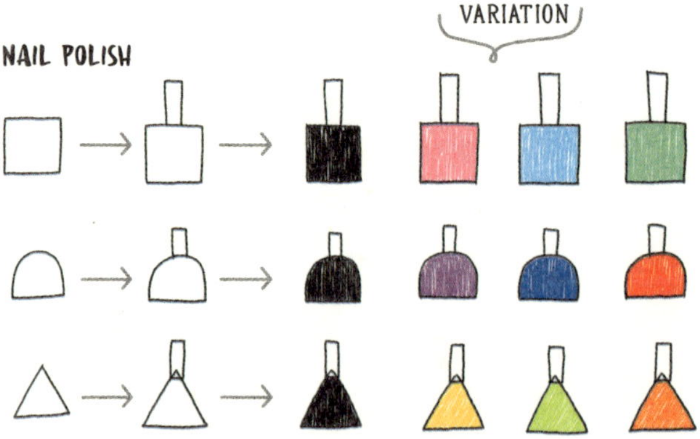

PERFUME BOTTLE

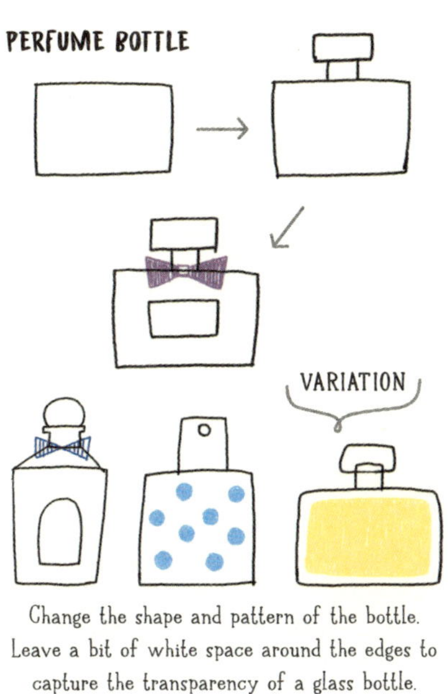

Change the shape and pattern of the bottle. Leave a bit of white space around the edges to capture the transparency of a glass bottle.

COSMETIC CASE

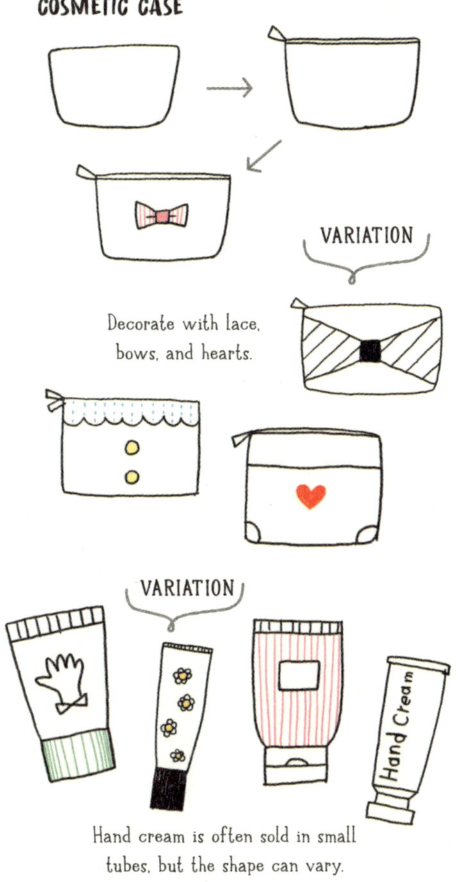

Decorate with lace, bows, and hearts.

HAND CREAM

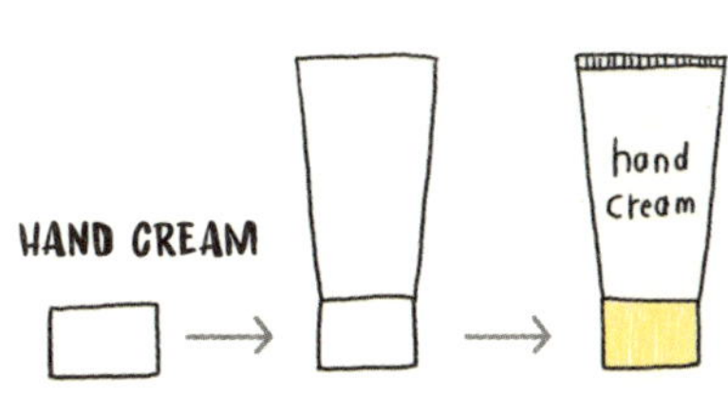

Hand cream is often sold in small tubes, but the shape can vary.

FALSE EYELASHES

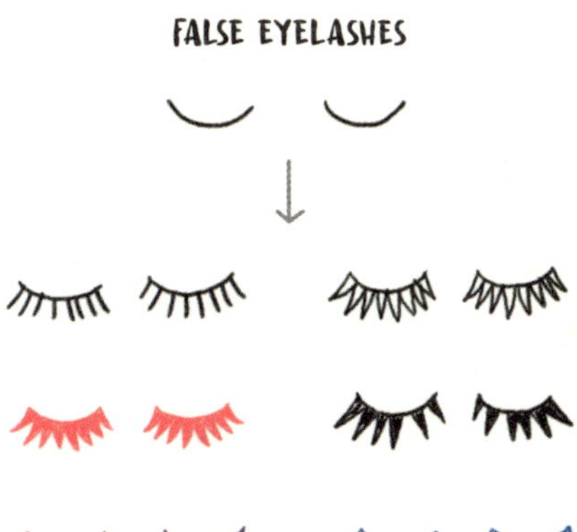

LIP GLOSS

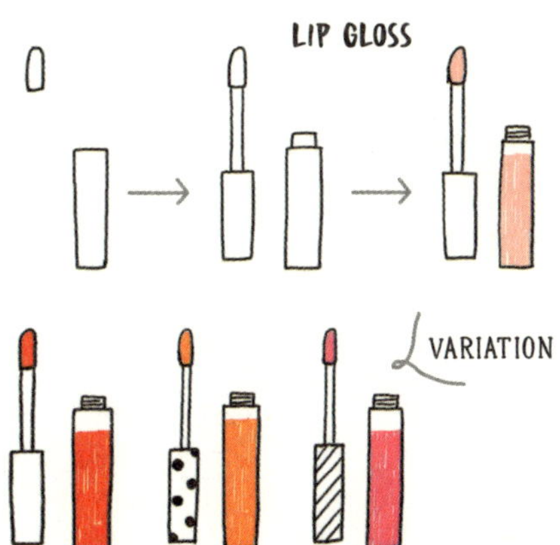

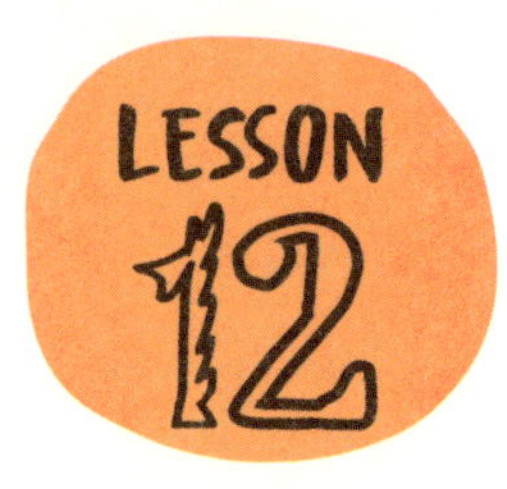

BUILDINGS & VEHICLES

You can draw complex structures like buildings and vehicles by combining simple shapes. Details, such as a patterned roof or uniquely-shaped windows, add character.

BUILDINGS

Start with a triangle or rectangle for the roof.

HOUSE

Start with a triangle.

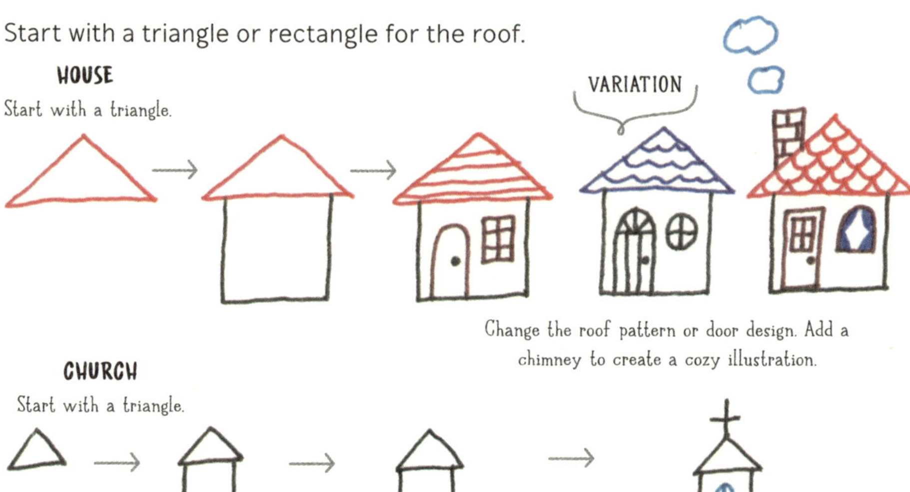

Change the roof pattern or door design. Add a chimney to create a cozy illustration.

CHURCH

Start with a triangle.

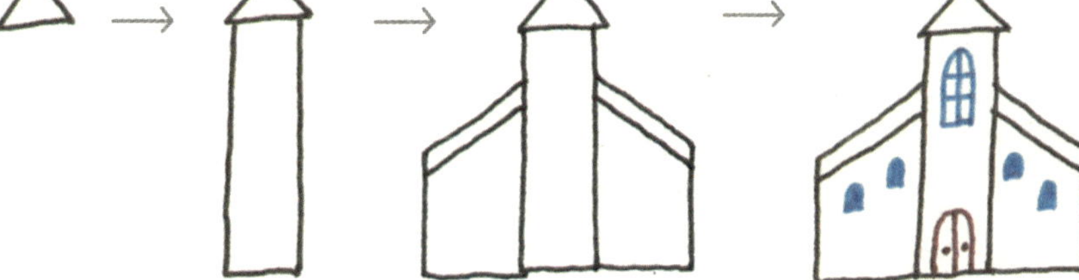

SHOPS

Start with a rectangle.

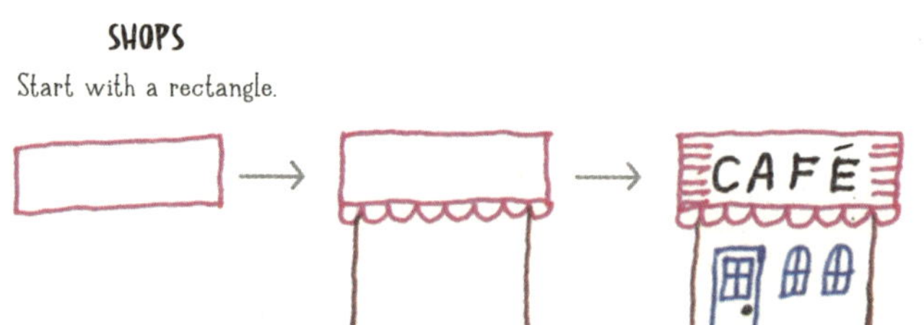

The striped roof creates a cafe-like atmosphere.

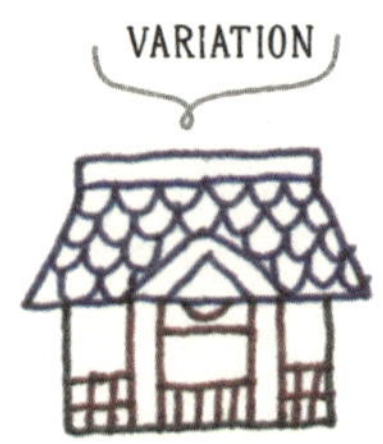

Change to a trapezoid-shaped roof with a semicircle pattern when drawing a temple.

VEHICLES

Start with a rectangle when drawing cars and trains, and use ovals and circles when drawing other vehicles.

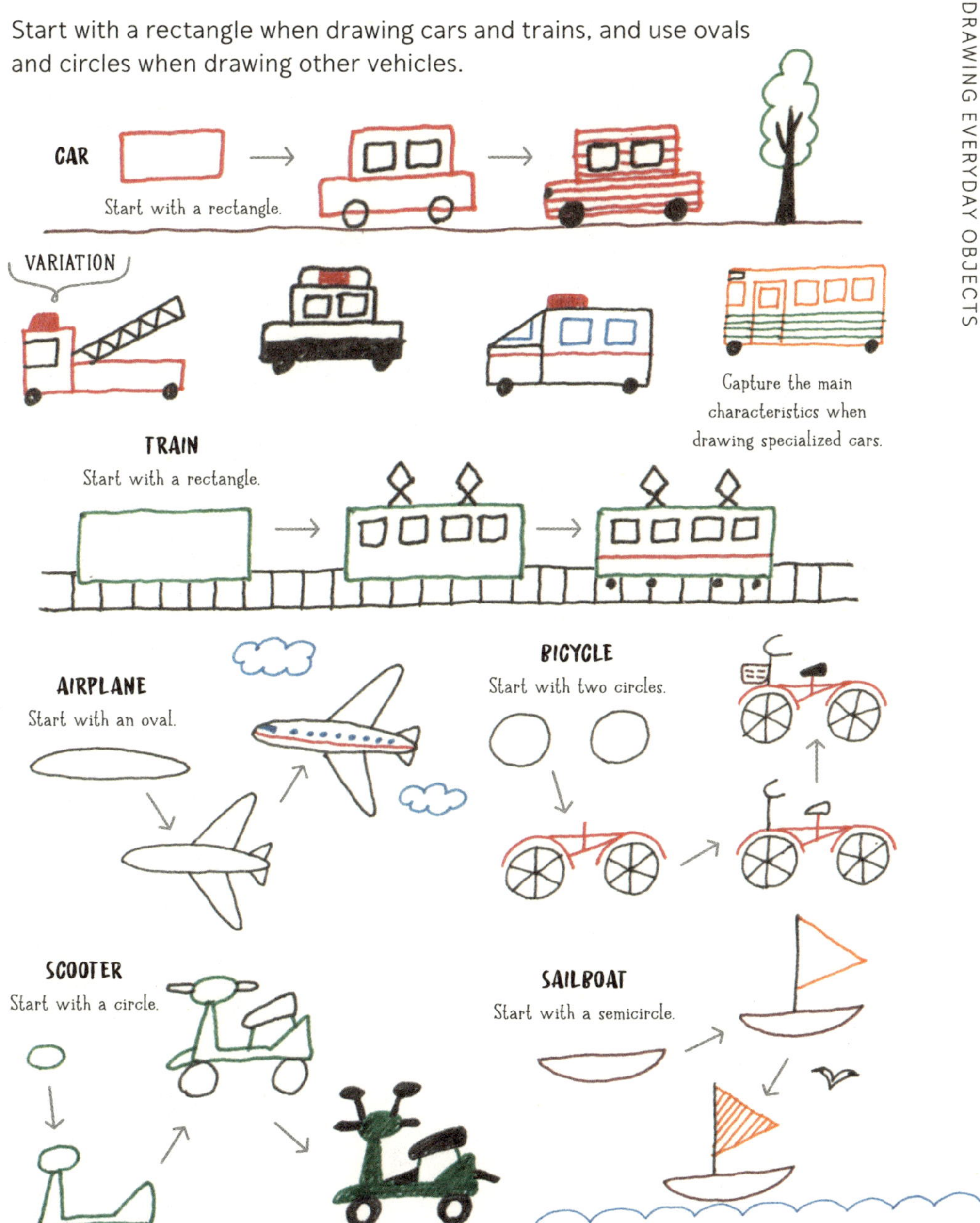

SPECIAL LESSON

PERSONIFY OBJECTS TO CREATE CHARACTERS

Use your imagination to add comical expressions and movement to the everyday objects you've learned to draw in this chapter and create original characters.

FLOWERS, LEAVES & TREES

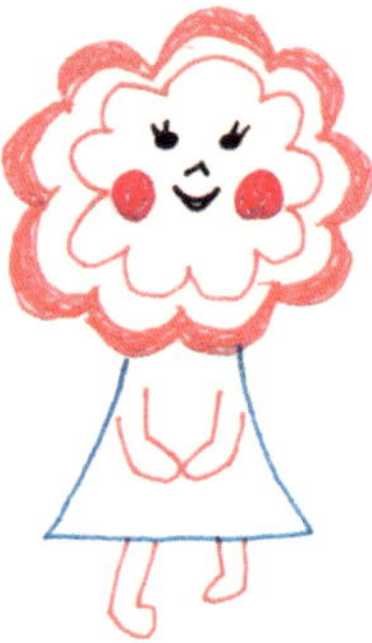

Draw red cheeks to create a shy flower girl.

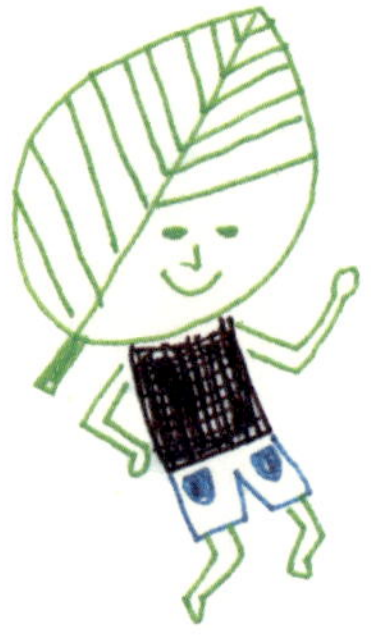

This lightweight leaf boy is very quick on his feet.

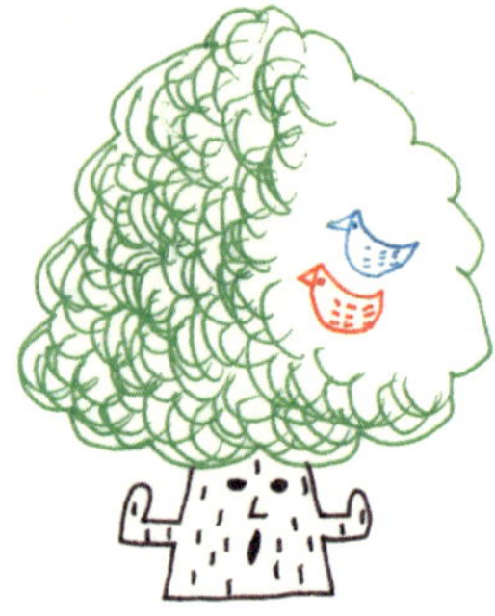

This massive tree calls to the birds.

FRUIT

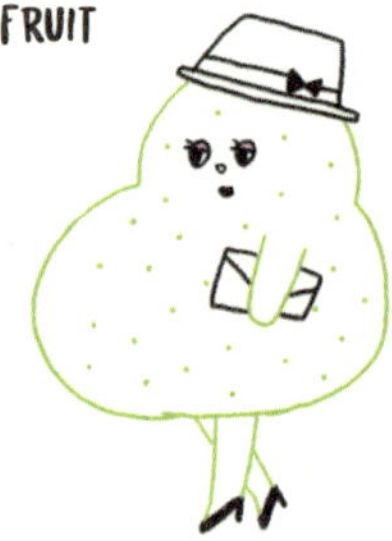

This chic pear character has a stylish wardrobe.

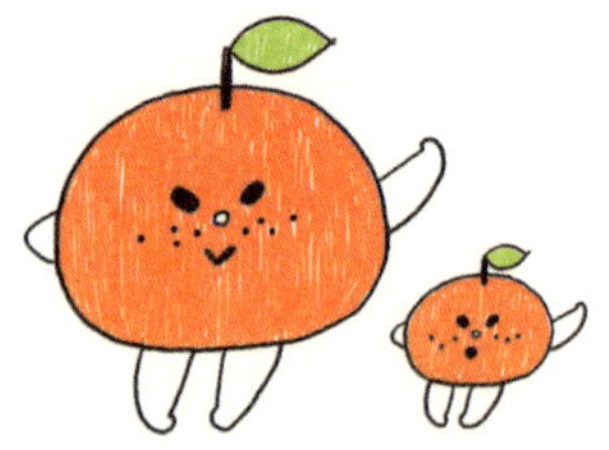

This parent and child orange duo both have charming freckles and leafy hairstyles.

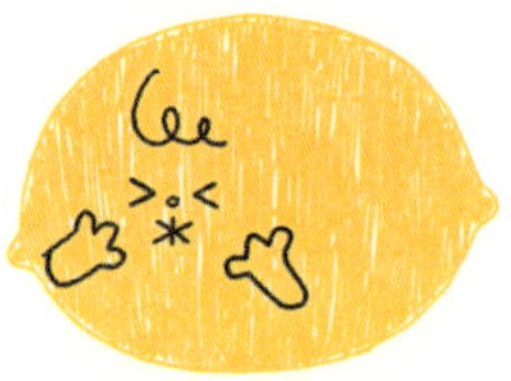

A sour facial expression and hands clutching the cheeks give this lemon character a funny look.

VEGETABLES

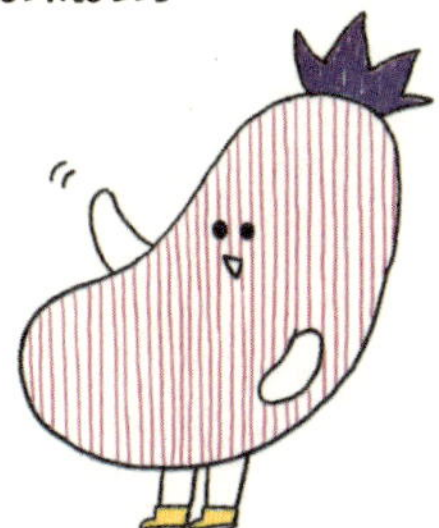

This quirky eggplant character waves hello to friends.

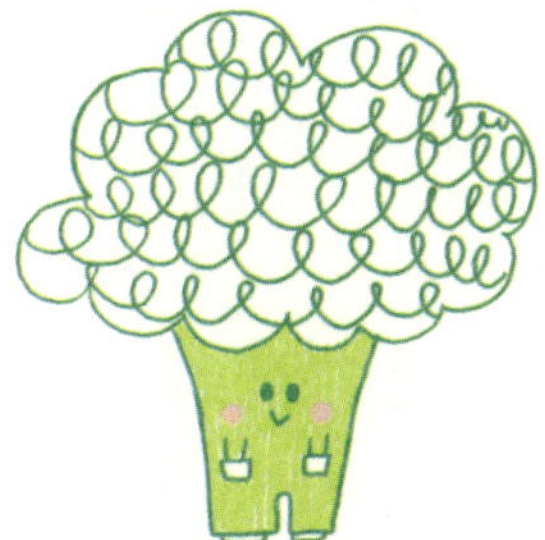

A shy expression and body language gives this broccoli character a cute look.

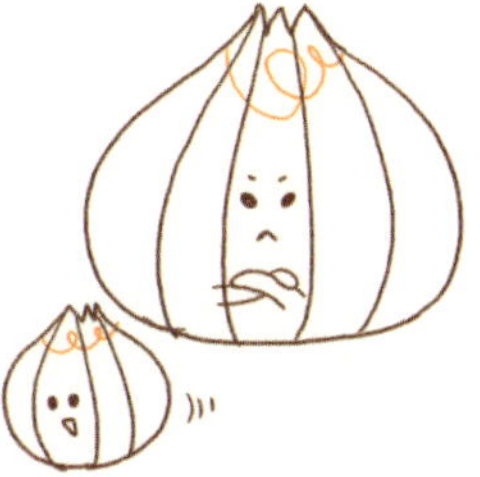

This onion parent disapproves of her child's wild behavior.

BREAD

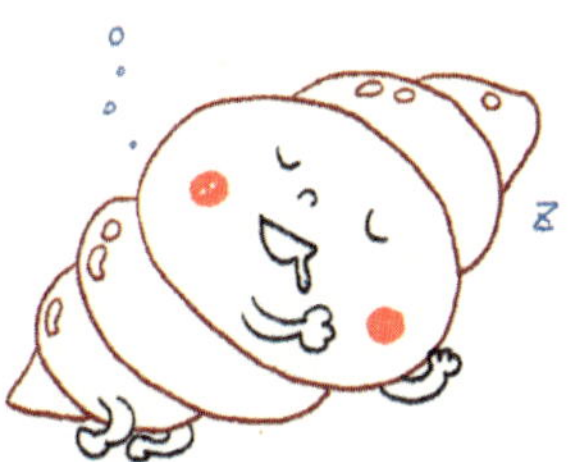

This croissant takes a nap on the bakery shelf while waiting to be sold.

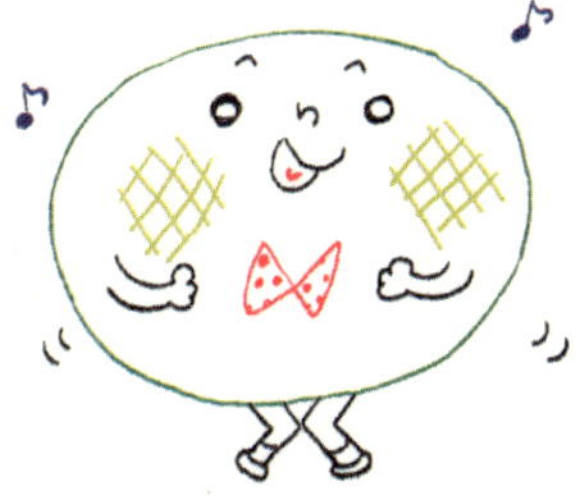

Score marks on the cheeks make this melonpan look like he's blushing.

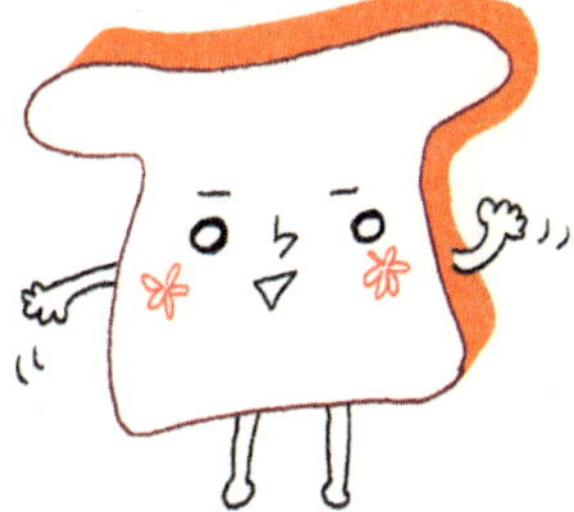

This superstar sandwich bread waves both hands.

SWEETS

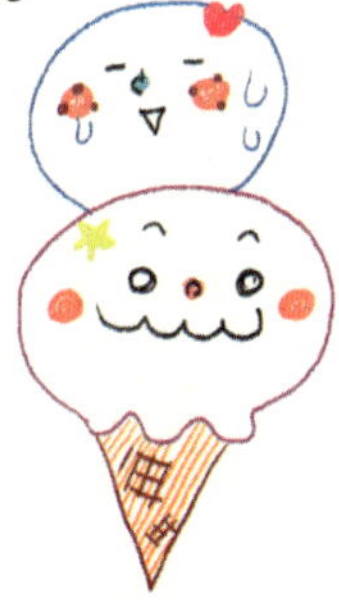

This ice cream cone cannot bear the heat!

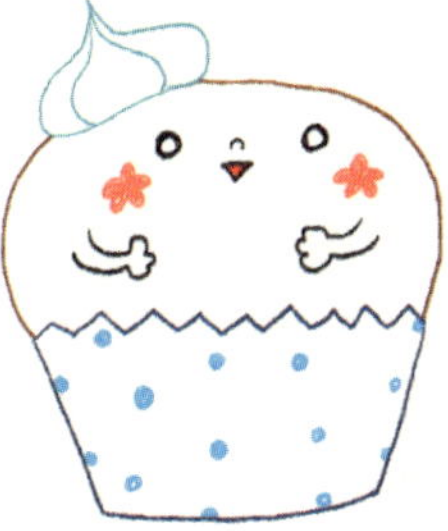

This cupcake girl wears a stylish whipped cream hat.

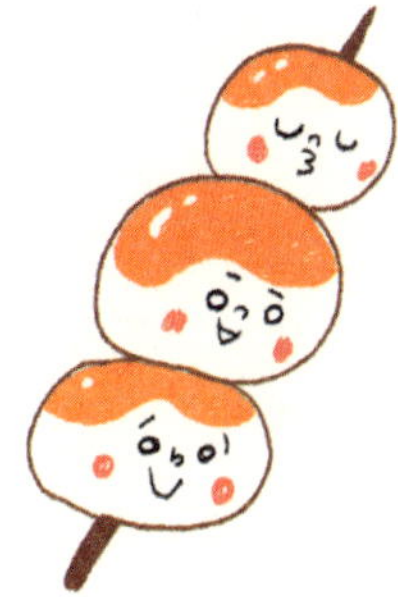

Each part of this mitarashi dango trio has a different facial expression.

DISHES, KITCHENWARE & FURNITURE

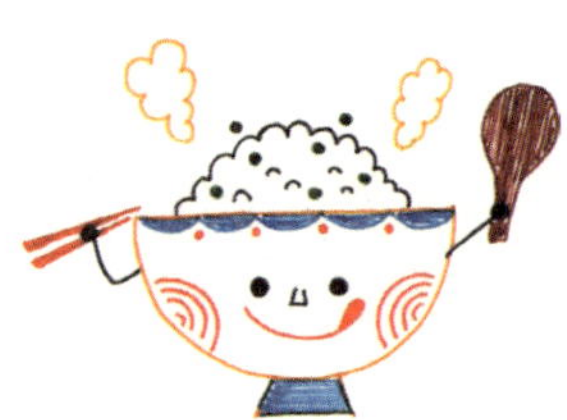

This hungry rice bowl boy serves himself.

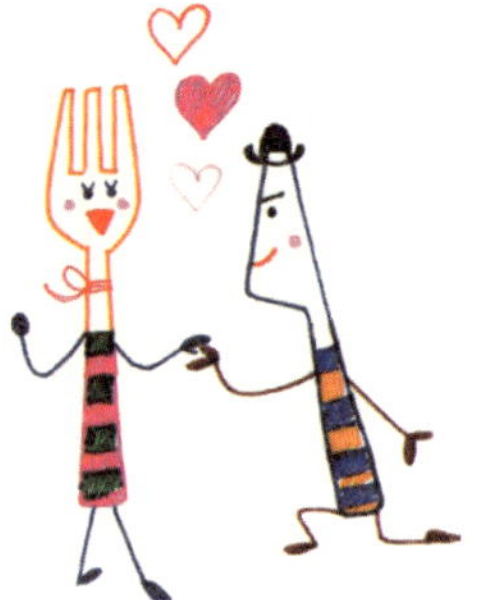

This fork and knife couple are happily in love.

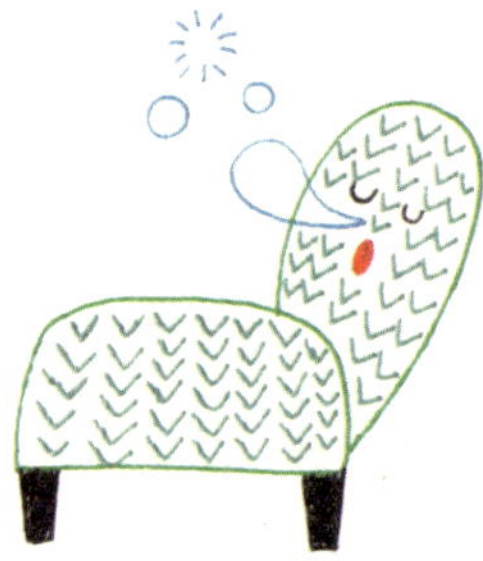

This chair enjoy a nice nap while his master is not home.

BUILDINGS & VEHICLES

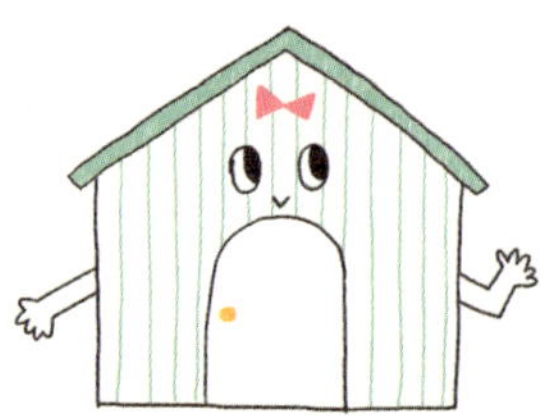

"Welcome!" This house character is very friendly.

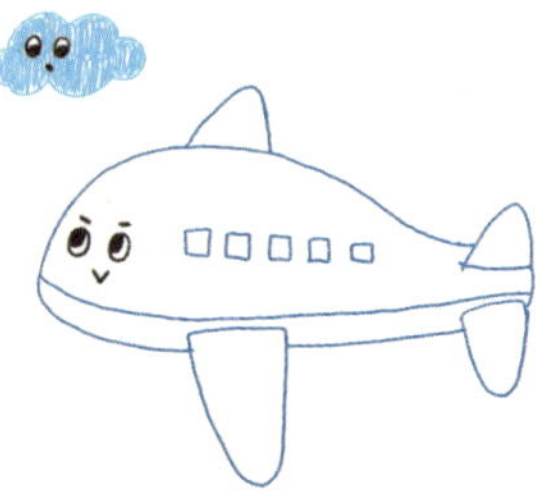

This jumbo jet flies fearlessly. Add clouds to create a cute illustration.

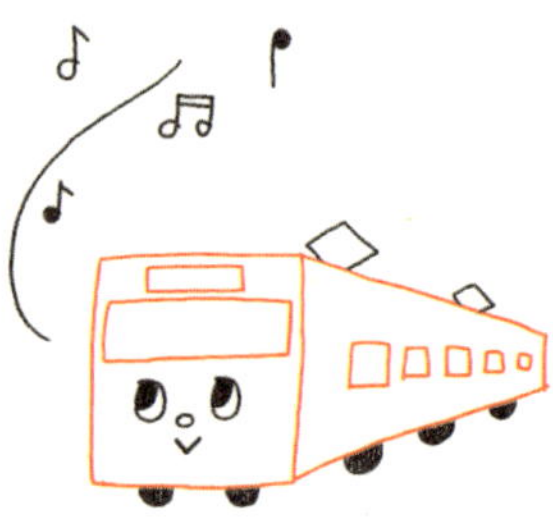

Add music notes to depict the train singing cheerfully as he chugs along.

HOUSEHOLD OBJECTS

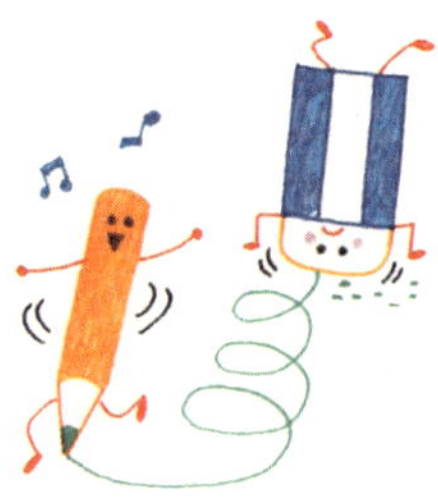

An eraser boy chases his pencil friend and erases his drawing in the process.

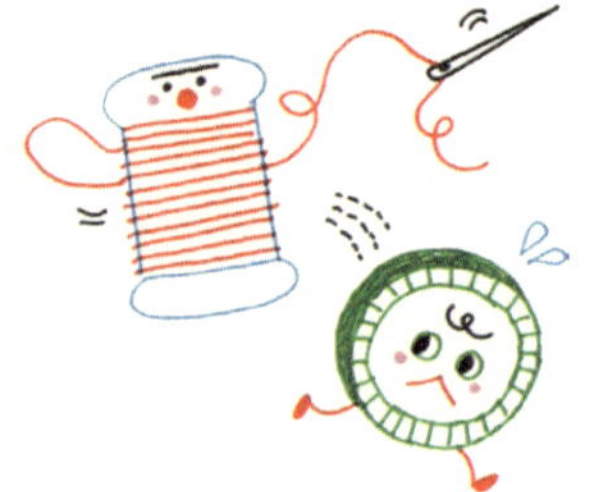

The button runs away from being attacked by the needle and thread.

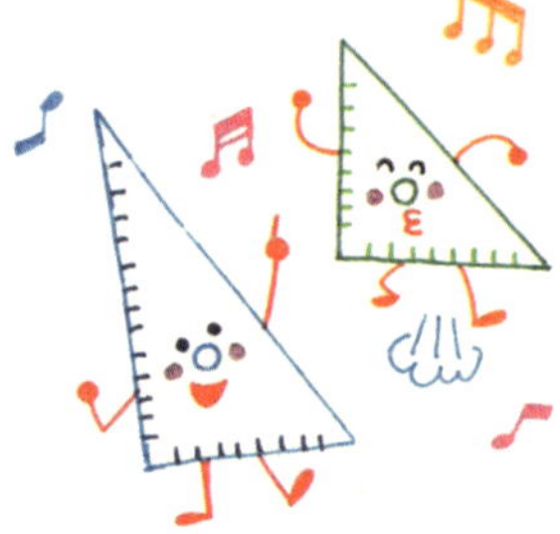

These ruler brothers are in such a good mood, they're dancing.

Chapter 4:

PATTERNS & BORDERS

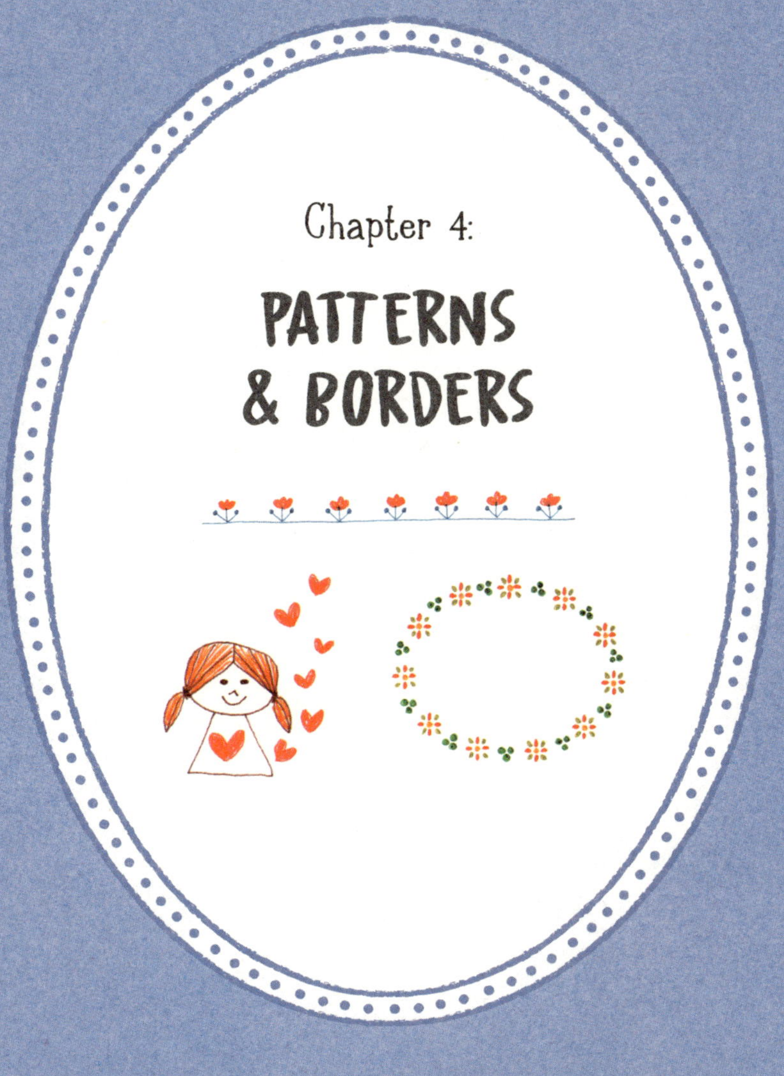

LESSON 1

MOTIFS

Use these cute little illustrations on notes and messages. There's always more than one way to draw a simple motif.

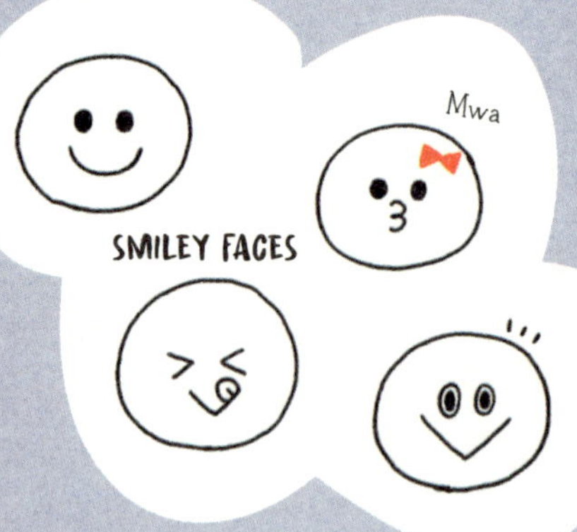

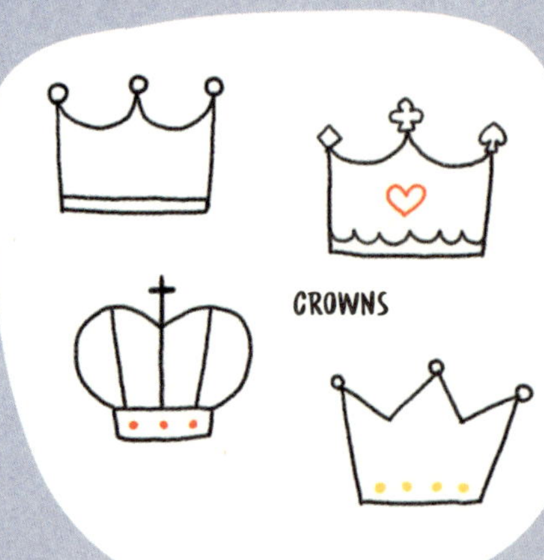

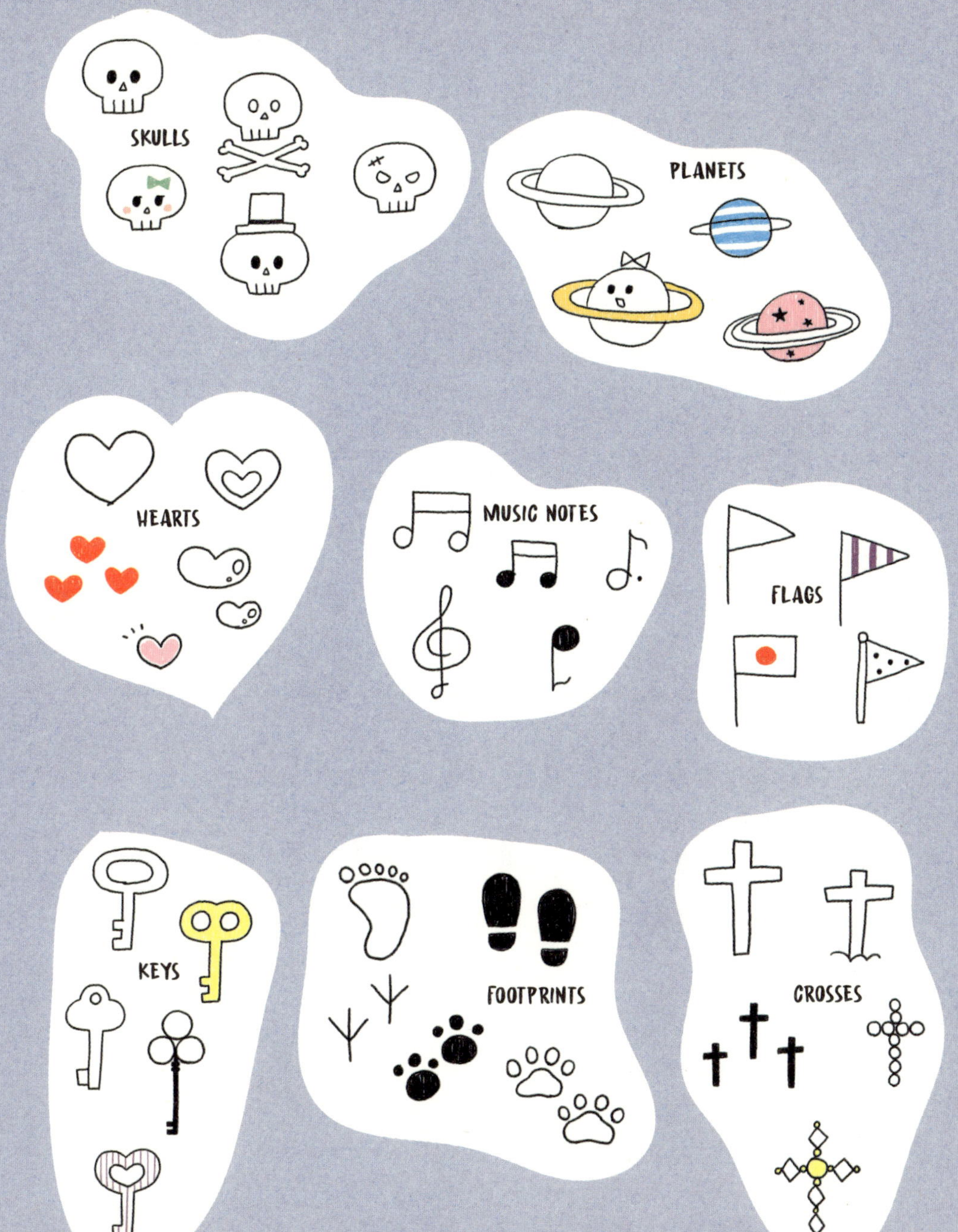
SKULLS
PLANETS
HEARTS
MUSIC NOTES
FLAGS
KEYS
FOOTPRINTS
CROSSES

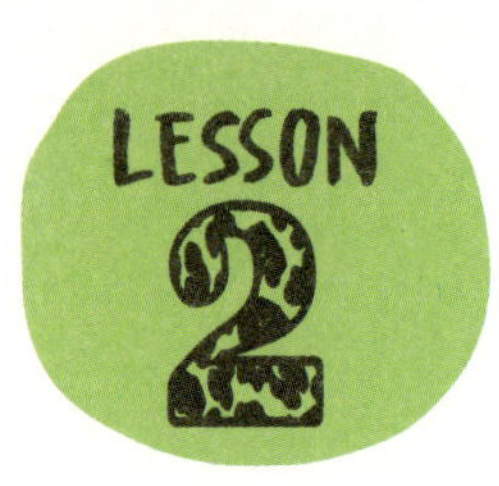

BORDERS & LINE MOTIFS

Decorative lines can be used on letters, cards, and other notes. Combine simple motifs to create stylish designs.

1 Repeat simple shapes or motifs along the line.

LINE + CIRCLES OR DOTS

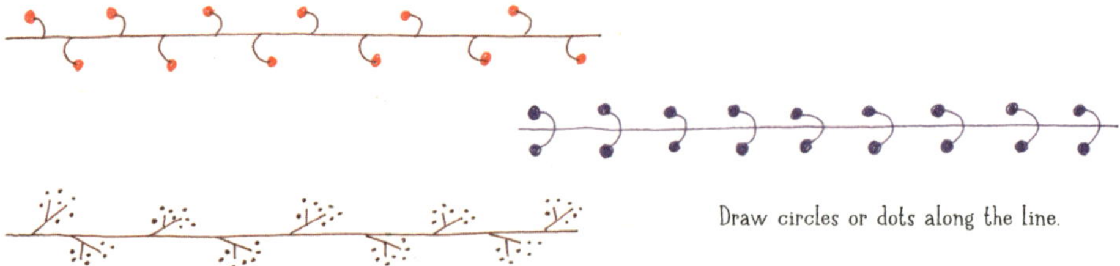

Draw circles or dots along the line.

LINE + PLANTS

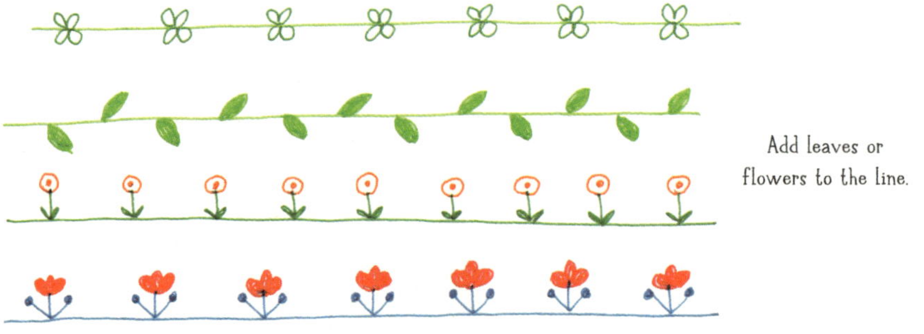

Add leaves or flowers to the line.

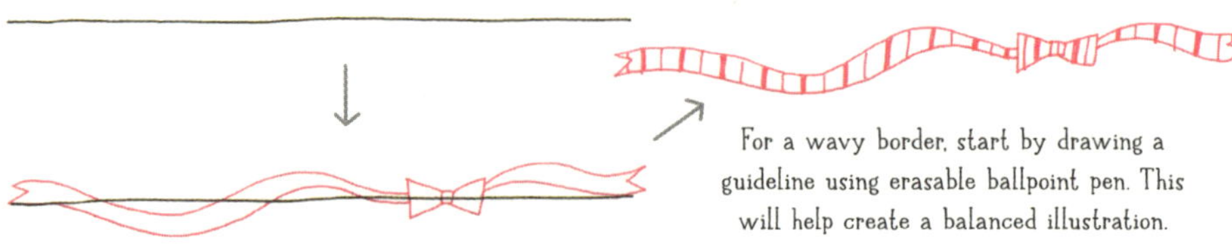

For a wavy border, start by drawing a guideline using erasable ballpoint pen. This will help create a balanced illustration.

2 Use continuous semicircles to create a lacy, decorative line.

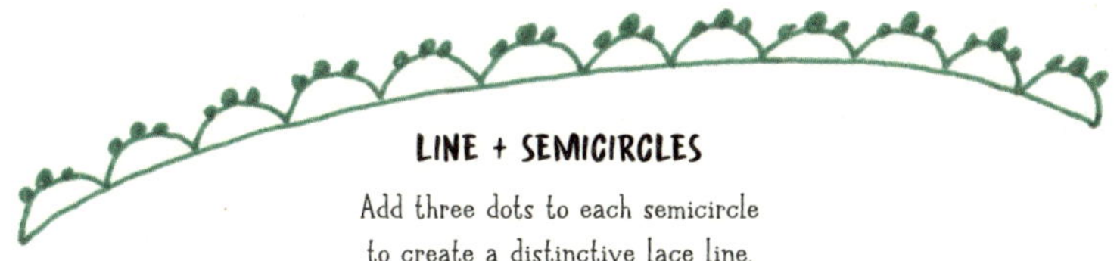

LINE + SEMICIRCLES

Add three dots to each semicircle to create a distinctive lace line.

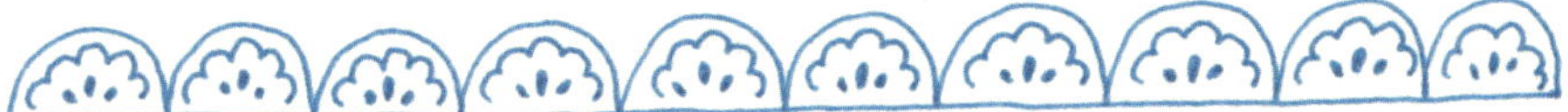

Add fluffy lines and three dots inside each semicircle to create a scalloped lace pattern.

Combine large and small semicircles for a more intricate design. Use pink for a feminine look.

Add several small semicircles along the outline of the larger semicircles for a frilly look.

TWO LINES + SEMICIRCLES

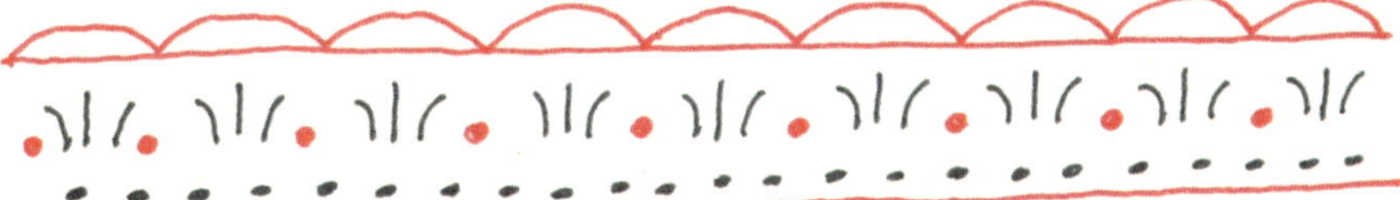

For a ribbon-inspired look, draw two horizontal lines, then add a decorative pattern inside.

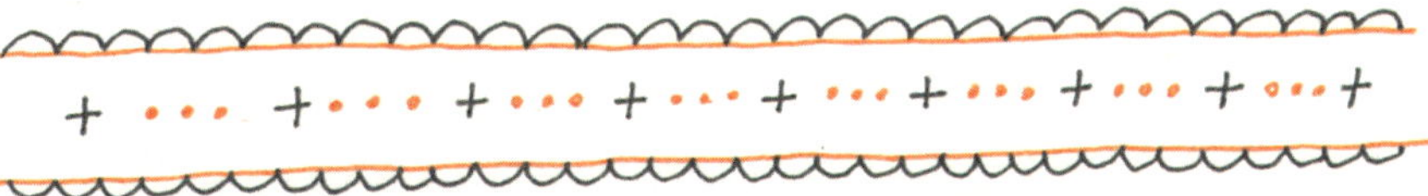

For folk-style ribbon, use scalloped lines and add a cross and dot pattern.

3 Repeat various motifs to create an original decorative line.

GEOMETRIC PATTERNS

Alternate between small and large decorative circles.

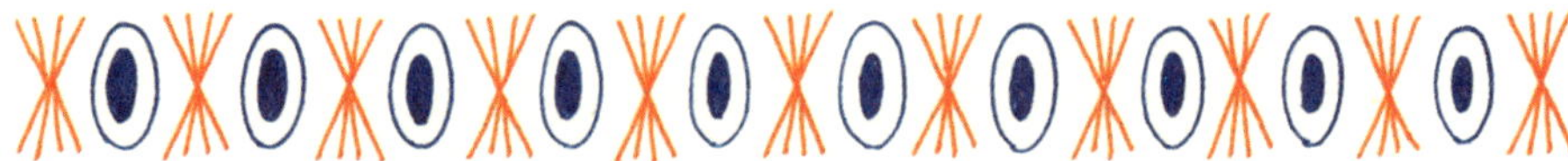

Use contrasting colors, such as blue and orange, to create a distinctive look.

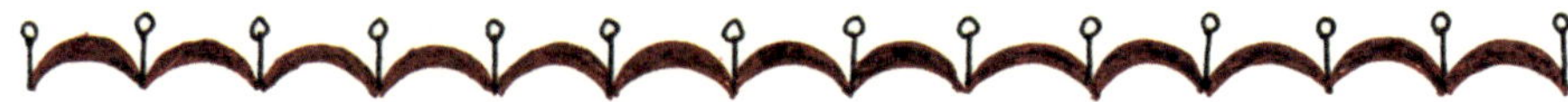

Draw a fluffy line, then add straight lines and circles.

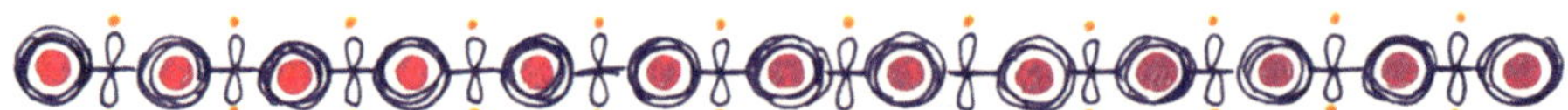

Add a figure-eight motif between circles for a loopy ribbon look.

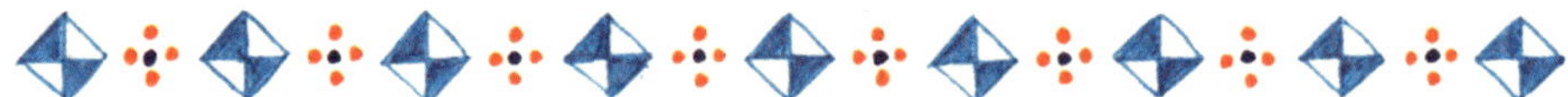

Square and dot motifs create a bold, geometric look.

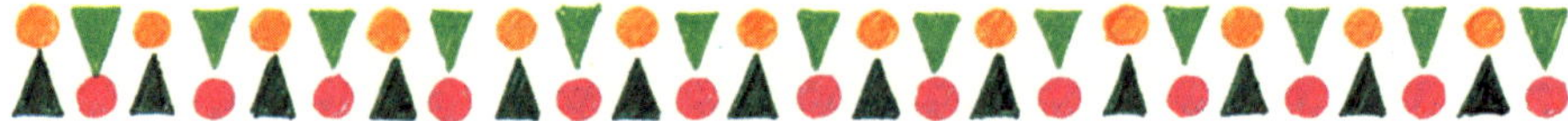

Combine triangle and circles for a zipper-inspired design.

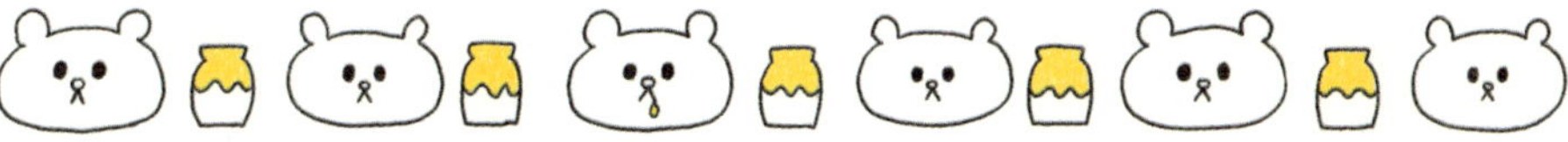

For an adorable design, combine bear faces with pots of honey.

This bread and milk motif makes the perfect border for recipes and shopping lists.

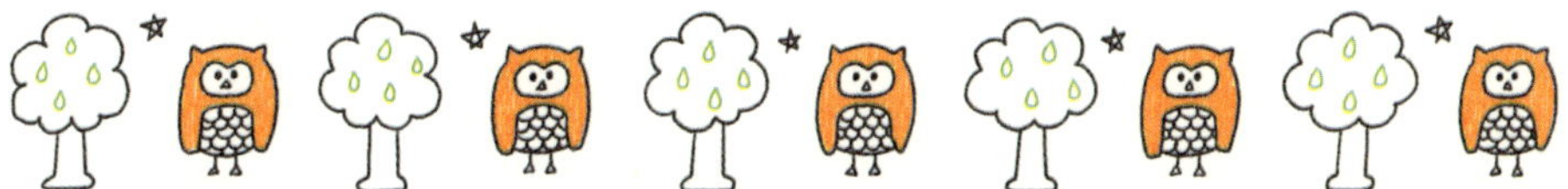

Draw an owl next to his favorite tree.

Bears, acorns, and mushrooms combine to create a fairytale forest-inspired line.

This simple, girlish motif features butterflies and flowers.

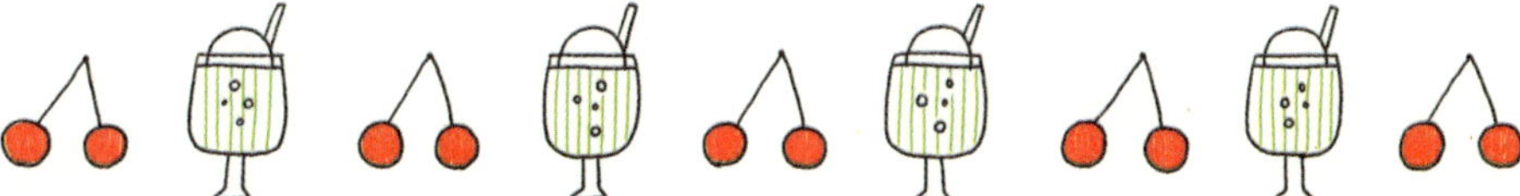

Ice cream sodas and cherries combine to create a retro line.

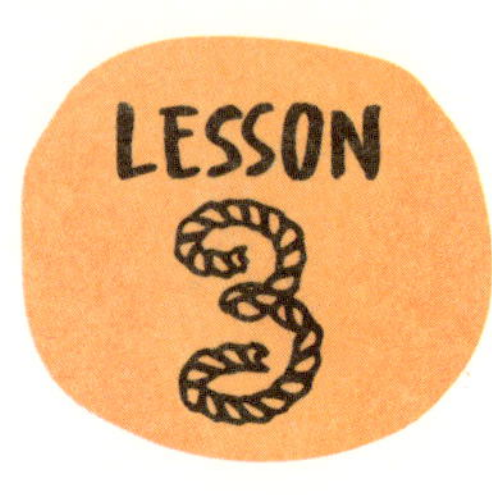

FRAMES

Draw a frame along the edges of letters, memos, and pictures. The frame will add emphasis to the text or drawings inside.

1 Draw a square or circular frame, then embellish with motifs along the outline.

Repeat semicircles and dots along the outline of a square frame. Imperfectly shaped semicircles make the design unique!

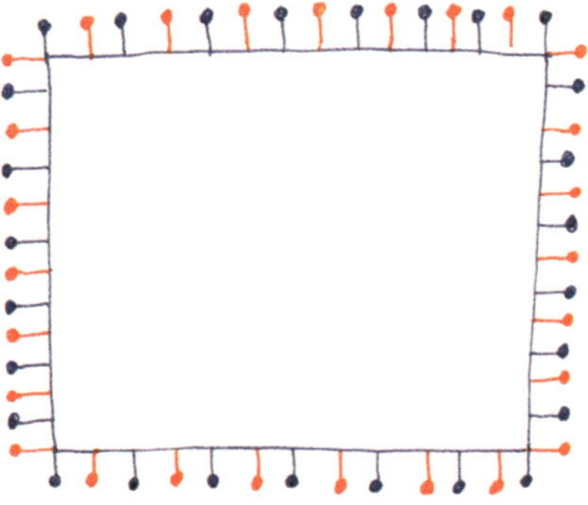

Draw a square frame, then add straight lines topped with circles. Use blue and red for a Parisian-inspired look.

A round frame with double semicircle frills creates an elegant, lovely look.

2 Repeat simple motifs in the shape of a square or circle without drawing a frame line.

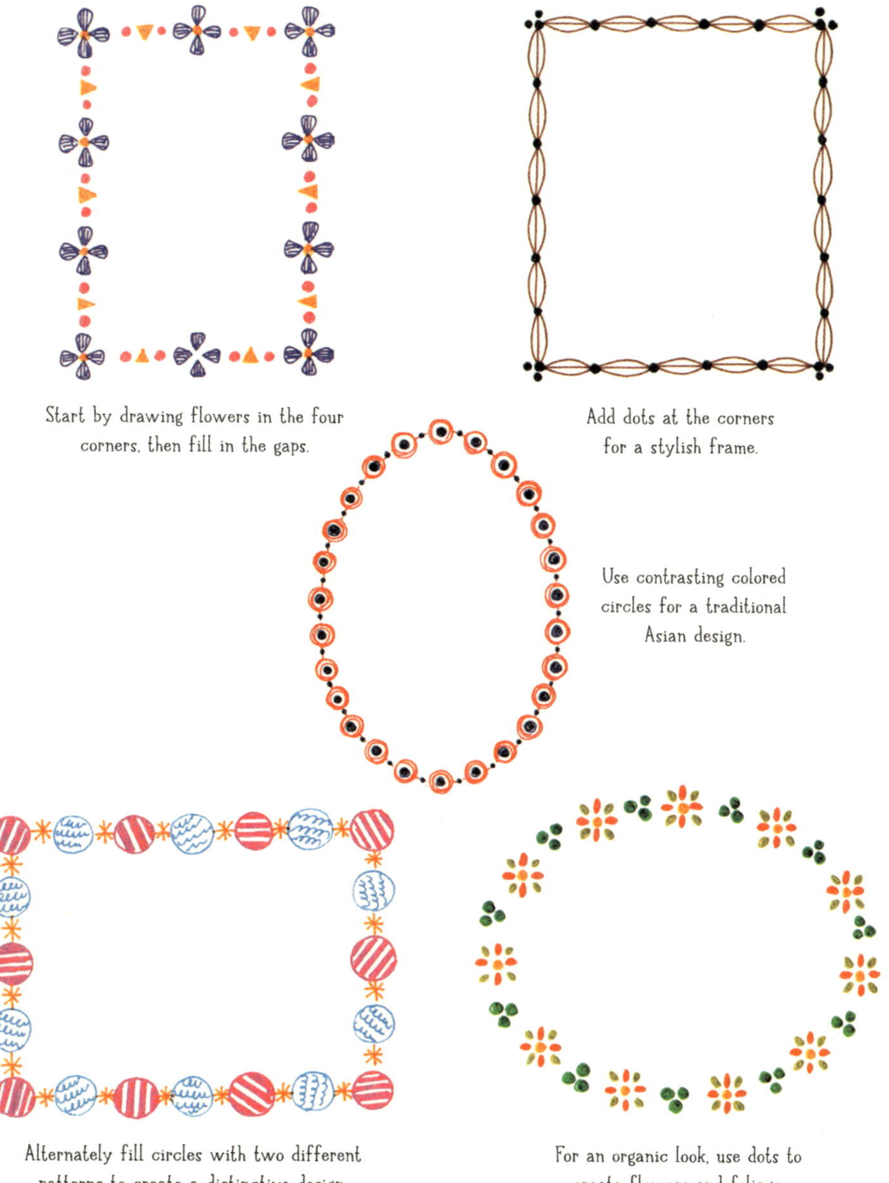

Start by drawing flowers in the four corners, then fill in the gaps.

Add dots at the corners for a stylish frame.

Use contrasting colored circles for a traditional Asian design.

Alternately fill circles with two different patterns to create a distinctive design.

For an organic look, use dots to create flowers and foliage.

3 Use the outline of objects to create distinctive decorative frames.

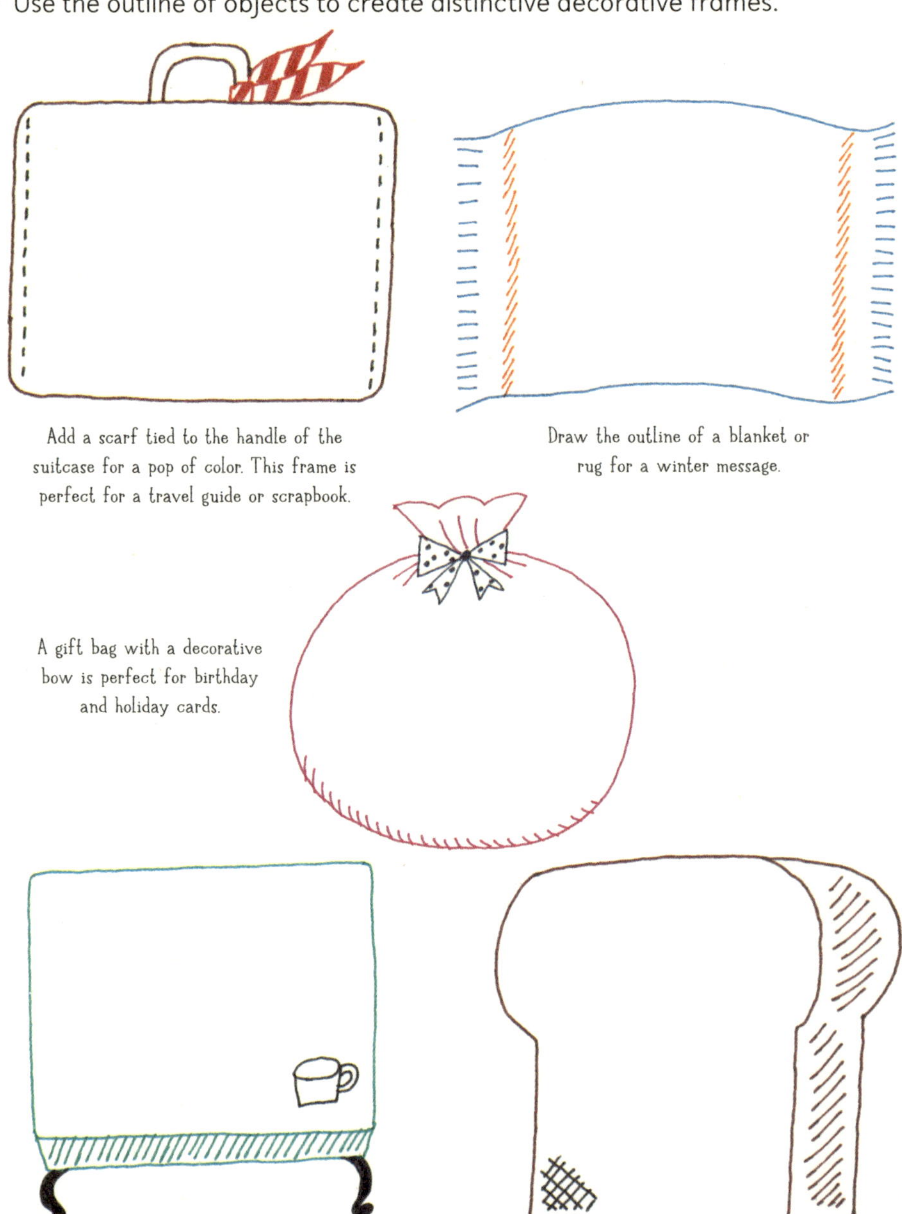

Add a scarf tied to the handle of the suitcase for a pop of color. This frame is perfect for a travel guide or scrapbook.

Draw the outline of a blanket or rug for a winter message.

A gift bag with a decorative bow is perfect for birthday and holiday cards.

Try a simple coffee cup on a square table for dinner party invitations.

A quirky sandwich bread frame adds humor to an invitation for a children's event.

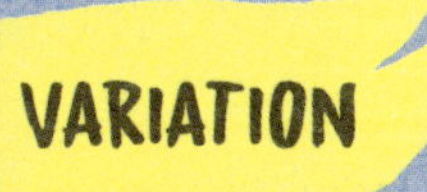

SPEECH BUBBLE FRAMES

Speech bubble frames are perfect for quick memos and notes. Use a design suited to the content of the message.

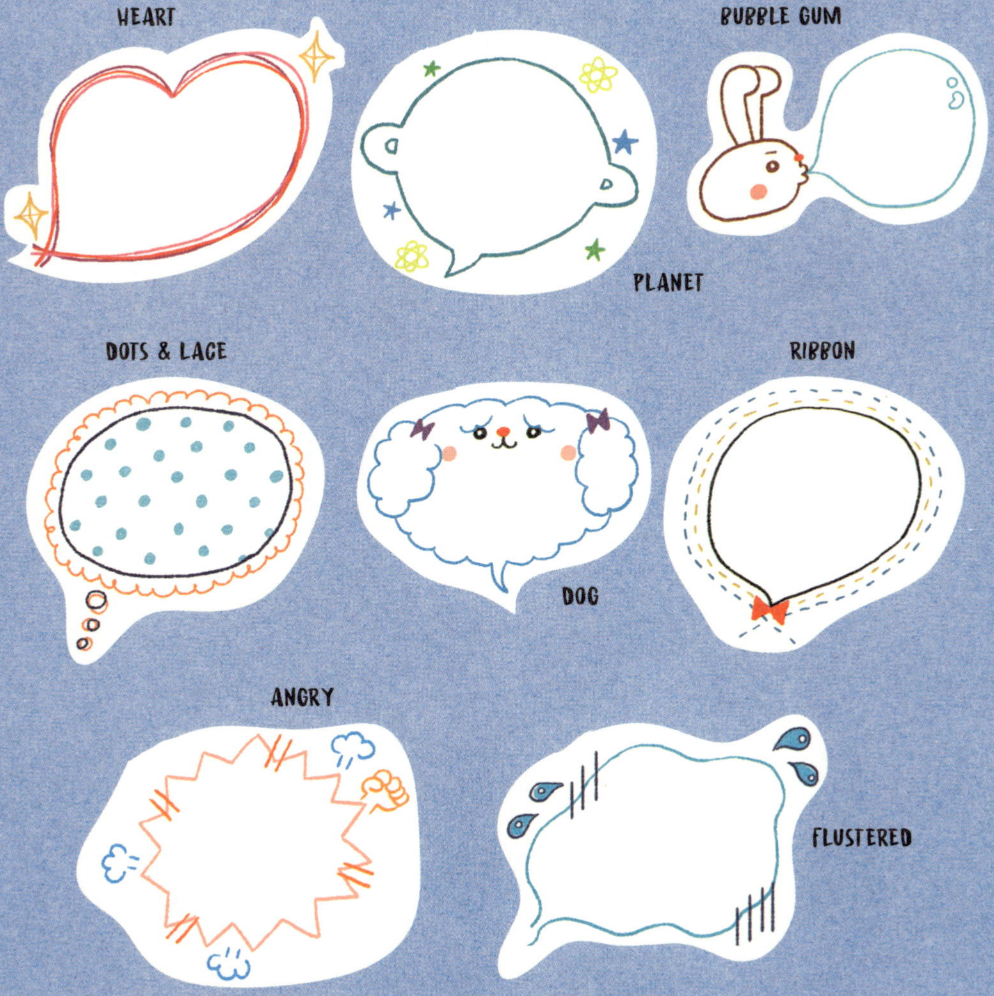

HEART

BUBBLE GUM

PLANET

DOTS & LACE

RIBBON

DOG

ANGRY

FLUSTERED

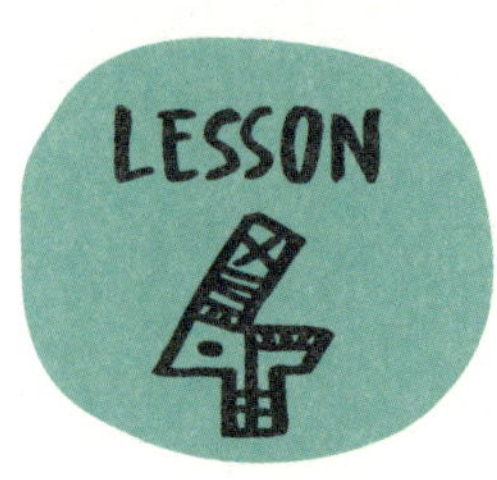

DECORATIVE TEXT

Add even more color and style to your illustrations by incorporating decorative text.

1 Draw thicker characters for "bubble letter" style illustrations.

ALPHABET (UPPERCASE)

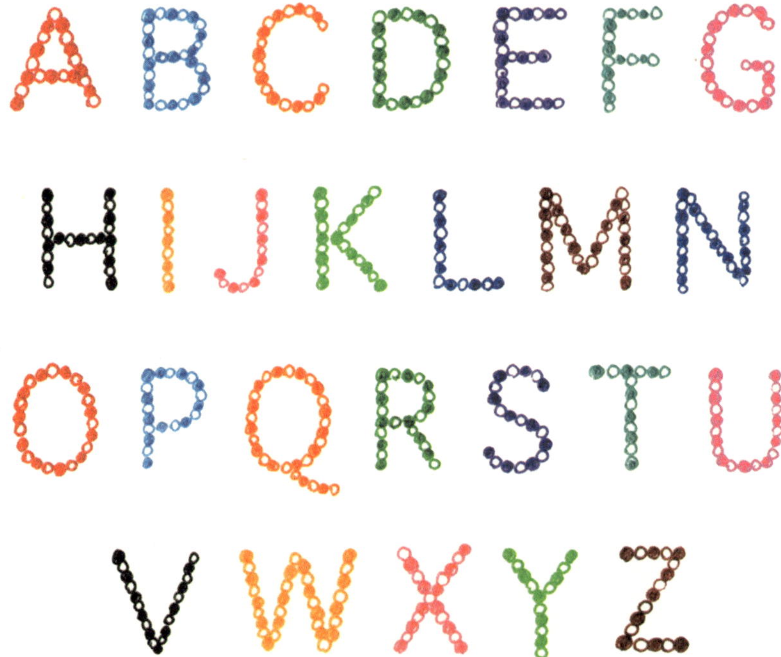

Use small circles to draw each letter.
Use one color for each letter and fill in alternate circles.

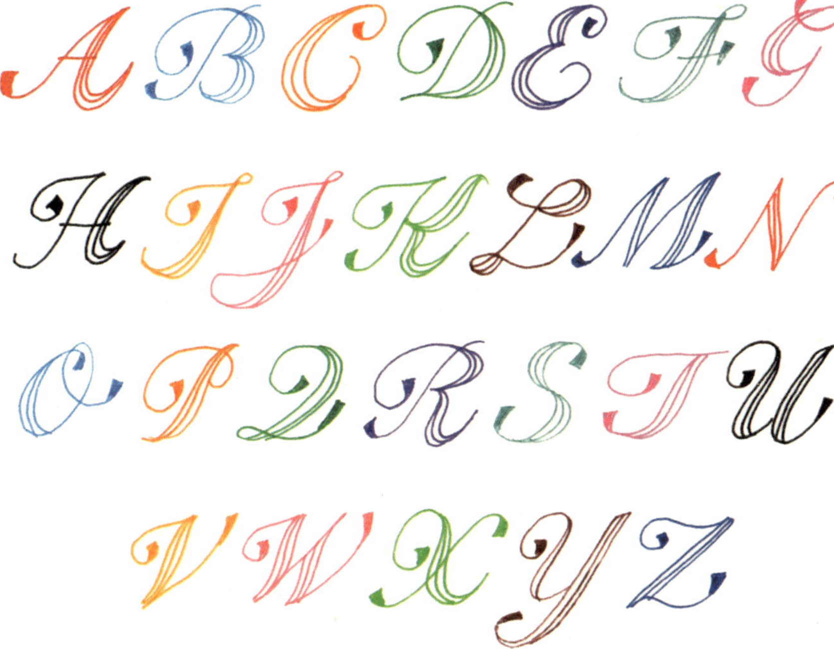

For a more elegant look, make certain parts of the letter thicker than others. This technique is recommended for cursive writing.

ALPHABET (LOWERCASE)

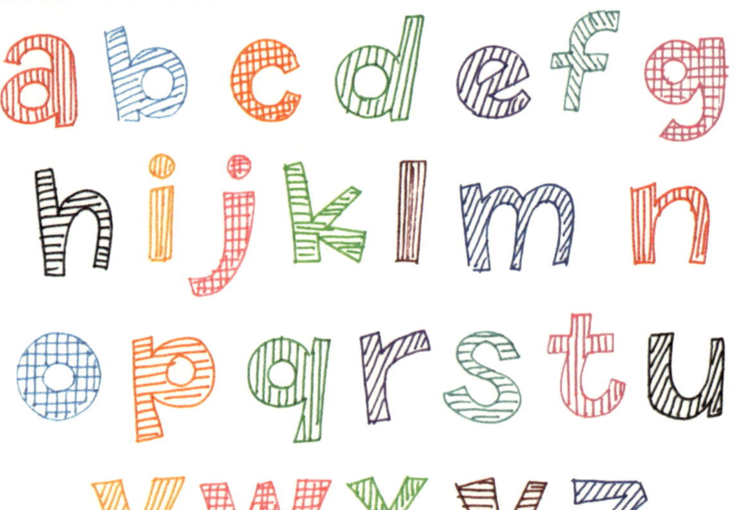

Use stripes or checkered patterns to fill in thick bubble letters.

a b c d e f g
h i j k l m n
o p q r s t u
v w x y z

Add dots to the tips of each letter for stylish text.

2 Add motifs or smiley faces to basic letters.

ALPHABET (LOWERCASE)

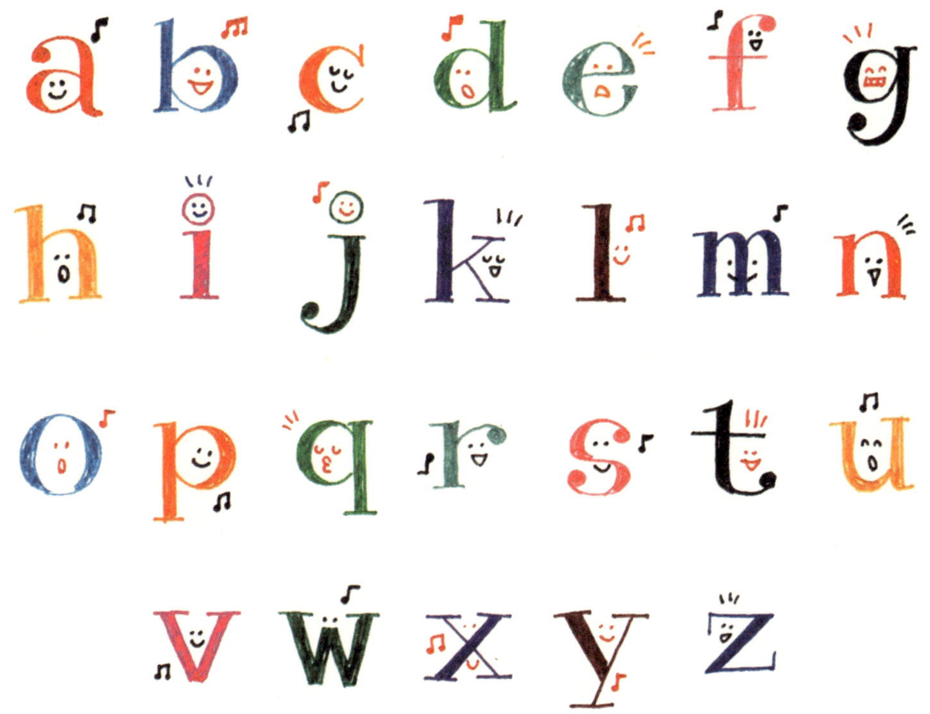

Draw various facial expressions inside each letter.
Add musical notes to suggest movement and sound.

ALPHABET (UPPERCASE)

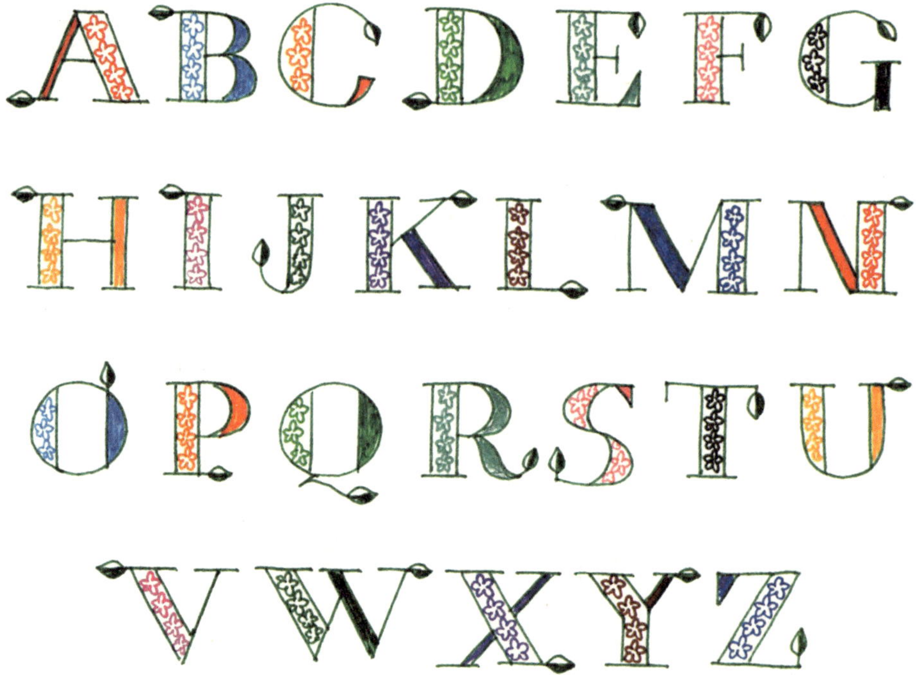

Fill the thick areas of each letter with small flower motifs.
Add leaves to the tip of each letter to emphasize the botanical theme.

VARIATION

EMOJI ILLUSTRATIONS

These fun illustrations are inspired by emojis. You can use them to express your feelings when creating handwritten messages.

SORRY

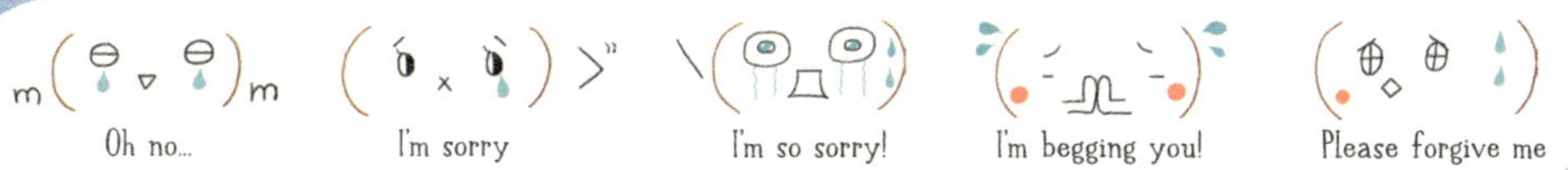

HAPPY

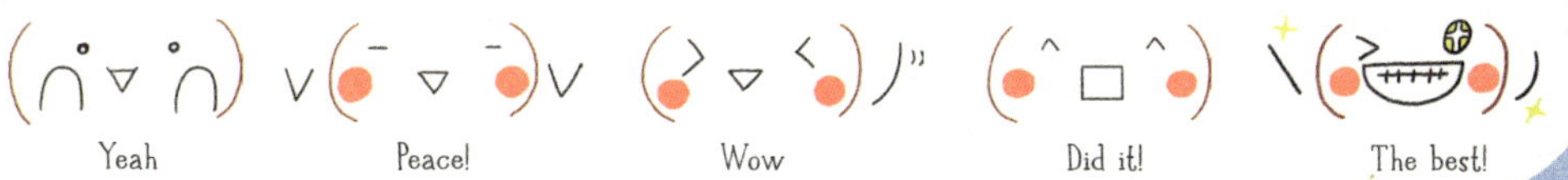

SURPRISED

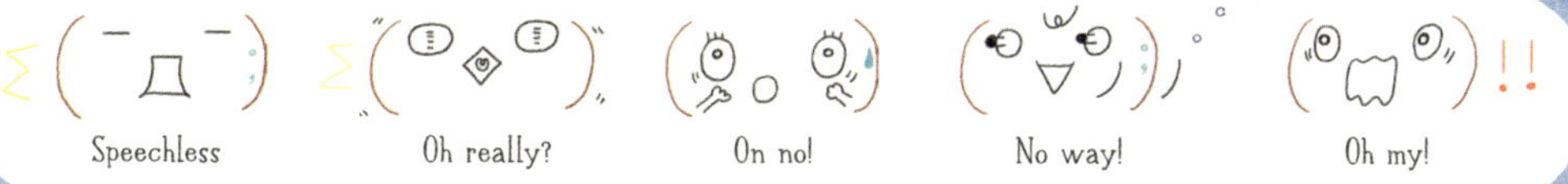

CRYING

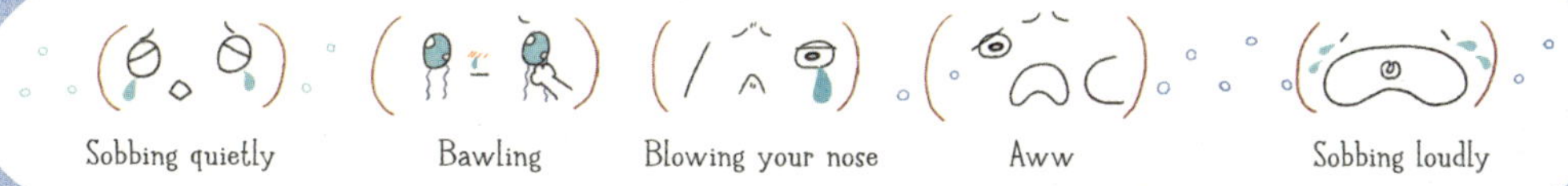

OK!

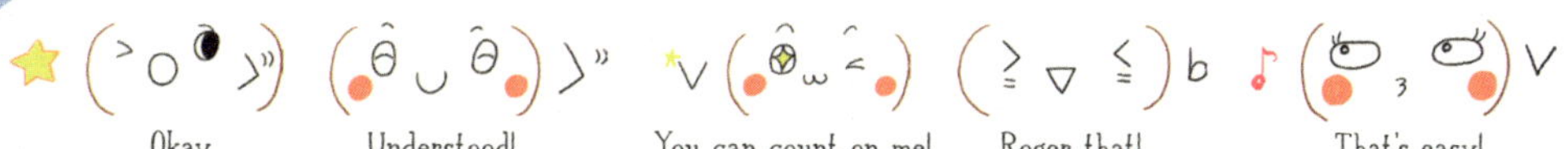

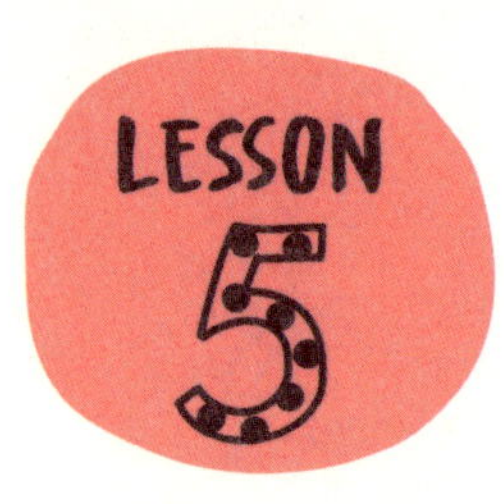

MESSAGES

Combine decorative text and cute illustrations to create messages perfect for greeting cards, memos, and other notes.

APPRECIATION

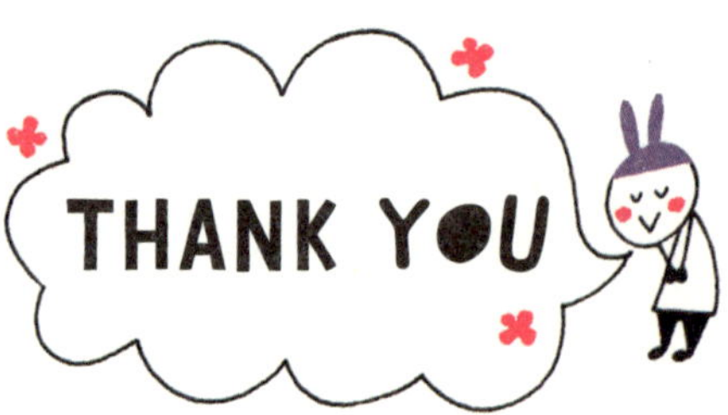

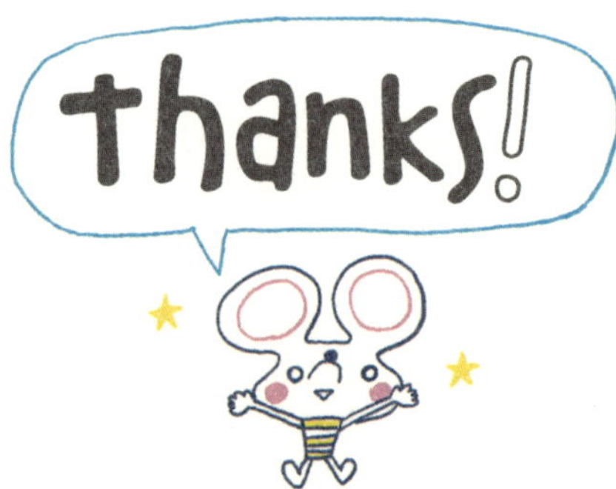

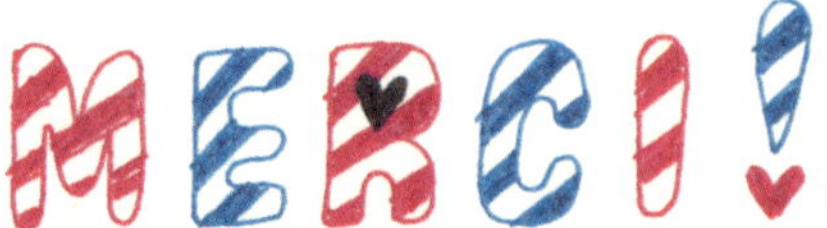

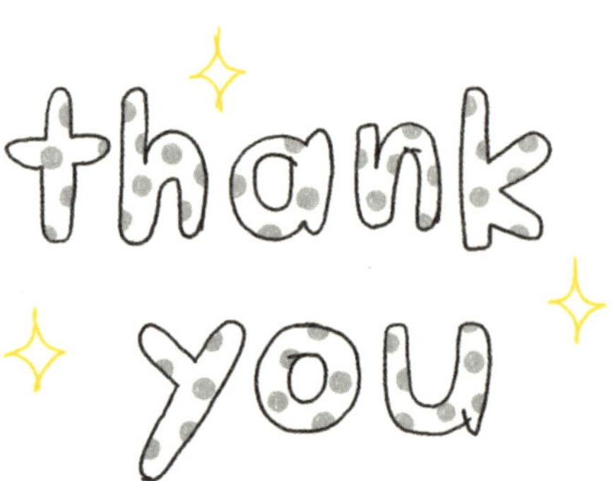

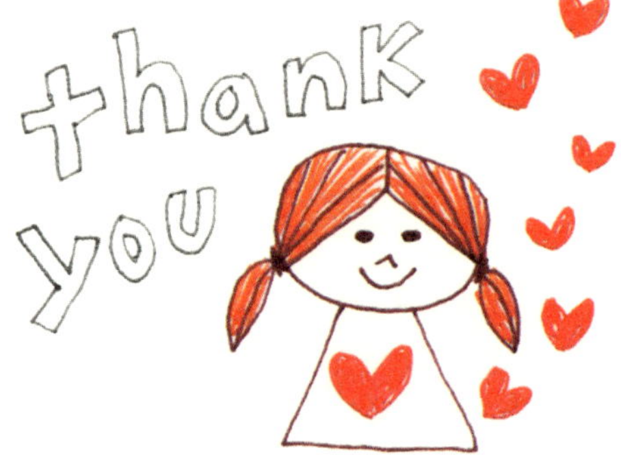

THOUGHTFUL EXPRESSIONS

thinking of you

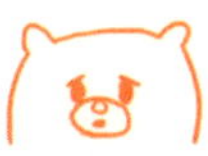

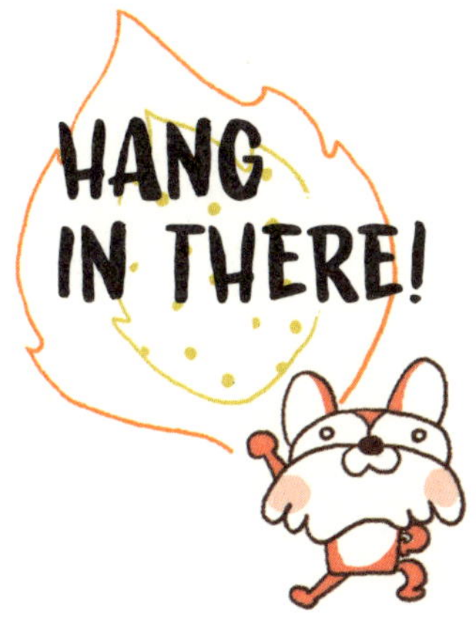

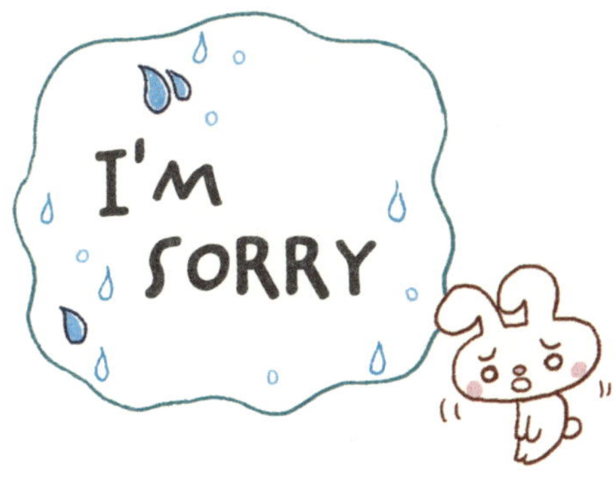

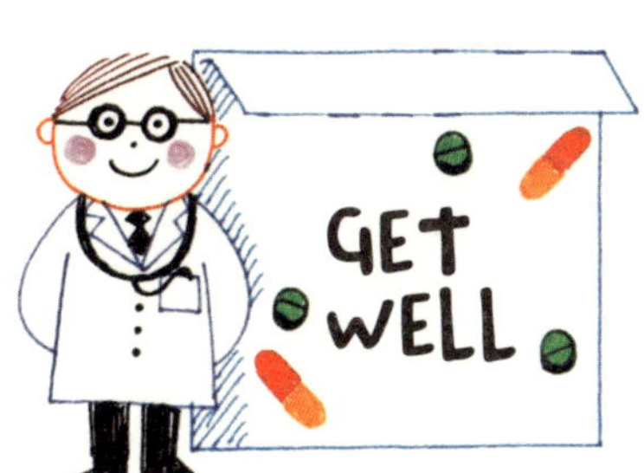

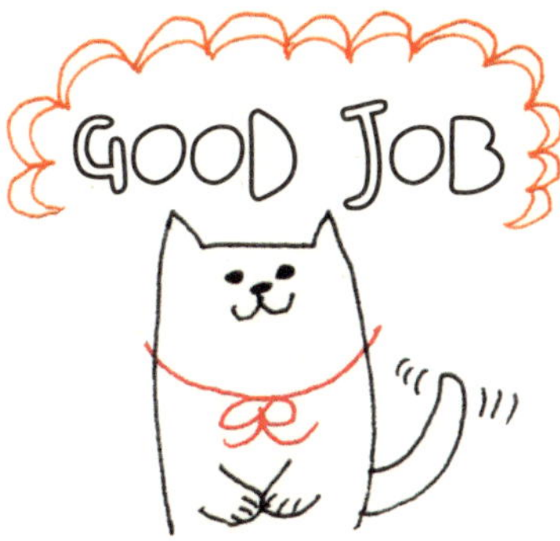

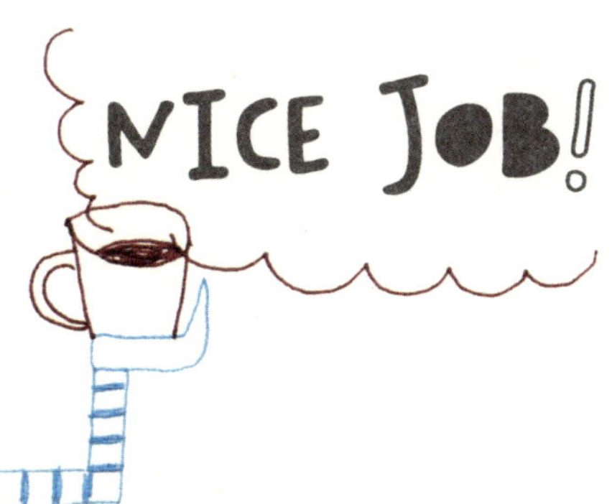

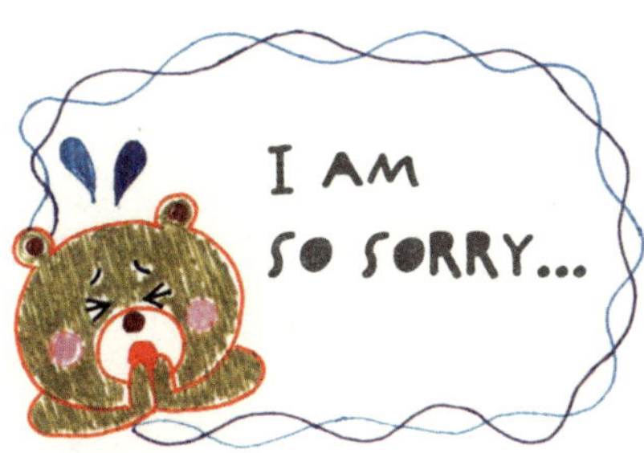

MESSAGES

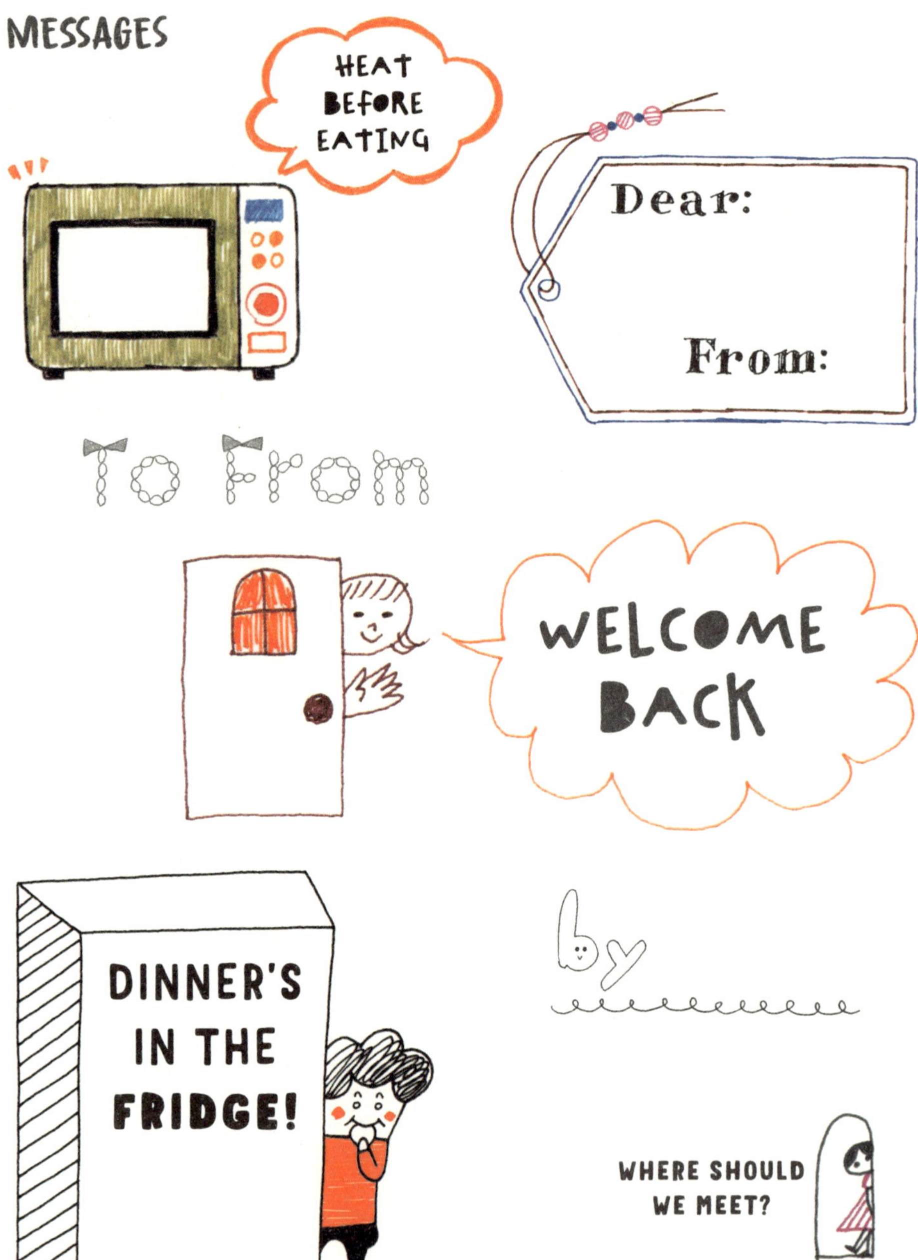
HEAT BEFORE EATING
Dear:
From:
To From
WELCOME BACK
by
DINNER'S IN THE FRIDGE!
WHERE SHOULD WE MEET?

INVITATIONS

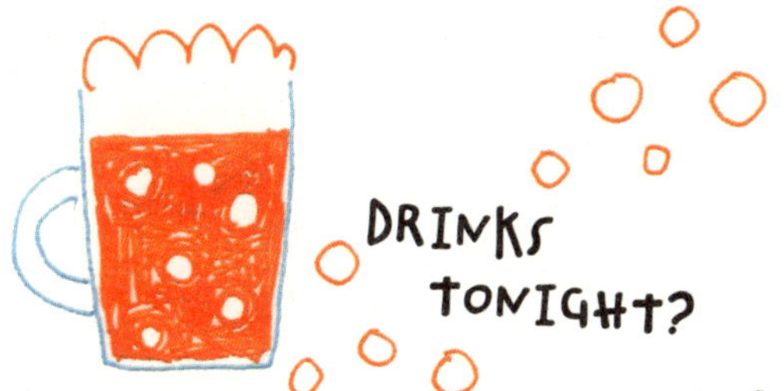

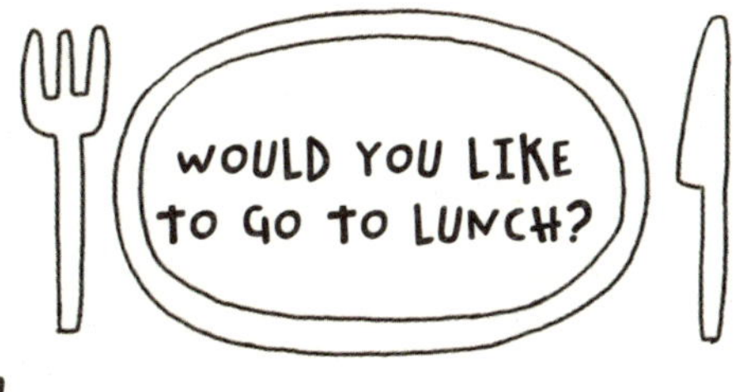

WOULD YOU
LIKE TO GO FOR
A DRINK?

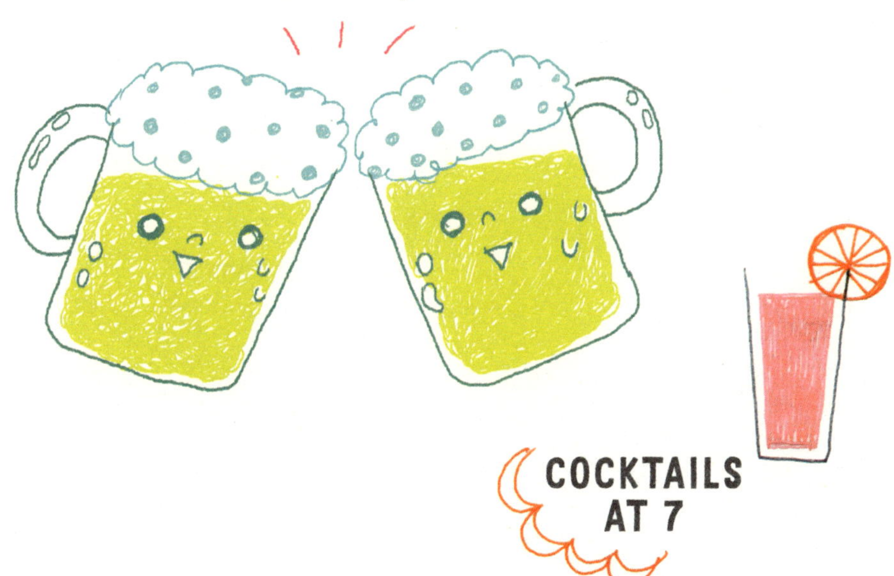

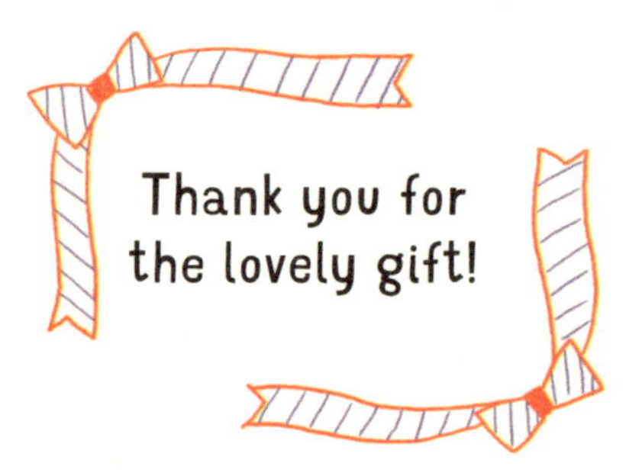
Thank you for
the lovely gift!

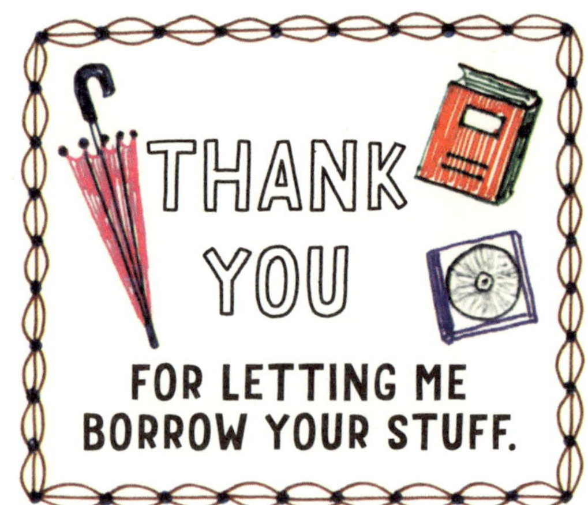
THANK
YOU
FOR LETTING ME
BORROW YOUR STUFF.

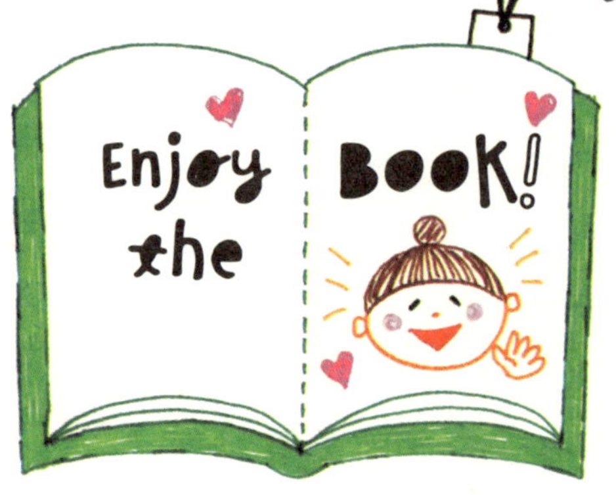
Enjoy
the
BOOK!

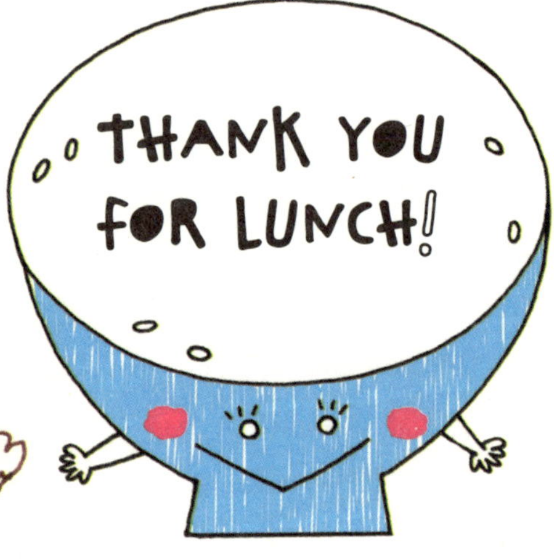
THANK YOU
FOR LUNCH!

Bon
voyage!

OFFICE NOTES

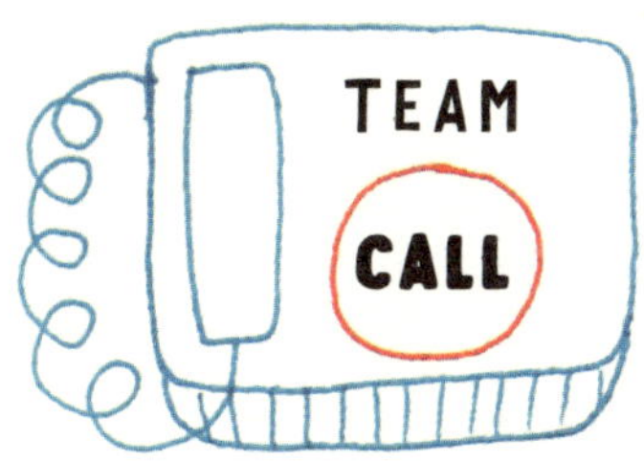

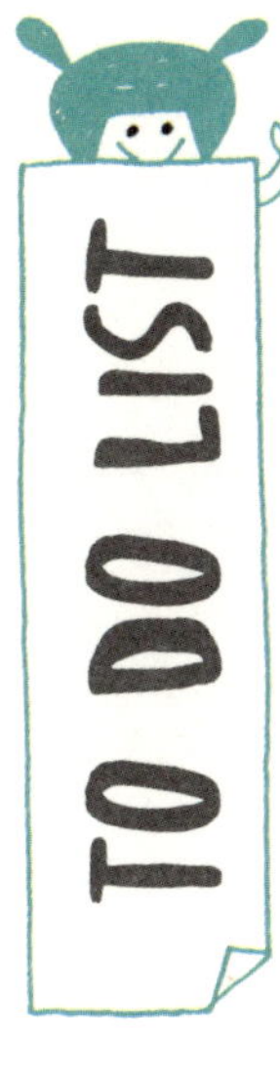

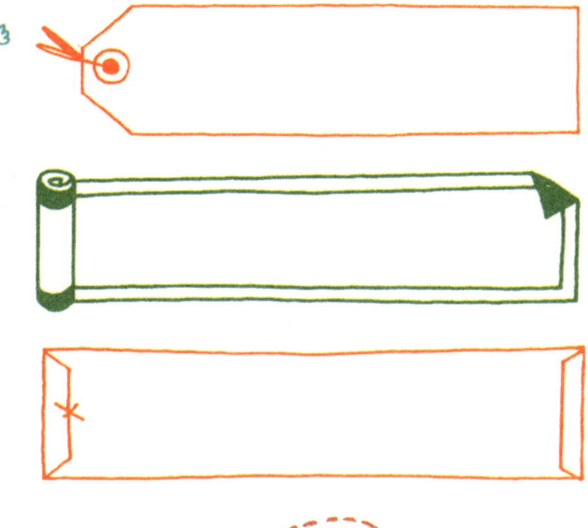

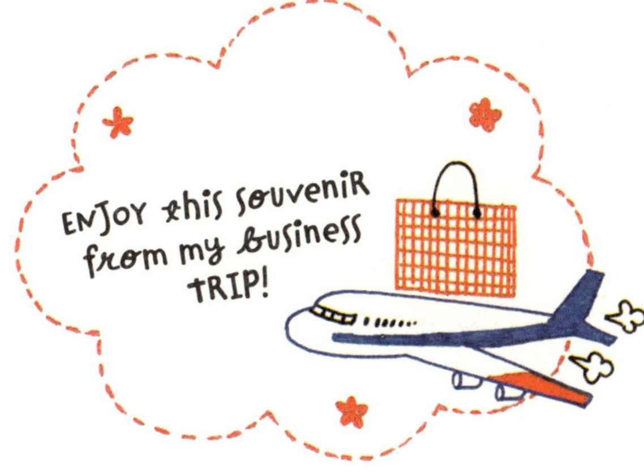

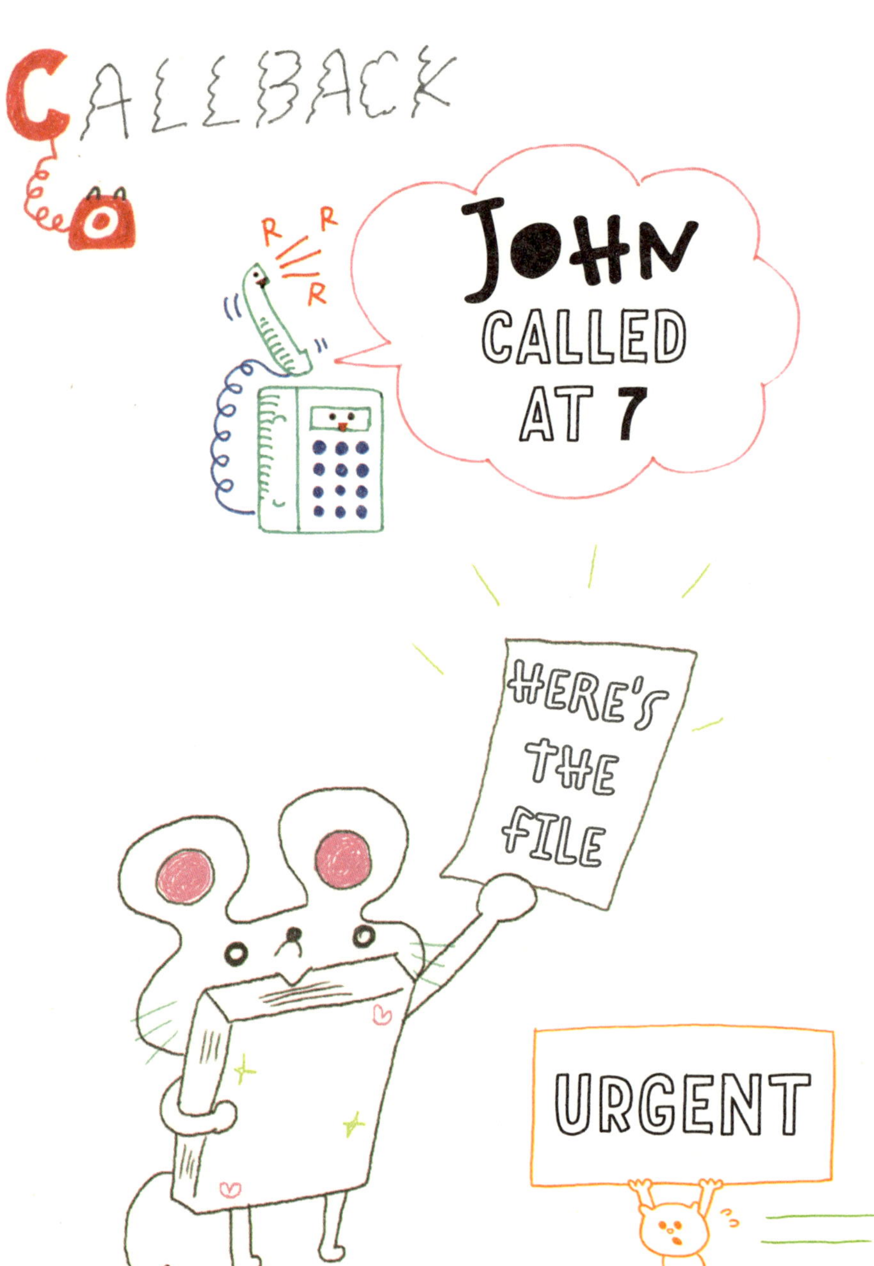
CALLBACK
R R R
JOHN CALLED AT 7
HERE'S THE FILE
URGENT

sample

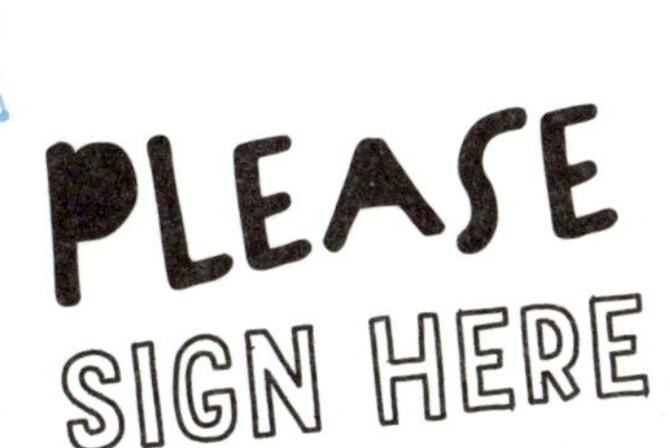

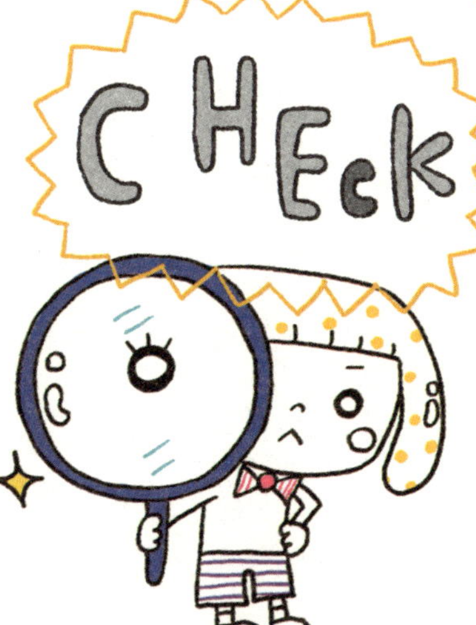

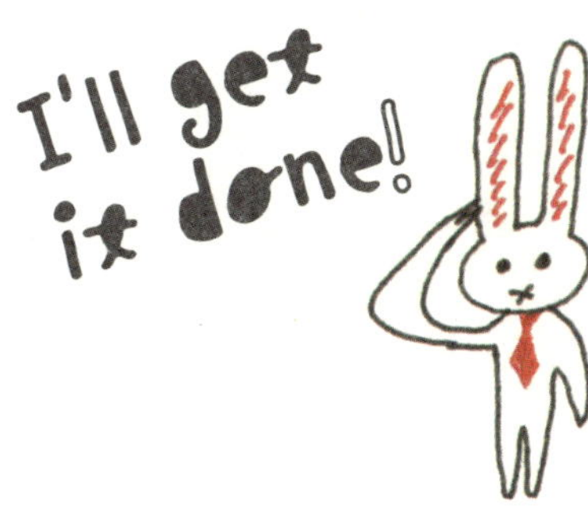

SHARING

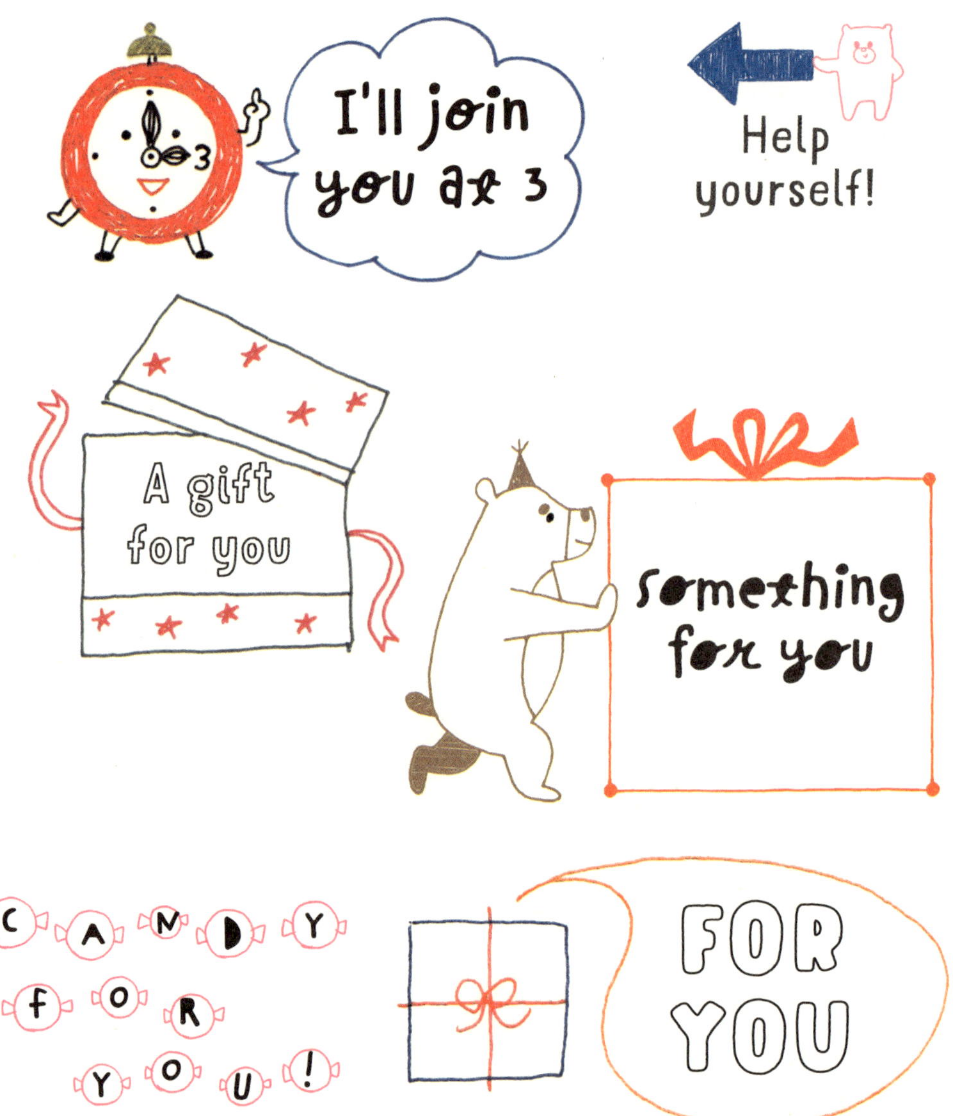
I'll join you at 3
Help yourself!
A gift for you
Something for you
CANDY FOR YOU!
FOR YOU

THIS CAME FOR YOU

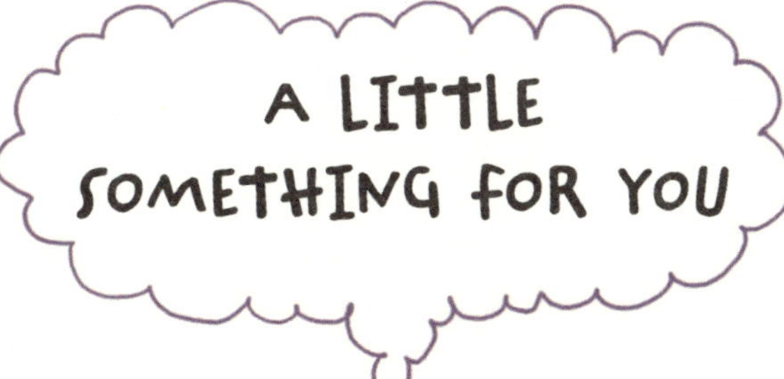

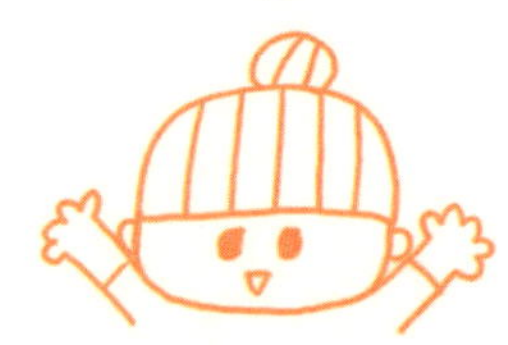

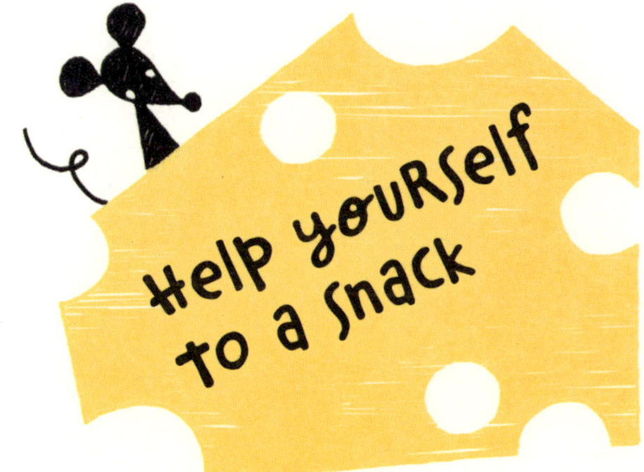

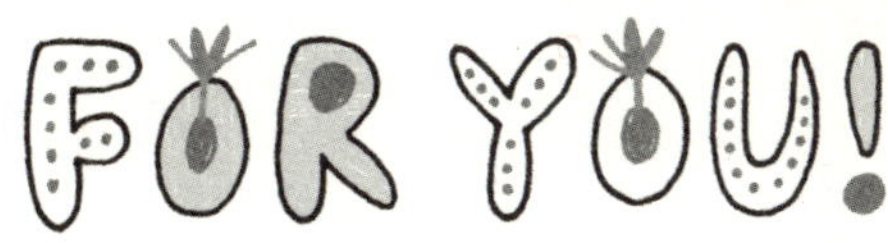

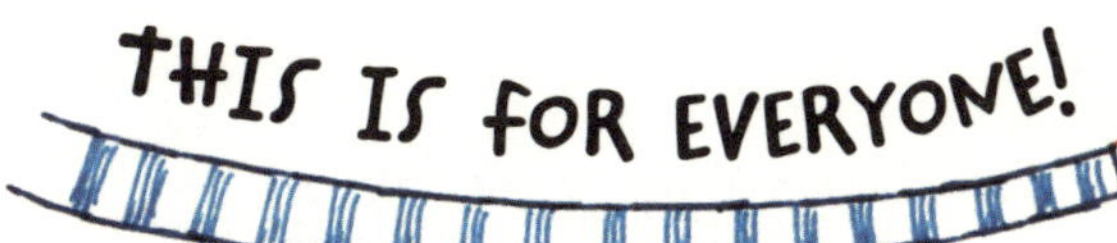

MONTHS

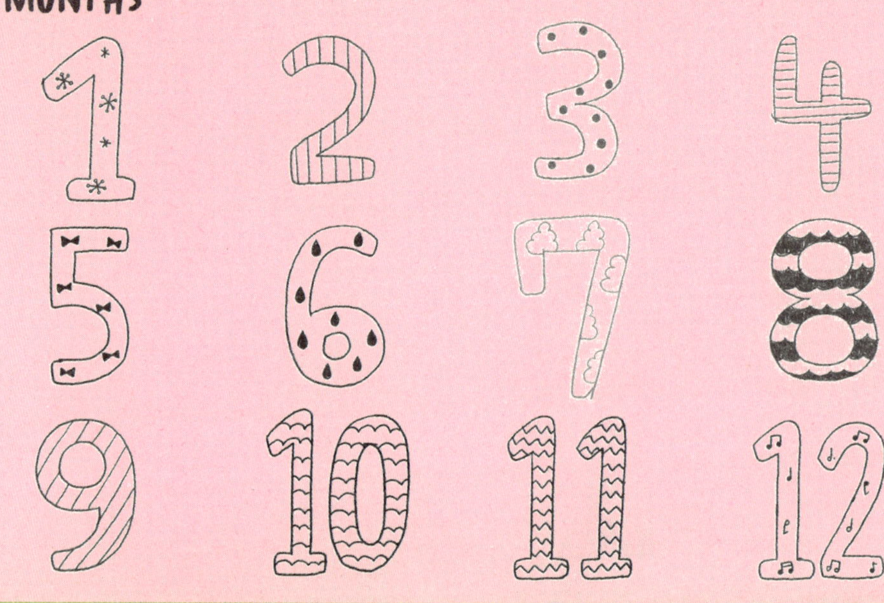

January February March April May

June July August September

October November December

Jan. Feb. Mar. Apr. May Jun.

Jul. Aug. Sep. Oct. Nov. Dec.

Chapter 5:

HOLIDAYS & SEASONAL ILLUSTRATIONS

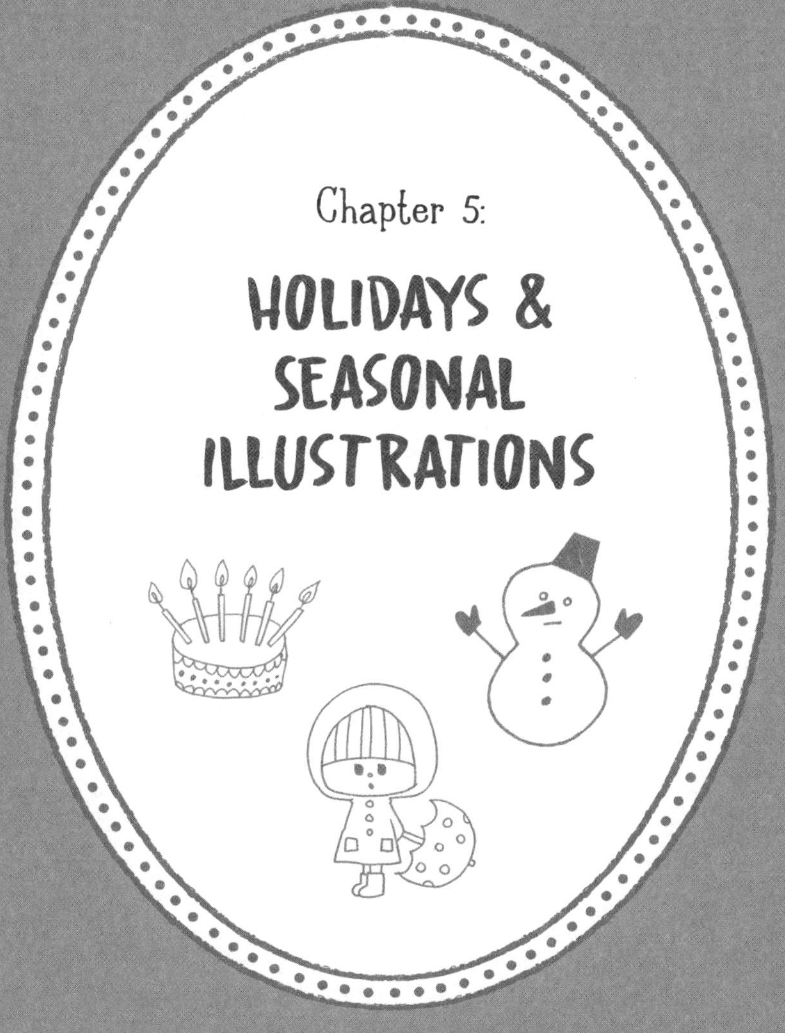

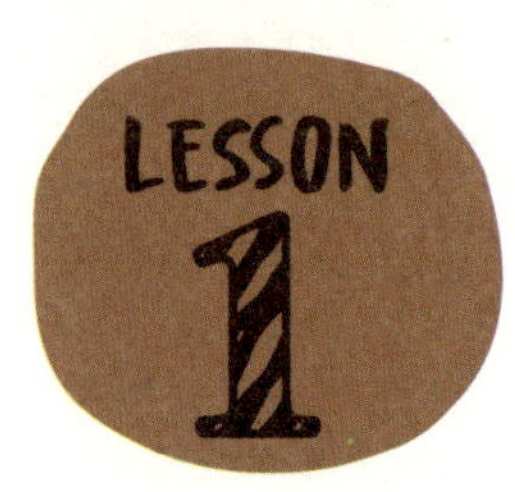

HOLIDAYS & SPECIAL EVENTS

These illustrations are perfect for cards celebrating holidays and important life events. Choose colors that match the theme of the illustration.

BIRTHDAY

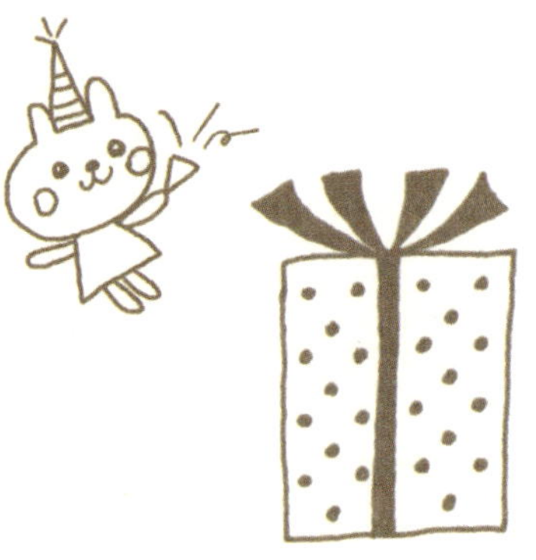

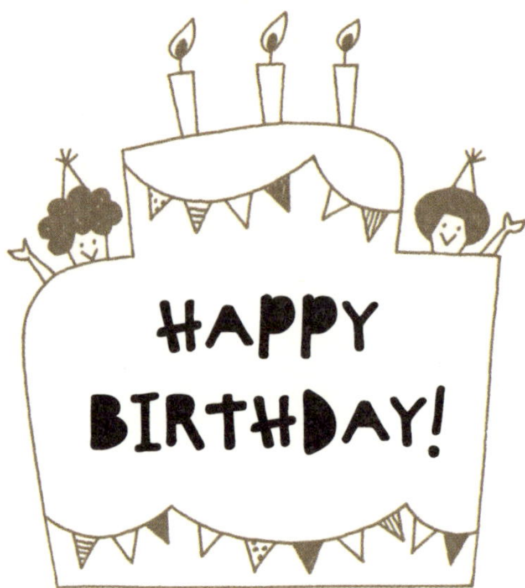

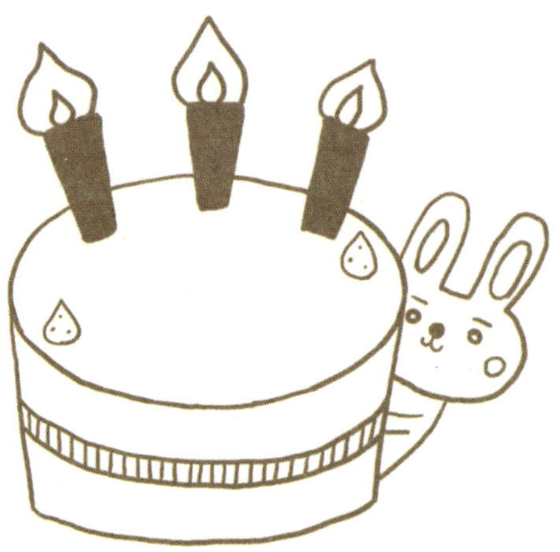

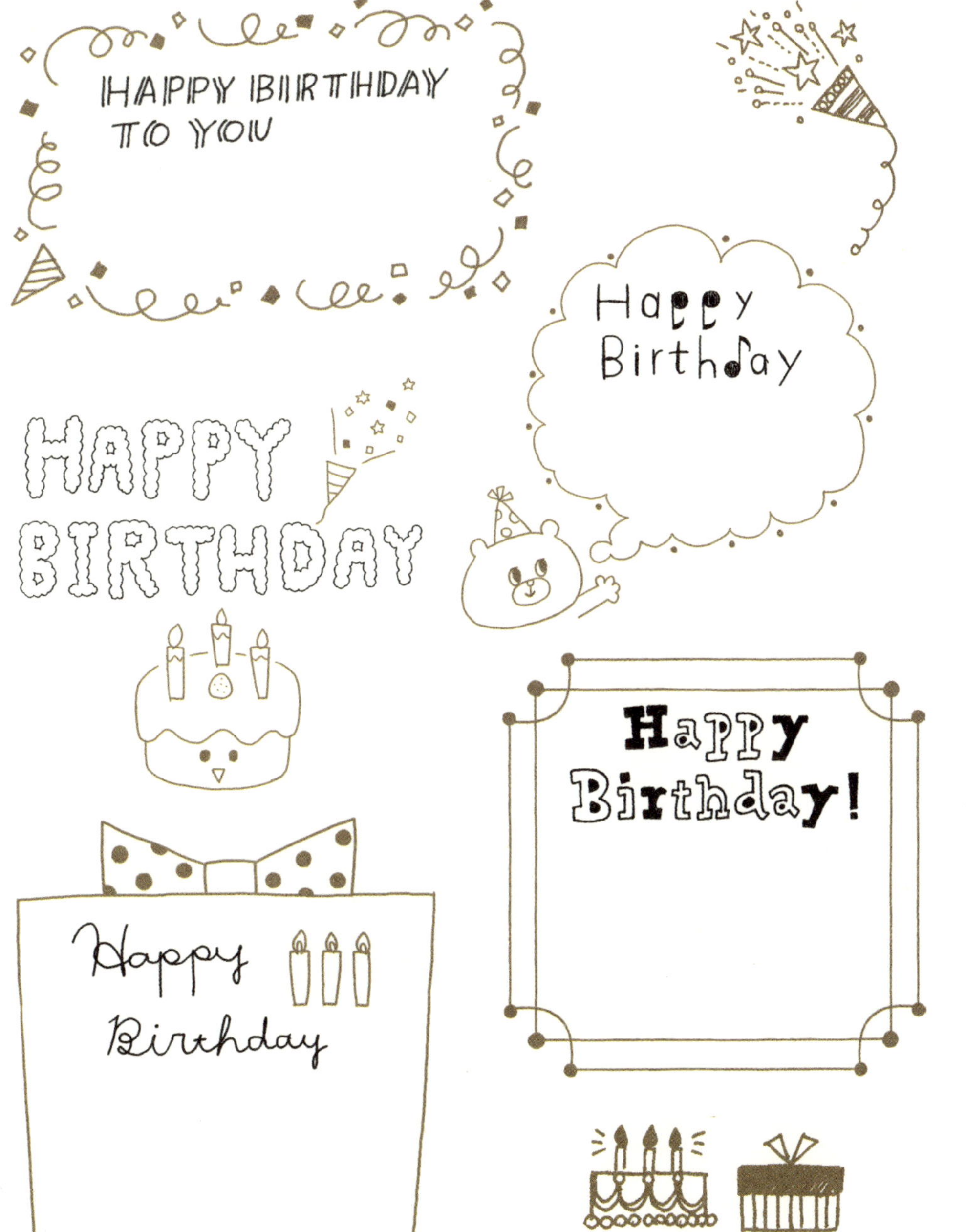
HAPPY BIRTHDAY
TO YOU
Happy
Birthday
HAPPY
BIRTHDAY
Happy
Birthday!
Happy
Birthday

CHRISTMAS

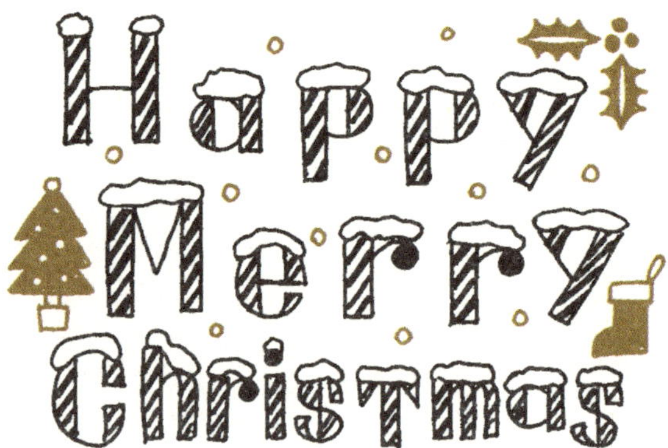

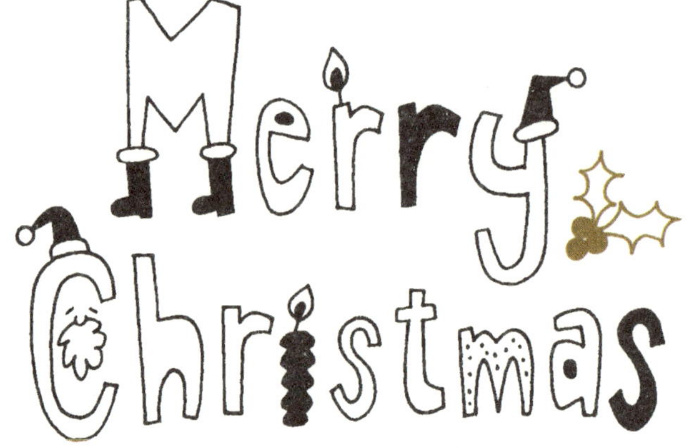

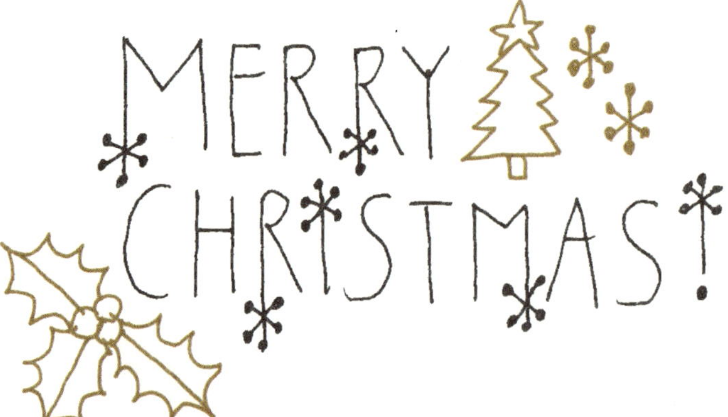

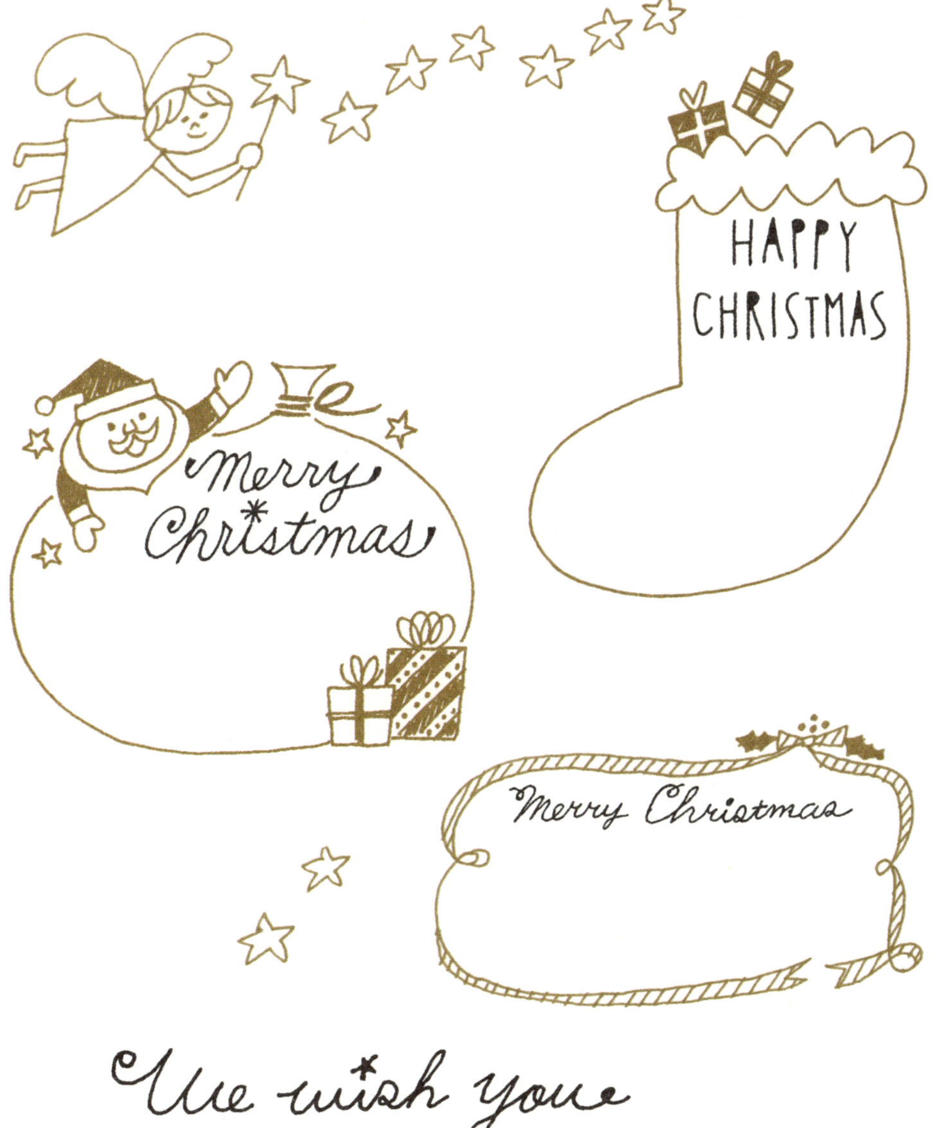

We wish you
a Merry Christmas

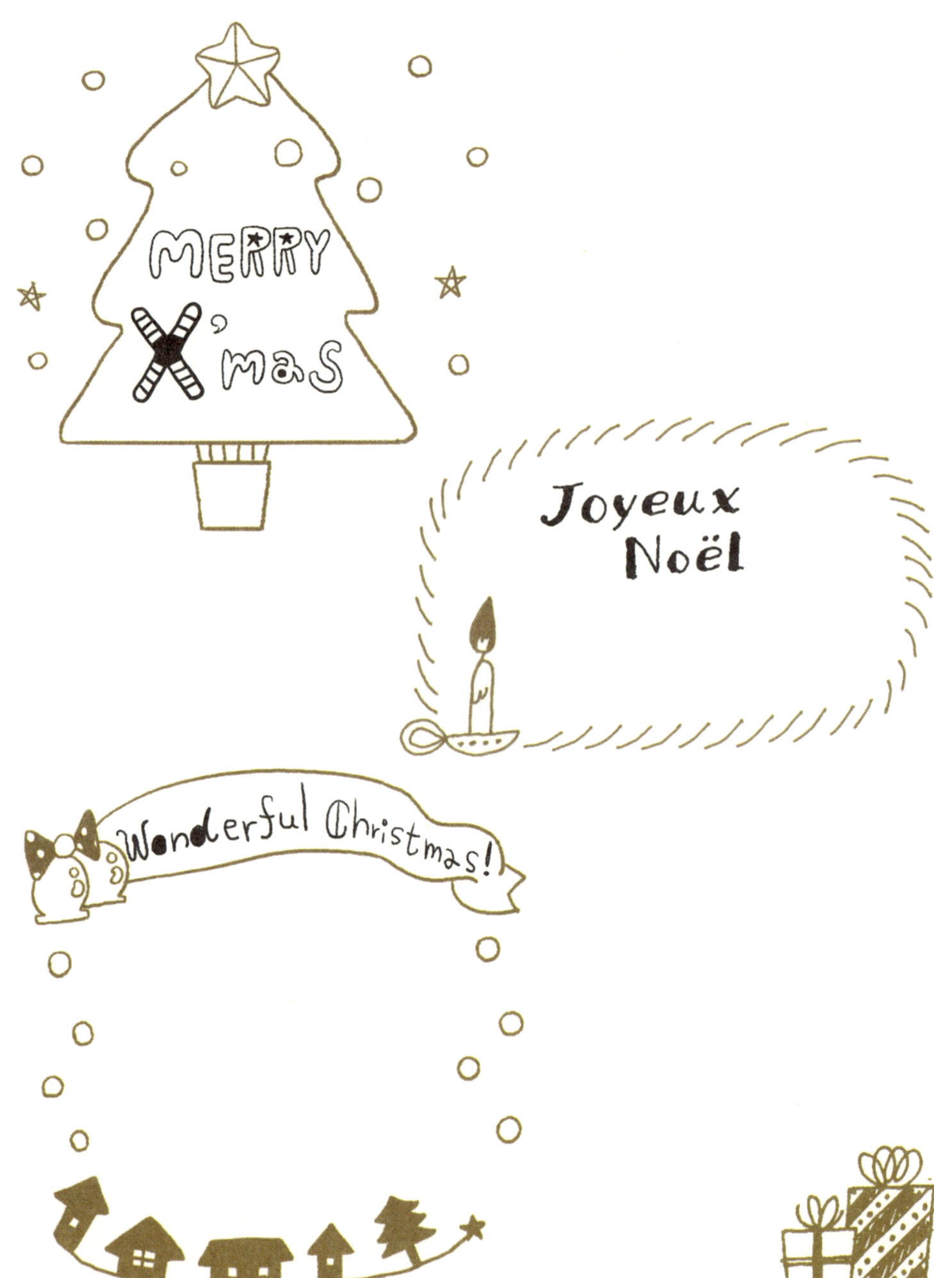
MERRY
X'mas
Joyeux
Noël
Wonderful Christmas!

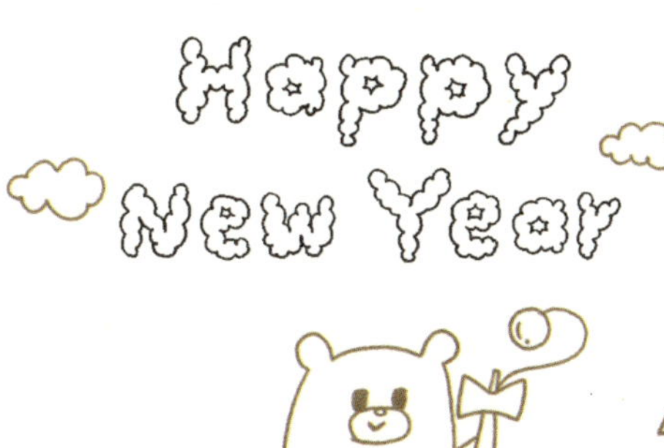

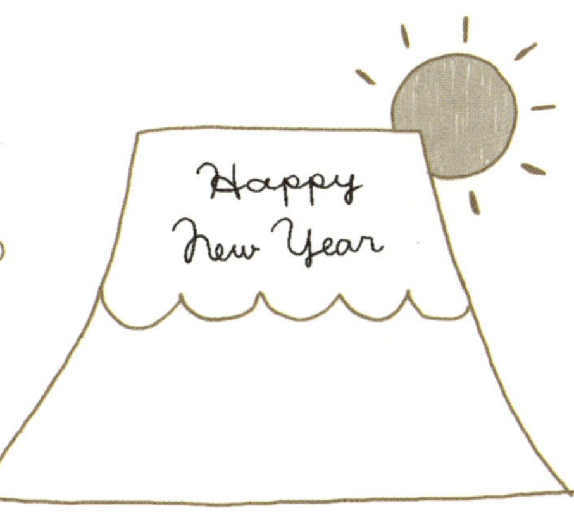

HAPPY
NEW
YEAR!

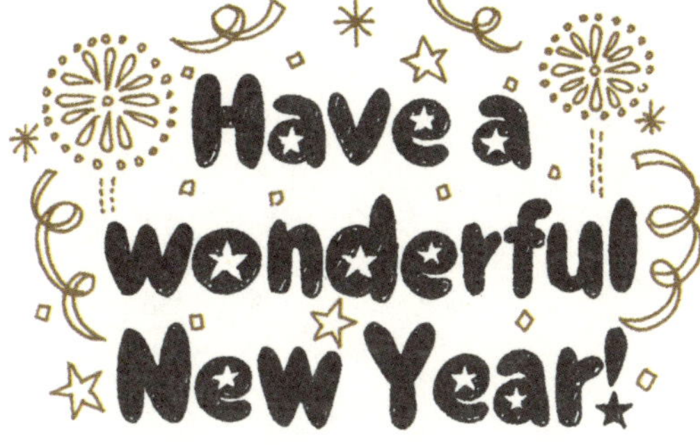

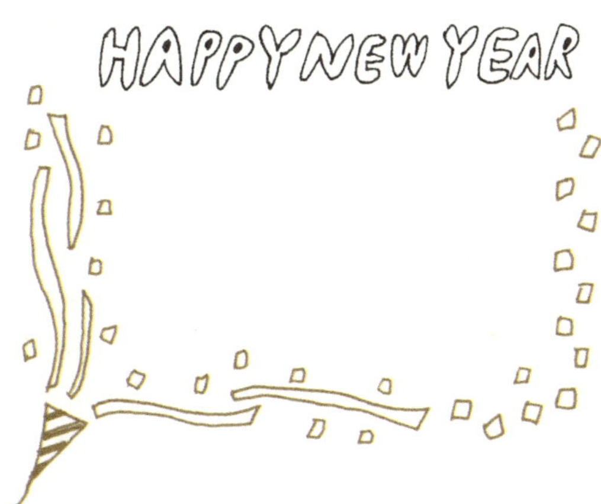

VALENTINE'S DAY

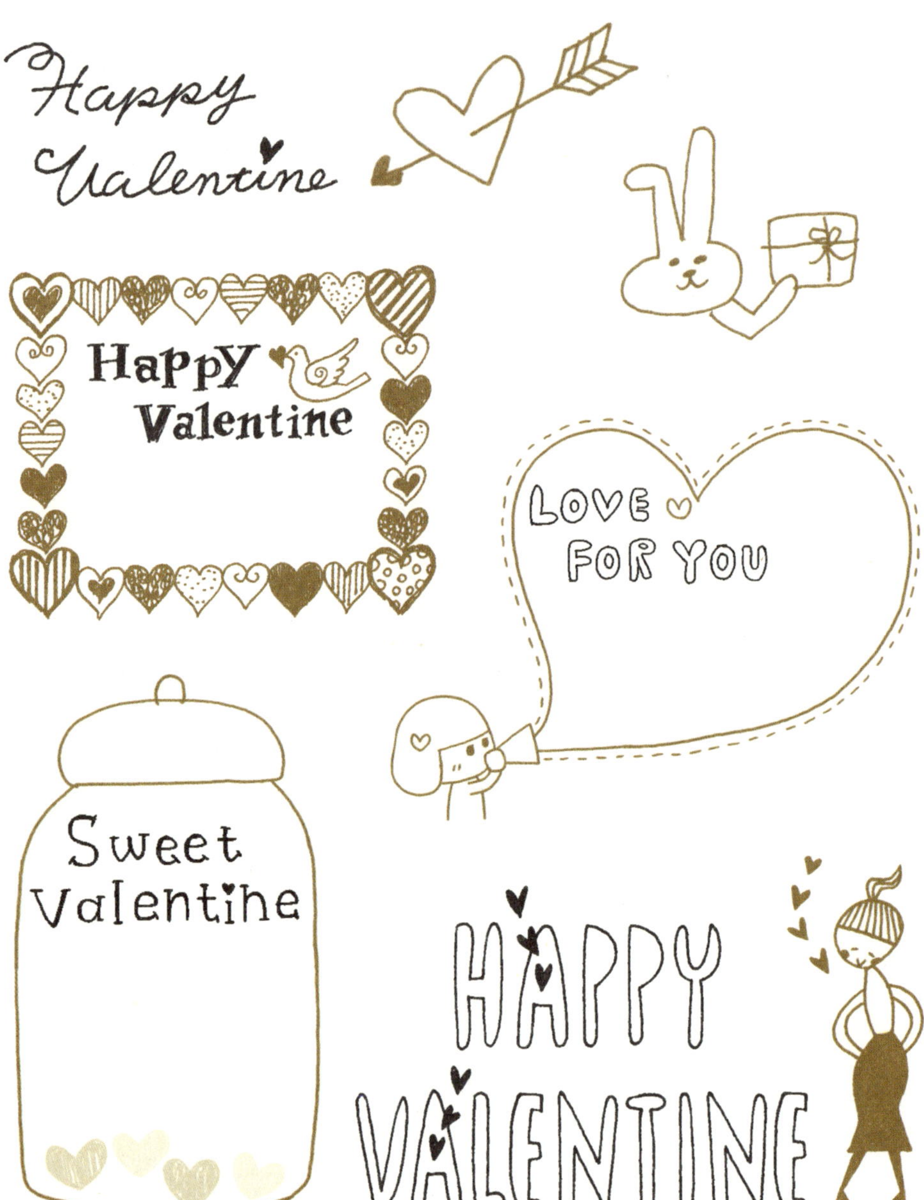

HALLOWEEN

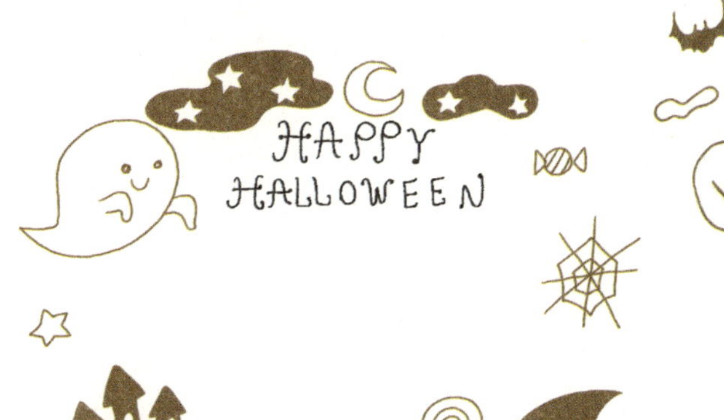
HAPPY
HALLOWEEN

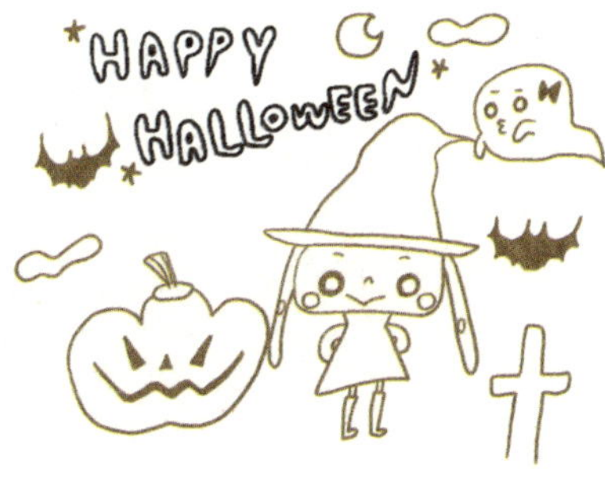
HAPPY
HALLOWEEN

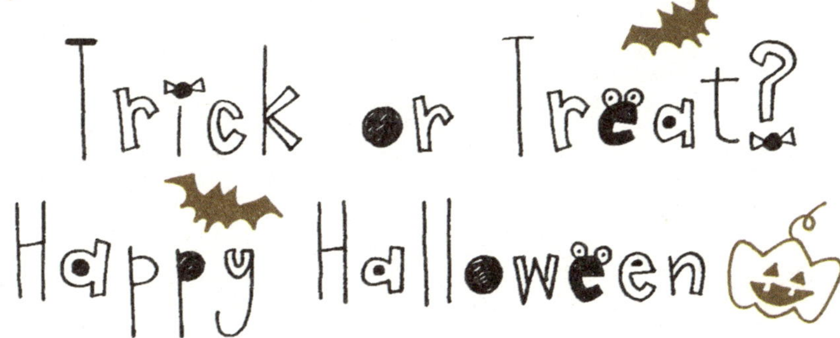
Trick or Treat?
Happy Halloween

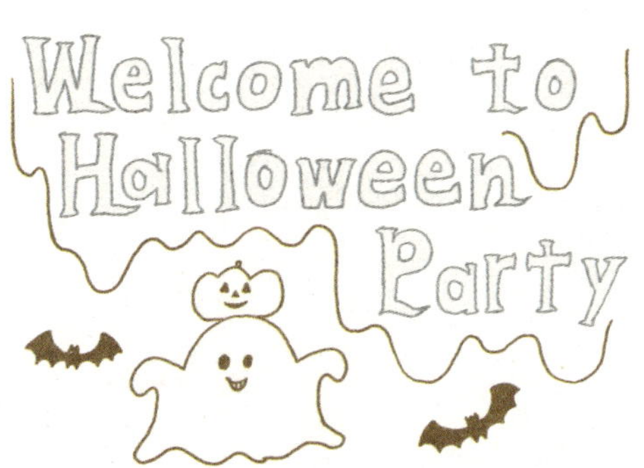
Welcome to
Halloween
Party

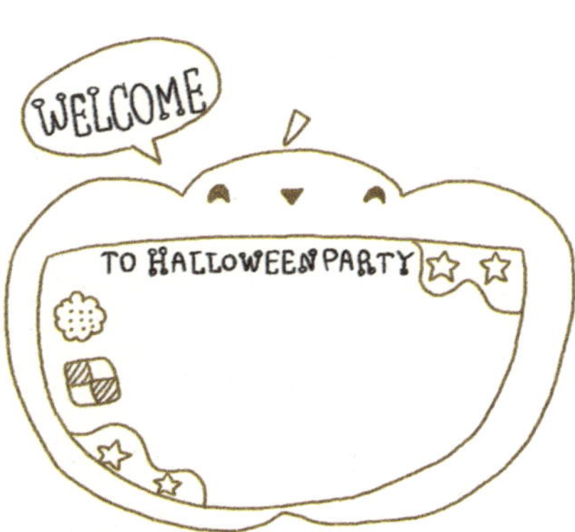
WELCOME
TO HALLOWEEN PARTY

MARRIAGE

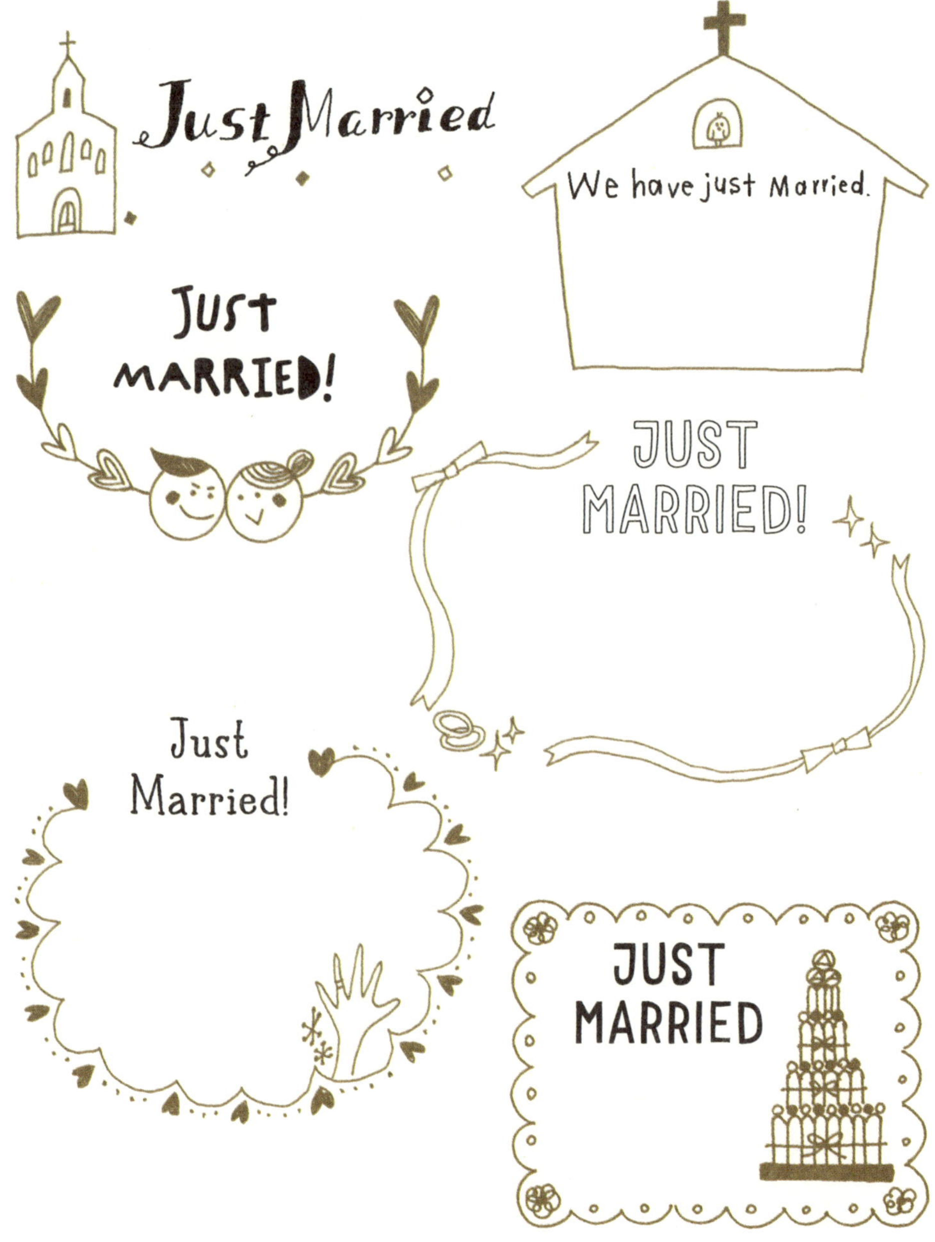
Just Married
We have just Married.
JUST
MARRIED!
JUST
MARRIED!
Just
Married!
JUST
MARRIED

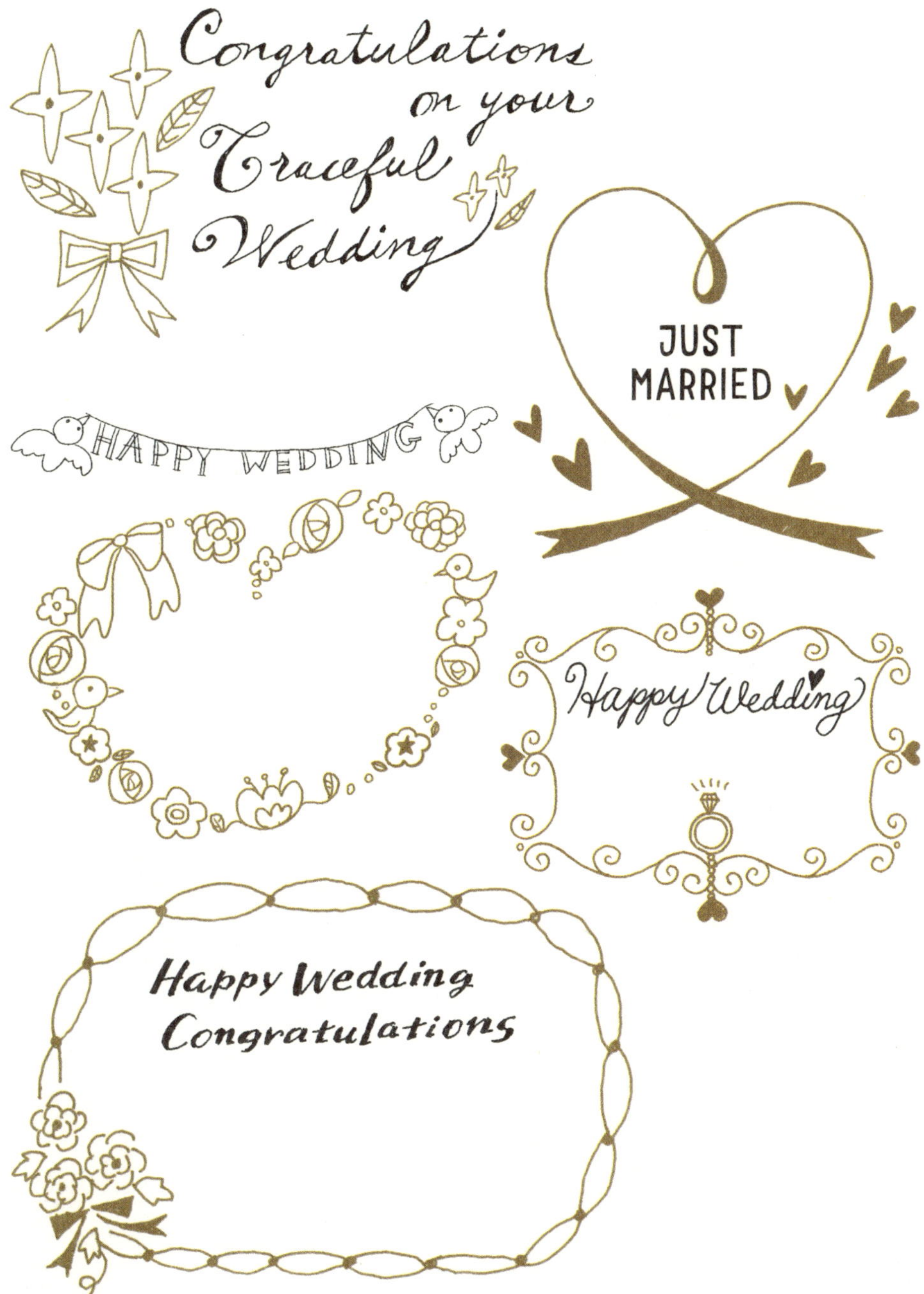
Congratulations on your Graceful Wedding
JUST MARRIED
HAPPY WEDDING
Happy Wedding
Happy Wedding
Congratulations

NEW BABY

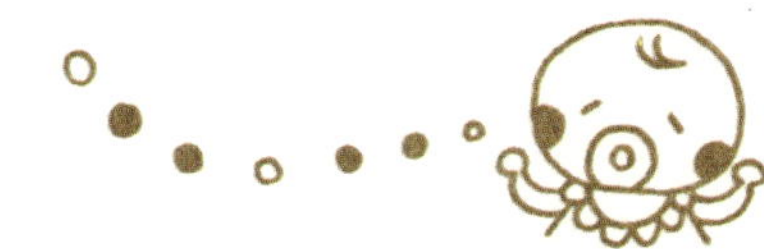

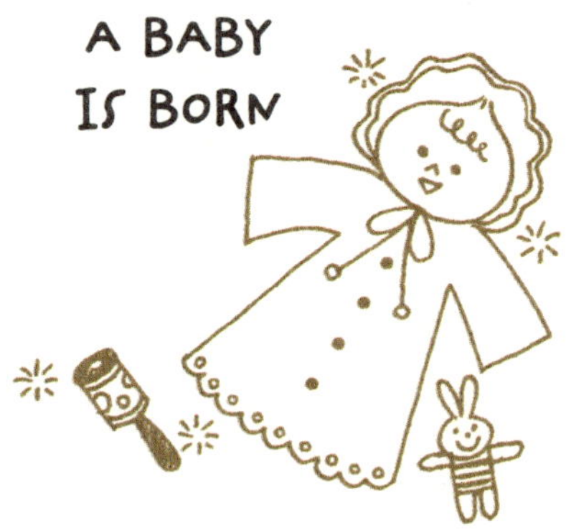

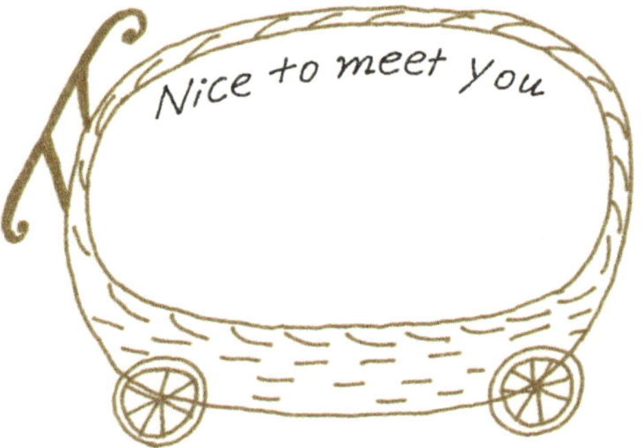

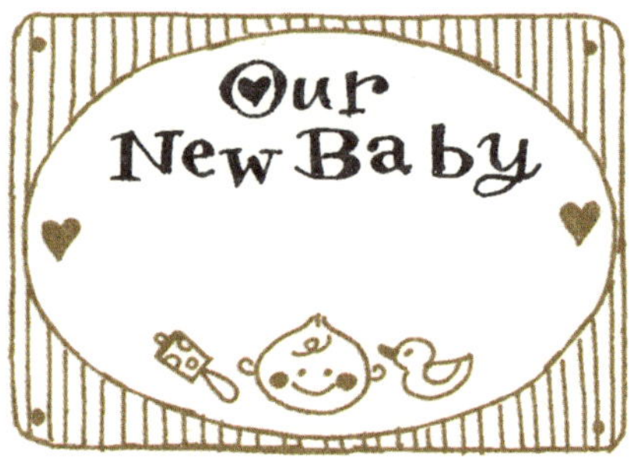

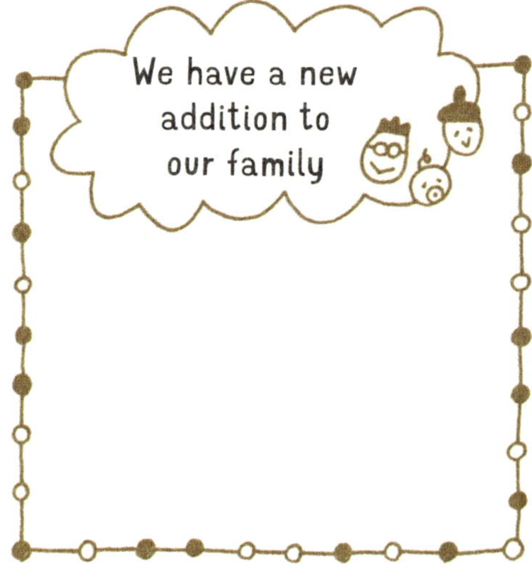

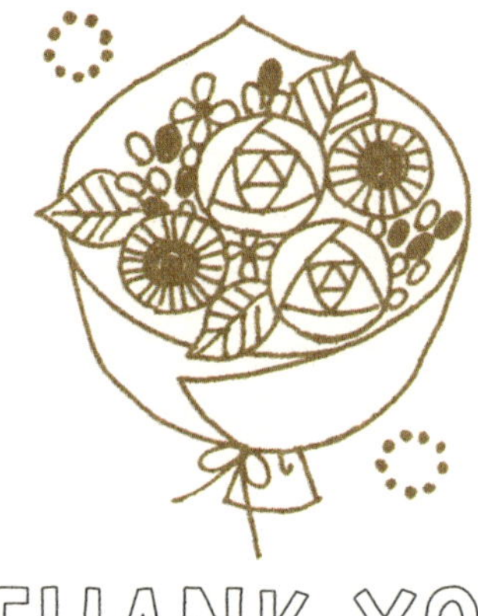

THANK YOU

FOR YOUR GIFT!

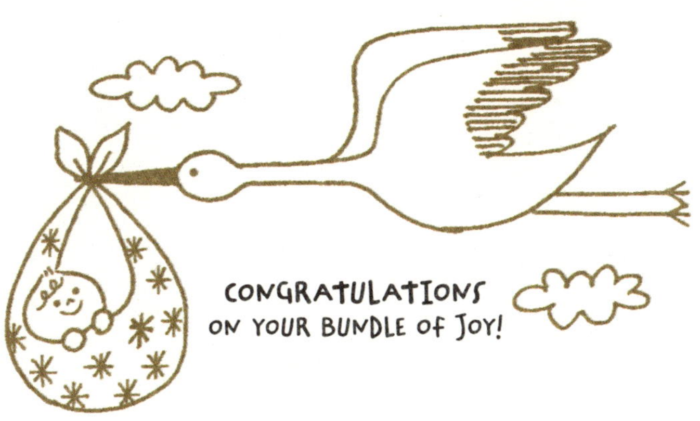

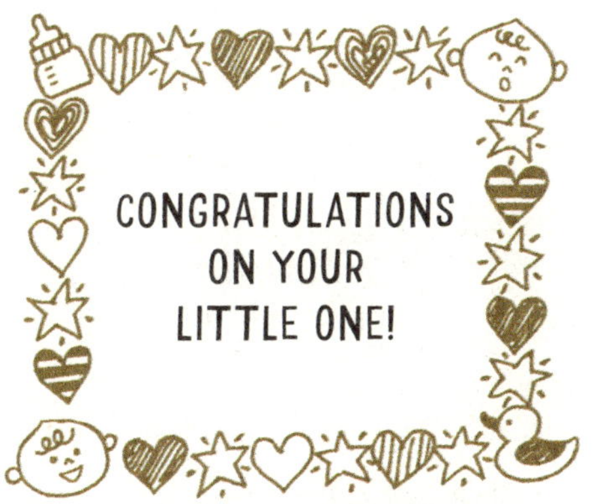

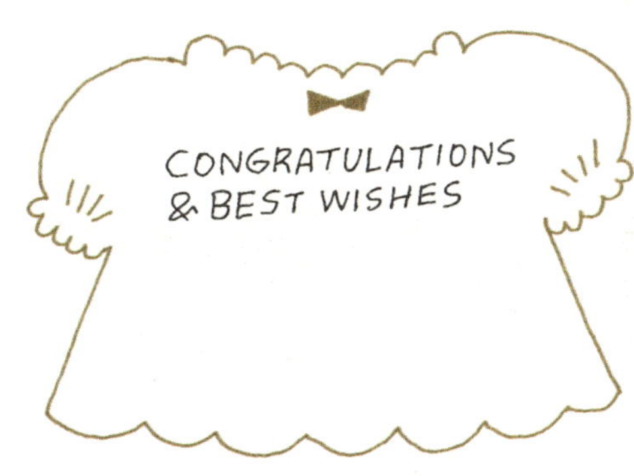

Congratulations

New Baby

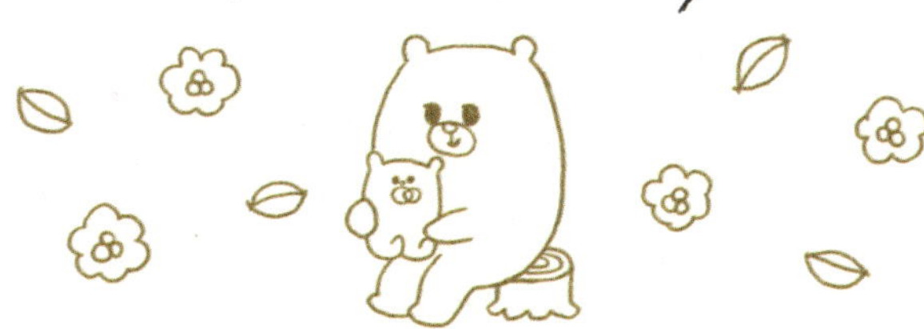

MOVING

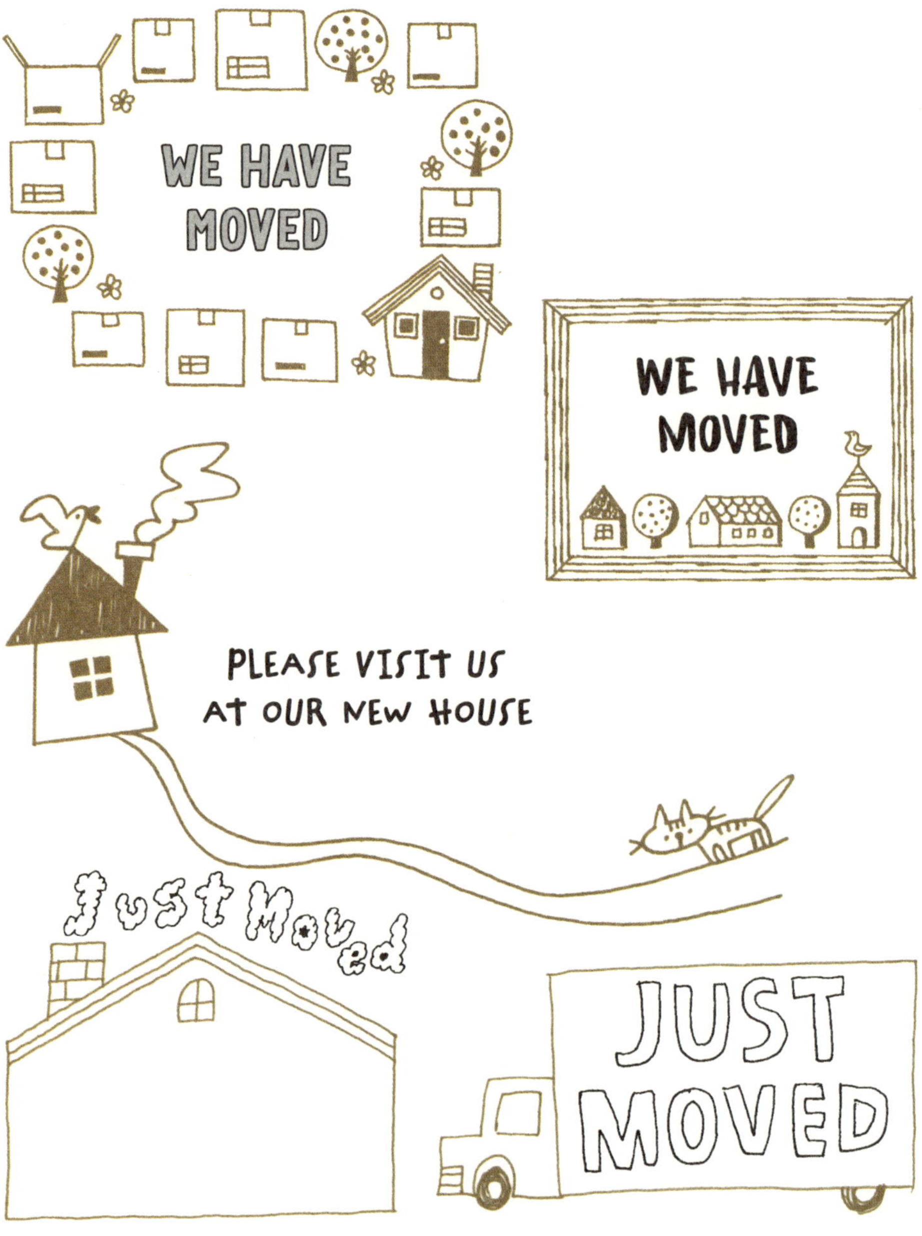
WE HAVE
MOVED
WE HAVE
MOVED
PLEASE VISIT US
AT OUR NEW HOUSE
Just Moved
JUST
MOVED

MOTHER'S DAY & FATHER'S DAY

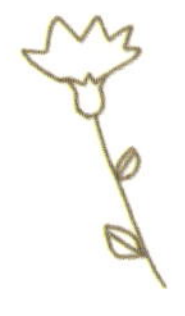

TO THE WORLD'S
BEST MOM

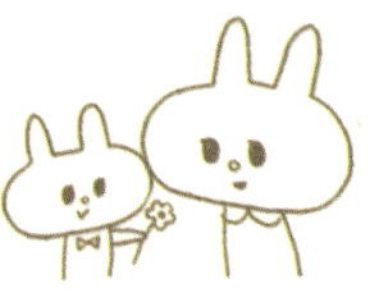

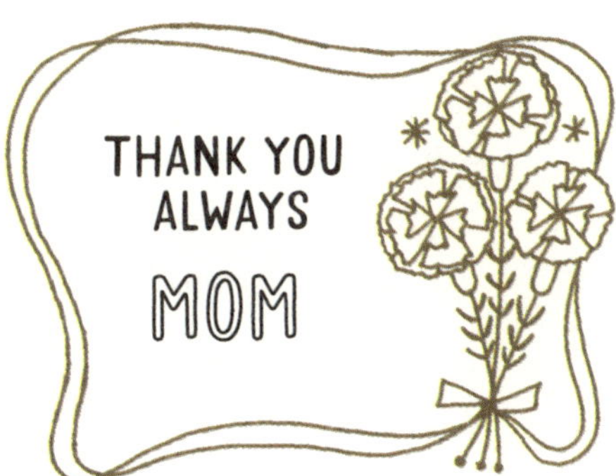

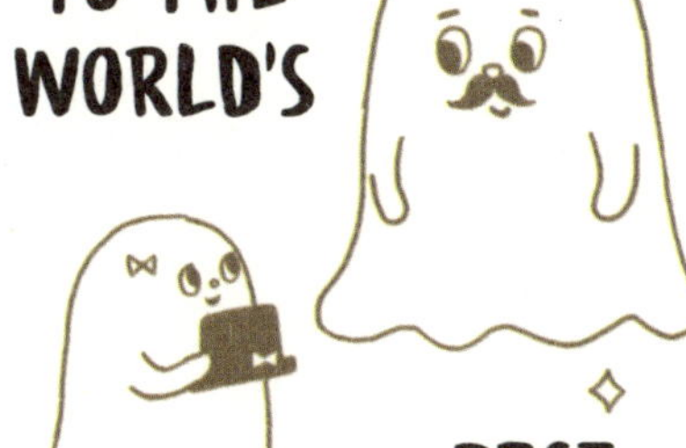

TO THE
WORLD'S

BEST
DAD

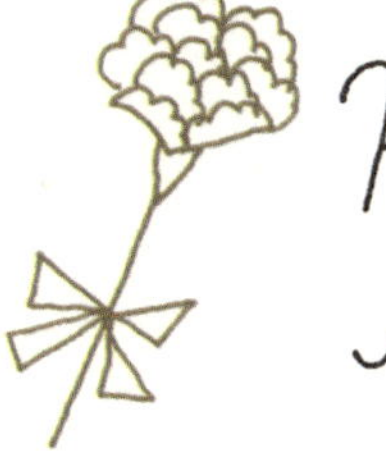

Happy
Mother's Day

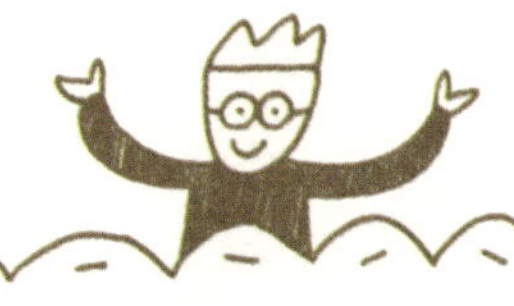

YOU'RE
THE BEST
DAD!

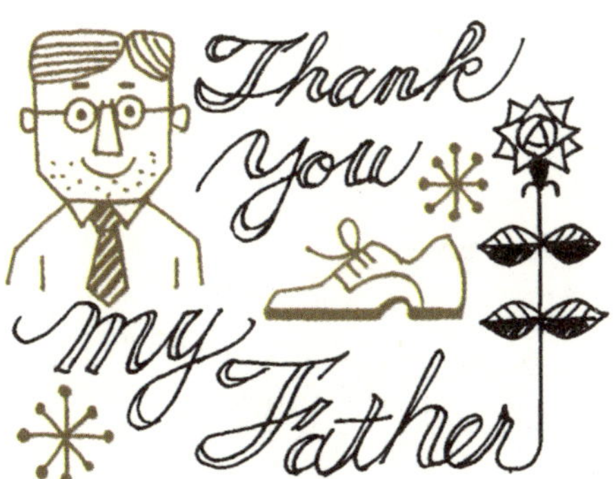

RETAIL

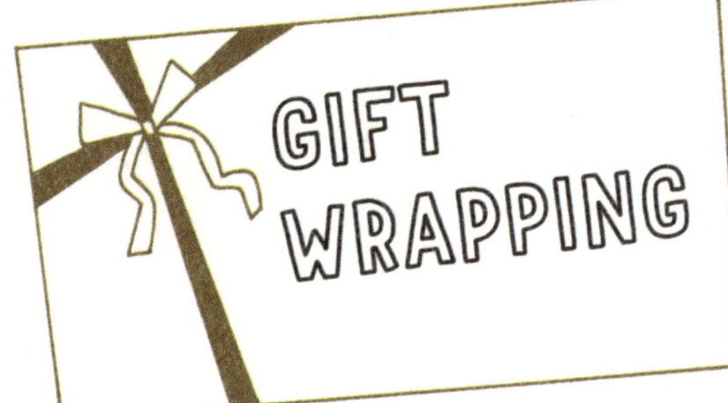

STAFF

Sale

RECOMMENDATION

BEST
SELLER!

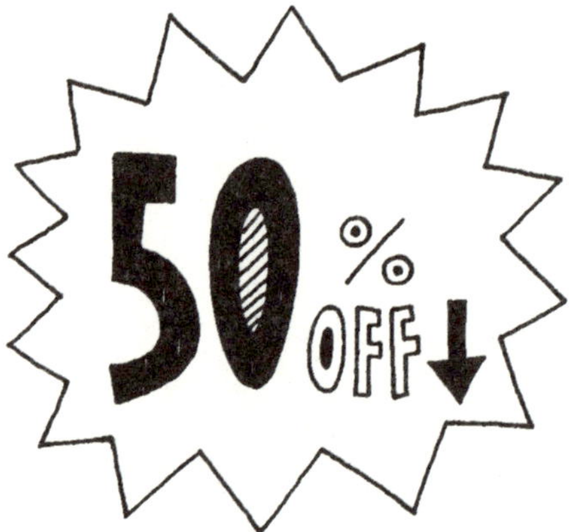

STAFF
FAVORITE

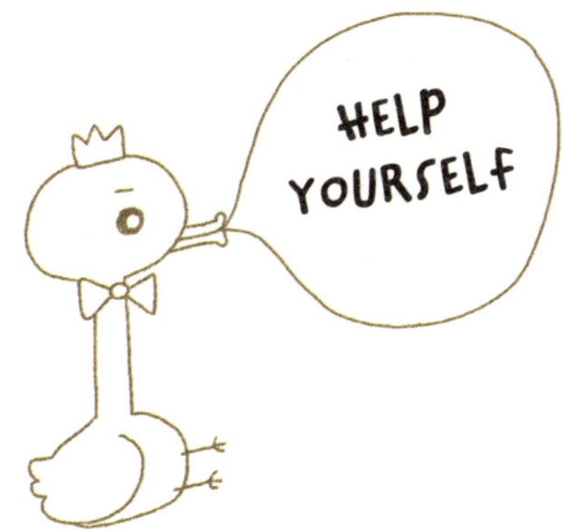

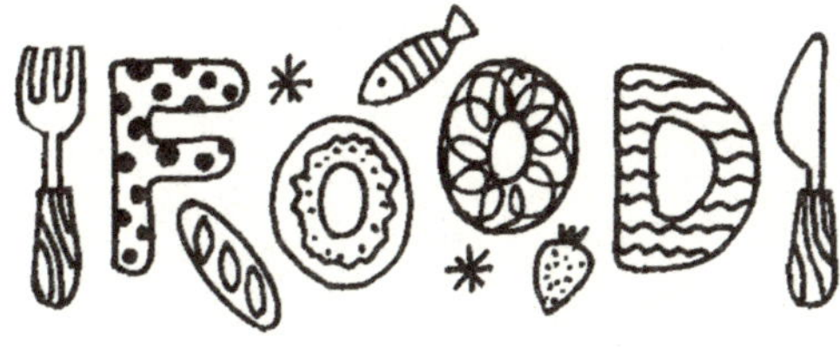

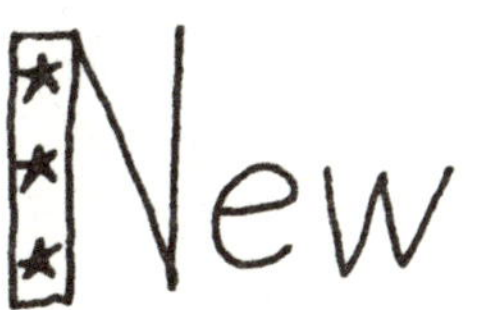

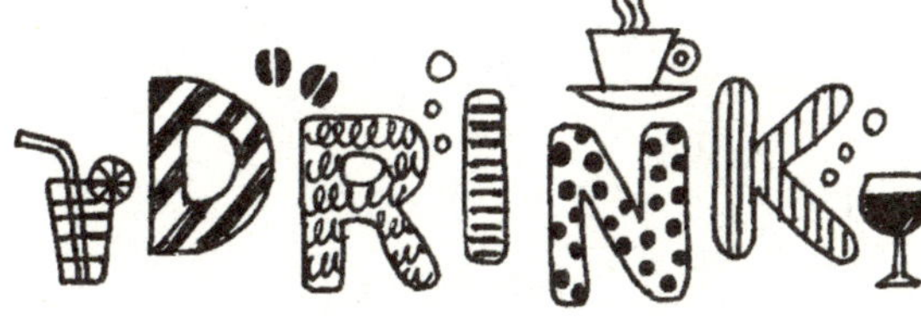

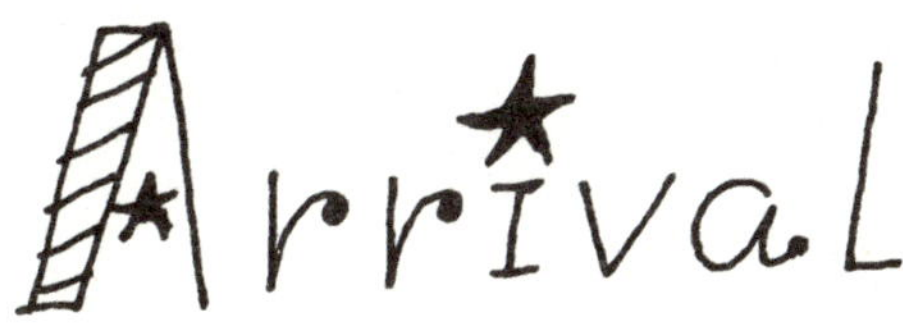

TAKEFREE

MENU

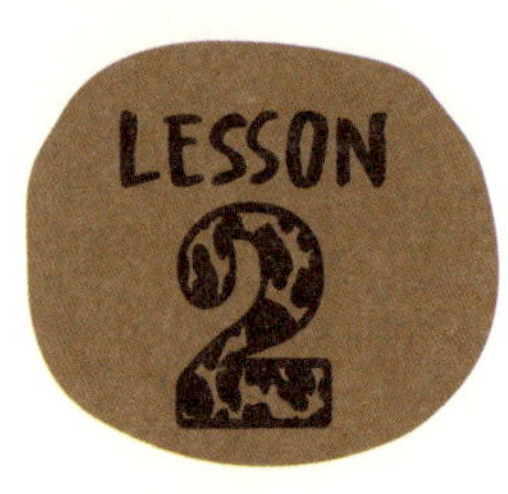

SEASONAL ILLUSTRATIONS

These small illustrations are inspired by seasonal events. Use on greeting cards, messages, and gifts.

SPRING

Field day

Plum blossom tree and nightingale

Cherry blossom tree

Tulips and butterfly

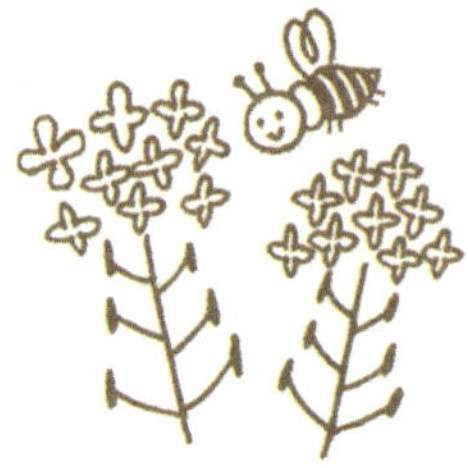

Flowers and honey bee

Bamboo shoots

Ladybug and clover

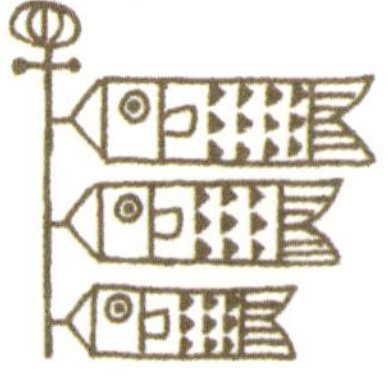

Children's Day streamer

Swallow

SUMMER

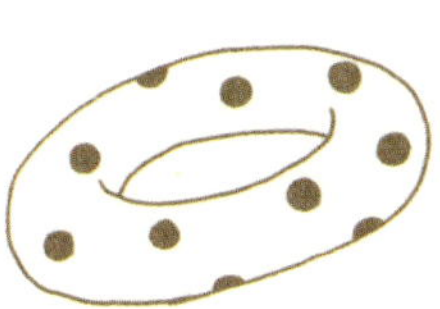

Inner tube

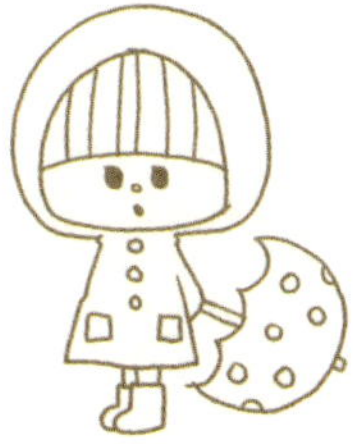

Rainy day

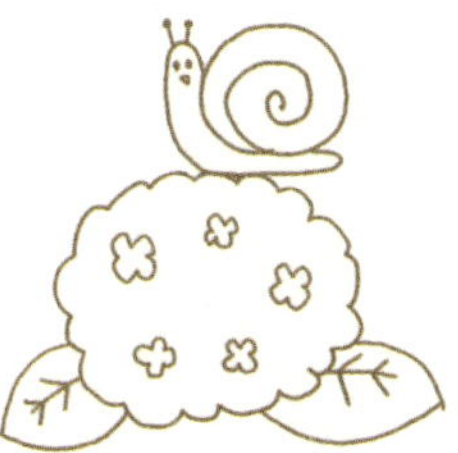

Hydrangea and snail

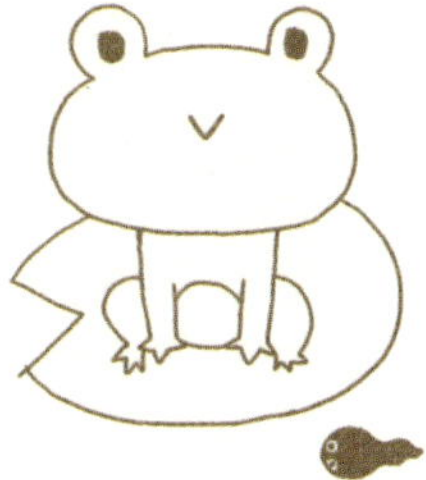

Frog and tadpole

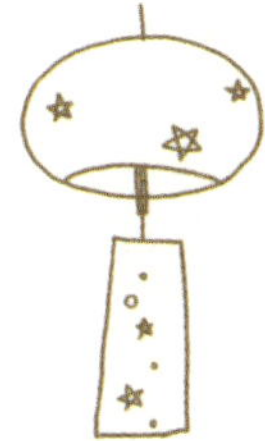

Wind chimes

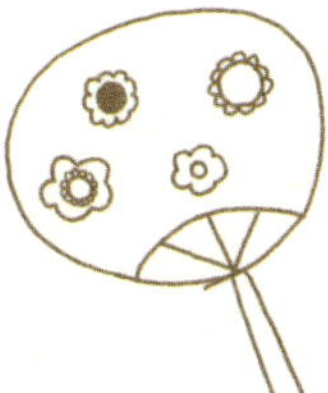

Fan

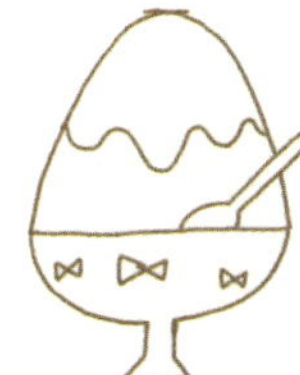

Shaved ice

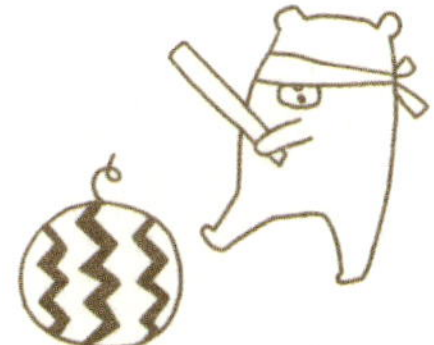

Summer games

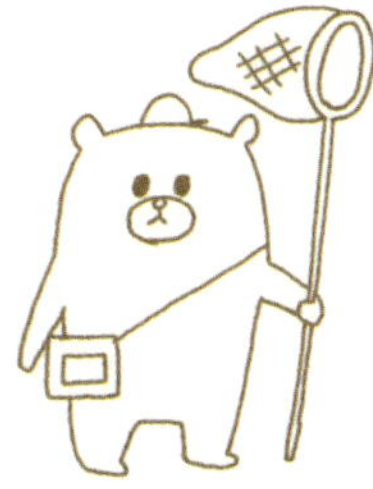

Collecting insects

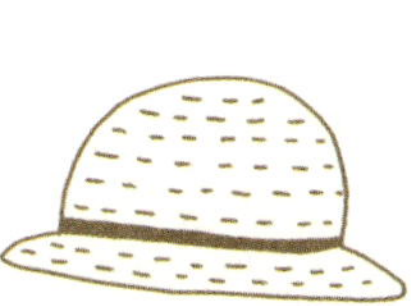

Straw hat

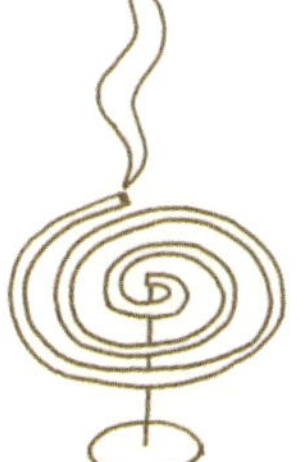

Mosquito incense

Fireworks

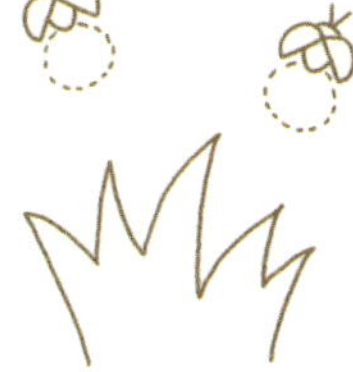

Fireflies

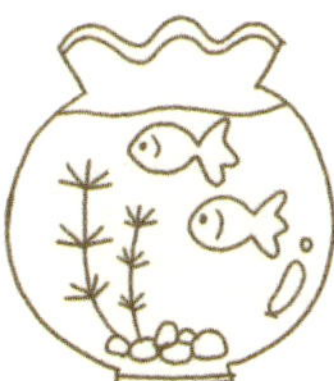

Goldfish

AUTUMN

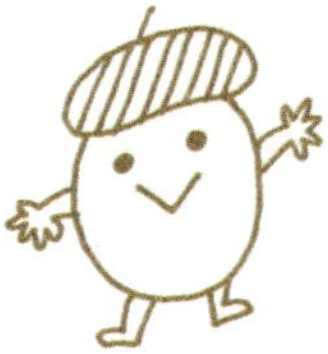

Acorn

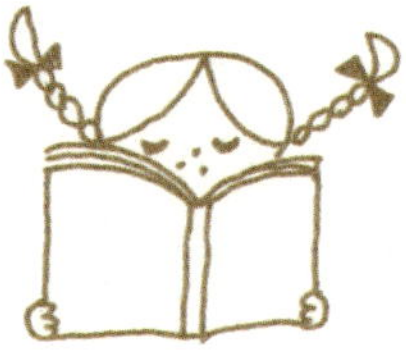

Reading books

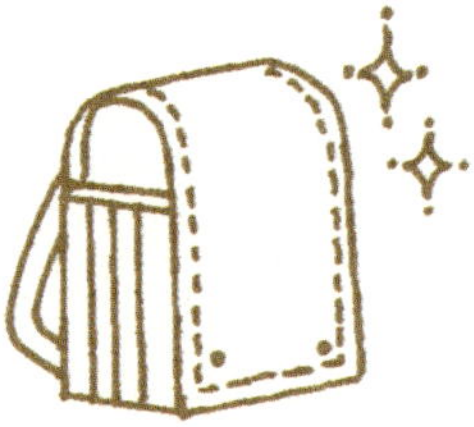

First day of school

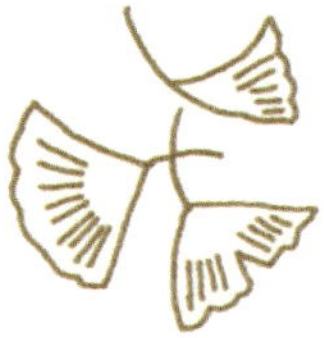

Collecting leaves

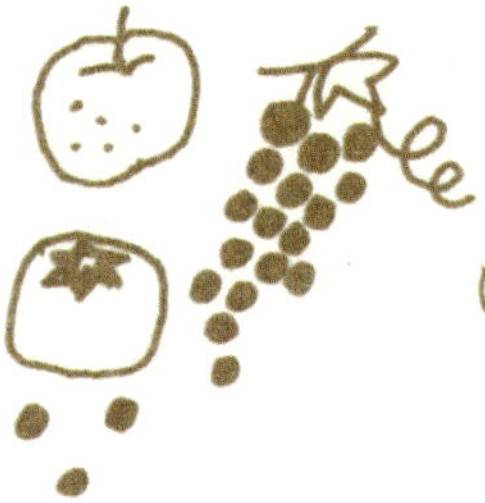

Fruit picking

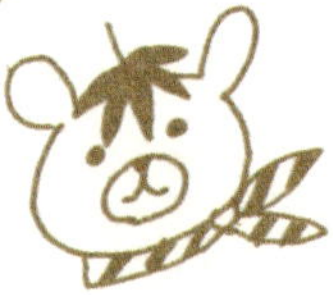

Playing in the leaves

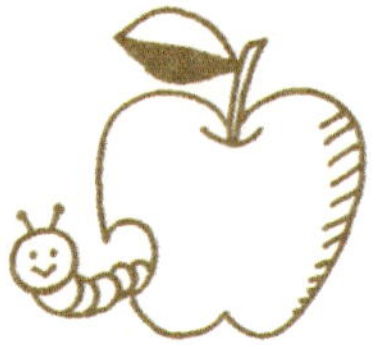

Apple and worm

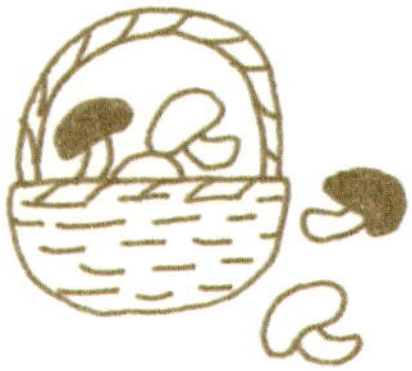

Mushroom hunting

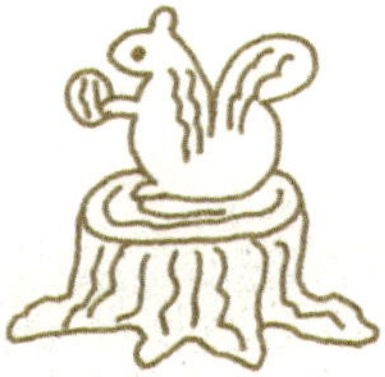

Squirrel

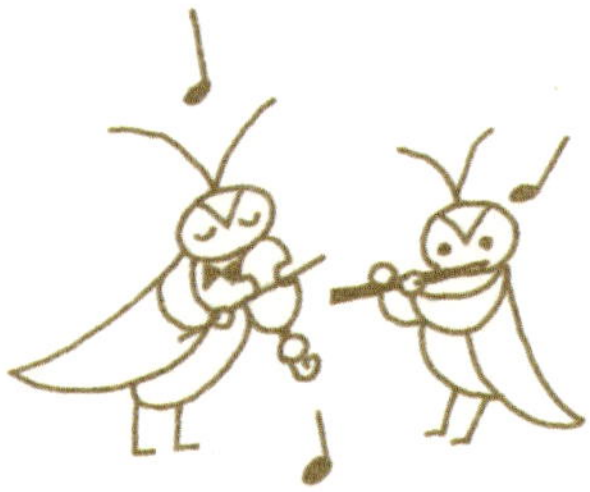

Concert of insects

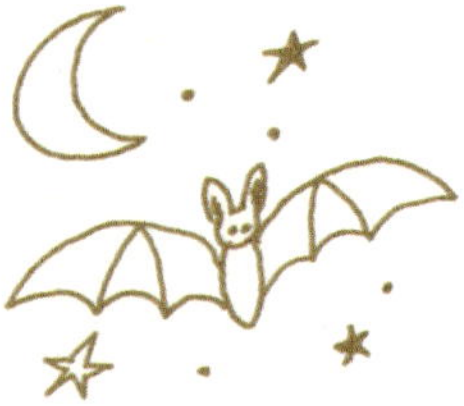

Crescent moon and bat

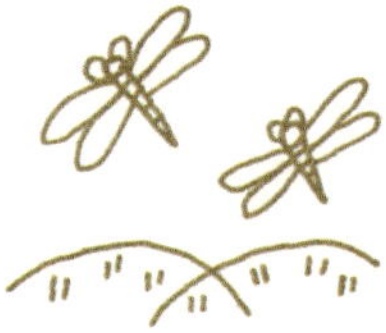

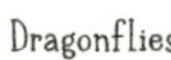

Dragonflies

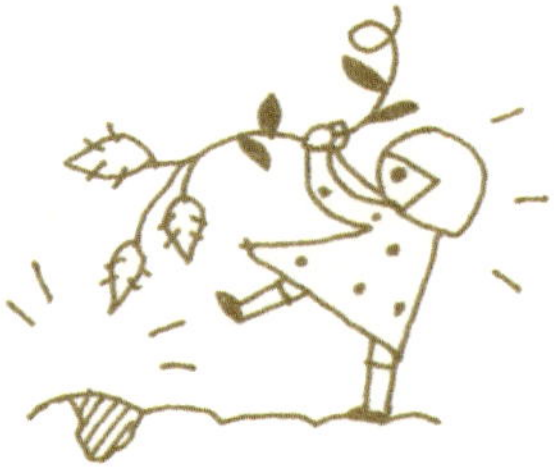

Harvest time

Halloween pumpkin and ghost

WINTER

Santa Claus

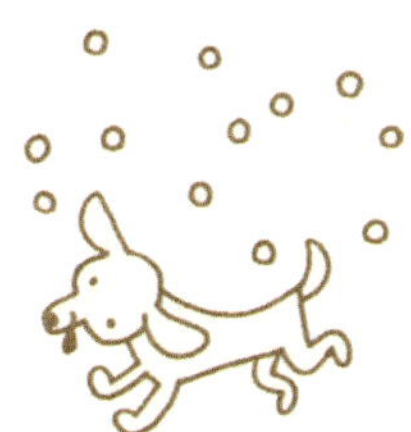

Playing in the snow

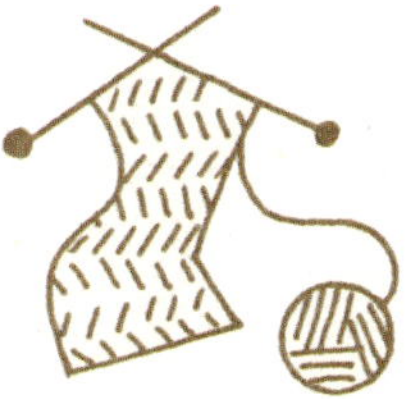

Knitting

Snowman

Christmas tree

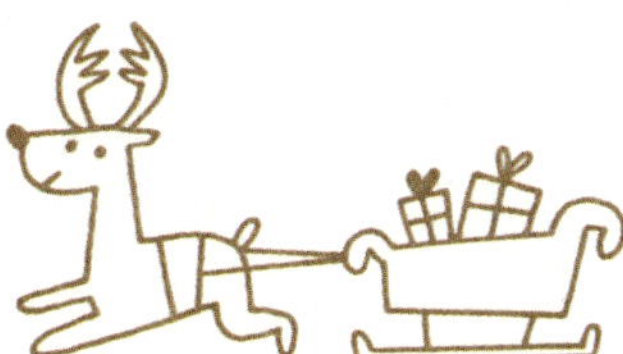

Reindeer

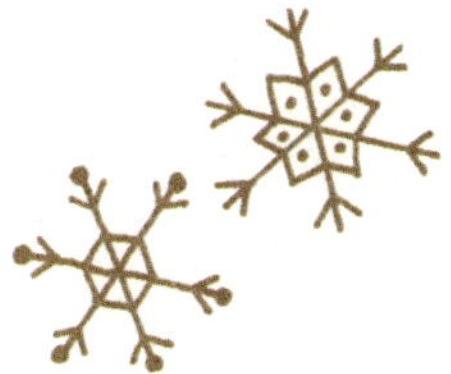

Snowflakes

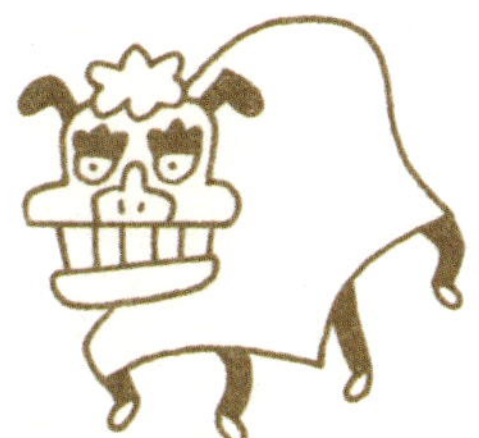

Lunar New Year

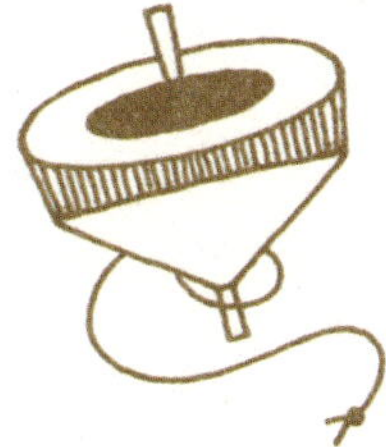

Spinning top

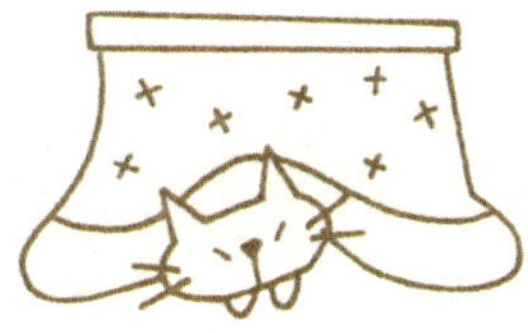

Staying cozy inside

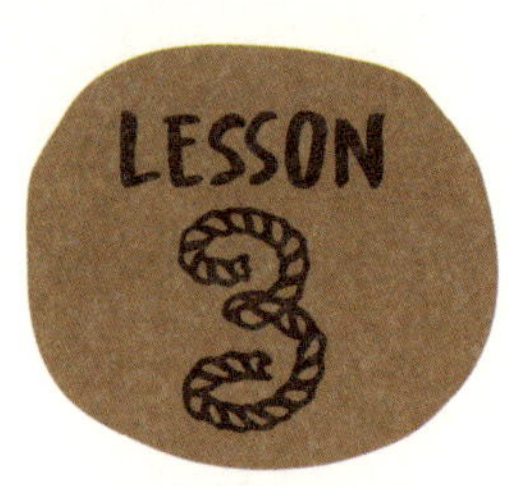

ICONS

These illustration icons can be used to decorate your calendar, planner, or diary. They are a creative way to commemorate special events.

EVERYDAY LIFE

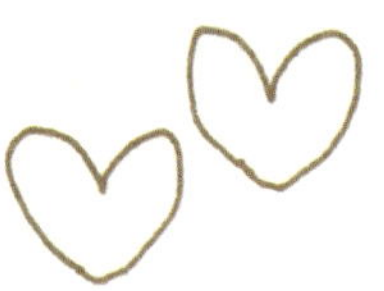
Anniversary

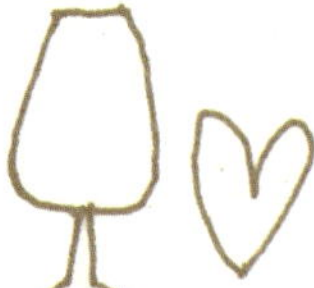
Date night

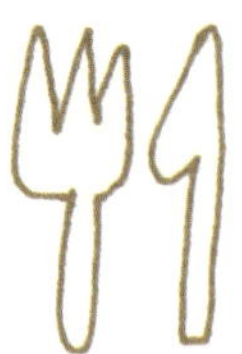
Dinner party

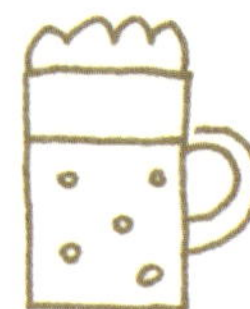
Cocktail party

Wedding

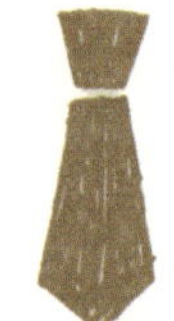
Memorial service

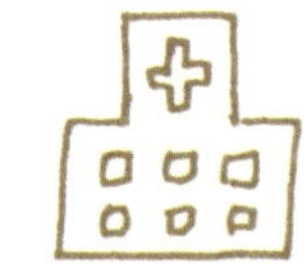
Doctors appointment

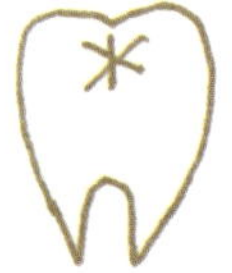
Dentist appointment

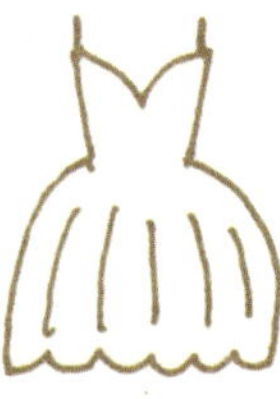
Party

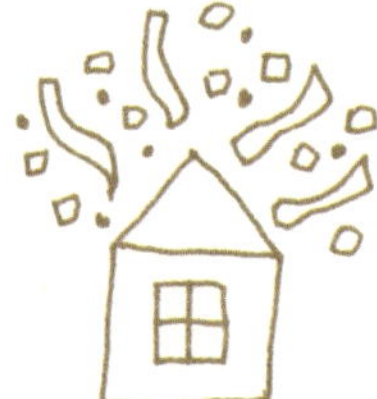
Housewarming party

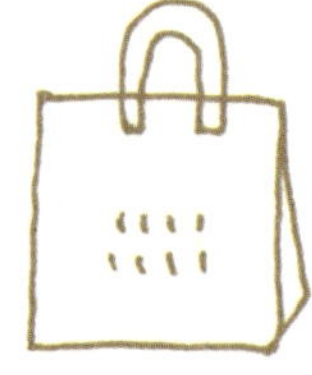
Shopping

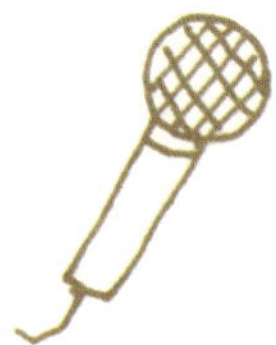
Karaoke

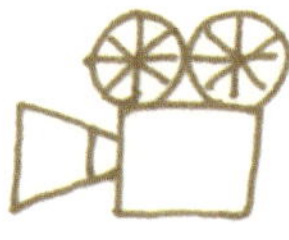
Movie night

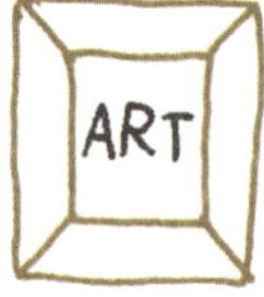

Art exhibition

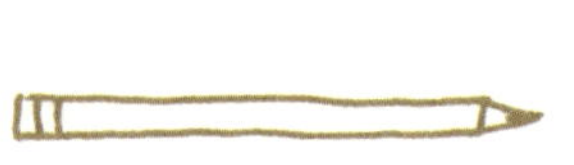
Homework due date

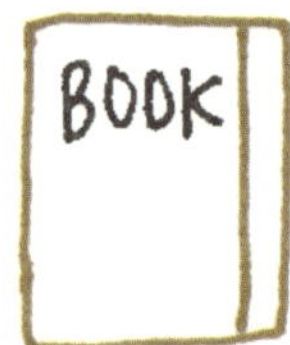

Study

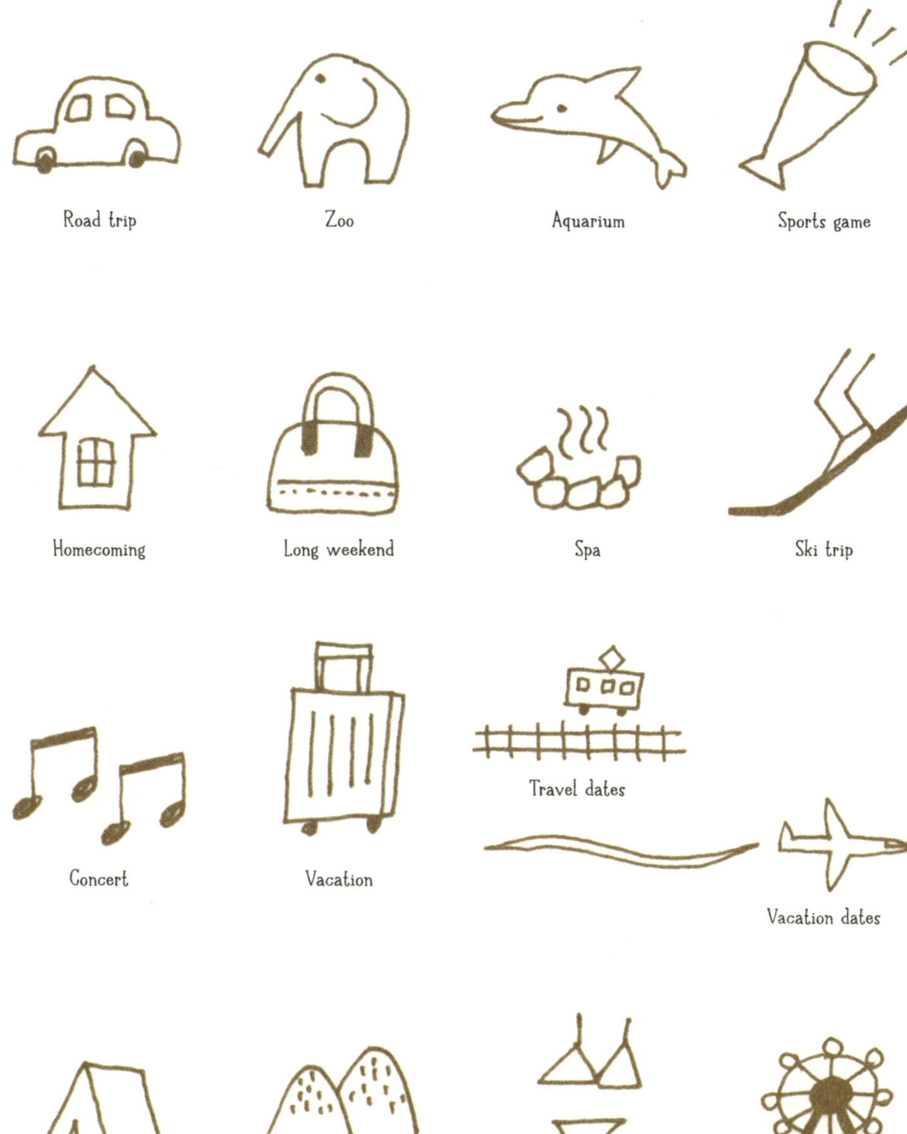
Road trip
Zoo
Aquarium
Sports game
Homecoming
Long weekend
Spa
Ski trip
Concert
Vacation
Travel dates
Vacation dates
Camping
Mountain climbing
Swimming
Amusement park

WORK

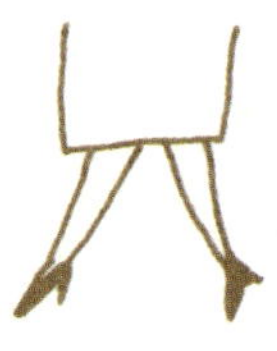
Office day

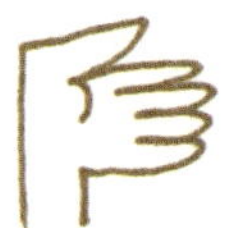
Vacation

Late shift

Early shift

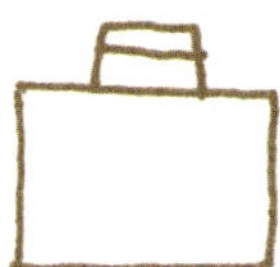
Business trip

Meeting

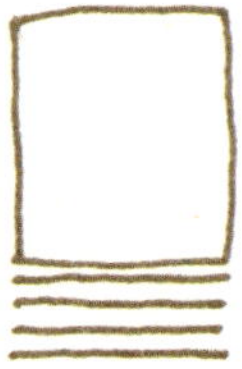
Staff meeting

Deadline

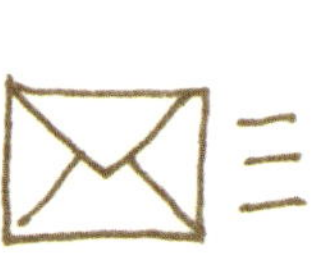
Email

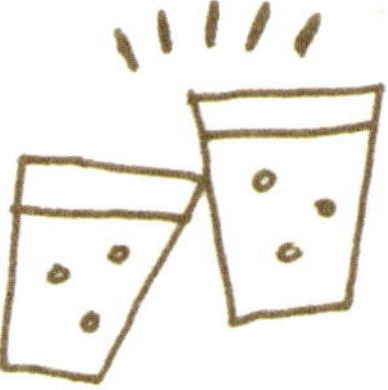
Office party

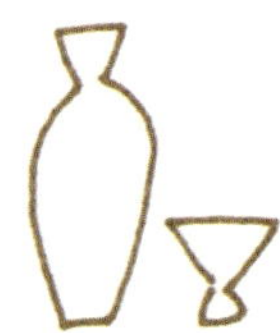
Client lunch

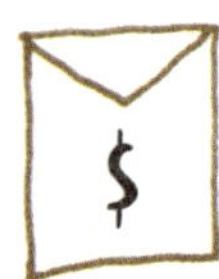

Payday

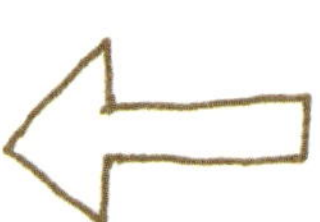
Client visit

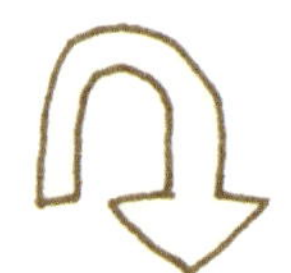
Leave work early

Interview

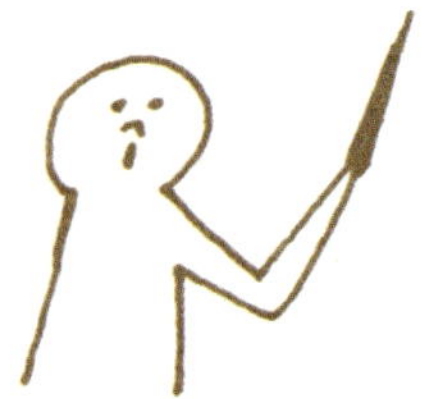
Presentation

LESSONS & APPOINTMENTS

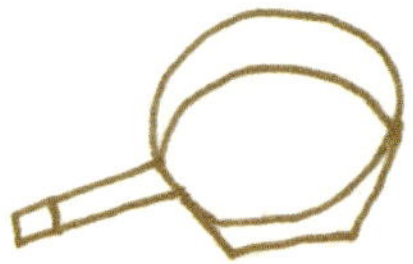
Cooking class

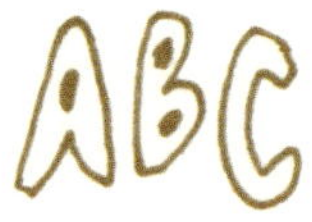

Language lessons

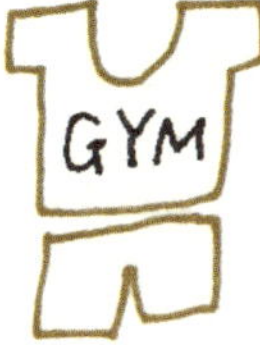

Gym

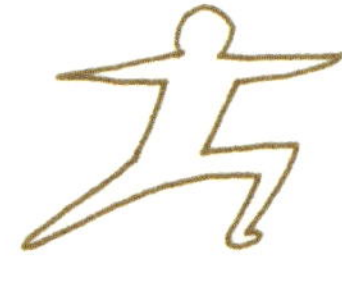
Yoga

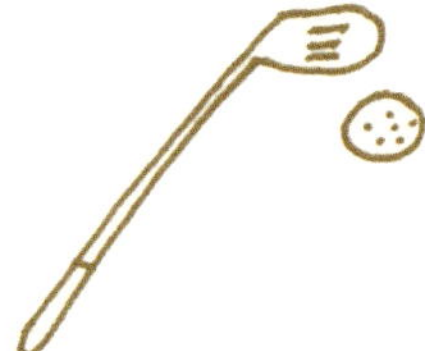
Golf

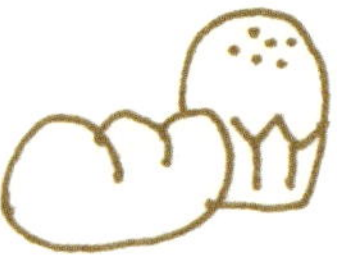
Baking class

Flower arranging class

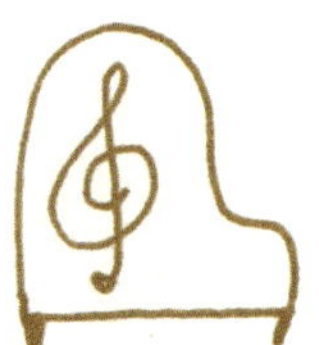
Piano

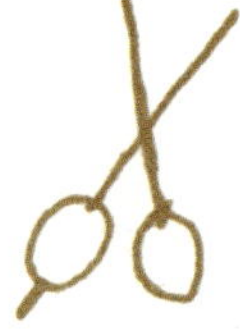
Beauty salon

Nail salon

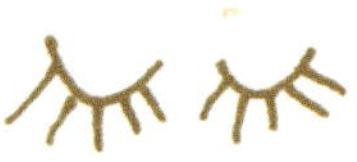
Eyelash extensions

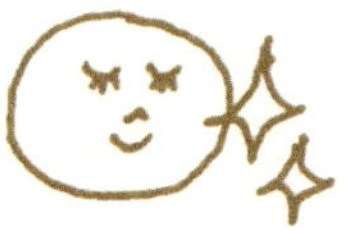
Beauty treatment

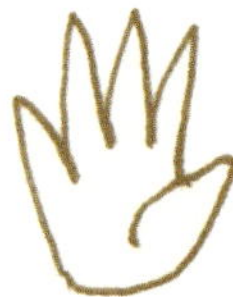
Massage

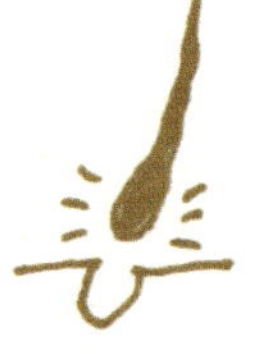
Hair removal

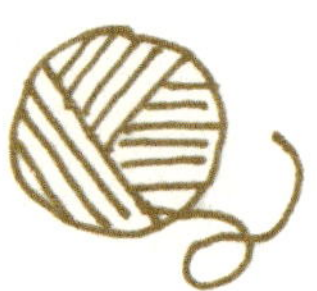
Knitting

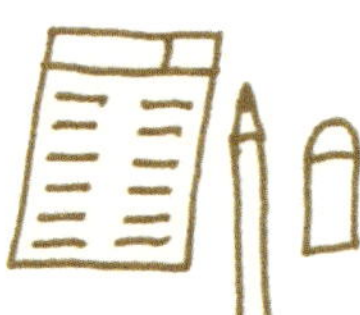
Test

NOTES

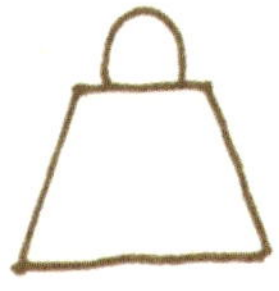
Weight

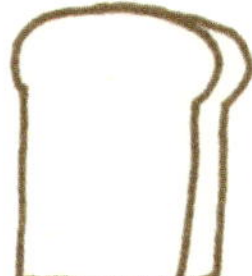
Breakfast

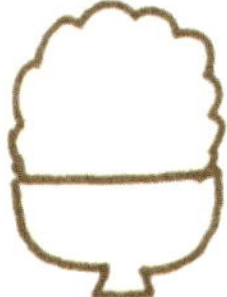
Lunch

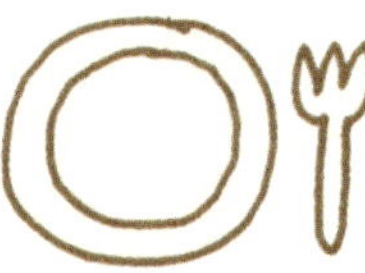
Dinner

Wake up time

Bedtime

Birthday

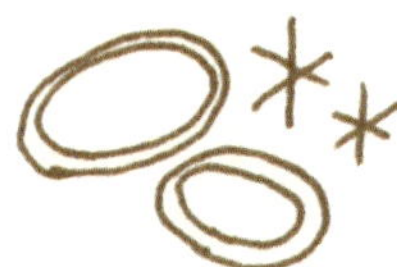
Wedding anniversary

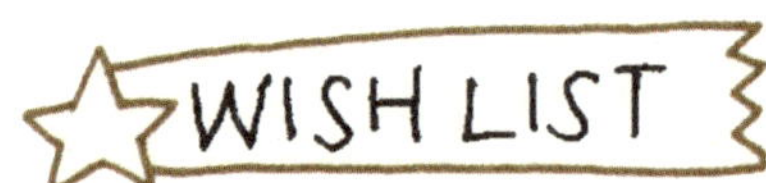

Wish list

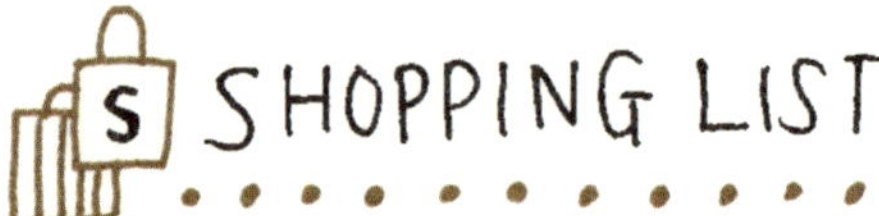

Shopping list

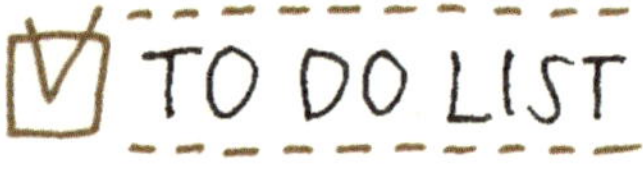

To do list

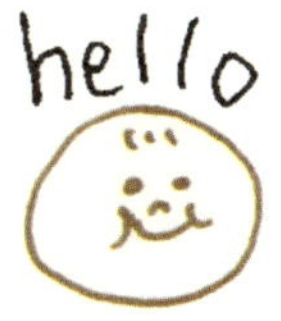

Estimated date of delivery

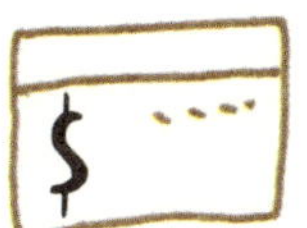

Credit card or license renewal

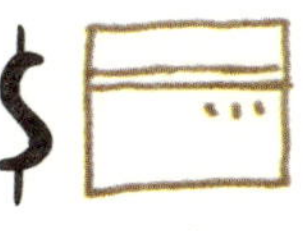

Credit card payment date

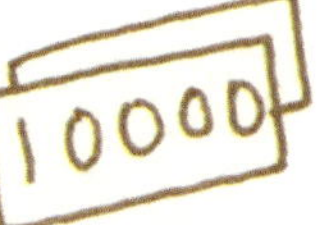

Bill due date

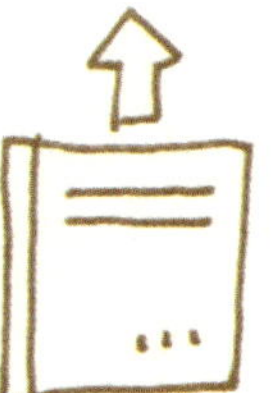
Library books due

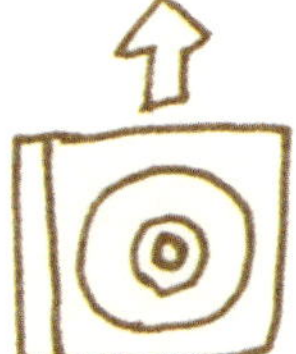
DVD return

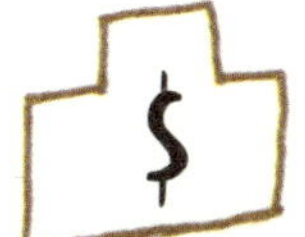

Bank

Post office

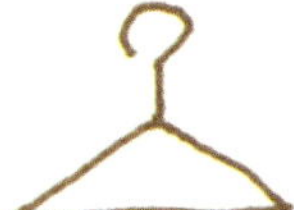
Dry cleaning

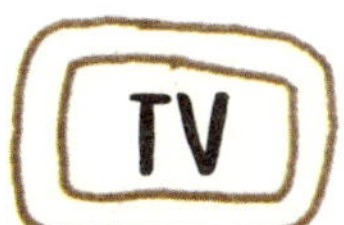

Record TV show

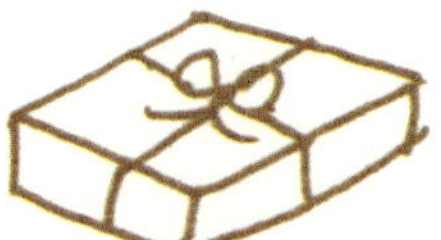
Buy gift

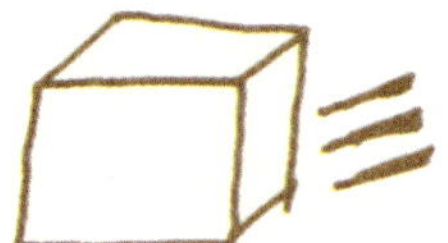
Package delivery

SCHOOL EVENTS

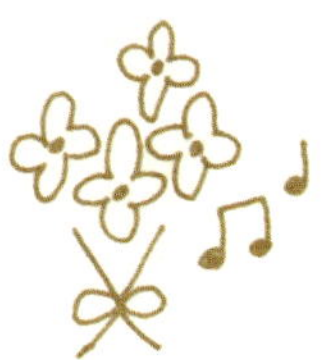
Music performance

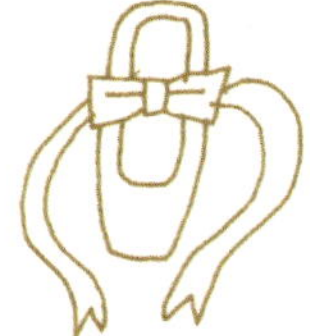
Ballet recital

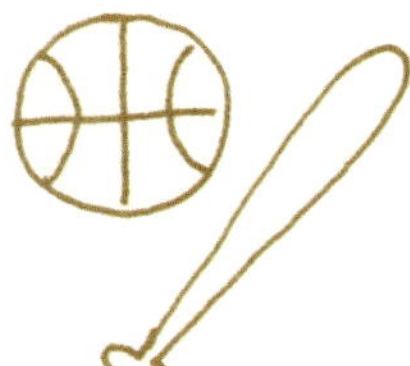
Sports games

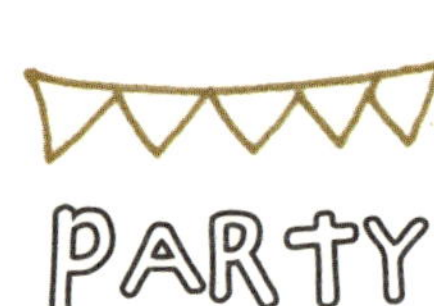

Celebration

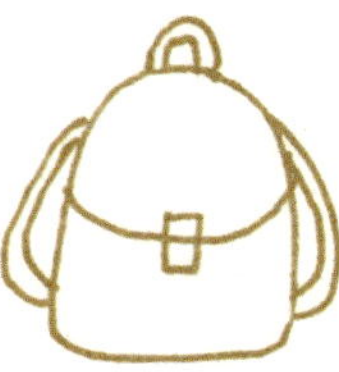
Field trip

First day of school

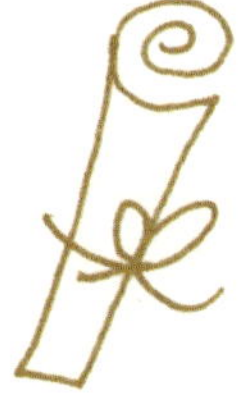
Graduation

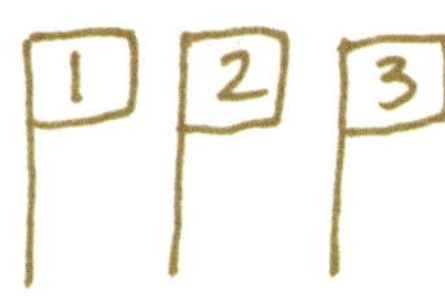

Field day

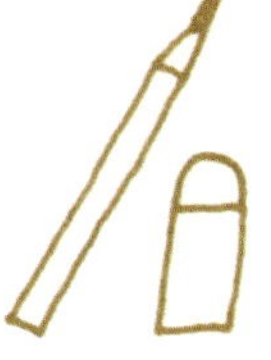
Test

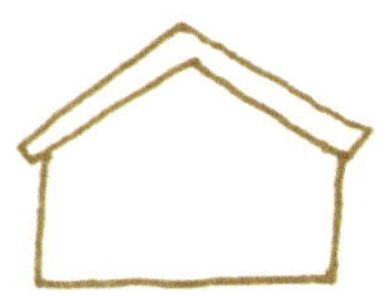
Open house

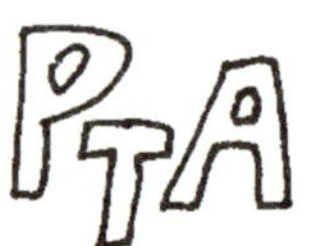

PTA meeting

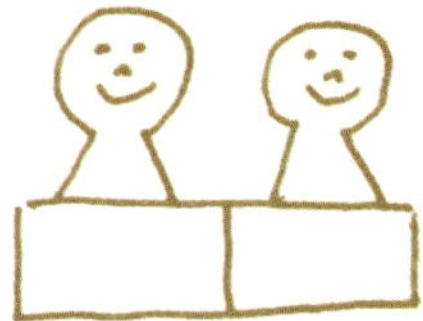
Parents' day

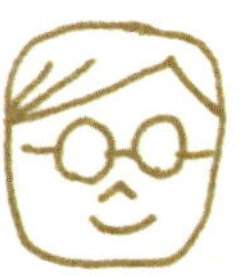
Teacher conference

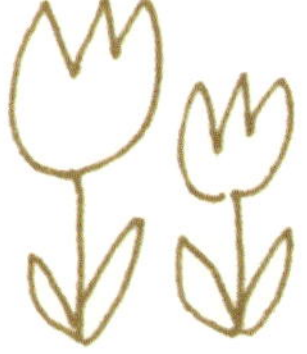
Spring break

Summer vacation

Winter break

WEATHER & MOOD

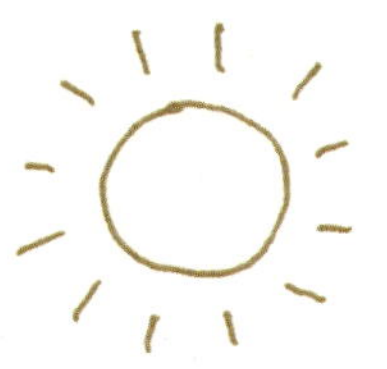
Sunny

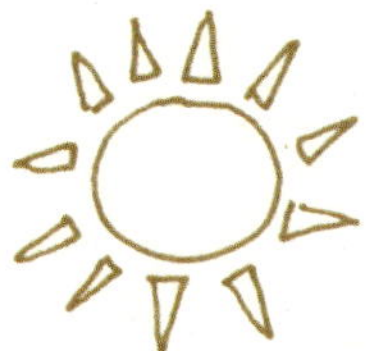
Heat wave

Cloudy

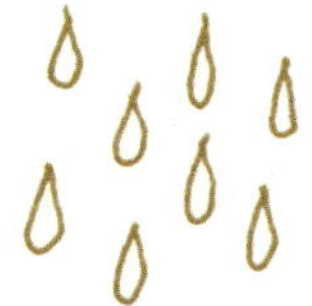
Rain

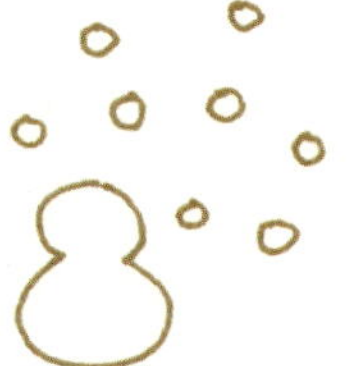
Snow

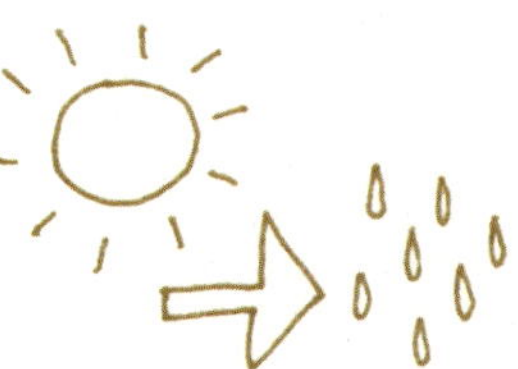
Rain after sun

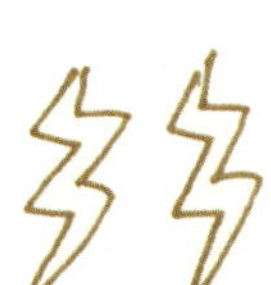
Thunder

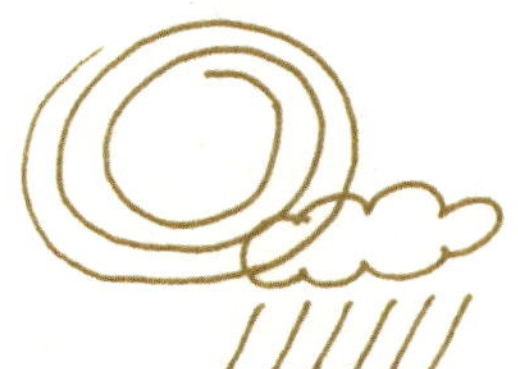
Hurricane

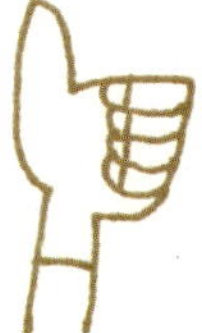
Good day

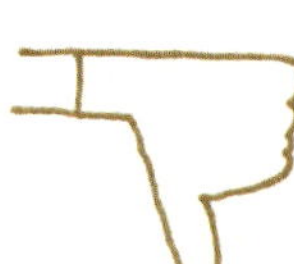
Bad day

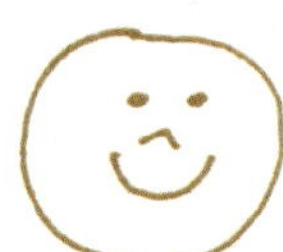
Happy

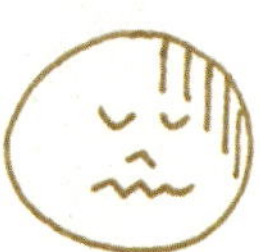
Sad

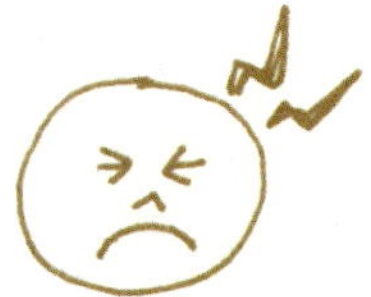
Headache

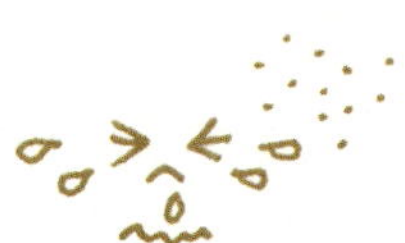
Heavy pollen

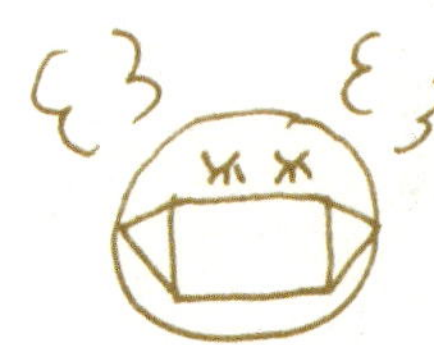
Cold

INSPIRATION GALLERY

Now that you've mastered the art of doodling with ballpoint pens, let's put your skills to good use! Have fun adding cute illustrations to everyday objects or create one-of-a-kind notes, cards, and gifts for your friends.

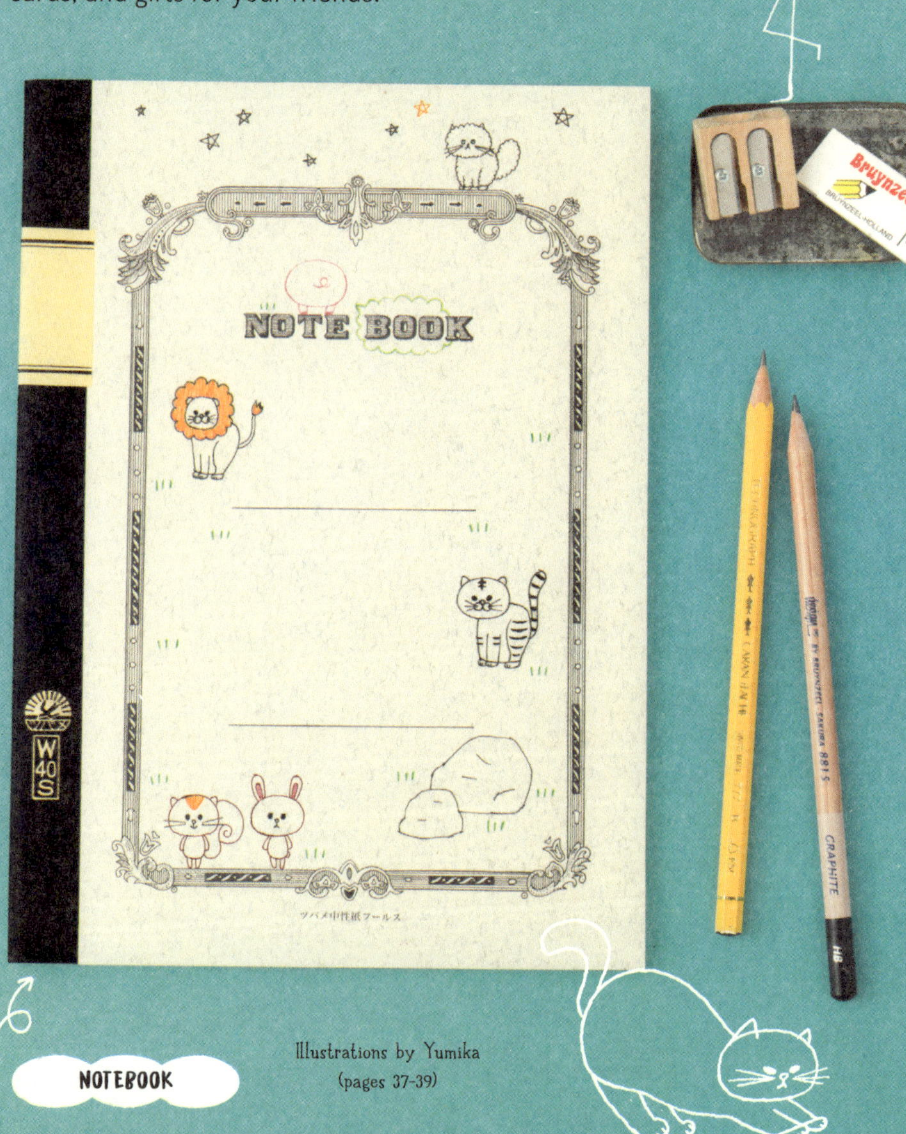

NOTEBOOK

Illustrations by Yumika
(pages 37-39)

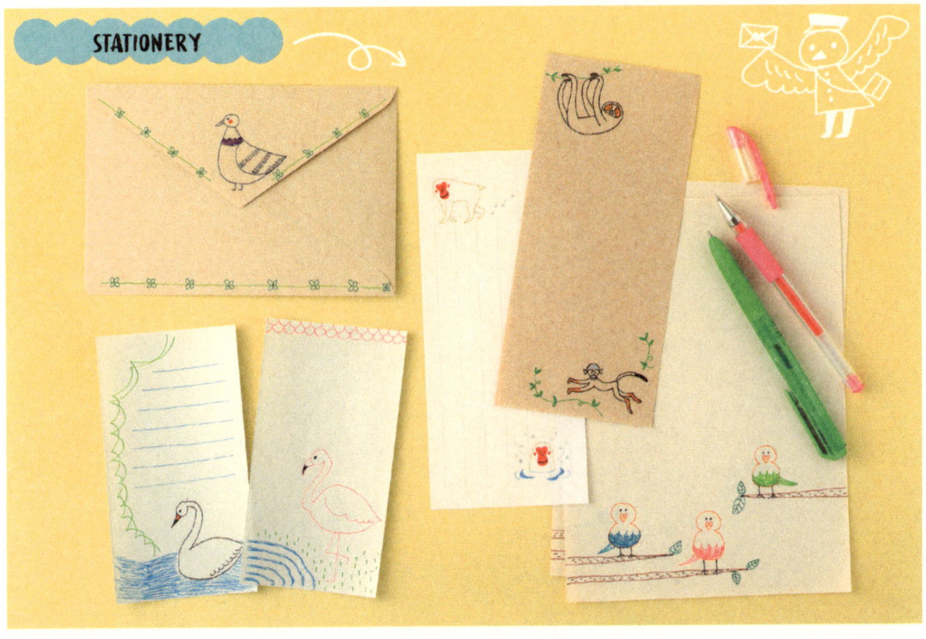

Illustrations by Azumi Saito (page 47) and macco (pages 52-54)

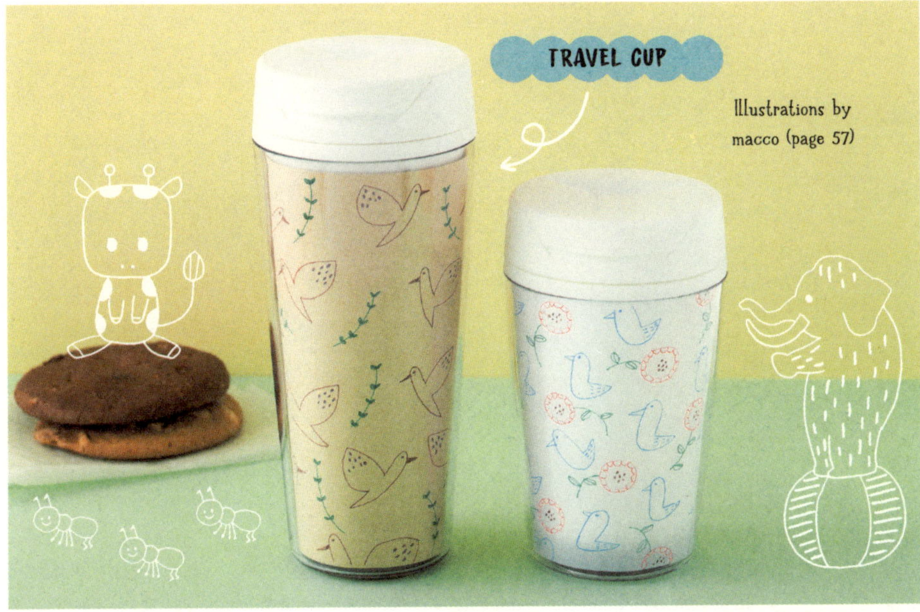

Illustrations by macco (page 57)

These adorable illustrations are perfect for lunch box notes and memos. Use friendly animal characters when labeling your food in a shared fridge or draw fun portraits of your friends when offering words of encouragement.

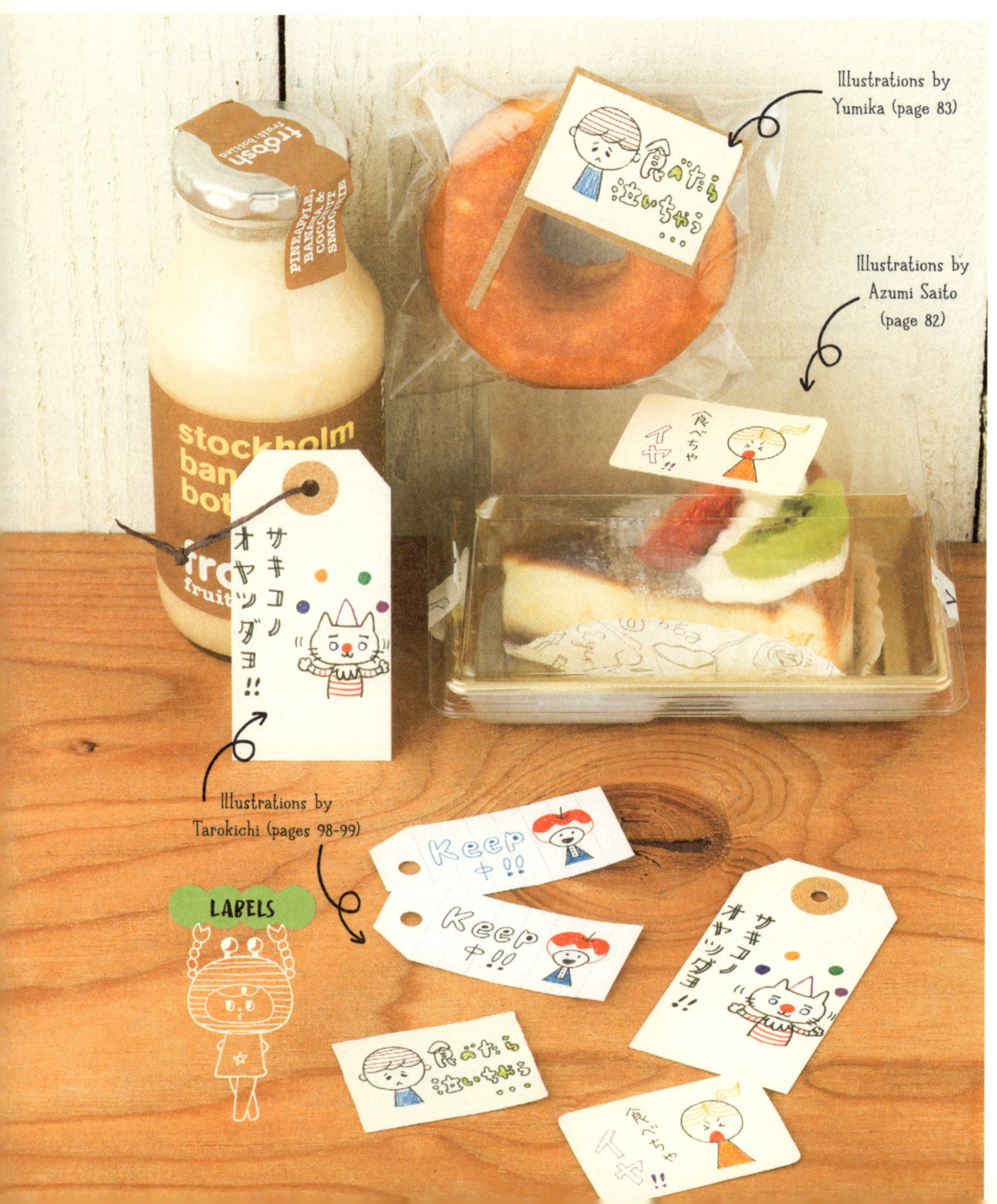

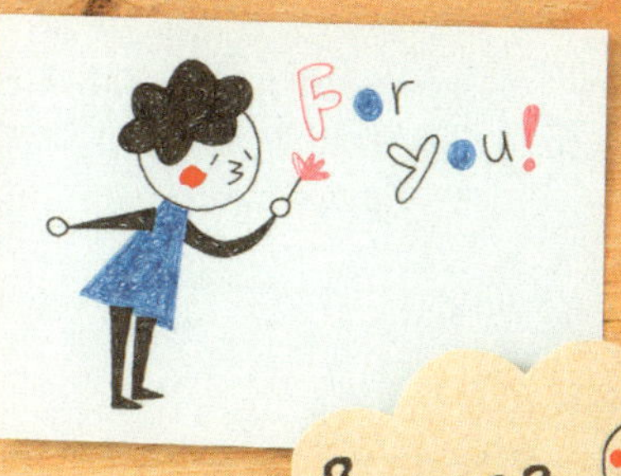

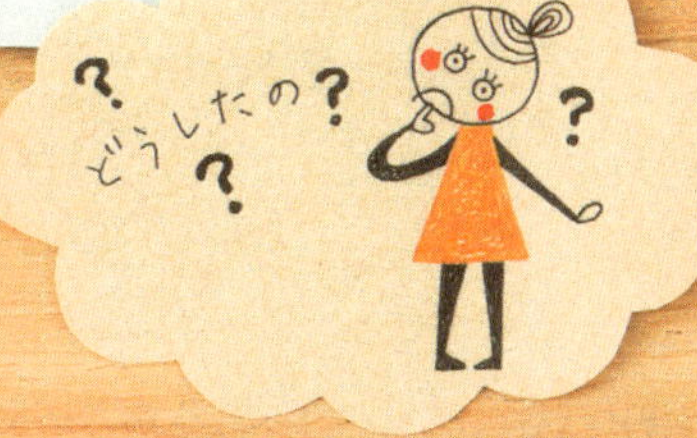

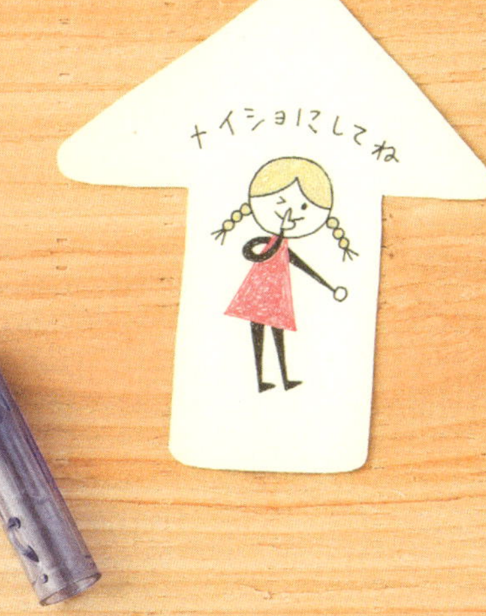

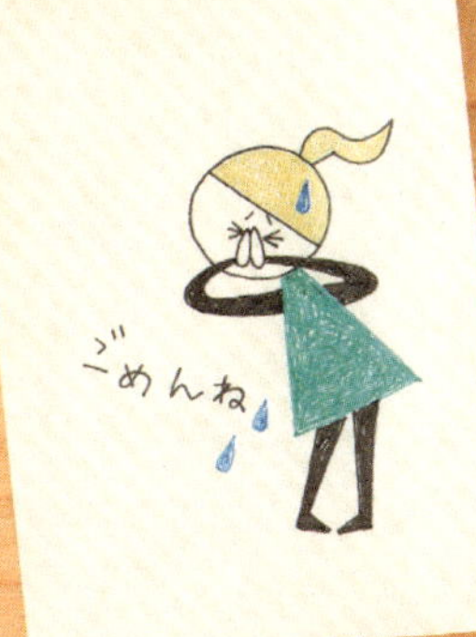

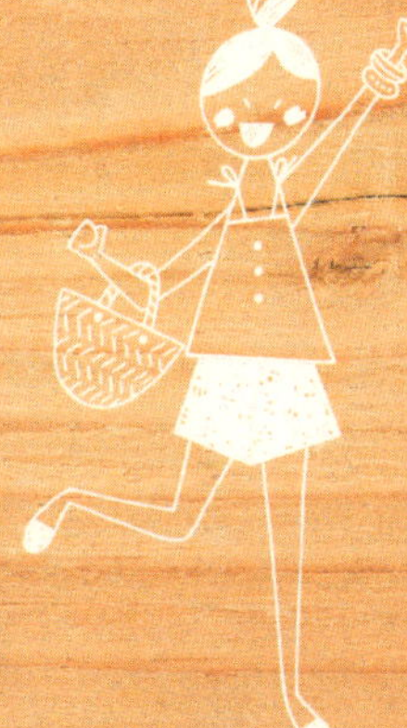

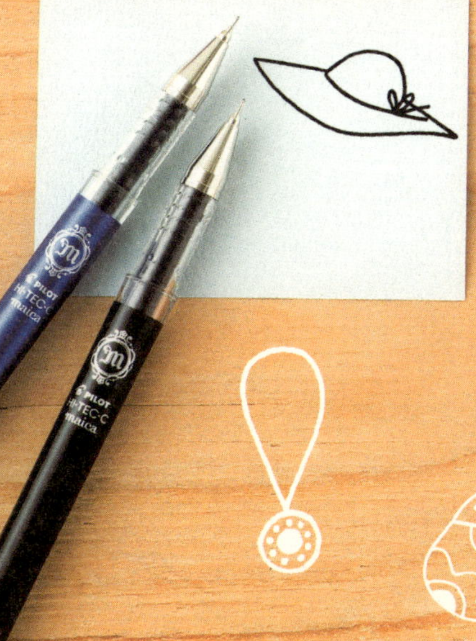

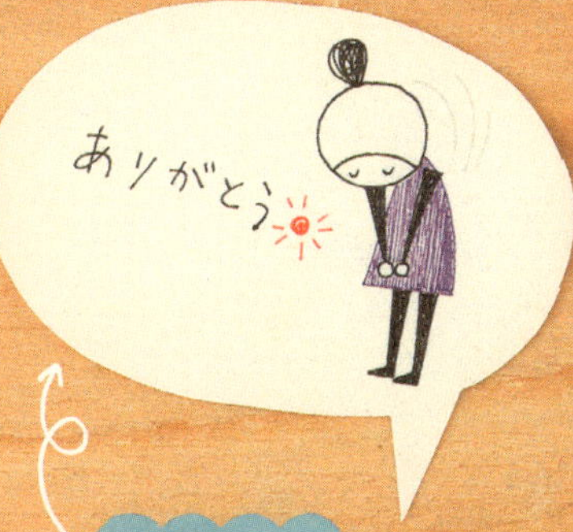

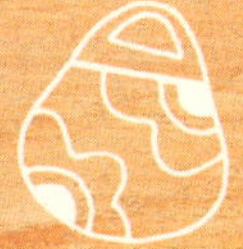

MEMOS

Illustrations by
Azumi Saito (pages 86-87)

Everyday objects, such as food, plants, and cosmetics can be transformed into stylish motifs when drawn in ballpoint pen. Draw on shrinkable plastic to create unique jewelry and accessories.

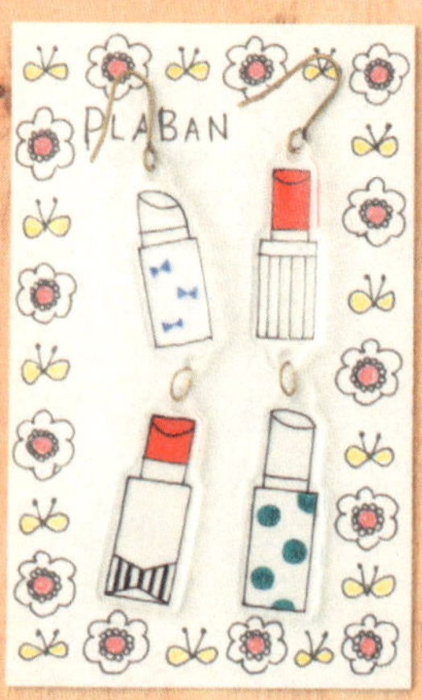

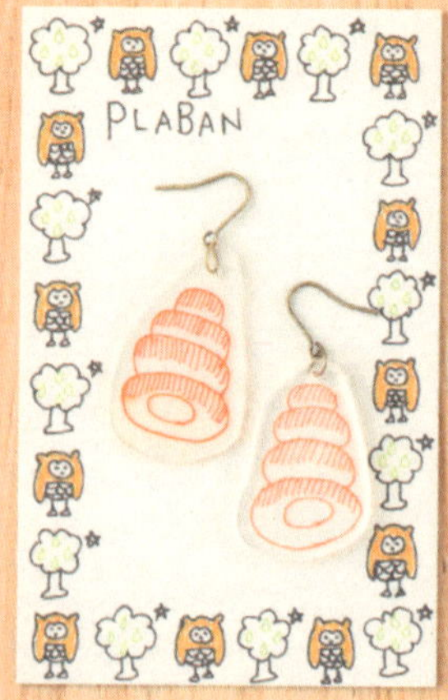

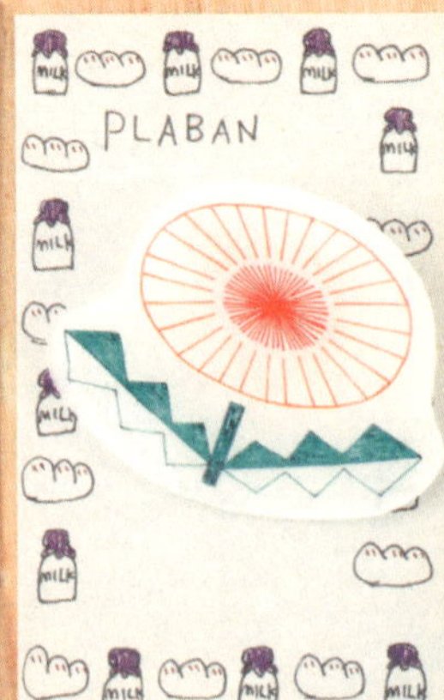

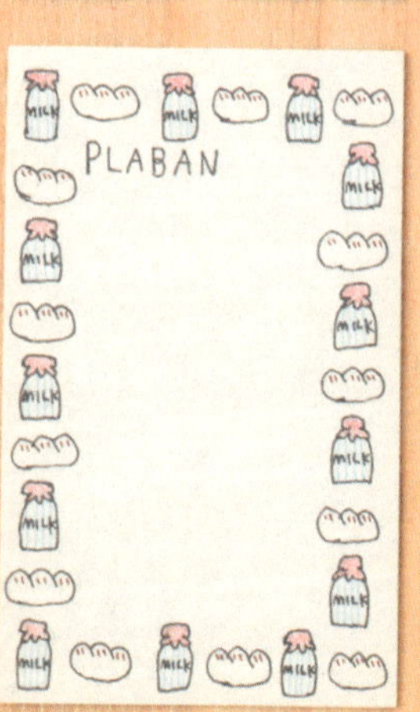

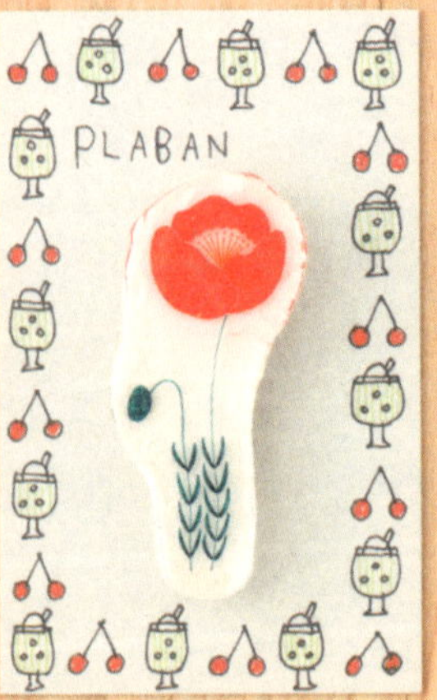

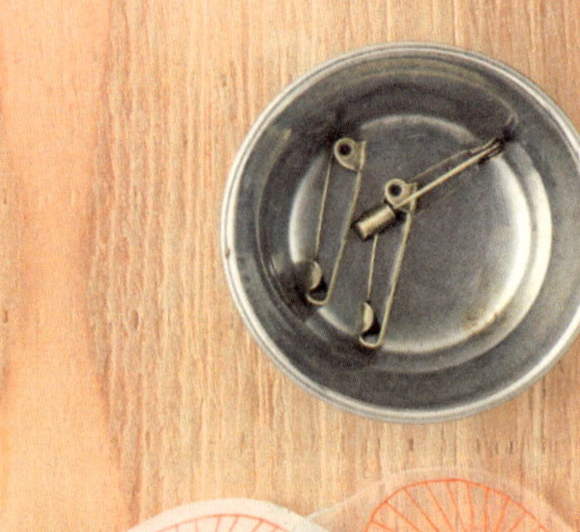
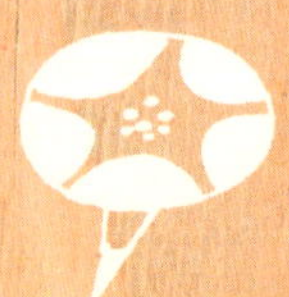
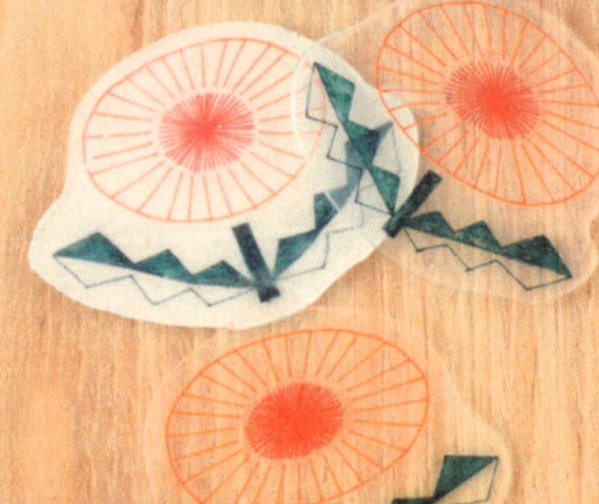

JEWELRY

Illustrations by Keiko Okada (page 110), macco (page 125), and Yumika (page 150)
Refer to page 163 for frame illustrations.

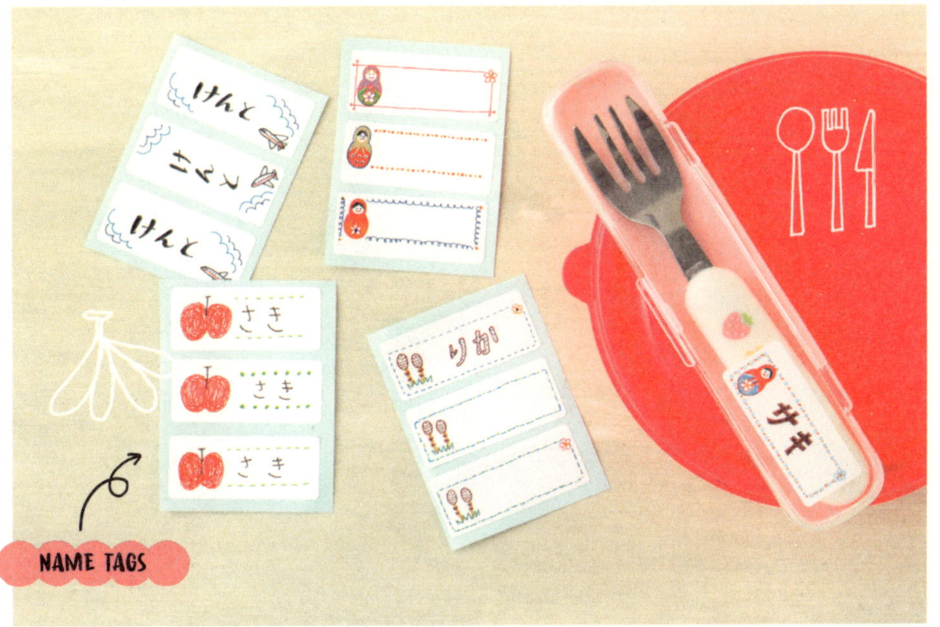

Illustrations by Keiko Okada (pages 110 and 145), macco (page 117), and Aki Kobayashi (page 153)

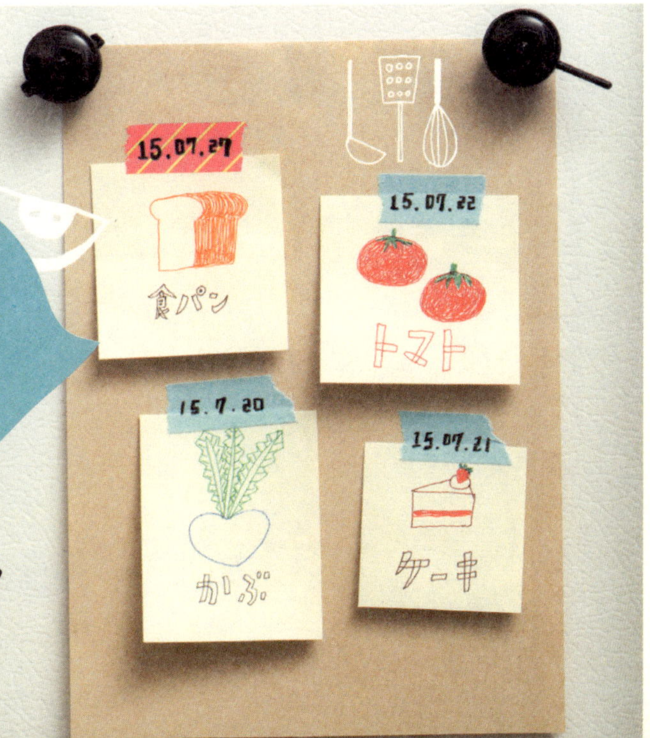

Write the expiration date on a strip of masking tape and use to affix food illustrations to your fridge.

Simply swap out the tape as necessary.

EXPIRATION DATE LIST

Illustrations by macco (pages 120, 124, and 127)

Use icon-style illustrations to embellish your calendar, planner, or diary, or send seasonal messages to friends and family. Illustrations are a fun way to express your feelings.

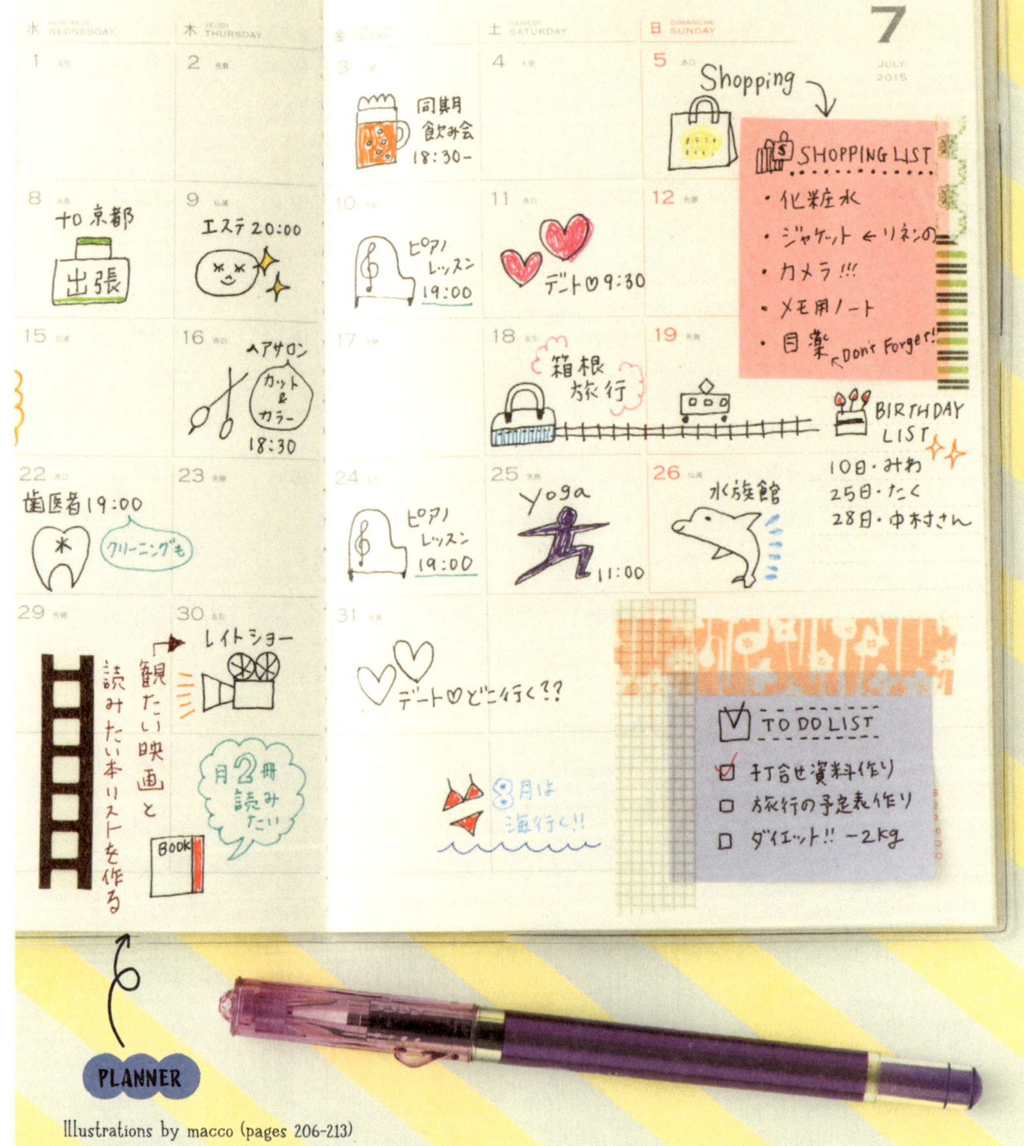

PLANNER

Illustrations by macco (pages 206-213)

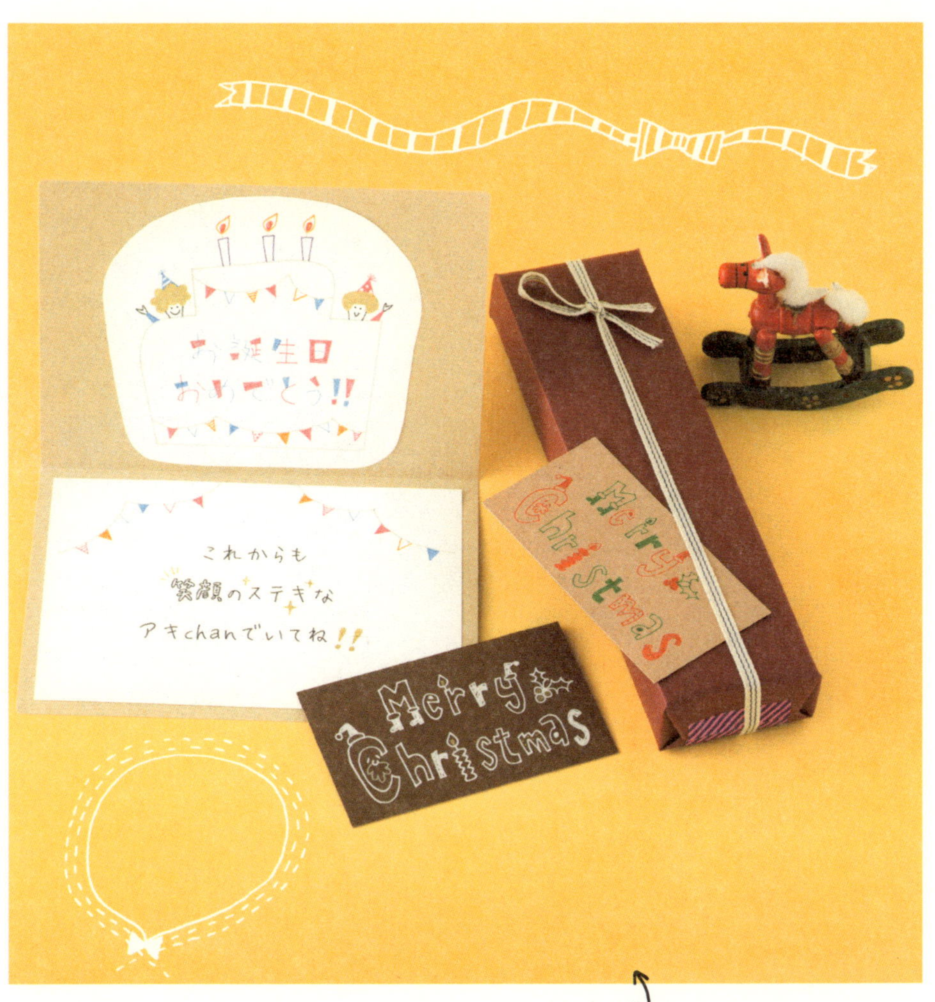

CHRISTMAS & BIRTHDAY CARDS

Illustrations by
Azumi Saito (pages 186 and 188)

ABOUT THE ILLUSTRATORS

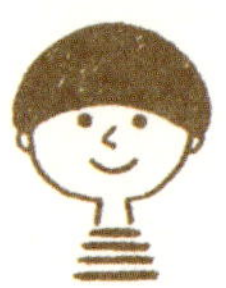

Keiko Okada majored in graphic design. She worked as a designer for a stationery company before becoming a freelance illustrator. Her illustrations often appear in children's books, picture books, academic books, and magazines. Visit her website at: okakei.jugem.jp

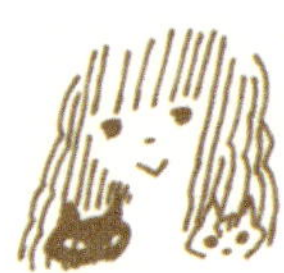

Aki Kobayashi graduated from Setsu Mode Seminar. As a freelance illustrator, her work has been featured in women's magazines, books, advertisements, and packaging. She is also engaged in interior design and product development through her brand Francegum. Visit her website at: www.francegum.com

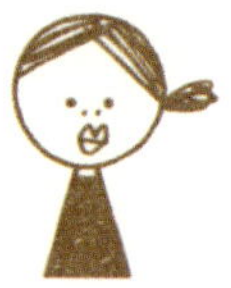

Azumi Saito is a freelance illustrator living in Japan. She previously worked as a book and magazine editor. Her cute and funny illustrations are often found in books and magazines, and her illustrations often feature pets, such as dogs, cats, and parrots.

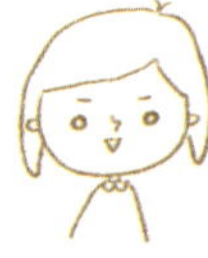

Tarokichi became a freelance illustrator after graduating from art school and is active in a wide range of genres, including mobile content, stationery goods, and advertisements. She enjoys manga, acrylic painting, and napping. Visit her website at: tarosumi.pupu.jp

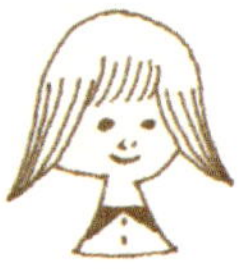

macco graduated from the PALETTE CLUB SCHOOL illustration class. She is an active freelance illustrator whose work has been featured in advertising, magazines, and books. She is known for her hand-painted, personalized illustrations and trendy color schemes. She has a pet corgi and plays the piano. Visit her website at: www.maccomac.com

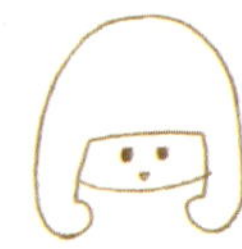

Yumika is known for her fairytale character illustrations. She specializes at drawing illustrations with story lines. In addition to working as a freelance illustrator, she also produces stationery. Visit her website at www.yumikasagawa.com

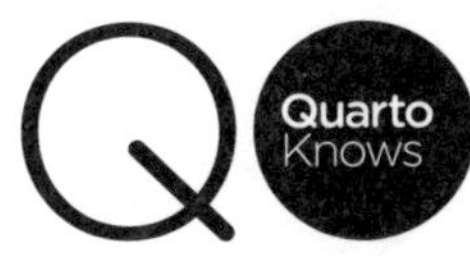

Brimming with creative inspiration, how-to projects, and useful information to enrich your everyday life, Quarto Knows is a favorite destination for those pursuing their interests and passions. Visit our site and dig deeper with our books into your area of interest: Quarto Creates, Quarto Cooks, Quarto Homes, Quarto Lives, Quarto Drives, Quarto Explores, Quarto Gifts, or Quarto Kids.

First published in the United States of America in 2020 by Quarry Books, an imprint of The Quarto Group
100 Cummings Center
Suite 265-D
Beverly, Massachusetts 01915-6101
Telephone: (978) 282-9590
Fax: (978) 283-2742
QuartoKnows.com

Some of the illustrations in the original Japanese edition include hand-lettered Japanese text. In instances where this occurs, an English translation replaces the Japanese hand-lettered text using Chinchilla font, Awesome Sauce font and Mr Dodo font.

Editor: Six Pommes
Illustrators: Keiko Okada, Azumi Saito, macco, Aki Kobayashi, Tarokichi & Yumika
Product Cooperation: PILOT CORPORATION & Mitsubishi Pencil Co., Ltd.
Design: Akira Hirano (Robitasha)
Photography: Yumiko Yokota (STUDIO BAN BAN)
Styling: Mariko Danno
Editorial Production: Fumika Miyoshi (Robitasha)

Translator: Kyoko Matthews
English Language Editor: Lindsay Fair

ISBN: 978-1-63159-846-3

10 9 8 7 6 5 4 3 2 1

Printed in China

ALSO AVAILABLE

How to Draw Almost Everything
An Illustrated Sourcebook
by Chika Miyata
ISBN: 9781631591402

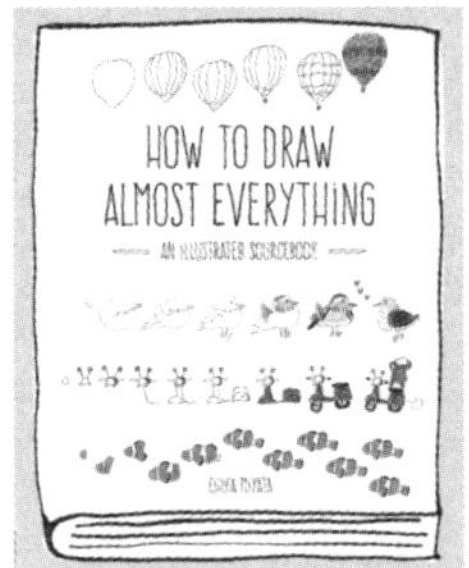

How to Draw Almost Every Day
An Illustrated Sourcebook
by Kamo
ISBN: 9781631593772

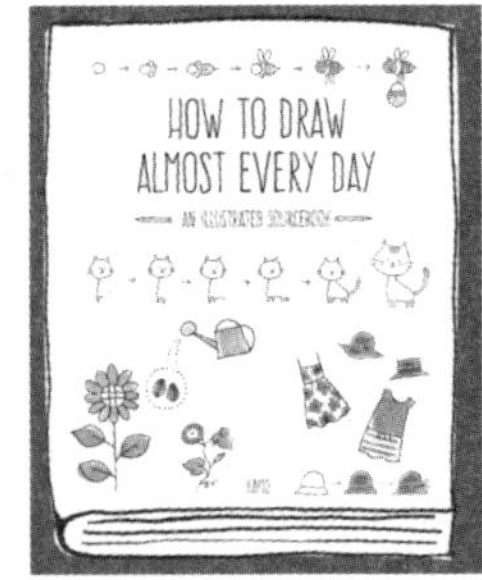

How to Draw Almost Every Animal
An Illustrated Sourcebook
by Chika Miyata
ISBN: 9781631593765

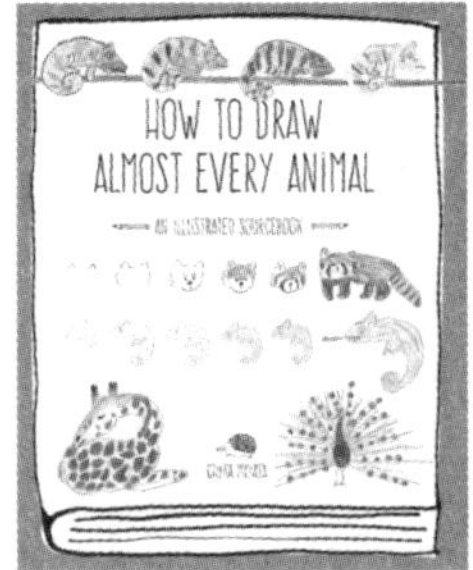

How to Draw Almost Everything for Kids
An Illustrated Sourcebook
by Naoko Sakamoto and Kamo
ISBN: 9781631594991

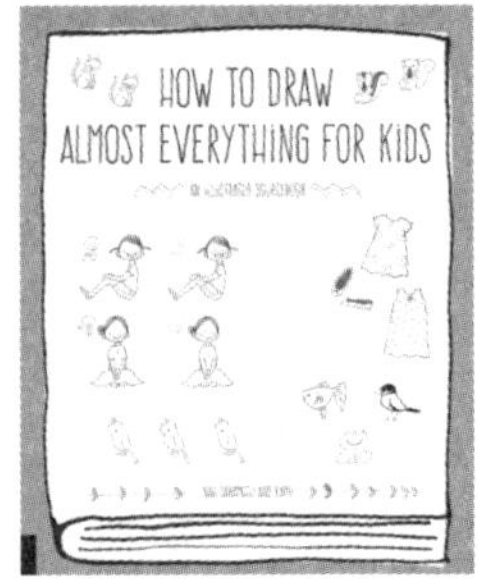

Draw 62 Animals and Make Them Cute
by Heegyum Kim
ISBN: 9781631596759

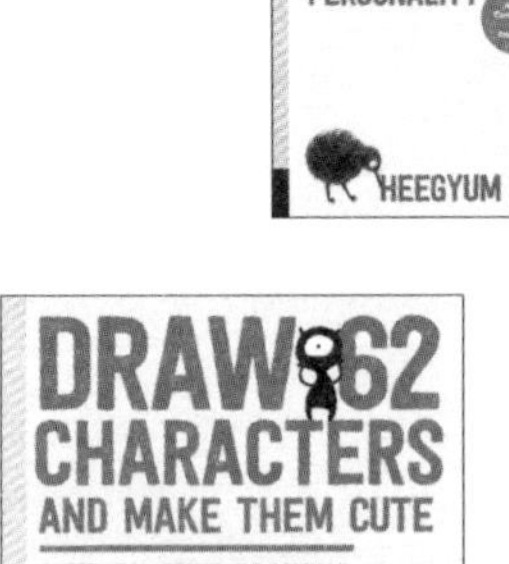

Draw 62 Characters and Make Them Cute
by Heegyum Kim
ISBN: 9781631598210

Draw 62 Magical Creatures and Make Them Cute
by Heegyum Kim
ISBN: 9781631596827

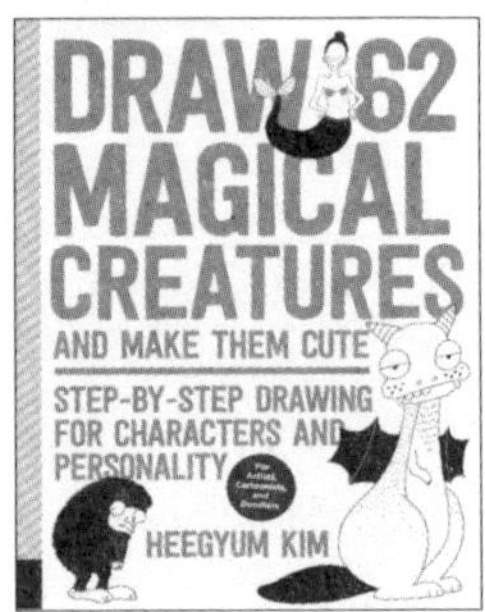